MY BRAVE BOYS

BOYS

To War with
Colonel Cross
and the
Fighting Fifth

Mike Pride and Mark Travis

With a Foreword by Walter Holden

University Press of New England
HANOVER AND LONDON

University Press of New England, 37 Lafayette St., Lebanon, NH 03766

First University Press of New England paperback edition 2003

Printed in the United States of America 5 4 3 2 1

Library of Congress Cataloging-in-Publication data
Pride, Mike, 1946–
    My brave boys : to war with Colonel Cross and the Fighting Fifth /
Mike Pride and Mark Travis ; with a foreword by Walter Holden
        p.   cm.
    Includes bibliographical references and index.
    ISBN 1-58465-075-3 (cl: alk. paper)   ISBN 1-58465-281-0 (pa: alk. paper)
    1. United States. Army. New Hampshire Infantry Regiment, 5th
(1861–1865) 2. New Hampshire—History—Civil War, 1861–1865—Regimental
histories. 3. United States—History—Civil War, 1861–1865—Regimental
histories. 4. Cross, Edward Ephraim, 1832–1863. I. Travis, Mark, 1957–
II. Title.
E520.5 5th .P75 2001
973.7'442—dc21   00–012376

Thanks to the New Hampshire Veterans Association for the use of several photos
from their Civil War Collection.

Thanks to Charlotte Thibault for her cover painting titled *Colonel Cross and the
Fighting Fifth at Antietam.*

For Monique Pride, my better half in all things.

—MIKE PRIDE

To my mother, who made all dreams possible.

—MARK TRAVIS

Contents

Maps

Foreword

I was born into a family that cherishes history. Our ancestors fought in every war from the French and Indian War through the Civil War. As a combat infantryman from World War II, I gained through firsthand experience respect for the soldier in battle, but also a lasting wonder at why and how the soldier perseveres and does his duty despite seemingly impossible dangers and trials. One place I sought answers was in Bruce Catton's great trilogy of the Army of the Potomac. It was here that I discovered Colonel Edward E. Cross and his brave boys of the Fifth New Hampshire Volunteers. Catton makes twelve glowing references to the man and the regiment. As soon as I could, I bought a copy of Doctor William Child's history of the Fifth and one of Thomas Livermore's memoir of the regiment—and I was hooked.

Everybody who becomes seriously interested in Cross travels to his birthplace, Lancaster, New Hampshire, and talks with Faith Kent, granddaughter of Cross's best friend, Henry Kent, and keeper of the flame. Miss Kent is liberal with her information and generously hands out copies of the many wartime letters that Cross wrote to Kent. After talking with her in the spring of 1963, I began to think that Colonel Cross's journal might still be around somewhere. It had been quoted by at least three writers: Child in his history of the regiment; Livermore in his highly readable *Days and Events*; and Benson Lossing in his contemporary history of the Civil War. Yet, sometime around the turn of the century, the journal had disappeared.

After a year of plugging away, I got my first solid lead. I have promised not to name names, but I will say that the rest of the story involves two doctors. The first doctor, an amateur historian, agreed to sit down with me, but I couldn't get any closer than telephone conversations. During one call, he hinted that he might possibly have some vague idea where the journal was. We finally set a "definite date" for a fall Saturday. When I called that morning, he confessed that he was about to leave for a Dartmouth football game; he had forgotten about our meeting. Although he had promised not to reveal the name of the owner of the journal, he could see that I was sincerely interested for historical purposes (and, although he didn't say it in so many words, he was sick of my badgering); he would give me the name if I promised not to tell on him.

He named a second doctor, to whom I wrote, requesting to see the journal. After I had about given up hope, I got a call. The journal was not for sale, the second doctor told me, but I could come up to see it. The last part was great news, but the first was a little strange. I hadn't said anything about buying.

This doctor was a short man with a mustache and thick glasses. When I visited him in December of 1964, he wore a tweed suit and a woolen tie. After inspecting me at his door, he led me into his drape-darkened parlor. He said he couldn't reveal how the journal had come into his possession. Suspecting some illegal action, I was satisfied not to know. He told me he was leaving the journal to his daughters. Again I was satisfied, but still frustrated.

Finally he left the room and returned with the journal clutched to his chest with both hands. "It's very fragile. I have to hold it myself." That might be the journal, I thought, but how could I tell? Mumbling something, he hurried out of the room and returned with a typed manuscript in a green folder. He read me the heading, "Private Journal of the Organization, March and Services of the Fifth New Hampshire Regiment, Colonel Edward E. Cross." I recognized the Crossian flourish; I had indeed been given a glimpse of the lost journal of Colonel Cross.

The little doctor grew more confidential. He would tell me how he had acquired the journal if I promised not to tell Faith Kent. I promised. Years back he had gone to Lancaster to an auction of property belonging to either an uncle or a cousin of hers. A stamp collector, he had bid on a barrel of old letters, gambling that he might find some valuable stamps. When he got home and dumped out the contents, there at the bottom of the barrel he found Colonel Cross's journal and other papers. Suddenly he seemed to feel he had said too much. Thanking him quickly, I left.

Time went by. I wrote, asking if I could look at the typescript in his house and maybe take notes. To indicate my seriousness, I said that I had already written 150,000 words of my manuscript on Cross and the Fifth and had submitted a chapter to *American Heritage*. I wrote that although the manuscript had been rejected, Catton himself had praised it: "The author has done a good, careful job. . . . I must admit that I liked it myself, but after all I am a dedicated Civil War something-or-other."

The doctor called. "Innumerable people," he told me, wanted the journal. He had given up the notion of writing his own "heroic biography of EEC," but he hoped one of his daughters might pick up the flag. He cautioned (as I already knew!) that he was careful about showing the journal: "I have let people see it only if I was sure they did not have a hidden camera and only if certain they had a poor memory."

I wrote him that whatever he decided to do eventually, I would still like to see the journal. Surprisingly, he called me as soon as he got the letter. Since his daughters had "not the slightest interest in the diary," he would sell me the journal and his other Cross papers for three hundred dollars. In those days three hundred dollars was serious money. Finally I wrote, offering one hundred, taking a chance that the sum, although it fractured our family budget, would not insult him. Within a few days, he wrote back: "I accept your offer and on receipt of your cheque will forward everything I have concerning Col. Cross."

I drove to his house the very next weekend, trusting neither the mail service nor the possibly capricious minds of the doctor and his daughters. On January 30, 1965, I gave him the "cheque" and picked up the journal, the typescript he had written, and the other papers. These papers, I found when I got back home and examined them, were a mine of material completely aside from the journal. There were clippings from contemporary newspapers; copies of some of Cross's reports and letters; a clerk's handwritten copy of the letter Major General Winfield Scott Hancock had sent to New Hampshire's U.S. senators demanding a general's star for the colonel; a letter from historian Benson Lossing to Cross's brother-in-law, Dexter Chase, returning the journal to him; and Cross's oversize passport to Mexico signed by Lewis Cass, secretary of state. Also in Cross's own handwriting were his official report after the battle of Fair Oaks, a letter to his father written right after he was wounded at Fredericksburg, his ten-page account of the battle of Chancellorsville, and lines evidently intended for an epic poem. Having visited Gettysburg and seen market prices for Civil War memorabilia, I feared that, despite the doctor's precautions, I did steal the Cross materials after all.

But he had said that he was happy to have someone use the materials. I eventually told Faith Kent I had the journal, although I couldn't tell her where I got it. She very graciously told me that she was pleased that I had found the journal.

Over the years, nothing I have written (and I have written a lot!) has come anywhere near capturing people's interest as much as my possession of the Colonel Cross journal. Among the authors I have corresponded with are MacKinley Kantor and a writer of historical books for Time-Life. Having read in Kantor's *Gettysburg* that Cross was a tyrant, I wrote him a polite rebuttal. Although I read later that "nobody challenged his historical accuracy," Kantor backed off and later even wrote a section for a book I was editing. The Time-Life writer traveled from New York to Southwest Virginia to see the journal because he was planning a book on the colonel. Shortly after he returned home, he wrote me that he had lost interest in Cross because he had discovered Cross's membership in the American Party—the "Know-

Nothings." I was a little surprised, thinking that a historian should judge a man's actions not by modern notions but against the standards of the time he lived in.

I kept at the work, with much tolerance from my wife—who put up with hours of my holing up to do my writing, with my purchasing reference works we couldn't afford, and with accompanying me to various Civil War battle-fields. I also had tremendous help from Pewilla Dick, a Boston editor who over many years maintained her generous and unflagging interest, close read-ing, and cogent comments. I spoke before Civil War roundtable groups. I had visits from other people whose interest in the journal brought them great dis-tances. But unfortunately, I have never managed to interest a publisher in my version of the story of Colonel Cross and the Fifth New Hampshire Volunteers.

Then one night I had a call from another person who had heard where the journal had landed. I welcomed such interest, of course, and invited the caller over to see the journal and to chat about the colonel and his brave boys. But it has turned out to be much more than a pleasant chat. The caller was Mark Travis. When he came to our house, he brought Mike Pride with him. I soon realized the connection we had made was important to them and could be important to me. Off and on for thirty years I had hacked away in the mine but had never quite reached the mother lode. The knowledge, enthusiasm, and sincerity of these two editors from Concord convinced me that they had a good chance of striking pay dirt. I let them take away a typescript of the jour-nal, my copy of the rare and valuable *Days and Events*, and a copy of the even rarer and much less valuable history of the Fifth New Hampshire written by me (and turned down by a distinguished list of publishers). Later we sat down and hashed out my part in the endeavor: besides going over the manuscript, I would write this foreword.

I was right about the potential of Mike and Mark. They have traveled far, walked the battlefields, dug deep in archives, and discovered personal letters and historical records that give their work an extra layer of personality and reality. The reader will see how an outstanding regiment was formed and out-fitted, how the men camped and marched, how they reacted to battle. Here are the deft personal touches that bring events to life. Here are the heroics but also the gripes and backbiting, the conflicts between leaders, and the subjuga-tion of the individual for the success of the group. Here is Colonel Cross showing both his inspiring leadership and his petty favoritism. Here is Doctor Child, the surgeon who became the regiment's chosen historian; here is Tom Livermore, a teenage sergeant who was to rise to command of his own regi-ment; here is James Larkin, whose letters home to his young wife show both his fortitude and his confusion over the abuse he and other officers sometimes suffered from the colonel; and here are the enlisted men, some surprisingly literate, the nineteenth-century GIs who did the dog work, who suffered deprivation and disease as well as danger and death.

The story of Colonel Cross and the Fifth New Hampshire is the story of the Army of the Potomac from General McClellan's futile Peninsula campaign through the cataclysm of Antietam, the bloody defeat at Fredericksburg under General Burnside, and the shocking rout at Chancellorsville under General Hooker to the climactic battle of Gettysburg under General Meade. There was a Fifth New Hampshire afterward, but it was only a shadow; the "Old Fifth" died on the battlefield of Gettysburg.

Thus, I feel it appropriate to paraphrase the heroic words of the colonel's refrain from an unfinished epic poem. Cross wrote: "It's tramp and hurrah for the Fifth! They were there!"

My version, with appreciation to the authors: "It's tramp and hurrah for Mike and for Mark! They are here!"

WALTER HOLDEN

MY BRAVE BOYS

1 The Fighting Fifth

"May a grateful country do the Fifth
New Hampshire Regiment of Volunteers justice—written history
never can."

—Major Otis Waite, *New Hampshire
in the Great Rebellion*, 1886

YOUNG CHARLES WRIGHT KNEW THAT THE GRAY OLD
farmer next door had served during the Civil War in the Fifth Regiment, New Hampshire Volunteers—the famous Fighting Fifth—and
he wanted to know more. So Wright tried to engage his reticent neighbor
whenever the two met: one evening on the dusty road by the pasture gate,
one day when both hired out to shovel snow for the town, each week when
Wright stopped by to deliver the local paper. On one such visit the boy announced that he had traded his rifle for an old shotgun, and sixty-nine-year-
old Leonard Howard finally rewarded the teenager's wide-eyed persistence.
"You know I've a buckshot in my left arm," the farmer said. "That so?" the
boy answered, his hopes rising. "How'd it happen?"

With that the veteran and his admirer sat for a visit beneath a framed Civil
War battle print. Over a plate of fresh cookies, Howard told Wright about
the wounds he had suffered in his arm at Fair Oaks and in the chest at Antietam, about the history he had witnessed at Gettysburg and Cold Harbor.
Most of what he said was true, but—perhaps feeling the pressure only a rapt
young audience can generate—Howard embellished a bit here and there. He
needn't have. He had been a good soldier, recommended for the Congressional Medal of Honor for his courage in returning to the ranks rather than
leaving the regiment after each of his injuries.

As for the Fifth, its story is even harder to match. Two thousand infantry
regiments fought in Union armies during the Civil War. None—not one—

suffered more deaths in combat than the Fifth. The toll was heaviest among the regiment's original 1,012 volunteers, in whose ranks Howard had marched. Nearly one in five of these men died in battle. Not one in ten remained with the regiment after two years of service. Even the few who emerged with their lives and health intact were changed forever by their experience. Charles Wright was fortunate to have heard Howard's account of this ordeal; a year after their talk together, at the age of seventy, the veteran died. "Dear Sirs," his widow told the government pension office. "It has become my very painful duty to inform you that Comrad Leonard W. Howard of Wentworth N.H. has been mustered out of service on Oct. 18th 1912."

Howard was luckier than many of those who marched off in the Fifth, in that he lived to march back, but in other respects he was a typical volunteer. He was nineteen when he enlisted, a farmer in his youth as in old age. Many who joined him in the regiment had also labored over New Hampshire's rocky soil before the war. Others were workers in the mills that drew power and profits from the state's tumbling rivers. The Fifth's ranks included shoe-makers and machinists, clerks and tanners, a scythe-maker and a sign-painter, students and teachers, immigrants and natives, fathers and sons, brothers and cousins. One was no older than eleven. Most were between eighteen and twenty-five, and on the whole they were taller than average.

Their home state was one of the nation's foundation stones. Once it had been a frontier, with thick forests and Indian dangers, but nature had yielded to civilization in New Hampshire generations before. Its jagged White Mountains were a tourist attraction, and when two men shot a bald eagle for sport, the newspapers noted its seven-foot wingspan with satisfaction. The train brought Boston, even New York within reach; the telegraph carried far more distant news quickly to hand.

Still, there were many in the Fifth whose home was their world—and the fact that theirs was a settled life did not make it easy. When a farmer was thrown from his wagon, there might be no treatment; when a daughter fell sick with a fever, there might be no cure. An injury as common as a hernia could render a healthy man an invalid, plunging his family into poverty unless the children were old enough to work in his place. Thus money was one reason men volunteered for the Fifth. Adventure was another. Those with loftier motives enlisted, by and large, to save the Union and not to free the slave— though the effect of their sacrifices was to help accomplish both.

At the center of their story was Colonel Edward Cross, the fierce commander who dominated the Fifth from the start, infusing it with his formidable personality. In part Cross was a teacher who showed his volunteer regiment how to soldier, in part a missionary who trumpeted the virtues of glory and honor. He frightened men into obedience, drawing his own sword on them more than once. He drove some officers harder than they could stand, while inspiring others and indulging those who were his favorites. He defied his superiors to see that his men were well fed, and when they fell sick or wounded he responded as a tender father. His pointed views and severe temper hurt his prospects for promotion even as the Fifth's performance in battle commanded recognition. Though the colonel's affection for his "brave boys" was deep, he led them not just dutifully but eagerly into harm's way. Many perished because of their willingness to follow.

The regiment, a unit of one thousand men when at full strength, was the basic component of Civil War armies. "It is to the army what a family is to the city," wrote Lieutenant Colonel William Fox, a Civil War veteran and historian. Today's army has regiments too, but they differ fundamentally from their Civil War counterparts. Civil War regiments were organized by the states, not the federal government. As the Fifth's name suggests, it was the fifth of eighteen Civil War regiments raised in New Hampshire. Its men were true volunteers who enlisted in the late summer and fall of 1861, after the first flush of war fever had passed but before victory came to seem so elusive and costly that men had to be enticed into the ranks with fat bonuses, or compelled to serve through a draft. Most in the Fifth knew some of their comrades before the war; many had even grown up together in small New Hampshire towns. Their intimacy was a powerful bond. With time they formed a new community, distant in experience and outlook from the people they had left behind.

Because they were composed of volunteers, hastily trained and often led by nonprofessionals, Civil War regiments varied widely in quality. The Fifth was known in its time as one of the Union's best, and Cross was considered the reason why. In 1863, after a year of hard service had thinned its ranks, Major General Winfield Scott Hancock referred to the regiment as "refined gold." The newspapers preferred to call it the Fighting Fifth, a more dramatic nickname. It was Fox, a post-war student of regimental losses, who determined that no other regiment had endured more battle-related deaths. "The losses of the Fifth New Hampshire occurred entirely in aggressive, stand-up fighting," he wrote. "None of it happened in routs or through blunders. Its loss includes eighteen officers killed, a number far in excess of the usual proportion, and indicates that the men were bravely led." The regiment's lustrous reputation has persisted over many years. The twentieth century's best-known Civil War historian, Bruce Catton, called the Fifth "one of the best combat units in the army" and considered Cross "an uncommonly talented regimental commander."

But neither this reputation nor the Fifth's story is widely known today. Its survivors, like Howard, are long gone; gone too are those, like Wright, who knew them firsthand. In fact, aside from Civil War buffs and a small group of re-enactors who march under its flag, the Fifth New Hampshire has been lost to time. Colonel Cross and his regiment deserve a bigger following, for theirs is a remarkable human story. It is more a story of loss than one of glory, because that is the reality of war. But it remains worthy of appreciation, and it is in service to that cause that we present it in the pages that follow. Our focus is the regiment's original volunteers, who endured the most of all. Our intention is to unfold their story as they experienced it. Because of how fully he defined the Fifth, our tale begins with Edward Cross and his life before the war. It ends, for reasons that will become clear, at Gettysburg—the battle that broke the Confederacy's strength, and the one in which Colonel Cross and the New Hampshire regiment he led gave the last they had to give.

Cross

"I am ready for the wars."
—Edward E. Cross, July 3, 1861

THE EDWARD EPHRAIM CROSS WHO STRODE INTO New Hampshire's State House on August 20, 1861, to present himself to the governor was twenty-nine years old, six feet, three inches tall, and so lean and upright that he likened himself to a fence post. He had flashing blue eyes, a long red-brown beard, and a complexion weathered by years of rugged living. His hair curled in wisps, forming a halo around his bald pate. Although he had no close female friends, he saw himself—and was seen —as a charmer. His gait was nervous and awkward, but a man who observed him on horseback wrote that he sat "tall in the saddle, straight as an arrow, lithe like an Indian, with a head on his shoulders that noted everything in the range of vision."

Cross had arrived in Concord expecting a military commission, a prize for which his whole life had prepared him. As a boy, he reveled in tales of New Hampshire men serving in colonial wars against the Indians, in the Revolution, and in the Mexican War; as a young man, he learned to write narrative prose by retelling these stories with a romantic flourish. The moment he was old enough to put on a uniform, he joined the militia. He loved to ride, shoot, and drill and even took sword-fighting lessons. As the years passed, Cross turned increasingly toward a life on the trail and in the lawless West. He crossed the country with a wagon train, rode as a volunteer with Indian scouting parties, and fought in a Mexican civil war.

The American Civil War could not have come at a better time for Cross. By 1861, after more than a decade of roaming the country and shaping his own destiny, he found himself not just on the frontier but beyond it, living among people he claimed to loathe. Wanderlust had taken him to Canada, New York City, Philadelphia, and Washington, D.C., to the South and to the West, but it was hard to see what his next move might have been if the war hadn't come along. Although his intelligence and wide-ranging interests made him many friends, he was a harsh judge of people wherever he went. As a journalist in Cincinnati, he threw himself into anti-Catholic, anti-Irish politics only to see the slavery debate wreck his incipient American Party. While his old friends back in New Hampshire moved easily to the new Republican Party, Cross clung to his nativist beliefs and despised abolitionists. He quit his job in Cincinnati to start Arizona's first newspaper, then lost the paper—and almost his life—in a duel. Although he seemed not to be looking for a wife, in moments of reflection he worried that no woman would have him and that the loneliness of a bachelor's life might be too great a price to pay for the personal freedom he had so cherished in his youth.

The young man who left Lancaster, New Hampshire, in 1850 to make his mark on the country could not have foreseen these doubts and shades of gray. He was too confident for that, too dynamic and daring. Even a growing country seemed too small for his ambition. Cross was eighteen years old at the time, but he was articulate and experienced beyond his years. He was already an accomplished printer, and his service in the local militia had given him a permanent taste for the soldier's life. Yet in a sense he never left Lancaster at all. Throughout his travels, he read New Hampshire newspapers to keep abreast of the politics of his native town and state. He came home to fish and visit with his old friends whenever he could. His mother wrote to him often, and another faithful correspondent, his childhood friend Henry O. Kent, became his touchstone, reminding Cross of the direction his life might have taken had he not been a rover. It wasn't that Cross envied Kent—they were simply friends for life, one who stayed home and one who, like thousands of others in the 1850s, sought his fortune in the West.

Cross was born on April 22, 1832, in Lancaster, a farming community of just over a thousand people and the shire town of Coos County, New Hampshire's northernmost. He experienced very early the tug-of-war between a life of words and a life of action. He liked to read and write, but he was vigorous, too, and the natural world, so immediate in the White Mountains south of town, enticed him to take long rides and climbs. In such an isolated village, which had been settled only seventy years before his birth, tales that had passed down from the Revolution were still alive with promise. Cross and his friends built rafts and forts but also staged plays, circuses, and shows. Later, writing to Kent, he fondly recalled "the varied and exciting scenes being exhibited to the public in your barn for the trifling consideration of 2 pins! Do you remember Fort Ticonderoga, the warlike stories and formidable weapons there collected? Ah! There's where you and I got our taste for the '*miling-*

tary,' which with me will always be a part of my existence." In the classroom, visions of buffalo and wild horses in the American West teased Cross's imagination. He never forgot the day, just before his eighth birthday, when his teacher, Mary Springer, made her class "hurrah for 'Tip and Tyler'"—William Henry Harrison and John Tyler, the Whig ticket in the presidential election of 1840. When Cross was in his teens, the town sent a contingent to fight in Mexico with the New England Volunteers. His father, Ephraim, was adjutant and, for a time, lieutenant colonel in the town militia. A hatter by trade, the elder Cross was known in Lancaster as Colonel Cross.

At the age of fifteen, Edward Cross went to work as a printer at the *Coos Democrat*. The newspaper was in a second-floor office on Main Street. As its name implied, the paper had a Jacksonian political agenda. Its editor, the former schoolmaster James Rix, lived the dual life of politician and journalist, rising to be president of the New Hampshire Senate. He earned a reputation for being honest, prickly, and impetuous. Cross learned at Rix's shoulder but did not admire him. "He was a strange, misanthropic man," Cross wrote years later. "The coarse weeds of *miserdom* had choked down nearly all the cordial and happy impulses of his heart." Cross saw in Rix "a relentless system of hatred towards all those who did not agree with him in politics."

Cross's brother, Richard, and his future brother-in-law, Dexter Chase, also worked at the *Democrat*, but its most celebrated employee was Charles Farrar Browne, who later became the humorist Artemus Ward. As foreman at the *Democrat*, Cross instructed Browne "in the mysteries and miseries of typesetting." Browne made an impression on him by dumping the contents of pots out of windows onto passersby and other "d——d foolery." Late one night, with a ball of chalk in hand, Browne mounted Cross's shoulders and transformed the red signpost above the entrance of the Temperance Inn into a barber's pole. In time, the two pranksters had a falling-out. As a lieutenant in the Coos Grays, Cross was, in Browne's view, "rather proud of his position." One day when Cross went to change for training, his clean, pressed uniform had disappeared. Rather than skip drill, he put on a red scarf and dug out an ancient cutlass. He looked foolish, but he did his duty. Late that night, the town drunk, who often pretended he was Napoleon, was found lying in a woodshed "in a state of extreme intoxication." He was wearing Cross's uniform, and it was covered with mud. Cross instantly guessed that it was Browne who had outfitted the local Napoleon in the style to which his delusions entitled him. He confronted Browne at the printing office, and the two fought desperately, winding up at the base of the stairs before the smaller Browne escaped. During the fight he had grabbed a printer's hammer, and as he fled down Main Street, he realized he still had it in his hand. Afraid that he might be accused of stealing it, he ran back and heaved it through the second-floor window, hitting Cross in the abdomen.

In 1850, Cross struck out on his own. He traveled to Canada, where his father was building ships, and to New York, where he apparently intended to join an expedition to liberate Cuba. By June, after the seizure of a ship scuttled the expedition, he had made his way to Cincinnati and taken a job as a printer at the *Cincinnati Times* for forty-five dollars a month. The *Times*, a daily newspaper with a weekly edition called the *Dollar Times*, operated thirteen steam presses and employed sixty men. The salary enabled Cross "to live well and save something."

The city offered him ample opportunity to carouse and to see things he never would have seen in Lancaster. "My powers of consumption, both of solids and of fluids, are unimpaired—and would disgrace no man," he assured Kent. He called eggnog "the immortal beverage," writing: "Angels could with propriety sip it, and no saints that I ever heard of would object to a foaming tumbler." One morning, after one too many tumblers and a street brawl, Cross awoke with a lump on his head from a policeman's baton. He attended the theater often, saw the singer Jenny Lind, and even took in a French ballet troupe. "The chief attraction of this," he wrote Kent, "consists in the ladies appearing in *very laconic* and brief dresses—and tights—and throwing those appendages to the human body known as legs into the air in a very surprising and elevated manner." The boys in the audience watched "in a steady and devout manner, occasionally slapping their hands and crying, 'Up a little higher!'"

Although Cross liked to talk about women, he had no lasting romances. When he wrote to Kent, who was nearly two years his junior, he relished the pose of the worldly sage. "Take the advice of 'one who knows,' and be cautious about your female correspondents," he wrote. "I have seen the danger of them." He expounded on this thought a month later: "Be very careful of what you put on paper to girls. . . . What a man says he can deny, or what he does he can often *wiggle out of*—but what he *writes*, there it is staring him in the face, his name over it." Cross claimed to be corresponding with half a dozen women and using a pseudonym with each. During a visit to Philadelphia, after sitting out on a hotel piazza watching the girls go by, he teased Kent with a tongue-in-cheek account of the city's "incredible number of beautiful harlots . . . not the brazen, bawdy sort, but the demure, sly, 'under the rose' description. Every evening the streets are alive with them in all possible disguises. Some as young widows—some as sewing girls—some as servant maids, or young ladies hurrying home late from school." The tale ended in a melodramatic warning from *The Inferno*. "Read Dante, and learn your doom," Cross wrote his friend.

Neither nightlife nor girl watching interfered with Cross's chief ambition. Through practice and study, he taught himself to write. He joined the Mercantile Library, which stocked fifteen thousand volumes and the major newspapers and magazines of the day, and spent "many a long night there." When Kent entered Norwich University, a military school in Vermont, Cross lamented that he could not join him. "I have the tide of life to breast alone and must trust to that best of schools—*experience*," he wrote. Already possessed of a good vocabulary and a sharp ear for the language, he made his own way as a writer and journalist. He enjoyed verse but found it limiting. "There is a certain stage in a person's existence that ought to be called the Poetic season —when a man feels as though he were a Moore, a Pope or a Bryant—but it soon fades away," he wrote. "I am going to try proze. That is useful to anyone." When Kent asked his advice on a flowery essay he had written for a class at Norwich, Cross obliged his friend with a critique. Though useful in some particulars, it was most notable for the critic's merciless manner. "1st I do not like the subject," Cross wrote. "2nd I do not like the style. 3rd I do not like so many adjectives. . . . It is more like a school girl's composition than the product of a military student."

Several of Cross's own literary efforts were patriotic stories based on New Hampshire military history. An early one, which appeared in the *Cincinnati Times*, was "The Young Volunteers; An Incident of the Mexican War." Following the custom of the day, Cross signed it with a pseudonym, the name of his late grandfather, the Revolutionary War veteran Richard Everett. The story delivered what its title promised: the heroic, if bloody, adventures of two members of a volunteer infantry regiment from New England. But the opening paragraph introduced the author, not the story. It was pure autobiography, showing how Cross saw himself and how he imagined his future.

"There is no class of men who have the passion for adventure, the love of excitement, so largely developed, as printers," he began. "They are continually wandering from city to city, from land to land—restless, unsettled, and ready to engage in any enterprise that promises honor and profit, or affords them an opportunity to 'see the world.' Being always intelligent, well-informed men (their business makes them so), they generally fall into the leading rank of adventurers. . . . There are few *old* printers; the business is followed awhile and then left for something more productive of that great necessity to human enjoyment—cash. It is an excellent business to *rise* from; it furnishes many of our most talented and popular men—authors, editors, speakers, lawyers, physicians, and even clergymen. A printer is well versed in human nature—there is no place like a printing office to sharpen a man's ideas, and give him a knowledge of the real motives, intents, and actions of humanity. Thus a printer grows wise, as it were, has an inexhaustible store of miscellaneous information, and no one can say that they do not do their part towards moving on the world. They are great lovers of the drama—many of them become actors, and good ones, too. . . . Printers are peculiar men; they have a tinge of melancholy in their natures, a sort of deep conviction that this world is a monstrous humbug—they have found it out—there's no sincerity, no confidence in it."

Beyond his writing ability and his powers of observation and analysis, Cross needed one further qualification to be a journalist: a political stance. This proved to be no obstacle. The American Party, or Know-Nothings, came into their own shortly after Cross's arrival in Cincinnati. The city was a Know-Nothing hotbed, the *Times* an American Party mouthpiece. Cross had grown up in a family of Democrats, but his roots were Anglo-Saxon Protestant. This was the essential trait of the Know-Nothings, who believed that the very idea of America was a protest against the corrupting power of both crown and church. Waves of immigrants fleeing the European turmoil of midcentury had entered the United States; many were Irish Catholics. In a story for the *Times*, Cross praised a bill in Congress aimed at slowing the flow of immigration, writing that it would "prevent America from becoming the poor-house and prison of Europe, as she has been for the last half century." Cross and his newspaper supported any measure that barred Catholics from holding public office. They favored requiring immigrants to wait twenty-one years to become naturalized citizens.

Cross's loyalty to American Party doctrine was genuine. In early 1853, on the eve of a city election, he wrote to Kent of the "mighty influence" of Catholics. "Great excitement is felt here in relation to the doings of the Priests, and I venture to predict some bloody riots ere many days. All the Catholic Churches keep arms in them and there is 60,000 Catholics in our city." His militancy toward Catholics was no less fervid than his hunger for territorial expansion. "Henry," he wrote, "I am anxious to see a war. I hope we shall have trouble with England. I want to see Canada annexed and the whole continent Americanized. I would volunteer at once in case of a rupture." After the American Party triumphed at the polls in 1854, Cross called it "a glorious election" and exclaimed: "Where is Popery? Where are the calculations of the old Hunkers? Gone!"

In his newspaper writings, Cross portrayed America as a culture built on the shoulders of Anglo-Saxon Protestants. He found clever ways to demean other ethnic groups. During a visit to Lancaster, he traveled in the White Mountains and wrote a piece for the *Times* extolling them as a tourist destination. He described a six-hour walk up Mount Washington, the tallest mountain in the Northeast, proudly listing the other peaks of over four thousand feet named after Adams, Jefferson, Monroe, and Jackson. "Thus you see our great men will have monuments that will endure when the puny works of man are crumbled into dust," he wrote. "The 'everlasting hills' bear their names, and they will tower skyward in their glory, while pyramids decay and marble statues are scattered into atoms." There were other mountains in the aptly named Whites, too, lesser mountains. "Many peaks have Indian titles," Cross wrote, "but they are too crooked and unpronounceable for me to chronicle."

Beyond his political criticisms of the Roman Catholic Church, Cross seldom mentioned religious or spiritual matters in his letters to Kent. One exception came after Kent wrote him that a mutual acquaintance had suddenly become "a bright light" of faithfulness after attending a revival meeting. "This is certainly a wonderful transformation, as his brightness has hitherto been hid under a bushel," Cross responded. "I consider these annual revivals as most unmitigated humbugs. There is no true religion in these excitements which come and go with cold weather. I admire true religion but detest hypocrisy. Fits of godliness every winter have always characterized Lancaster, and sin the remaining seasons. This sort of holiness reminds me very much of a blacksmith's fire which only burns while somebody blows the bellows." However skeptical he might be of religious conversion—"I am not very easy to humbug," he wrote—Cross was taken with spiritualism. He sometimes sat with a circle of friends attempting to contact the dead. "My boy," he wrote to Kent, "*there's something in it!* I have investigated for the past year and am convinced of the Truth." Cross named Rix, the late editor from Lancaster, as "one of my particular spirit friends. I have had many talks with him." He expected Kent to doubt him. "Go ahead," he wrote. "We only know enough in this world to be aware that we know nothing."

During the winters of the mid-1850s, the *Times* sent Cross to Washington as a correspondent. Still writing as Richard Everett, he produced a gush of copy nearly every day. His rambling reports touched on a wide variety of events, from squabbles in Congress to the deplorable condition of George Washington's home at Mount Vernon to the launching of a warship. Legislators opposed a thousand-dollar appropriation to buy coal and wood for the city's destitute population in the dead of winter, arguing that it would encourage paupers to move to Washington from other cities. "There is much truth in this argument, but very little charity," Cross wrote. He reported with mock surprise of the presence of many senators and other "first citizens" in one of the capital's notorious gambling dens. He scoffed at President Pierce, a fellow New Hampshireman who would one day be his confidant, as a feckless leader whose only answer to the violence in Kansas was to issue proclamations.

Although Cross had no affection for the South, he saw abolitionists, including John P. Hale of New Hampshire, as a threat to peace. He toured the southern states in 1855. "I do not like the South at all," he wrote Kent from Charleston, South Carolina. "It ought to be numbered among the heathen lands of the earth." And from Raleigh, North Carolina: "This is a miserable country. God only knows how the people subsist. Nothing but tar and pitch, varied by resin and turpentine." Despite these criticisms of the South, Cross urged Kent to work against Hale's candidacy for the U.S. Senate. "If he is elected, the whole South will rear and plunge out of its traces," he wrote. "An Abolitionist is a fanatic and nothing else. I am opposed to the extension of slavery, but consider its immediate abolition a chimera, an impossibility, an insane idea." His visit to the South convinced him "that if you and I live to be fifty years old, we shall see the dissolution of the American Union. It is a dreadful thing to contemplate, but it is inevitable, unless you can hang, or otherwise get rid of the fanatics of N. England." With the bravado of a twenty-two-year-old, Cross personally welcomed the burden of sustaining the union. "My friend," he wrote Kent, "the government and destiny of America is coming into our hands . . . and we should prepare for that trust, and labor for the common good and common honor of the mighty confederacy."

Cross left the capital in early 1856 to cover the American Party's council in Philadelphia, an assignment that proved painful to him. Before the opening gavel fell, the party had split along sectional lines when its northern branch endorsed admitting Kansas as a free state. Its future was bleak. Cross tried to put the best face on the proceedings but fell to chronicling petty disputes. His story on the fight over whether to seat the Louisiana delegation was typical. The Lousianans considered themselves "Gallicans" — Catholics by birth who had renounced papal and priestly power. The delegation's chairman convinced party leaders to seat the Gallicans, but his arguments did not sway Cross. "There is an enormous amount of Jesuitism among even the Gallican Catholics," he wrote, "and when once it is decided to admit them, a broad road is opened to the whole Papal system, and we once more take the serpent to our bosom." Let the Louisianans in, and "we shall have the veriest Papists among us now, putting on the Gallican mask and claiming a brotherhood with the American party!"

As the brotherhood dwindled, Cross held to his beliefs and cast about for a party that would accommodate them. "The American Party may dissolve," he wrote Kent, "but its doctrines are to stand inviolate. Whatever may come, I shall stand by them to the last, and never so help me the Eternal God will I cast a vote for a foreigner or a Roman Catholic!" Initially he could not bring himself to return to the Democratic Party, which he found as different from the party of Jackson "as the Lord's prayer and the Devil's dream." Nor could he support "the 'Republican' doctrines—in fact I have not yet found out what they are. Slavery cannot be interfered with in the states where it exists, and the Constitution declares that a state shall be admitted with such institutions as she may elect. So what does this agitation amount to? Simply the placing in power of ignorant, stubborn, hollow-hearted demagogues." He backed Millard Fillmore, the American Party nominee, in the presidential election of 1856. "I enlisted in the American ranks for the war and intend to stand by our colors until we gain the victory or go down like brave men with our flag flying in defiance." The next year, with his party extinct, James Buchanan elected, and the Dred Scott decision inspiriting the North, Cross relented and became a Democrat. Kent was a Republican, and Cross chided him for it, ridiculing the new party as "a good hobby to ride" and stating his convictions in stark terms. "Negroes are *not citizens* and never should be," he wrote. "This is a white man's government."

Although Cross ran the *Cincinnati Times*'s eight-man editorial staff by 1857, commanding an annual salary of eleven hundred dollars, he began planning to pull up stakes and move farther west when offered a new job in Arizona. He was wistful about this move. "True, I love New England well . . . but the *West* is my future field of action," he wrote Kent. "Sometimes I think I shall return to dwell beneath the shadow of our ancient mountains, but each day the boyish charm grows fainter and fainter as new associations cluster around the heart and ties of interest and friendship grow stronger and stronger." After years of urging Kent to leave Lancaster and join his adventure, he now advised him to stay put. "Good men—talented men are rare in the old Granite State," he wrote. "Stay by her in her old age, as it were, when her children are scattered."

Cross's new employer was the Santa Rita Silver Mining Company. Three years earlier, Major Samuel Heintzelman of Cincinnati had organized the first silver mining company sent to Arizona, and the venture had prospered. The owners of the new company intended to follow Heintzelman's lead, setting up operations in the Santa Rita mountains twelve miles from Tubac, Arizona, an old Spanish mission settlement. One owner, a Cincinnati editor named William Wrightson, decided to start a newspaper to promote the company's interests. He planned to haul a printing press west—it would be Arizona's first—and he hired Cross as his editor. The deal included a share in the mine. "It is a venture of some magnitude, but well suited to my roving disposition," Cross wrote Kent.

In a series of articles for the *Cincinnati Times* beginning in August 1858, Cross took his readers with him on the journey with the wagon train carrying equipment and provisions to the Santa Rita mines. He was by now a twenty-six-year-old man, secure in his opinions and expert in his skills as a reporter. He was equal parts historian, social commentator, naturalist, humorist, polemicist, and promoter. Whatever the material prospects of the expedition, it was the journey itself that captivated Cross. Life in the saddle, the presence of danger, the company of men, the days of prairie tedium broken by mountain vistas, and above all the allure of adventure in a vast, young, and expanding country—all these filled him with a wonder that enlivened his accounts.

Cross's journey began with passage aboard the *Fanny Bullitt* down the Ohio and Mississippi Rivers from Cincinnati to New Orleans. To his dismay, the riverboat departed thirty-two hours late, carried so much cargo that it could run only by day, and took twelve days to inch from Louisville to New Orleans. "Nothing can be more dull and monotonous than the scenery of the Mississippi once the first impression of immensity and grandeur has worn away," Cross wrote. "For hours you sail through a wilderness, whose giant trees hang over the dark waters, and then perhaps pass a small clearing, where some adventurous 'Sucker,' or 'Corncracker,' or 'Puke,' as the inhabitants of Illinois, Tennessee and Missouri are severally termed, has established a wood-yard." On his earlier trip south, Cross had stopped in Napoleon, a town at the mouth of the Arkansas River, and found it to be "a nest of thieves, gamblers, drunkards, bullies and knaves." Now, when the *Fanny Bullitt* docked there to take on passengers, "the few individuals who came on board walked straight to the bar, and deigned to converse with no man until they were 'liquored.' As usual, they were of the sallow miserable, hard-up, aguish race which inhabits the small villages of the Mississippi."

The departure point for the Santa Rita party's overland journey was Port Lavaca, Texas, a hundred miles southwest of Galveston and four hundred miles by water from New Orleans. Cross had little good to report about his stay in New Orleans, where "a green putrid water" ran in the gutters, adding to the stench of rotten vegetables and garbage in the streets. Yellow fever was epidemic. "Funeral processions are seen on almost every street," Cross wrote. Fifty-two people died of the fever in a single day during his stay. Though happy to leave, he and his party only grudgingly paid the price for passage down the Gulf of Mexico aboard the steamer *Matagorda*. The cost was twenty dollars per person, plus a dollar per hundred pounds of heavy freight. Once on the gulf, Cross marveled at the porpoises that raced alongside the ship, but he soon succumbed to seasickness, "like death . . . a common leveler." After thirty-six hours, the *Matagorda* reached Galveston and steamed on to Indianola, where Cross and company caught a sloop to Port Lavaca.

All across Texas, first to San Antonio, then on to El Paso, on a mule train journey of nearly six hundred miles, Cross portrayed the people he encountered through the filter of his own opinions. He ridiculed Mexicans and blamed the Catholic Church for failing to raise them up. "The children are commonly quite pretty," he wrote, "but as they grow up both sexes assume the Aztec physiognomy, which is far from being beautiful. They all have a profusion of jet black hair, and it is one source of occupation to relieve each other of the 'live stock' which inhabits it, and in the performance of this to them, very pleasant duty, they manifest a surprising dexterity, cracking the 'animals' on their thumb nails and then (must the awful truth be told?) *eating them*!" Even when praising the skill of the hired Mexican muleteers who drove the wagon train, Cross could not resist an insult. "Nearly all of them cherish beneath their pleasant exterior the treachery and falsehood of the true Spanish and Mexican blood, and brood over the slightest affront until chance offers for their knives to take revenge," he wrote. "On this account they are never furnished with arms by the proprietors for whom they drive." In the crumbling Jesuit missions and poor settlements along the way, Cross saw evidence that the Catholic Church had failed in Texas by imposing religion on the natives without laying the necessary foundation. "The clearing up of the forests, the plow which follows the log cabin, the villager, the free school, the newspaper, all these forms of true civilization, are left for the practical Saxon, who believes that before men can be converted they must be enlightened. It is impossible to stamp Christianity upon the darkened mind of the savage with any permanence."

In Texas's German villages, Cross found a counterpoint to both the depravity of the Mexicans and the sloth of the Southerners who had settled in Texas. Since many of his readers in Cincinnati were German-Americans, it was only natural that he praise the Germans, but the contrasts he drew were stark. Slavery, Cross wrote, had made the cotton farmers lazy. Despite the fertility of Texas soil, most Southerners grew only cotton, buying dairy products and vegetables elsewhere at high prices. The German settlements, on the other hand, were "the oases of civilization. A neat village, clean and well laid out, the houses adorned with paint and green blinds, with a flower garden in front, and a broad-acre of vegetables in the rear. Here also you shall find butter, cheese, milk and fruit, as good as can be found in the fatherland. The Germans, *tidy and industrious, temperate*, and comparatively refined, are missionaries in Texas, and bless every locality where they are found." The Germans were "not insane upon the subject of cotton; neither demented concerning 'the nigger business,' but prefer, like rational beings, to enjoy the good things of life, and have property in something else besides lands and Negroes." Southerners called German immigrants the "d——d free-labor Dutch," but why they failed to follow the German example Cross could not fathom. Of one obstinate Southerner, he wrote: "The most charitable opinion of such a person must be, that he is a fool, when before his eyes are the abundant evidences of the blessings of free labor to give the lie to his senseless denunciations."

On a less caustic note, Cross often wrote of the trials he endured in camp, from the minor annoyances of life under the open skies to the monotony of a cuisine heavy on bacon and beans. He catalogued the reptiles and insects he encountered, admitting to a fear of snakes, especially rattlers and moccasins, and cursing the assortment of tarantulas, ants, ticks, mosquitoes, and roaches that thrived in the late-summer heat. "No sooner do you lie down at night than exploring parties start up your trousers legs, and the fleas commence the practice of phlebotomy with all the zeal of 'old school' doctors," he wrote. One night during a storm, Cross experienced a more stunning natural phenomenon. He was standing with a group of men "engaged in the praiseworthy operation of tapping a five gallon keg of whiskey" when a ball of fire shot from the sky. As thunder pealed, "I felt a sudden blow upon my right foot as though struck by a sledgehammer, a fearful shock of electricity and was conscious of being pitched violently to the ground." He lay insensible for half an hour, struck not by a sledgehammer but by lightning. The same bolt hit at least three other men and two mules. In quieter times in camp, he had other preoccupations. He was "elevated to the dignity of chief cook of mess number two" and had to satisfy "seven invincible appetites." One article included Cross's recipe for fresh venison; another extolled "a sort of Meg Merriles stew" that the doctor in the party had concocted from mule rabbits, prairie hens, quails, and turtles.

The Rio Grande was a milestone on the journey, and Cross rode with the advance party of five horsemen when the train approached it. One of his companions, who was riding a lame horse, challenged the other four to race for the river and offered a bottle of El Paso wine to the winner. "In an instant, flourishing our rifles, and whooping a la Camanche, four of us were off, spurring our horses to their utmost speed," Cross wrote. Two fell away after two hundred yards, leaving Cross neck and neck with one last challenger. "With a tremendous leap, clear over a bunch of mesquite, my gallant old mustang, 'Grey Devil,' forged ahead, and, keeping up his pace, came out in triumph, and was the first horse to plunge his nose in the Rio Grande—an event which his rider duly celebrated by a series of Indian yells, and a fusilade from his 'six-shooter.'" Cross vowed that when the party reached El Paso, he would split the prize bottle of wine with Grey Devil.

It was in El Paso that Cross committed an act out of character for a man who saw himself as a paragon of virtue in a land of infidels. He visited the old

Roman Catholic Church, whose construction had begun in 1620, the year the Pilgrims came to Massachusetts. Cross noted this fact with patriotic feeling and described the cathedral in respectful terms. He and another member of the Santa Rita mining party climbed into the ancient belfry to enjoy the view. As they were leaving, they decided to pilfer a souvenir. They stole two iron pieces of a bell tongue, which lay "temptingly in view worn out and useless for their purpose," Cross wrote. He was quick to make excuses for himself. "If there was any sacrilege in the act it must be charged to a spirit of veneration for the time-honored edifice and not to a vulgar desire of plunder, nor intentional desecration," he wrote. "My portion of the prize I value highly, and shall long keep it as a memento of one of the oldest religious edifices on the continent."

As the party headed farther west, a new danger grew. Cross knew his readers were interested in stories about hostile Indians, and he did not disappoint them. He wrote about a Cincinnati lawyer who had traveled to Texas looking for a new home. During his visit, the body of a German was brought into town with a three-foot arrow sticking through it. The lawyer's "numerous friends," Cross wrote, "will no doubt have lively hopes that he may avoid such penetrating evidence of savage regard." When Cross's party came upon the grave of five men killed by Indians, he reported: "They have a wild and romantic resting place, where the wolf howls and the raven croaks in dreary lonesomeness." Despite the light and sentimental touches Cross brought to these stories, the danger of Indian attack was real. One measure of its seriousness was the arsenal the party carried. "A company of twenty-five Americans, armed as we are armed, can safely defy two hundred Indians, unless we are besieged at a distance from water," Cross wrote. One morning in camp, he inventoried the weapons. Along with twenty-four hundred rounds of ammunition, he counted eight Bowie knives, eight Colt cavalry carbines, ten U.S. rifles, six double-barreled guns, twenty-seven Colt cavalry pistols, and twelve Burnside carbines. The Burnside was a relatively new model, named after Ambrose Burnside, who manufactured it in Rhode Island. After watching a member of the party use one to shoot a coyote at more than three hundred yards, Cross pronounced it "a splendid weapon for frontier service." It would, in other words, be useful for shooting Indians.

And yet in one article Cross seemed to view Indians as a natural feature of the landscape and to regard their way of life with admiration. This occurred on December 1, the day the party crossed the Continental Divide. Winter was coming, but the Ohioans had left their warmest clothes behind. When frigid weather gave them "a pretty good idea of the celebrated retreat from Moscow," they improvised. "Our camp is now worthy of Jack Falstaff's brigade," Cross wrote. "Coats, pants and over-alls, temporized for the season from blankets, corn-bags, and every available material, cut and made in quaint styles, give to the wearers a very motley appearance." While he took his turn on guard duty at four o'clock that morning, the clouds cleared away, revealing more stars than he had ever seen. "Between watching for Apaches, and keeping warm, there was little time for star-gazing," he wrote, "but as day broke the scene was more than glorious—it was divine—and at the risk of getting an arrow through my body, I sat down on a rock to scribble in my note book some doggerel verses on the occasion." One stanza read:

> Daylight is breaking,
> Nature is waking,
> Slowly the moon fades away in the blue;
> The bright tint of morning
> The East is adorning,
> And the heavens are gay with the sun's golden hue.

When the men of the Santa Rita company reached the Continental Divide's western (Pacific) slope, in southern New Mexico, they unfurled the American flag and gave three cheers. Cross paused to admire the view. To the north he noted the Copper Mine Range, home to Mangus Colorado and his Apache band. The men could count Apache campfires at night and see signs by day that their train was being watched. "No Indians are more vigilant, wary and active than the Apaches," Cross wrote. "Mounted on their fleet horses, and armed with their long bows and keen lances, they sally forth from their strongholds in the hills on expeditions of war and plunder, carrying their forays far into Mexico, returning laden with spoil and driving great herds of mules and horses."

In early January 1859, Cross and his party reached Tubac, a town just south of Tucson. Tubac was headquarters to Heintzelman's Sonora Silver Mining Company, and now the Santa Rita. A trading post had transformed the town into a commercial and social center of a thousand people. Cross hoped to make his fortune through his shares in the silver mine while editing the company newspaper, but it was a perilous place. "We have no law here," he wrote Kent. "Everyone goes around with six-shooter, rifle and bowie knife for between Apaches, Mexicans & bad white men, one needs arms always." In six months, in a radius of sixty miles, Cross counted thirteen violent deaths. Writing for several newspapers back east under the fanciful nom de plume "Gila," he described a bleak frontier outpost in desperate need of a judicial system and more Anglo immigrants. His readers should disregard the overblown population figures they might have seen elsewhere, he wrote, as there were fewer than 250 white Americans in all of Arizona. A man who had visited every village had counted nineteen American women. "I had previously heard the number stated at twenty-four, and of that number we can count thirteen within a circle of forty-five miles from us," Cross wrote. "Were it not for bringing our limited assortment of fair ones into unenviable notoriety, I would give the names of the entire lot."

While supplying readers in the East with such accounts, Cross also started Arizona's first newspaper, the *Weekly Arizonian*. It ran four pages and was printed on a hand-operated cast-iron Washington press. In his first editorial, Cross wrote that circulation would be small and expenses great. "It is not, therefore, with very bright prospects of pecuniary return that we begin our labors." He described the anarchy of the territory and wrote that "one great object" of the *Arizonian* would be "to advocate the establishment of law and government in Arizona." Cross opened the editorial quest for forcible seizure of Sonora, the Mexican state just south of Arizona. The goal was access to gulf ports that would make the transport of goods and mining equipment to Arizona cheaper, faster, and safer. Captain Richard Ewell, the commandant at Fort Buchanan, was willing to wage war on the Apaches and to seize Sonora —if only he had twenty-five hundred American soldiers. Cross lamented that a measure to supply such a force had failed in Congress by a single vote. On national political affairs, the *Arizonian* vowed neutrality. The paper held strong views, Cross wrote, but they were irrelevant "until government extends to us the right of suffrage," and thus he promised to keep them to himself. This reticence raised suspicions. Within months Cross felt obliged to write: "Some malicious persons have circulated a report that this paper was Black Republican. . . . Because we have endeavored to avoid politics, for the present, some people imagine we have Black Republican proclivities, which is very far from the fact."

For an editor, jostling over politics came with the territory, but in a frontier setting with a small white population, Cross's incendiary style invited trouble. Until he arrived, Sylvester Mowry, a mine owner from Tucson, had enjoyed a near monopoly in creating the impressions of Arizona appearing in the newspapers of the important eastern cities. When Cross raised questions about the way Arizona had been portrayed, he did so at Mowry's expense. In a snide passage on the front page of the very first edition of the *Arizonian*, Cross baited Mowry. He had seen an account in a New York newspaper asserting that a rich silver vein had been found on Mowry's land and that "an excited mining fever" was running through Arizona. Cross goaded the *New York Times* to document this great discovery and to "designate some particular locality where a few cases of the above mentioned 'mining fever' may be found!" Mowry was in Washington and thus not immediately aware of this ridicule, but he had seen a scathing letter from Cross, writing as Gila, in the *Washington (D.C.) States*. Mowry struck back, writing to the *States* that Gila "has never seen enough of Arizona to write intelligibly about it."

Cross read into Mowry's criticism an assault on his character, and Gila's pen went for the jugular. Before coming to Arizona, Cross wrote to the *States*, he had read and trusted Mowry's "voluminous" accounts of conditions there. Now Cross falsely claimed that Mowry had never even lived in Arizona and that Mowry's "productions" were "fabulous." "In representing Arizona to be a good agricultural country, he was absolutely injuring the Territory, and deluding people into a long and dangerous journey to a country whose agricultural resources, in all, are not equal to one first-class corn-growing county in Ohio," Cross wrote. He called Mowry's letters and pamphlets "the laughing stock of the western portion of the Territory."

By the time Mowry returned to Arizona, words no longer sufficed as weapons in his rivalry with Cross. He challenged the *Arizonian*'s editor to a duel. Mowry was no stranger to firearms or codes of honor. He had graduated from West Point and served five years in the army before resigning to enter the mining business. Cross had called him dishonest and threatened his interests, and he had but one recourse. "It is a part of the freedom of the press that any man may mapoon another in the papers, and to this fact I am indebted for the blackguardism to which Mr. Cross has resorted," Mowry wrote to the *States*. "The fact that I have raised him to the level of a gentleman, by demanding of him personal satisfaction for the scurrilous language he has used towards me, prevents my showing him in his true light."

On the morning of July 8, 1859, a strong wind swept across the dusty streets of Tubac as miners and farmers from miles around made their way to the central plaza, where the local editor and the Tucson firebrand had vowed to shoot it out. Mowry and Cross had reputations as marksmen, and the particulars of the duel almost assured that one of them would die: they had agreed to use Burnside carbines at forty paces. The principals arrived in the square, and the crowd parted, creating an ample field of fire. Mowry and Cross took the carbines from their seconds and counted the steps to their assigned places. On cue, they turned, aimed, and fired. Neither was hit. Three more times, each man broke his barrel, inserted a brass cartridge, aimed anew, and pulled the trigger. On the fourth round, only Cross's carbine fired, but Mowry stood unbloodied. A dispute broke out about whether, because of the misfire, Mowry should be granted a free shot. He seemed inclined to take one, but many in the crowd warned him against it. Voices cried out, "Hold your fire!

Don't shoot, Mowry!" After a few moments in which the duel threatened to grow into a wider conflict, Cross settled the issue. He handed his carbine to his second, folded his arms across his chest, and told Mowry to take his shot. Mowry reloaded, brought his Burnside to his shoulder, pointed it sky-ward, and fired. He declared himself satisfied, and the duel was over. "It was bad shooting, but the wind saved us," Cross wrote Kent. "It blew a perfect gale across the line of fire. His second ball tore the skin on my right ear, while my ball No. 3 ripped his coat across the heart." He added a couplet: "Alas, what perils do environ / The man who meddles with old iron."

The combatants observed the rituals of shaking hands and making public apologies, but even without drawing blood, Mowry found a way to win the duel. Both the *States* and the *Arizonian* published the apologies. Cross, the item read, "withdraws the offensive language used by him, and disclaims any intention to reflect upon Mr. Mowry's veracity or upon his reputation as a gentleman." Mowry declared himself "satisfied from personal explanations that he has done an injustice to Mr. Cross' character and motives . . . and takes pleasure in withdrawing the imputations against Mr. Cross." Any difference of opinion they might have about Arizona was "an honest one," the two men asserted. Despite the conciliatory words, the incident had taught Mowry that a printing press in the wrong hands—especially if it was the only printing press—could threaten his designs for Arizona, his political ambitions, and even his life. The week after the apology appeared, the *Arizonian* carried the news that Mowry had bought the paper and the press and would take them to Tucson. The price was twenty-five hundred dollars. The new owners did not question either Cross's "honesty of purpose" or ability to run the paper, but they intended to turn the *Arizonian* into a partisan sheet. Cross, the paper reported in a bit of fanciful phrasing, "has retired to the country to rusticate."

Cross offered both private and a public assessments of the sale of the paper he had edited for a scant four and a half months. "Couldn't stand it—too many fights—might as well try to issue a paper in the hot place where gates 'stand open night & day,' as the hymn says," he wrote Kent. In a farewell message in the paper itself, he called the editor's job "perilous, precarious, and thankless." He had given the *Arizonian* his full attention, and "time will prove the right or wrong of my exertions. At present I would not alter a line that has been written. Some kind friends have cheered me, some people have found fault. To the former I am thankful, to the latter I have no apologies to offer."

In the ensuing weeks, a story spread across the country that Cross was dead. Almost certainly it began with a column by Cross's old Lancaster sidekick, the prankster Charles Farrar Browne, now writing as Artemus Ward in the *Cleveland Plain Dealer*. Ward's column, titled "The Fighting Editor," reported that not long after Cross had survived the duel, several Mexican men became angry with him over the incessant barking of his dogs. These "Mexicans fell on Cross and cut him to pieces," Ward wrote. "Thus goes the story," he added. "It may or may not be true." Cross read a notice of his own death in the *Boston Post* and was not amused. "Who the devil started such a cruel hoax?" he wrote Kent. "If 'Fungus' Browne wrote that infernal lie I'll have a bit of satisfaction that he will remember to his dying day."

From the time he lost the editorship of the *Arizonian* until the outbreak of the Civil War, Cross remained on the move, sometimes with little direction. He traveled cross-country to New Hampshire in late 1859. Along the way he stopped to see his younger brother Richard, an army engineer stationed at Fort Fillmore on the Rio Grande. He returned to Arizona to look after his interest in the Santa Rita silver mine. He had made two thousand dollars the previous year and used some of it to pay his mother's grocery bills in Lancaster, a responsibility he had shouldered for years. Because his father had alcohol and money problems, Cross paid local merchants directly to make sure the provisions reached his mother. In 1860, as a volunteer, he joined Captain Ewell, the local army commander and future Confederate general, on a scouting party to search for Apaches. One correspondent wrote of Ewell and his mission: "It is expected he will bring the redskins to their senses, and to his terms, which will be peace with the whites, for the Apache will steal, and mule and horse meat is a delicacy with them." Cross spent several months commanding an army garrison in Sonora in a Mexican civil war. He took the side of Benito Juarez's Liberal Army, which sought to restore an 1857 constitution based on democratic principles. As he had in his writings in the *Arizonian*, Cross approved of Juarez's efforts toward popular government and against the entrenched powers in Mexico City, especially the Roman Catholic Church.

The wayward nature of Cross's endeavors during these months had counterparts in both his political outlook and his personal life. His initial optimism about President Buchanan quickly faded. "Sick of old Buck and the crowd of Harpies that hang around him," he wrote Kent. But he still could not abide the abolitionist tint of the Republican Party. His real hope was for a revival of the American Party. "Truth squashed to earth will rise again," he wrote, quoting the mayor of Chicago. In the meantime, he decided early on his choice in the 1860 presidential election. He supported Stephen Douglas, the Democrat from Illinois. "I am a Douglas man—can't go Seward & hate Hale," he wrote. But Cross was losing touch with events back home. When his mother wrote him that Kent had married, he congratulated his old friend but wasn't sure who the bride was. He correctly assumed it was Kent's longtime companion, but even that caused him a tinge of melancholy, in part because he had once had romantic feelings toward the woman himself. "What is life without woman's love to hope and struggle for?" he wrote Kent. "Full well do I know the lonely days and desolate periods which mark the existence of one who has no dear object around which to garner up the treasures of his heart." He worried that he was "fast becoming a withered, part-bitten cabbage stalk in the garden of the world, in the interesting position of caring for nobody while nobody cares for me—a misanthropic wanderer up and down the broad aisles of the world, having, like the old gentleman in the Bible, no 'abiding city!' However, I intend to appear before you some day like the ancient Marriner returned from his voyaging, though I trust not with the same bad fortune that haunted that worthy individual." A few months later, Cross revisited the same theme in a letter from Tubac. "I have had an adventurous life here, but having accrued an ample interest in the rich silver mines hope to be able to 'settle down' soon. Of course, nobody will marry me—that is, no one I want." These reflections flowed from the pen of a twenty-seven-year-old man whose vast hungers and energies had carried him far from the hills and the conventions of a small town north of New Hampshire's White Mountains.

Sooner than he expected, the outbreak of the Civil War offered Cross a way back. He could have taken a commission as a captain in a regiment of mounted rifles in Arizona but chose instead to return to his native state. By July 3, 1861, he had settled his affairs in Arizona and traveled to San Francisco. He wrote Kent from there, beginning with these words: "I am ready for the wars." Kent, who was by now a rising Republican, was in a perfect position to help his old friend. In April, days after the Rebels fired on Fort Sumter, Kent had been appointed to assist New Hampshire's adjutant general in organizing the state's recruiting efforts. Cross let Kent know he was prepared to accept almost any position Governor Nathaniel Berry offered, but he preferred "mounted service, with which I am familiar, as three years of Indian fighting has made me a tolerable partisan officer."

By the time Cross reached home in August, the Union defeat at Bull Run had already snuffed out optimism in the North about a brief war, and the volunteer infantry regiments then forming in New Hampshire were committed to three years' service. Berry needed experienced military men to run them. He offered Cross a colonel's commission to lead the Fifth Regiment, New Hampshire Volunteers. The governor granted him several requests, including the right to choose his senior officers, but it is hard to imagine Cross would have turned down this opportunity under any circumstances. It was the chance of a lifetime, and everything he had dreamed and done had prepared him for it. Just when he needed it most, the Civil War had given him a story to live. Now he could hardly contain his desire to begin seeing to every detail of his new command and molding the Fifth New Hampshire in his own image.

Coming Together

"A more noble set of men never left
N.H., and never will."

 — *National Eagle* of Claremont,
  November 14, 1861

I N SEPTEMBER OF 1861 THE CENTER OF ATTENTION IN Concord was not the State House but a bullet-scarred tent in its yard. The man responsible for erecting it was thirty-five-year-old Edward Sturtevant, a well-known, well-liked, and well-practiced master of the dramatic gesture. The tent had been captured from the British in the War of 1812 and delivered to Concord during a visit from President Andrew Jackson in 1833. Sturtevant delighted in the patriotic heritage it evoked, believing it would help attract one hundred men to serve as a company under his command in the Fifth New Hampshire Volunteers. Though Sturtevant's approach was promising, the circumstances seemed less so, because the five months since the war's outbreak had been full of setbacks. But the Union's struggle did not discourage Sturtevant, and it did little to discourage others from following him. He recruited most of his company in less than a week. Nine other captains recruiting companies for the Fifth around the state enjoyed similar success, and their commander-to-be, Colonel Cross, was pleased with the reports reaching him in Concord. On September 15, two and half weeks after Cross became the regiment's first member, he wrote to Henry Kent. "Everything goes on first rate with the 5th," Cross said. "Over 650 men are reported. What regiment was ever raised so soon in this State? Every article of equipment is under contract. I shall start the camp at once and call in the men."

As these recruits gathered under Cross's command, they thought of themselves not as federal troops but as New Hampshire men, and they viewed the rebellion crisis through the window that was their state. As they knew, the first months of the war had been a trial for New Hampshire as well as the

Union. These months are the setting from which the Fifth rose, and so they are important to its story. Unlike Cross, who had been away in the West, Sturtevant experienced New Hampshire's war from the very beginning.

Sturtevant was a natural leader, like the colonel, but was easy rather than edgy in temperament. As a youth learning the printer's trade, he passed lazy summer evenings with friends who gathered to swim in the Merrimack River as it flowed behind the railroad yard in Concord. It was Sturtevant's habit to place the lighted end of his cigar in his mouth before slipping under the warm water. When he surfaced, he withdrew the cigar and puffed smoke like a loco-motive as he continued deliberately toward the far side. Sturtevant was suffi-ciently adventurous to move as a young man to Richmond, Virginia, where he worked as a printer for a pro-slavery paper; he was sufficiently bold to wrangle an invitation to a White House ball, where he delighted in playfully stepping on the hems of the pretty ladies' gowns. By 1855, at the age of twenty-nine, Sturtevant was back in Concord, where he served as night constable and became a fixture in the community. As an officer of the law, he was a willing soldier in the temperance movement. But in the spring of 1861, as true war grew near, he became eager to enlist in the nation's cause instead. At last, on April 12, a drizzly day in Concord, rebel forces attacked the federal Fort Sumter in South Carolina. "The storm has burst," a friend told Sturtevant. "Yes," he answered, "and I shall be in the thickest of it." The fort surrendered the next day, and as Sturtevant made his rounds that evening, he told friends that he would be the first to answer the expected call for volunteers. It came on the morning of April 15, reaching Concord by telegraph at eight. Friends rushed to the Phenix Hotel, where he lived, and roused Sturtevant, who hur-ried the two blocks to the State House, marched into the adjutant general's office, and offered his services. He was, as he had hoped to be, New Hamp-shire's first Civil War volunteer. By day's end, he had recruited fifty others; by month's end, he had recruited 226, the second-highest total in the state. His success made Sturtevant a captain in the First New Hampshire Volun-teers, a regiment of eager men enlisted for only three months of service.

In the days after Fort Sumter, three months seemed more than enough time to save the nation. The United States was not yet eighty years old; it was as much a family heirloom as a political entity, a treasure handed successfully through several generations and not to be lost by the latest. Across all of New Hampshire, young men buzzed over the prospect of enlisting in a glorious crusade. Selectmen called town meetings that surpassed any in memory for attendance and excitement. Editors of newspapers defined by their politics demanded that politics be put aside. Clergymen took to the pulpit and cele-brated the Union's holy cause. Voters raised taxes to arm soldiers and support

their families. Women convened in churches to make shirts, socks, and drawers. And the first volunteers who stepped forward were treated, prematurely,
like conquering heroes.

There were sixteen such volunteers in Amherst, a proud town with handsome white homes arrayed around a village green. The volunteers were celebrated a week after Fort Sumter by a gathering that newspaperman Edward
Boylston called "the most enthusiastic meeting in this place since that which
followed the announcing of the Declaration of Independence from the old
Rock on the Common." The audience sustained its enthusiasm through fourteen speeches, a vote to pay the volunteers eighteen dollars a month, and the
adoption of this resolution: "That, inasmuch as we regard the Constitutional
liberties secured to us by the Fathers of the Revolution as the most valuable
legacy we can bequeath to our children, no efforts or sacrifices shall be lacking
on our part to preserve them in their original purity, and to hand them down
unimpaired to posterity." The next day, eleven of the volunteers marched with
the accompaniment of a fife and a drum to the adjoining town of Milford,
where they paid their respects to the volunteers there. Along the way they
stopped at a Daguerrian photography salon, where they posed before the
American flag. Two threw back their shoulders and puffed out their chests
with belligerent pride.

In Concord, the capital and a burgeoning railroad center, the stars and
stripes appeared everywhere at once: at city hall and the railroad station, on
lapels or locomotives, outside homes or in shop windows. The *New Hampshire Patriot* was a leading Democratic paper that had warned of disaster if
Abraham Lincoln and his Republicans gained power, but now its editor,
William Butterfield, made his allegiance clear: "The policy which has brought
this terrible catastrophe upon us, is not [the Democrats'] policy; but the Government is their Government, by whomsoever administered. The country is
their country; the Constitution is their Constitution; the Flag, the glorious
stars and stripes, is their Flag; and that country, that Government, that Constitution, and that Flag have been for sixty years their peculiar charge. . . . The
same is true now; and their duty is plain and imperative, and it must and will
be performed." The city council appropriated ten thousand dollars for the
families of volunteers, and doctors offered them free care. At a public meeting
on April 19, the Reverend Henry Parker of the South Congregational Church
rose to address the crowd. "We ought to rejoice that we are permitted to live
in this country," he said, "to strive, and fight, and die, if need be, for the great
principle that underlies this government. The great crime that is sought to
be committed is the destruction of our republican form of government. We
must prove our title to our patriotic ancestry by fighting on the battlefield in

defense of the blessings which they have left us." Parker's speech came on the eighty-sixth anniversary of the Revolutionary War's first battles at Lexington and Concord, Massachusetts.

In Claremont, long a prosperous farming community and now an emerging manufacturing center too, there was no need to put partisan politics aside, because the town was Republican to the core. "We are glad and proud to say that the popular current is rushing on in loyalty," said the *Northern Advocate*, "with a patriotic determination to sustain the Flag and the Honor of the country." The current carried through three packed public meetings and at least twenty-seven speeches in the week after Sumter. On the evening of April 29, two weeks after President Lincoln called for volunteers, the town prepared to send eighty-five recruits to war. Their recruiting agent and captain, William Austin, received a sword. The soldiers received revolvers and dirks; the Claremont Manufacturing Company presented them with pocket Bibles. "The ladies gave to each two pairs of flannel drawers, two flannel shirts, woolen socks, towels, pocket handkerchiefs and a needlebook well filled with useful articles," reported Otis Waite. The recruits marched to the railroad station at six the next morning, where a crowd of four hundred gathered—one in every ten Claremont residents. The men received one more gift—a day's supply of cold meats, breads, and pickles—before departing for Concord amid cheers and tears.

Lost in the frenzy was one salient fact: few knew what they were doing. The First New Hampshire Volunteers was commanded by Colonel Mason Tappan, who owed his position to politics rather than aptitude or experience. Tappan was an anti-slavery congressman with wild hair and an unruly mustache, and, like the governor who appointed him, he was a Republican. The officers in the regiment's ten companies were typically beginners whose preparation consisted of studying a manual on infantry tactics and drill. The soldiers were amateurs too, and spirited ones. To volunteers who had risen in defense of a free nation, taking orders from any man seemed unnatural and drilling seemed inglorious.

The combination of uncertain leaders and headstrong followers posed disciplinary issues that were not resolved during the regiment's month-long stay at Camp Union in Concord. Reports filed by officers of the guard, charged with maintaining order in camp, reveal unending struggles. "Seized and destroyed five gallons of Ardent Spirritts," one report said. On May 11, a private was arrested for swearing at an officer, "You are a damned son of a bitch, and I don't care a damn for you." The private was fined three dollars. On the fifteenth: "The musicians are very negligent in beating the taps." The nineteenth: "2 females were ordered to retreat from camp at breakfast roll call."

On the twentieth, the officer of the guard discovered a loose board in the wooden fence surrounding the camp, which had obviously served as a "passageway to the city." A patrol of five men was dispatched, and it returned with six prisoners.

Despite the First's troublesome nature (if not because of it), Concord treated its departure for the field on May 25 as a grand event. The men, clad in new uniforms of cadet gray, were escorted by the Governor's Horse Guards, Concord Engine Company Number Two, and two bands. Noisy well-wishers crowded the streets, while others leaned from windows and shouted from rooftops. Sturtevant's company was given the honor of leading the way, carrying the stars and stripes and reveling in the loudest cheers. As the soldiers prepared to board their train at the depot, the crowd surged around the men in a frenzy of red, white, and blue excitement. The regiment of one thousand men was accompanied by twenty women, who were to serve as nurses and laundresses. The train that carried them all south was forty cars long.

In the field, the First continued to be hampered by its undisciplined character. The regiment spent its first two weeks in camp outside Washington, where the soldiers persisted in their adventuresome habits. "The necessity for a systematic punishment of the disgraceful misdemeanors of some of our men is urgently desired by the majority and orderly portion of the troops," one high-minded officer wrote. On June 10, the regiment was ordered to occupy a ferry forty miles up the Potomac River. It took the men five days to reach their destination, a ponderous pace. On the morning of June 17, the men of the First came under fire for the first time, from Rebels with muskets and cannon on the far side of the river. The two sides shot at each other with little effect for about an hour.

That was the end of the First's war-making, save for the loss of five men captured after swimming across the Potomac River for a playful foray in rebel territory. The regiment played no role in the startling federal defeat at Bull Run on July 21, a battle that sent Union soldiers and sight-seeing civilians streaming toward Washington in disarray and discouragement. On August 5, its term of service up, the First arrived back in Concord. The men were treated to a breakfast of cold beef and tongue, white and brown bread, cheese, crackers, and coffee in the State House yard. "The soldiers looked in good health generally," reported the *New Hampshire Patriot*, "but were rough and rusty, and many of them very ragged—showing the shameful neglect of the Government they volunteered to serve and to save. But notwithstanding all this neglect and ill-treatment, we are assured that they have done their duty manfully and promptly, in every respect; and although they have neither won battles nor captured cities, they have done much hard work, have rendered valuable service, and have experienced a large share of the soldier's hardships. They have generally enjoyed good health and have returned in good spirits— many of them prepared, after a brief rest, to enter the ranks again, in the hope of rendering efficient aid in 'conquering a peace.' "

The question of how to prosecute the war already seemed more complicated than when the First New Hampshire was recruited. Democrats continued to wave the flag but grew increasingly critical of Lincoln and Republican war aims. Some said Bull Run was Lincoln's fault, because he rushed the Union army into the field; others said Lincoln's decision to restrict civil liberties showed the government could be as serious a threat to national ideals as the Rebels themselves. Republicans, they warned, were waging war not to restore the Union but to destroy slavery, even if achieving that required them to destroy the nation. Republicans, on the other hand, equated dissent with treason and stressed the limited nature of their aims. "We are not disposed to deny that some ultra abolitionists voted the Republican ticket," said the *National Eagle* of Claremont, "but the most of that class, as is very well known, never vote with any party.—They are quite too pure and sinless for this world."

The war dominated state politics too, as the Republican-controlled Legislature debated how much money to commit to the war effort and under what terms. Lawmakers authorized Republican Governor Nathaniel Berry to spend one million dollars, some of it to repay money his predecessor had borrowed on his own authority to put the First into the field. Democrats tried to halve the spending and failed; they tried to limit spending to "lawful" calls to arms, and failed in that too. Twice repulsed, the Democrats read their frustrations into the record—frustrations that were clearly more fundamental than the issues at hand. "We have asked whether this war contemplates reunion, and if so, in what manner arms are to achieve that object," House Democrats said. "We have asked whether it means the desolation of Southern homes, the overthrow of Southern institutions, and the destruction of our own race there." Two Senate Democrats all but blamed the North for the rebellion. "Our government had its origin in compromise," they said. "It has been preserved by compromise. And have we grown so much wiser and better than our fathers that we have no compromise to offer; that we may with impunity disregard their example?"

More critical still was a Concord newspaper called the *Democratic Standard*, and its harsh words led to violence. The *Standard* assailed Lincoln for his "imbecility, blunders, defeats, and disgrace," and, on August 8, denounced the Union army as "Old Abe's Mob." Word of that reference quickly reached the men of the First, and some seemed intent on proving it apt. A handful of soldiers visited the *Standard*'s office and demanded copies of the paper. They

were given partial editions omitting the offensive remark, but insisted on seeing the rest. "They complained of the paper because it opposed the war," wrote
John Palmer, the publisher. "I told them in the end they would acknowledge
the *Standard* was right. . . . They left without any hard words." In less than
an hour, however, a crowd of civilians and men from the First began gathering outside the *Standard*'s office. Palmer and one of his sons appeared bearing weapons in their second-floor windows, and two law officers struggled
to maintain control of the crowd, which soon numbered in the hundreds.
Finally, led by a fifteen-year-old who was a servant to an officer in the First,
the crowd surged inside. Two shots were fired but no one was seriously injured; the rioters pillaged the office and heaped type, paper, furniture, and
other spoils in the street for a bonfire. For safety's sake, the Palmers were
taken to the state prison in Concord, and debate focused on the extent to
which the men of the First were responsible for the riot. The *Patriot* said
civilian instigators were really to blame, as did Palmer, who struck a note both
defiant and plaintive in a letter two weeks after: "I will close by saying to the
public that I have now no hat, coat or boots to wear—that my clothing was
destroyed with the rest of my property."

For many in New Hampshire, regardless of their politics, the war now
seemed a much more serious matter than it had in the spring. "DULL," sighed
the *Eagle* of Claremont in early August. "Business is dull; the spirits of our
people are duller, and the prospects of any improvement are dullest of all. The
factories are running less time, paying less wages, and employing fewer hands
than usual. It is said that the owners talk of shutting down altogether. The
clerks at the stores lounge about listlessly, and are rather astonished at the
sight of a customer. Everybody is coming down to a war footing, and beginning to realize the difference between peace and war." One difference, of
course, was wounded men, as well as coffins, returning from the field. The
body of Wyman Clement, who had died of typhoid fever, arrived in Claremont on the evening of August 3, about the same time as a letter from Private
Charles Putnam of the Second New Hampshire to his brother about the horrors of Bull Run. "I tell you what it is, George, that was the hardest day's
work I ever did," Putnam wrote. "We fought them nine hours, and looked in
vain for reenforcements. Many were out of ammunition, and we were compelled to retreat. Sometimes the cannon balls struck so near that they would
throw the dirt all over me, but I kept on until I got to the hospital, where I
stopped a few moments to see some of our wounded. I pray God that I may
never witness another such sight. I left and came on about ten rods, and
found two of our own company that were wounded. One was Jack Straw. He
had his leg shot off below the thigh—wanted water—got them some and

started on. I was obliged to pull my boots off and walk in my stocking feet. During thirty-six hours we marched over sixty miles, besides being on the field seven hours, with nothing to eat but hard bread, and nothing to drink but muddy water." Grim as his experience had been, Putnam was certain that the single battle would not—and should not—settle matters. "We had four men killed in our company, nine wounded and five missing," he concluded. "I am entirely well now. They say we must try them again next week. I am ready to go, and if I fall I know I shall be avenged. I know it is a just cause, and am willing to go where duty calls." In Littleton, the *People's Journal* dressed the same sentiment in grander fabric: "Remember, we say, that the blood of those martyrs to the cause of liberty and right, cries out to each one of us, 'send soldiers,' more soldiers to avenge the dead and save those who are still struggling against fearful odds from a similar fate."

Edward Sturtevant tapped this spirit of hard determination when he erected his historic tent in the State House yard in late summer and began recruiting for the Fifth New Hampshire Volunteers. The reality of war had changed the terms of service. Now Sturtevant was looking for men willing to serve three years, not three months, with a bounty of ten dollars, plus one hundred dollars payable at war's end. Many would-be recruits were familiar to Sturtevant; he took the measure of others as they took the measure of him. The captain had an unimposing build and a lazy left eye, but his energy was unflagging as he filled his company and transformed the State House lawn into a training ground, teaching the men how to march in step, turn as one, and otherwise grow accustomed to orders. William Butterfield's newspaper office overlooked the scene from across the street, and he liked what he saw. "Capt. Sturtevant's Company are picked men," Butterfield wrote, "well behaved, and will obey orders and do their duty—so we judge them from three weeks' observation, from our window, of their movements while enlisting."

The Fifth was recruited from across New Hampshire, its ten companies roughly corresponding to the state's ten counties. For the most part, like Sturtevant, the Fifth's company captains were prominent men in their communities, though it did not always follow that they were well suited to military command. One with potential was Charles Hapgood, the son of a gunsmith who had become a merchant in Amherst. Hapgood had served as secretary during April's exuberant war meetings, and by summer found he could no longer resist the conflict's call. He sold his interest in a dry goods store to his partner and began recruiting for the Fifth. "Captain Hapgood is a soldier per se," said the local *Farmer's Cabinet*, "with all the qualities inborn and acquired to fit him for the station he is to occupy. Of commanding form, stentorian voice, excellent judgment, and thoroughly skilled in military tactics.

We thank the authorities for the appointment, and stand sponsor for the result, with not a little pride." Hapgood placed an advertisement in the same edition calling for volunteers between the ages of eighteen and forty-five. "The Fifth will be a regiment of light infantry, and will be commanded by COL. EDWARD E. CROSS," it said. "The Field and Staff Officers will be selected from among the very best military men in the State, and as far as possible will be those who have seen service. Young men of Hillsboro' County, will you not respond to the call of your Country?"

Ira Barton was a captain who, like Sturtevant, had seen service in the First New Hampshire. But he was fourteen years younger, just twenty-one, a schoolteacher who owed his nascent military career to his devoted father, a lawyer and Republican politician. Levi Barton had used those connections to push his son forward with the war's outbreak, seeing an opportunity for Ira to raise his standing and, through an officer's pay, help conquer the family's debts. The father had placed the son in a difficult position, however, because Ira was a bookish young man with an air of entitlement, and not a warrior. In the winter of 1861, Barton was preoccupied with securing speakers for a lecture series in Newport. Just a few months later, due to his father's hand, he was recruiting a company of soldiers for war. Barton enlisted only forty men but was still named a company captain. When Levi Barton visited the First's camp in early May, he came away concerned that his son was overmatched. "For the short time I was present I could but see the evil tendency of camp life," he wrote on May 12. "One must have high and honorable motives, a firm purpose to act from, a sense of right to come off uncontaminated." In the end, Ira Barton felt that he had risen to the challenge of leadership; after the First disbanded, he began recruiting a company for service in the Fifth. His sense of maturity growing with his confidence, he also proposed marriage to Helen Wilcox, another teacher who, at twenty-four, was three years his senior.

State authorities named Charles Long as captain to recruit for the Fifth in Claremont; he was a prosperous farmer and a logical choice. Long had received a military education at Norwich University in Vermont, and in the first months of the war he had traveled the state as a drillmaster for recruits. "His ambition is to show a company so well-disciplined as to secure 'the right' of the regiment, which is the post of honor," said the *National Eagle*. Long's company was at half strength and already busy by mid-September, two weeks after recruiting began. "Rub-a-dub," said the *Eagle* on September 12. "Martial sounds again fill the air. Twice or thrice daily, Capt. Long's company, enlisted for the Fifth Regiment, parade upon the Park for inspections and drill. They number about 50, and fast filling up. Many of our best young men have gone into this crack company." By the end of September, Long had more than eighty recruits, sixty of them from Claremont. Twenty-three were farmers and twenty-one laborers. Nine were carpenters, six spinners, and three clerks; the rest included machinists, shoemakers, painters, masons, a bookkeeper, and a weaver.

As with April's volunteers, men who enlisted in the Fifth were celebrated in their communities, but now there was a more sober, even melancholy aspect to their send-off. "Be Patient," the *Granite State Free Press* of Lebanon editorialized. "We want everything to go by steam. We are impatient of all delays in the accomplishment of plans and enterprises. It is make haste in everything, and, as a natural consequence, our progress is not always of a substantial character." The Union's early embarrassments were not due to cowardice, the paper said, but to rushing unprepared men into action. At a farewell for Lebanon men bound for the Fifth, Lieutenant Nathan Randlett's remarks were brief but to the same point. "Give us time," he said, "and we will speak for ourselves." September 27 was a national fast day; in Claremont, every church opened for special services, which were well attended. That evening, the community gathered to honor Captain Long's soldiers. There were nine speeches, five of them by ministers. Long was given a revolver and a sword; each soldier received a pocket Bible. "The audience were dismissed," reported the *Northern Advocate*, "and left the house with mingled emotions of gladness and grief—that our soldiers had received such a noble expression of confidence and sympathy, and a silent grief that so many of our young men should be called from the associations of home to meet upon the field of deadly strife the enemies of the best government ever established by the wisdom of man." At seven the next morning the company departed for training camp in Concord; family members and well-wishers followed on horseback and in carriages, unwilling to turn back until the column reached Newport, seven miles away. If anxiety was high, so was confidence in the company. "They are already well advanced in the drill, moving with the steadiness and precision of veterans," said the *Eagle*. "We do not believe it can be matched by any company not yet mustered into the service. A few days acquaintance with the uniform, knapsack and rifle musket, and a week's experience under canvass, and these men will be soldiers, ready to meet the enemy in battle."

Before meeting the enemy there was the matter of meeting the imposing Colonel Cross—not quite a foe, but by no means a friend. The colonel was known by recruits to be an adventurer tested in the distant West; his driving manner made a large presence larger still. It had been a month since Cross was given command of the Fifth, and he had seen to every aspect of its creation. Free as promised from political interference, he selected his senior officers, obtained tents, purchased wagons and blankets, bought flour and meat, and

THE FIFTH NEW HAMPSHIRE

The state they came from

Lancaster
Littleton
Bath
N
White Mountains
Lebanon
Croydon
Newport
Rochester
Claremont
Concord
Portsmouth
Antrim
Manchester
Keene
Milford
Amherst
Nashua

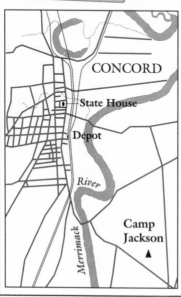

CONCORD

State House
Depot
River
Camp Jackson
Merrimack

Places they went

Oct. 29, 1861: **Leave Concord by rail.**

Oct. 31–Nov. 28: **Bladensburg, Md.**

Nov. 29–March 10, 1862: **Camp California, near Alexandria, Va.**

March 10–April 3: **Three-week march, vicinity of Manassas Junction, Va.**

April 4: **To the Peninsula.**

May 28–29: **Built the Grapevine Bridge, Chickahominy River.**

June 1: **Battle of Fair Oaks.**

June 1–27: **Camp near Fair Oaks Station.**

June 28–July 1: **Seven Days battles: Orchard Station, Savage's Station, White Oak Swamp, Glendale, Malvern Hill.**

July 2–Aug. 15: **Harrison's Landing, Va.**

Aug. 16: **To Newport News, Va.**

Aug. 28–29: **Camp California.**

Sept. 5–16: **March to Sharpsburg, Md.**

Sept. 17: **Battle of Antietam.**

Sept. 22–Oct. 31: **Bolivar Heights, Va.**

Oct. 31–Nov. 17: **March along the Blue Ridge Mountains.**

Nov. 17–Dec. 12: **Falmouth, Va.**

Dec. 13: **Battle of Fredericksburg.**

Dec. 14–April 28, 1863: **Falmouth.**

April 28–May 5: **Chancellorsville campaign.**

May 6–June 6: **Falmouth.**

June 9: **Brandy Station.**

June 14–July 1: **Gettysburg campaign.**

July 2: **Engaged at Wheatfield.**

Aug. 3, 1863: **Return to Concord.**

even chose the training ground on Glover's Hill, off the old Pembroke Road. Cross owed his life's great opportunity to a Republican governor, but he named the camp for Andrew Jackson, the greatest of Democratic heroes. On September 26, in expectation of the first arrivals, Cross issued General Order No. 1 from Camp Jackson. It forbade liquor in the camp, prohibited anyone but an official sutler from selling goods to the soldiers, established a school of "practical and theoretical instruction" for officers and first sergeants, and closed with an admonition: "Soldiers will remember that they have no responsibility farther than to obey the orders of their superiors with promptness and good faith; and the commanding officer trusts that each officer and soldier will endeavor to be distinguished for ready obedience, gentlemanly conduct, and soldierly bearing."

The first company into camp was Sturtevant's, which made the march from the State House on September 28. Long's Claremont company arrived the same day, as did a company under Captain Richard Welch, whose men were drawn from south-central New Hampshire. Welch would prove an undistinguished officer, but in his ranks were two men who would become astute chroniclers of the Fifth—and whose first impressions of camp were positive ones.

One of these men was Sergeant Thomas Livermore, at seventeen a year too young to be in the army but in fact already a veteran of the First New Hampshire. He was the grandson of a prominent New Hampshire lawyer named Solomon Livermore, an anti-slavery man who liked to follow Sunday scripture readings from his pew—but in the original Greek. Thomas's father, not content with a life of quiet prominence in New Hampshire, had sought his fortune first in the lead-mining boomtown of Galena, Illinois, and then amid the Gold Rush in California. Thomas had been just seven years old when he journeyed west with his family, a trip he made on horseback. His father valued education as well as adventure and saw to it that Thomas was well schooled, in part by sending him east to New Hampshire for a time to live with his distinguished grandfather. When war broke out, the Livermores were back in Galena, which was home to a volunteer company being drilled by an ex–regular army officer named Ulysses Grant. But everyone expected the war's climactic battle to be fought soon near Washington, so that is where Thomas Livermore resolved to go, with his father's blessing, a Bowie knife, a revolver, and eighty dollars. He joined the First New Hampshire in the field as a private; Colonel Tappan, who knew his grandfather, assigned him an officer's duties. Even so, Livermore had been frustrated by the First's amateurish ways. His expectations were high when he arrived in the Fifth's camp, and he was pleased by its orderly layout, dictated by Cross in what the colonel called the

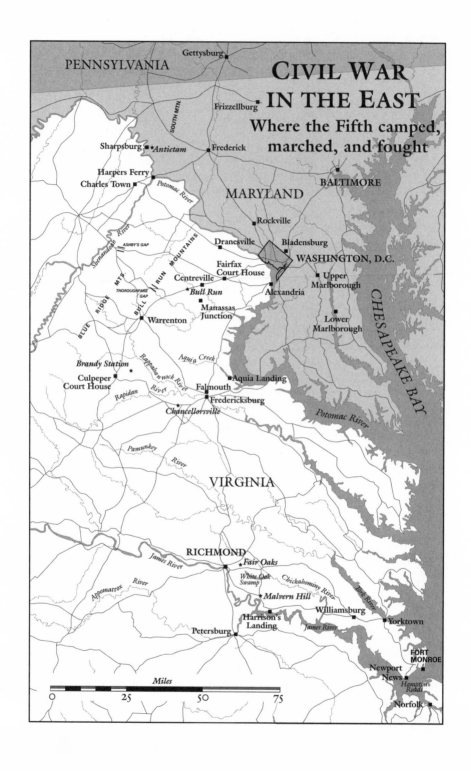

CIVIL WAR
IN THE EAST
Where the Fifth camped,
marched, and fought

PENNSYLVANIA

Gettysburg

Frizzellburg

SOUTH MTN.

Sharpsburg *Antietam

Frederick

Harpers Ferry
Charles Town

Potomac River

BALTIMORE

MARYLAND

Rockville

Shenandoah River

ASHBY'S GAP

Drancsville

Bladensburg

Fairfax
Court House

WASHINGTON, D.C.

BULL RUN MOUNTAINS

Centreville

MTS.

Upper
Marlborough

THOROUGHFARE
GAP

*Bull Run

Alexandria

BLUE RIDGE

BULL RUN

Manassas
Junction

Warrenton

Lower
Marlborough

Aquia Creek

CHESAPEAKE BAY

Brandy Station

Rappahannock River

Culpeper
Court House

Aquia Landing

Rapidan River

Falmouth

River

Fredericksburg

*Chancellorsville

Potomac River

Pamunkey River

VIRGINIA

RICHMOND

James River

Fair Oaks

White Oak
Swamp

Chickahominy River

York River

*Malvern Hill

Appomattox River

Williamsburg

Yorktown

Harrison's
Landing

James River

Petersburg

FORT
MONROE

Newport
News

Hampton
Roads

Miles

Norfolk

0   25   50   75

Spanish style. "There were five rows of tents," Livermore wrote, "each ending on a square of which they made one side. On the other side were an equal number, on the third were the tents of the field and staff, and in the center of the fourth side the guardhouse was the only obstacle between the square and the parade grounds." The young veteran also studied Cross, an angular figure with red-brown hair who moved in bursts, leaning forward, hands clasped behind his back: "The colonel, whose reputation had excited my curiosity, was seen busily engaged around the camp in every department, now directing the quartermaster, now receiving new detachments, now superintending drill, and now trying a horse."

A private in Livermore's company named Miles Peabody also surveyed the camp with interest; he was Livermore's match in curiosity but, as a newcomer to soldiering, lacked his practiced eye. Peabody was twenty-one, a strapping six-footer and a pessimist by nature. His parents made bedsteads at their sawmill along a bubbling stream in Antrim; his father was not well, and the prospect of a long separation deepened Peabody's concern for his parents' welfare and that of the family business. He would prove a natural soldier in two respects, his preoccupation with food and his tendency to complain, or croak, but only one of those traits asserted itself in his first letter home, written the day after arriving in camp. "Dear Parents," he began, "I supose that you would like to hear something about camplife. Well in the first place we left Bennington Friday at half past six. We arived at Concord at ten. We formed into line at the depot, marched up to the state house, received orders to go into Camp Jackson about 1½ miles east of the City. We arrived at the camp about eleven when I and 5 other of our squad were put on guard. We stood on guard until one when we got our dinner. We had beefsteak and potatoes, wheat and brown bread for dinner, enough of it and well cooked. The first night it rained hard, but we had good tents and blankets and we slept as nice is if we were in Howards hall. There are about 400 men in camp now. We shall probably stay here 3 or 4 weeks. Nichols left us last Thursday without leave and we have not seen him since. Frank says that he will have him arrested. There is a reward of $30 for every deserter. Well, it is most dinner time and I will close. From your son, Miles."

Peabody and his colleagues had much to learn, and they spent most waking hours learning it. The men were up each day at six; they drilled for two and a half hours each morning and afternoon; they gathered for a dress parade each evening; and by nine each night the camp was still. Each day Cross schooled his officers and first sergeants in the manual of arms, infantry tactics, and his expectations. His task was eased by the presence of several trained and tested army veterans, including his brother Richard, a lieutenant in the Fifth.

Together the experienced officers taught the farmers and factory workers who filled the regiment the basics, starting with small squads and building toward the day when the entire regiment of one thousand could respond as one to extensive and intricate commands issued by voice, bugle, or drum. The men learned to move in a column of twos or fours for speed. They learned to deploy in a long line of battle, two rows deep, men shoulder to shoulder, "file closers" to the rear, ready to manage the regiment's firing and maneuvers. They learned loading by nines, a reference to the nine steps required to arm, aim, and fire a musket. There was little emphasis on accuracy and a great concern for quickness, both of movement and gunfire. The target of one mass of men was to be another mass of men, and victory was to be a matter of hurling more lead in the enemy's general direction than the enemy could hurl in return.

Colonel Cross knew it would take fortitude to stand in the face of such fire, and he could not teach fortitude. But he would insist on discipline, believing it to be the foundation of good soldiering. One day as Cross tested a horse, a group of recruits urged him to demonstrate his dramatic western riding style. Their familiar manner incensed the colonel, who promptly wheeled and charged them, scattering the group in panic. Cross's temper caught officers and men alike by surprise, sending tension and anxiety rippling through the camp. But the colonel had allies, including veterans such as Livermore who preferred a taut regiment like the Fifth to a lax one like the First. And when those who were discontented asserted themselves, Cross's response was immediate and sword-edged. "The men found out that they must obey or suffer the severest consequences," the colonel wrote in his diary. "One slight mutiny occurred among some men from Portsmouth, which resulted in their entire defeat and humiliation before the entire regiment."

Harshness was not Cross's only weapon. In his Order No. 4, he sought to motivate men by promising to select four sergeants and eight corporals in each company based on "good behavior and soldierly deportment." While permitting the first passes into Concord, Cross made his expectations clear: "It is the wish of the Colonel that every man shall behave himself in a soldierly and gentlemanly manner, so as to reflect credit upon the Regiment and himself; and it is to be hoped that every visit to the city and elsewhere, will be signalized by good behavior and soldierly deportment. The officers will endeavor to set their men a good example." The order included words of fatherly support—"The commander wishes to encourage all athletic exercise and amusement in camp, and it is his desire that the men employ their leisure time in such recreation as shall render them happy and contented with camp life"—and stiff severity: "The first duty of a soldier is strict obedience to orders. It is only by such obedience that the Regiment can arrive at the high state of discipline which is desired by the commander."

The Fifth New Hampshire was the fourth regiment to train in Concord, providing the capital's residents a solid basis for comparisons. The regiment's behavior left them little negative to say. "The 4th Regiment N.H.V. left Camp Sullivan last Friday at 12 o'clock a.m.," one state official reported to the *National Eagle*. "This regiment was better equipped than either of those that preceded it. But look out for the 5th Regiment, Col. Cross. This will be the crack regiment from New Hampshire. It will not be merely a fancy regiment, but one for hard service if it is required." Said the *Statesman*: "There have been no quarrels by day—no brawls at night. A very large portion of the regiment consists of men with whom obedience to constituted authority is a spontaneous act." Indeed, Cross was not the only positive influence at work in the camp; every man in the Claremont company signed a temperance pledge, and a prayer meeting held shortly after the company entered camp was well attended. The one blemish on the regiment's reputation may have been its marching song: "One-Ball Riley," a favorite of Cross's. Neither the tune nor the bawdy lyrics proved to be favorites of the governor. Nevertheless, the abundance of glowing reports cast the Fifth in the warm light of celebrity. The regiment's nightly dress parades often attracted an audience numbering in the hundreds, many of whom came to see Sturtevant and his Concord company.

The birth of the regiment's personality did not strip its men of theirs. Their ranks included single men, like Sturtevant, who once proclaimed, "I . . . am, what I suppose I have a right to be, an 'old bachelor,' enjoying all the rights and privileges of 'single blessedness.'" But there were family men too, like Sturtevant's first lieutenant, James Larkin of Concord. From the moment he left home for training camp, not two miles away, Larkin desperately missed his wife Jenny and their young children: his namesake James, whom he called Bubby, just fourteen months old, and his month-old daughter Lizzie, already nicknamed Belle. "I never thought you would leeve your wife and children who you love dearer than life," his mother wrote Larkin when she heard of his enlistment. "James, never show enny cowerdis, stand firm to your post and your contry and may the Lord bee with you and bring you to your family again." Despite Colonel Cross's nativist views, a smattering of immigrants gathered under his command. Private Daniel Harrington was an illiterate Irishman who proved a natural soldier. Lieutenant Jacob Keller was a Prussian whose heavy accent became a source of amusement to his comrades. Lieutenant William Moore, on the other hand, was a native son. He was descended from the founder of his hometown, Littleton, and from Revolutionary War veterans on both sides. Sergeant George Gove was a muscular six-footer while Private Peter Thebeaux was a wisp too small to be in the army, but both had the makings of stolid soldiers. Less suited to military life was Corporal Thomas Wier, a forty-five-year-old shoemaker who fell sick shortly after camp opened and was sent home to recuperate. Wier was a likable man, though his excitability on religious topics made others uneasy. Captain Hapgood's piety was more restrained but his faith was deep, and his well-tempered behavior stood in contrast to that of Major William Cook, whose fondness for drink was not unusual but whose inability to handle alcohol was. Corporal Benjamin Chase, "Bennie" to his devoted mother, was one of eleven children. His father was disabled and the family was poor, and Chase had enlisted in answer to his father's complaints that he did not earn enough to justify his keep. Private Samuel Crowther's aging mother was so ardent a patriot that she nailed a flag to her roof and vowed to shoot anyone who would tear it down. (Her home being in Connecticut, Rebels would be hard-pressed to try.)

Some in the Fifth were men of sophistication and accomplishment. Lieutenant Charles Ballou had gone west after gold in 1850; once in California he cultivated fruits and vegetables and worked as a bookkeeper in a clothing store. He learned Spanish so well that he became an interpreter on ships anchored in San Francisco harbor. He was short and could be testy, but after Captain Long recruited him, he adapted quickly to the army. Less adept in all respects was Captain Welch, who suffered this dissection by Sergeant Livermore's hand: "a man of medium height with a decidedly Roman, perhaps Israelite nose, black whiskers, owing part of their color to dye, a face wrinkled very much at the corners of his eyes, which twinkled in a manner half common to rogues and half to good-natured numbskulls."

Whether as individuals they were superb or not, Colonel Cross intended to clothe and equip every man in his regiment in the best the Union had to offer. The Fifth was to have been dressed in light gray, the traditional color of New Hampshire militia but not that of the federal army in the field. Cross rejected the gray uniforms as shoddy and instead secured Concord-made uniforms intended for the Sixth Regiment: "a uniform," Livermore wrote, "consisting of brogans, light-blue trousers and overcoat with cape, and dark-blue blouse and frock coat, and to cap us a helmet-like structure of dark gray or blue-mixed waterproof cloth, with a vizor before and behind, the top resembling a squash, and the whole lined and padded. This was a New Hampshire cap, and although it would do in a row to keep blows from the head and was good to protect the neck from rain, yet in summer it was a sweltering concern." When the uniforms were distributed, the quartermaster ran short of large sizes; an unusual number of men in the Fifth were taller than five feet eight inches. The men took pride in this—or at least those with clothes that fit did—seeing their size as yet more evidence of the regiment's stature. Not all of Cross's efforts on behalf of his men were successful. The Fifth trained with heavy smoothbore muskets known as Belgians; for active duty, Cross wanted Springfields, rifled muskets prized for their lightness and durability. The colonel traveled to Washington in early October in an effort to obtain Springfields, but he was rebuffed—to his deep and long-lasting chagrin. Cross concerned himself with his men's comfort, too, as a note in the October 15 *Northern Advocate* demonstrated: "In a letter from Capt. Long, he writes, 'Col. Cross wishes one hundred sacks made for our company to keep their straw in, as it will keep the camp looking better. Will the Ladies in Claremont make them?'" In fact, sacks were not all Claremont had to offer. The women of the Claremont Auxiliary Commission had been hard at work for months on everything from stockings to pillow cases, dressing gowns, and crab apple jelly. After farmer John Blodgett harvested a thirty-four pound turnip, thirty-eight inches around, he sent it to Long's company at Camp Jackson. "The boys will probably mistake it at first for a new fangled bombshell," said the *Eagle*, "but they won't turnup their noses at this when properly b'iled and served up with their rations."

Between October 12 and October 23, the ten companies of the Fifth were officially mustered into the government's service. Once that formality was accomplished, each company got three days' leave. Captain Barton used his time home to get married. In Claremont, Lieutenants Keller and Ballou were presented with swords like that given to Captain Long before the company left for camp. There was one meaningful difference: Keller and Ballou were bachelors, and their swords were purchased by the ladies of the community. The entire Claremont company found itself the featured attraction at a hastily organized town fair, complete with sheep, swine, squash, and, due perhaps to the short notice, a poor showing of butter and cheese. There was no disappointment with the parade that wound through town that afternoon: "Wm. Breck, Esq., of West Claremont with his beautiful matched blacks headed a procession of about three-fourths of a mile in length," reported the *Eagle*, "followed up by Lewis Perry's dashing black stallions, Rufus Carlton's dainty stepping sorrels and an endless number of beauties. This procession was escorted by Capt. Long's Company of soldiers with the full band. It made an extended march through the principal streets. In the procession rode Gen. Erastus Glidden on his elegant and spirited horse, looking like a veteran chief in the midst of an army on the march." Glidden, sixty-nine, was a general in name only, having commanded a state militia brigade in 1830. "It was the pageant of the day," the *Eagle* said of the parade, "and attracted, literally, thousands of spectators."

The regiment's last days in camp were a stage for Colonel Cross, whose performance demonstrated his capacity to inspire, intimidate, and infuriate. On October 24, Cross was ordered to close camp and bring the regiment to Washington. But several companies were still on leave, putting the colonel in a difficult position to which he responded with bared teeth. Cross demanded more time, offered no explanation to authorities, and threatened to resign if his request was not granted. On October 26, the field and staff officers were mustered in, and Cross issued an order detailing plans for the regiment's departure. It was meticulous and pointed. "No expense will be spared to arrest any man who deserts his regiment on the eve of its entering service," it said, "nor will punishment be remitted to any soldier who gets drunk and disgraces himself and the regiment on the morning of departure." On October 28, Cross posted another order formally naming the company's officers, sergeants, and corporals and awarding Sturtevant's Company A the regiment's most prestigious posting—a position on the regiment's right, when deployed, which Claremont's Company G had longed for. Disappointed, the *National Eagle* suggested that, as with wine, perhaps the last would be best.

Late that morning, Governor Berry came to Camp Jackson to present the state and federal flags the regiment would carry into the field. "We were drawn up in a hollow square to receive them," Livermore wrote, "and after they were presented Colonel Cross stepped out, and in a clear voice which all could hear made a speech considerably different in tone from those of roseate hue which recruits were accustomed to hear. The import was that we took those colors to fight under; that it was not to be play and glitter of glory altogether, but that we might expect to leave many of our number on the fields where we were to uphold them; and that we should brace ourselves with the resolution to maintain their glory and our honor even at the cost of life and limb to all or any. It was a grand speech; it did not excite the greatest enthusiasm, I think." At five o'clock, in a precise response to a bugler's call, the regiment's tall, conical tents were struck. All fell in the same direction as the last note faded, an insignificant moment but for Cross's orchestration, which filled it with drama. "Everything loaded in our wagons," Livermore wrote, "accouterments, canteens, knapsacks, and haversacks on our shoulders, we marched to Concord, where we slept in halls overnight."

The regiment was up at dawn on its day of departure. It was a frosty and windy October morning, but Concord residents warmed it by serving hot coffee. At half past six, the regiment formed in front of the courthouse: 1,012 men, bound for war. Despite the early hour, a crowd gathered and watched with anticipation as the regiment's flags were unfurled. When all was ready, the order rang out: "Attention! Right face! Forward march!" With that, the Fifth began its march to the railroad depot, its colors waving and its band playing "The Girl I Left Behind Me." Each man carried one day's ration of dried beef and soft bread in his haversack; waiting on the train were two days' rations of boiled ham and hardtack in barrels. The regiment's thirteen wagons were already on board, as were several officers' horses. The rest would be issued, along with the regiment's weapons, when the Fifth arrived outside Washington. Captain Sturtevant, the former Concord police officer, remained with a detachment to search out any stragglers or deserters who lingered in the city.

Colonel Cross's spirits soared as his men clambered aboard the train, twenty-two cars long. It pulled out of Concord just before eight in the morning, carrying Governor Berry for a portion of the trip. "For myself I never felt better," Cross wrote in his diary. "That morning I bid farewell to my Mother, & having been inured to partings, felt calm and happy." One newspaper said the regiment was expected to be assigned to a division under General Ambrose Burnside, "designed for operations along the southern coast." The *Eagle* chose not to speculate on the Fifth's destination but rather to toss a final bouquet its way: "Col. Cross is on all hands complimented as the best specimen of military man that has yet been seen in this State at the head of a Regiment," it said. "We expect great things from the Fifth."

Overlooked in the excitement was the ordeal of Frederick Manning of Lyndeborough, who became the regiment's first casualty that morning. Manning was a twenty-six-year-old private in Captain Hapgood's company. He had been holding a pistol with the muzzle in the palm of his hand when it went off; the ball entered at his wrist and lodged in his arm. "He was carried to the surgeon's quarters," the *Nashua Telegraph* reported, "and somebody —he supposes it was the surgeon, but we hope it was nobody who is entrusted with the life and limbs of any body—cut four great ugly gashes in his arm at different points between the wrist and the elbow, without finding the ball." Manning was told he had better go home, and was sent to the depot with an orderly to obtain a pass. Somehow he ended up on board, rolling south with the regiment; no one took notice of his plight until the train arrived in Nashua, forty miles south of Concord. "When he arrived here he was on the floor of the car, nearly insensible," the *Telegraph* reported. "He was taken to the Central House and taken care of. Gov. Berry hearing of it, sent to Dr. James B. Greely to attend to him. By inserting a probe the ball was found about three inches above the point of entering, and was easily removed. The gashes cut by the bungler in camp were left gaping open—and his arm presents the spectacle which is a poor comment upon the fitness of the operator for any position having to do with the life and limbs of the brave soldiers." Manning would recover and rejoin the regiment, only to be wounded in one battle in 1862 and killed in another the year after.

The trip south took two days and was largely uneventful. The train passed through Worcester, Massachusetts, and Norwich, Connecticut, before stopping on Long Island Sound. There the men boarded the steamer *Connecticut* for Jersey City, where they met a new train for the rest of their journey. Cross had ordered his officers to remain with their men throughout, and to inspect their canteens and haversacks periodically for liquor. On board the steamer, mulatto stewards were caught trying to peddle alcohol; Cross had them handcuffed and bundled onto the train with the regiment. The colonel chose a remote New Jersey stretch, stopped the train, and put the stewards off, still in irons. One soldier found the scenery wanting: "I can make a picture of New Jersey and all I shall want will be hogs, goats, niggers, mules, red sand, clay banks and a canal," he wrote. On the night of October 30, the train rolled into Philadelphia, where the regiment was treated to a hot meal and clean washrooms in the great hall of the Cooper Refreshment Saloon. "I say three cheers for the City of Brotherly Love," wrote Livermore. The train arrived the next morning in Baltimore, a city so hostile to the Union that the Sixth Massachusetts had been attacked there by a mob in April. The Fifth marched anxiously from one depot to another past grumbling onlookers, and continued quickly on toward Washington.

Before the capital came within sight, however, the train stopped and the regiment disembarked. They were in an army camp outside the small town of Bladensburg, Maryland, on a gentle, grassy slope that had been vacated earlier that day by the Second New Hampshire. Unfortunately, the men had been separated from their food and baggage during the journey, leaving them with blankets and cups and little more. Their new neighbors in camp, the Fourth Rhode Island Volunteers, learned of their predicament and, company by company, sought out the Fifth and shared their food. Having eaten, the men of the Fifth rolled up in their blankets for their first night's sleep in the field.

It was October 31. It had been only thirty-four days since Cross opened Camp Jackson and the men of Sturtevant's Company A marched in. It had been just over three months since the rebel triumph at Bull Run, the war's first great battle, fought not far from the Fifth's new campsite. It had been only seven months since the rebel attack on Fort Sumter threw the young nation into war with itself. As it happened, the arrival of the Fifth in the field coincided with the death of the last Revolutionary War pensioner in New Hampshire. Lieutenant Joel McGregory—age one hundred years, eleven months, and nine days—passed away in Newport on the thirty-first. McGregory had been a prisoner during the Revolution, spending eight months in the Old Sugar House prison in New York. After the war he made nails by hand, and tacks so small that a thousand could fit in an eggshell. "He has enjoyed good health in his last years," the *National Eagle* reported, "though his mind has been somewhat impaired."

So it was that Cross's men, beneficiaries of Revolutionary sacrifices, came to answer their own generation's call to duty. But for all the colonel had taught them in their month together, their transition from civilians of New Hampshire to soldiers of the Fifth had just begun.

Winter's Trials

"A man here will do about right, if he
knows what is best for himself."
—A soldier to the *Farmer's Cabinet*,
December 5, 1861

WHEN LIEUTENANT JAMES LARKIN AWOKE TO HIS
first morning at war, his outlook was brighter than the gilded
dome atop the State House in his hometown of Concord. The
Fifth New Hampshire's tents, baggage, and new muskets would soon arrive
at camp in Bladensburg, Maryland, and there would be much to do. But for
the moment his duties could wait, so Larkin sat on a box and spread a fresh
sheet of paper on a barrelhead before him. "Onward to Victory," his stationery said. "1776. 1861." Larkin was a devoted family man whose wife and
children were hundreds of miles distant now. Yet it was excitement, not longing, that gripped Larkin as he wrote for the first time from the field: "Dear
wife and children. The morning Sun is shining brightly upon me and my
sheet of paper as I write. We have had a splended passage here—no axident of
any kind. The men are all in good spirits and enjoy it much. It is a splended
place for an encampment. I am writing amid the jaber of a thousand men and
you must not expect a very good account of our journey at present. We are
preparing to pitch our tents and everything is in a bustle. It is beautiful
weather. The provisions you put in my haversac went well, I azure you."

From beginning to end, the Fifth's first winter in the field was a season of
plenty. But it was a trying time too, for it tempered the spirit of men like
Larkin with the realities of army life—particularly as lived under a demanding
leader like Colonel Cross. There were hours of drills, day upon day, and night
classes established by Cross for the regiment's officers. The men experienced
long slogs through gluey mud, skittish forays into rebel territory, and their
first encounters with the Negro. Tensions emerged within the regiment and

even with those at home, the most dramatic of which had Cross at their center. There were no shots fired in anger, but the men suffered before a foe as deadly as combat: disease. The effect of all this, by and large, was to draw the men together. When spring came, and with it a campaign to take the rebel capital, the Fifth was ready, harder for its experiences and better prepared for the struggles to come.

Larkin's first-day exuberance did not go untested for long. After he finished his letter, he and his men turned to preparing the Fifth's campground to Cross's specifications. The colonel expected the site to be cleaned of the broken boxes, empty barrels, and other residue left by previous occupants. He ordered fresh sinks dug at a safe distance from camp, screened by boughs so that men might have privacy as they tended to their needs. When the regiment's baggage arrived, he dictated the arrangement of tents in a white array as precise as any headquarters inspector might demand. All this was an exercise for which training camp had prepared the men well, so it was not the work but the weather that diluted the morning's enthusiasm. No sooner were the tents pitched than the skies opened. It rained for two days, transforming the Fifth's neat grounds into what Cross called "a perfect bed of sticky mortar." "Last night it commenced to rain," one soldier wrote home, "and the wind blew as you never saw it blow in N.H. It is raining and blowing now with no prospect of stopping, and the mud! It sticks as tight as a burdock burr in your hair."

On the evening of November 2 the rain turned cold, and the sodden regiment received unexpected instructions. The men were to march at nine the next morning, carrying two days' rations and forty rounds of ammunition. "The General regrets the imperative necessity which calls for this march on the Sabbath day," read the orders issued by their evangelistic commander, Brigadier General Oliver O. Howard. "Prayers will be holden in each Regiment just before commencing the march." Cross's priority was preparation, not prayer. The cooking and packing lasted well into the night; the colonel insisted that the men clean their newly issued Enfield rifles and other equipment before turning in for a short sleep. The morning would bring not a review or a drill, but a military mission—a soldier's duty—and Cross intended his command to be ready.

The coming Tuesday was election day, and the Fifth's assignment was to help ensure order at the polls in eastern Maryland. Because Maryland was a slave state, uneasy in the Union, such precautions made sense. But this was no simple march. The roads were muddy, the creek beds awash, and the men not yet hardened to the field. As the hours passed, the tramping soldiers began to sag under their wet burdens; each carried a bulging knapsack, blanket, overcoat, musket, cartridge box, canteen, and more. Their feet hurt, but no more than skin rubbed raw under their arms or between their legs. The men did not halt for the night until nine o'clock. They had covered about a dozen miles, but thought their march had been longer. "We lay down like tired dogs, every man glad to close his eyes," wrote Colonel Cross. The next morning, Cross had the Fifth up for coffee early—earlier than other outfits on the march, he noted with satisfaction. The regiment soon reached Upper Marlborough, a "dilapidated, unthrifty Southern village," and left two companies under Captain Edward Sturtevant to watch the polls there. The rest continued another dozen miles or so toward Lower Marlborough, where they would camp near the Patuxent River alongside the Fourth Rhode Island. Weary men fell asleep at every stop, only to be shouted awake by their officers and ordered on. "About nine o'clock we saw the camp fires of the advanced guard glimmering through the trees," Cross wrote. "The band at once struck up a lively tune and we marched into camp and a more wretchedly fatigued set of men it would have been hard to find."

Election day was uneventful, but the regiment's surroundings were interesting. Curiosity drew Private Miles Peabody into conversation with blacks, as foreign to most New Hampshire men as war or the army. Peabody recorded his initial impressions—positive impressions—in a surprised tone. "They are a good eal more intelegent than I had suposed," he wrote home. "I had a chance to talk to several of them when we was on the march. I asked a number of them if they would like to be free and if they could take care of themselves. They said they would like no better than to try." On the return march, one teenage slave acted on just that impulse. When the boy approached the long blue column, Captain Richard Welch told him he could come along. Peabody found the runaway a "very intelegent little fellow." His master valued him too, as became evident when he and two men approached the column in pursuit. The soldiers put a cap and overcoat on the boy and hid him in the ranks to thwart his pursuers. "They rode along the lines but they did not see him," Peabody wrote. "After they had got by we told him where we shuld camp that night." The runaway rejoined the company the next morning. "When we got into line his master came along and examined us again," Peabody wrote, "but we hid him in one of the bagage wagons. They followed us to Bladenburg and serched the wagons but they did not get him for we have got him in camp."

Despite the blisters this first assignment raised, the Fifth viewed it as a challenge met. "We did well and had but few stragglers," Cross wrote. The many small adventures of the march grew larger with each retelling, easing the anxiety natural among newcomers to a grand crusade. Each hour a train rumbled by the camp, carrying more Union men into the field. "The supplies and troops which poured in convinced us of the magnitude of the strife expected," Sergeant Thomas Livermore wrote, "and we longed for the day when our dreams should no longer be disturbed by those who passed us in advance."

Cross knew his men were not ready for a true campaign. The regiment reestablished its training camp routine of drill in the morning, drill in the after-noon, and dress parade in the evening. The colonel supplemented this work with more training for officers, better preparing them to teach the men. On Tuesday, Thursday, and Friday evenings, Lieutenant Colonel Samuel Langley led classes for the regiment's twenty lieutenants. On Monday, Wednesday, and Saturday evenings, Cross conducted classes for the ten company captains. All officers were expected to master the regulations by which the regiment lived and the tactics by which it would fight.

Drill was neither pleasant nor stimulating, and so grumbling about it was to be expected. When the grumbles took form, however, the consequences were severe. In contrast to Colonel Tappan, the commander of the ill-disciplined First New Hampshire, Cross tolerated no challenges from the ranks. Private Patrick Maley believed he could handle a musket as well as his sergeant, Emery Gould, and told him so one day during drill. That led to a struggle over the cocked and loaded weapon, ending when Maley struck the sergeant in the head with the barrel. A court-martial conducted in a captain's tent ordered Maley to forfeit ten dollars' pay and wear a thirty-two-pound ball and chain on his right leg for thirty days while performing hard labor. A verbal outburst sufficed to land Corporal John Sutton before a court-martial, too. Sutton had been lingering with the company cooks, a common temptation at drill time, when Sergeant O'Neil Twitchell ordered him to duty. Sutton was unmoved. "You little God-damned snotty-nosed sergeant around here using your God-damned little mean authority," he snapped. "God damn you, O'Neil Twitchell. I shall meet you sometime when you have not got your stripes on and I'll show you what your face is made of." For this failure to control his temper Sutton was sentenced to three hours of marching a day for six days with fifty pounds in his knapsack, plus two hours of camp policing per day and the loss of a half month's pay. The colonel lightened his load, quite literally, by reducing his sentence. Instead of fifty pounds, Cross said, Sutton would carry twenty-five.

That intervention reflected Cross's effort to strike a difficult balance. He insisted on obedience, but he also recognized that the Fifth's citizen volun-teers were too spirited and too fresh to respond to absolute authority as regu-lar army men might. His orders often reflected dual purposes: to demand and to explain. Both were apparent in his effort to prevent tent fires caused by poorly tended stoves. The tents, called Sibley tents, were shaped like Indian tepees and could accommodate eighteen men, who slept like the spokes of a wheel with the stove as its hub. Cross ordered a daily inspection of all tents, and made the sergeant in each tent responsible for extinguishing the stove at taps and not rekindling it until reveille. Should a tent be damaged, he ordered, it would be fixed within twenty-four hours or the squad would lose its stove; should a tent be destroyed, the squad would pay sixty dollars to replace it. That was all Cross really needed to say, but he closed with an appeal to his men's common sense, as a town father might back home: "Officers and soldiers should remember that carelessness in the use of stoves may cause the most horrible accidents for in a gale of wind the whole camp would be in flames in a moment."

Soon it became clear that Cross's sense of justice, while strong, was also partial. When Fourth Sergeant George Currier turned up drunk, Cross stripped him of his rank. "The Colonel deeply regrets the necessity to which he is forced but non-commissioned officers must set examples of good conduct," he wrote. But it was the officers, not the enlisted men, who had easy access to alcohol—and so it was the officers who most often abused it. None did so more flagrantly than Major William Cook, whose intemperate ways were well known. "Our Major has had another spree. He went to the city, was got tight and is to be tried by a court martial," Private Peabody wrote home. Yet no court-martial came to pass. In fact, due to Cross's indulgence, Cook survived a drunken moment of supreme embarrassment to himself and the regiment. "One day we were on the field with all our sashes and scales on, drawn up in array for review," Sergeant Livermore wrote, "and waiting for the reviewing officer to appear and receive our salute, when Major Cook came out of his quarters, and staggered down the rear of our line, and just as we were ready for the salute, he appeared in front of the brigade, and roared out in stentorian tones, 'Shoulder! Arms!' As everything and everybody was silent, and no one expecting such a *contretemps*, he made a sensation, and finally, after some confusion around him, he was got away and we could once more keep our eyes to the front. There was some fuss about this, but an apology or something of the kind fixed it, and the major retained his commission." Livermore considered Cook a bully but a brave one, and so thought the outcome to be just. Others took a dimmer view. "Had we been drunk as many times as Major Cook has been we should have been sent home disgraced," two officers later complained to the governor, "but he is allowed to drink and get drunk—nothing said of it."

The Fifth had arrived in the field not long before Thanksgiving, and the spirit of the holiday was afoot both in camp and back home. "The Amherst boys of the 5th Regiment will have a fine Thanksgiving dinner," the *Farmer's*

Cabinet happily reported, "made up of Roast Turkies, Pig, Chickens, Boiled Hams, Plums, Puddings, Pies, and an endless variety forwarded by friends from this place—enough to feast half the regiment. This is as it should be." Word of this bounty reached camp long before the food did, raising delicious expectations. Cross made his own plans for a regimental celebration: a day free of drills, with athletic contests, oysters, fresh milk, and hot mince pies. Lieutenant Larkin and his colleague in Company A, Lieutenant Stephen Twombly, arranged to share a roast turkey, while Cross and the regimental band were invited to the nearby camp of another outfit, Berdan's Sharpshooters.

All these plans came to naught. The Amherst shipment did not arrive in time for the holiday, and on Thanksgiving eve, the Fifth received orders to march to new quarters the next morning. "We then took occasion to grumble a little," wrote Sergeant Livermore, "but it's an ill wind that blows nobody good." This gust was to carry the Fifth through Washington, D.C., to an extensive army encampment outside Alexandria, Virginia—rebel territory. Reveille was sounded at 3:30 Thanksgiving morning. By five o'clock the regiment's tents were struck and the men were on the march, with fresh turkey on their minds but pickled beef and hard bread in their haversacks. "I suppose you had a grand time Thanksgiving," Private Charles Chase wrote home later. "I hope about the time you got hold of the turkey's leg you thought of us."

The Fifth put its best foot forward for the march through the capital. The colors were flying and the band playing as the regiment strode down Pennsylvania Avenue. The column was formally reviewed by Senator Henry Wilson of Massachusetts, a New Hampshire native, and less formally so by a crowd of soldiers and civilians gathered at the National Hotel. By sunset the regiment was in Virginia, where the reception was chillier. Driving rain, biting wind, and a lack of tents or firewood made for a miserable night. "I took a violent cold," Cross wrote, "and of course had one of my old fever and ague attacks, so severe I was not able to march with the Regiment the next day, much to my regret, and I remained at the house of some very kind people on the road."

The next morning the Fifth completed the march to what would be its winter quarters: Camp California. The regiment was home in a military sense as well. Along with the rest of Howard's brigade, comprising four regiments in all, the Fifth was assigned to Brigadier General Edwin "Bull" Sumner's division in the Army of the Potomac's Second Corps. Though command of the brigade, the division, and the corps would change with time, the Fifth would remain part of all three throughout the long ordeal to come. The men's first and greatest allegiance was to their regiment, but their sense of belonging, pride, and hardships borne together eventually extended to the larger units, too.

Camp California was located along the Little River Turnpike, in rolling farmland about three miles west of Alexandria. It was named in honor of Sumner, a regular army general fresh from command of the Department of the Pacific. The Fifth was told to camp beside the turnpike, on uneven ground at the base of a hill crowned by a fort. The land had been wooded until the army stripped it for firewood, so the regiment's first task was hacking away the roots and stumps left behind. Then each company aligned its tents along a company street, with its officers at the end. As in any community, some neighborhoods enjoyed loftier status than others; Cross's tent stood apart, with senior officers grouped around him. Their surroundings, once quiet countryside, were a vast, bristling sprawl of forts and soldiers. "White tents covered the hills; brilliant flags went up and fluttered out in the morning breezes only to be taken in when the sun went down," Sergeant Livermore wrote. "Blue-clad soldiers were exercising on every open spot, orderlies came and went from different headquarters, and to aid the scene the pleasing clangor of bugles and roll of drums, with the screaming of fifes, rolled over the hills and kept alive the listeners, while the flash of the glistening guns of the batteries as they wheeled in the sun, and the occasional roar of a gun from the forts assured us of an attempt to keep the Lord on our side." The inspiring scene turned beautiful by night, when candles and campfires flickered all over the hillsides. One soldier in the Fifth found the thought that Rebels were nearby more thrilling still. "Here we are in sight of our own game — and if we don't bag them, they probably will us!" he wrote.

The regiment's routines were reestablished immediately. The men drilled in companies for two hours each morning and in larger groups for two hours each afternoon. Cross put a particular emphasis on the speed with which men could load, aim, and fire their muskets. Each evening the Fifth turned out at sunset for a dress parade, which lacked the audience of appreciative civilians the regiment had enjoyed in Concord but remained a popular ritual. "This, when everyone was in dress uniform, when the bands played beautifully, and everything was done in a dignified and deliberate way, was a pleasant duty," Livermore wrote. Less pleasant was the extra training for officers, which Cross extended at Camp California. In the early afternoons, officers practiced the lunges and parries of the bayonet drill until their arms ached, preparing them to teach the same skills to their men. Three nights a week, Lieutenant Colonel Langley met with the regiment's ten first lieutenants. Major Cook worked with the most junior officers, the second lieutenants. Cross now supplemented his classes for captains by meeting on two other nights with the first sergeants, "with a view, no doubt," wrote Livermore, one of his students, "to making good officers of them in the future."

Though just seventeen, Livermore was a quick study, impressed by Cross and intent on learning the art of leadership. That he had a knack for it was clear already to his superiors and his men. One of his duties was calling his company's roll after reveille each morning. Sergeants in the other companies were forced to hold their men in line while waiting for enough light to see their paperwork. But Livermore memorized the ninety-eight names in his company and called the roll in darkness, providing himself and his men with more time to lounge before the day's duties began. This practice made Livermore a popular figure in Company K but the subject of suspicion and envy elsewhere in the regiment; eventually, no sergeant was allowed to call the roll until the regiment's drums sounded, and none was allowed to dismiss his men before reporting the results. It was one thing to bend regimental rules, of course, and another to enforce them. Livermore proved equally adept at both, as three men who neglected to keep themselves sufficiently clean learned one wintry day. Livermore marched the scruffy trio to an "ice-fringed brook" and ordered them to strip and jump in. Leaders being expected to face danger even more bravely than their men, Livermore removed his clothes and leapt in, too.

Although Sergeant Livermore took his work seriously, Company K's Captain Welch did not, and Livermore found his commander's behavior galling. Men angered by Livermore's orders sometimes went to the captain, who undermined his first sergeant by making empty promises to intervene on their behalf. The orders required to carry out maneuvers occasionally escaped Welch during drill, leading him to blurt nonsensical commands in frustration. "Get out there as skirmishers, every one of you," he shouted one day, "or I'll put you all in the guardhouse." Welch compounded these professional sins by putting Livermore's neat penmanship to personal use by night. "He would say, 'Orderly, you can write a better hand than I can, so just sit down here and write what I tell you,'" Livermore recalled. "Seated I would write his dictation. 'My dear Mrs. ———' (for the wicked old man wrote to married ladies sometimes), 'I have not heard from you for a long time'; a little more of the same sort and he would pause, and with that I, too, would pause. He would say, 'Go on.' 'What shall I say?' 'Oh, anything, damn it! write a good letter'; and I would then indite an Oriental epistle which he would pronounce first-rate and send off."

A more pressing preoccupation than romance was disease, a poorly understood threat that had already laid waste to many regiments. On average, each Union soldier could expect to be stricken seriously twice each year. Five soldiers in every hundred would die annually of disease, more than were killed in battle. Word circulated through the Fifth of regiments that had seen one hundred men die since fall, and so it was not surprising that many letters home from Camp California began with references to the health of the writer and his messmates. Even attempts at assurance had a sobering side. "It is very sickly here now," Private Peabody wrote his parents in November. "There is about 50 sick in this regiment. Three died last night but my health was never better. I have not been sick a day since I enlisted and I can stand most enything if I am well."

Cross's insistence on sanitary matters—including regular bathing and careful placement and policing of the sinks—held off illness better in the Fifth than in some regiments. But the toll was considerable nonetheless, particularly during stretches of cold, wet weather or at times of demanding duty. Most days in November, for example, Company B reported no more than four men absent due to sickness. But after the rainy night that followed the march through Washington, twenty men were reported sick. There were times when the men could do nothing to protect themselves from the elements. One night Lieutenant William Moore had to sleep in open air without a blanket or overcoat. "I thought as I lay down upon the damp ground," he wrote his sister Bettie, "how many kind mothers would cry out, as they were wont to do, when we chanced to sit upon the ground just as evening came on, 'You will certainly get your death a cold.'"

The men were exposed to an array of ailments, some familiar and others not. One officer, writing home in midwinter, offered an overview. "Since we came to camp," he wrote, "there have been admitted into the hospital one hundred and eighty-two patients. Of these, forty had the common continued fever, twenty-five the typhoid, twelve pneumonia, and of the remainder, more than one-half were down with the bilious fever so common in this climate. The balance had mumps, measles and slighter maladies."

Often, there was little the doctors could do for their miserable patients. On one especially grim day, Captain Ira Barton, suffering from "a very severe cold and the worst sore throat I ever had in my life," wrote to tell his father that he had ten men sick in the hospital and thirteen more sick in quarters—a quarter of his company. One of his men had died the week before and another, Private Robert Ash, had died that morning. "His suffering has been fearful," Barton wrote, "for the last four days he has not drawn breath without a groan. He has been in the hospital since the march to Marlborough. He has had a fever, mumps, measels, another fever and finally died with the bleeding dysentary. I fear that Wm. T. Dudley will not recover. He is in a critical state, perfectly deranged." Barton was right; Dudley died the next day. The captain triumphed over his cold, however, having dosed himself with a series of remedies. "Col Crosses good old mother had just sent him some herbs," Barton wrote. "He gave me some of them and they did me a 'power of good.' It broke up my fever but left my sore throat. The Dr. smoked it out once or twice, gave me an infernal gargle. I stayed in quarters and am now nearly well."

By the end of December, ten men had died of disease; by the end of the winter, thirty men would. Many others would be discharged because of illness. An official accounting published back home stressed not just the toll but the context. "The average strength of the Regiment has been 1,000 officers and men," it said, "therefore the loss is considered small, considering the change of climate—the exposure of the men,—exposed as soldiers always are, especially during the winter months." Still, each loss was deeply felt, in the ranks and by the colonel. The first to die was Private Frank Heywood, like Cross a Lancaster man. "He was an excellent young man," Cross wrote in his diary, "and a great favourite of mine. I closed his eyes. He died just at reveille—the last bugle ushered his soul into the land of spirits." Corporal Harrison Mann's meticulous personal habits were no defense against typhoid fever, to which he succumbed after a long struggle. "His father was with him and took the remains home," a soldier wrote to the *Farmer's Cabinet*. "The funeral was at 11 o'clock. The troops formed a hollow square, around the hearse. We accompanied the remains a half a mile, with reversed arms, the band playing a death march. Coming into line, the band played 'Home, Sweet Home,' and we returned to camp. While gone, another soldier, a private of Co. H, died, making the eleventh death since we left Concord, mostly of fever." Those whose bodies did not go home were buried near camp, with their name, company, regiment, and date and cause of death written with care on a wooden grave marker. Cross worried that the thicket of markers would depress morale, and the living were foremost in his mind when he shared the news of Robert Ash's death with the regiment at evening dress parade. "As I sat by the bedside of that dying boy and saw the tide of life slowing ebbing away," the colonel said, "and beheld with what bravery and Christian fortitude he awaited death, I thought then how, in his humble life and death he had set us a glorious example, not only as a soldier, but as a man. The heroism of a soldier's life and death is not confined to the battlefield. It requires more courage to suffer a lingering illness and 'die in hospital' than to meet death amid the din of arms."

The threat of illness made even civilian life uncertain, and soldiers in camp worried as much about their families' health as the families worried about them. Some men sought reassurance in faith. "We have a prayer meeting on the Sabbath and Tuesday evening, and a Class meeting Thursday evening, at the Chaplain's tent," a soldier told the *Farmer's Cabinet*. "The surgeon is a pious man, and many of the solders are professors of religion. The meetings are well attended and very interesting. Capt. Hapgood has commenced a Bible class, and the General has given him the use of a room in the house which was used by the Second as a Hospital. Twelve were present in the class to-day." However promising their start, the classes proved hard to sustain. "The days are all alike here, only Sunday is a little more so," another soldier wrote not long after. "Our Sunday School has 'caved in.'"

On December 6, two weeks after arriving at Camp California, the Fifth's routine was disturbed again. It was the regiment's turn for a five-day tour of duty on the picket line, an outpost intended to safeguard against surprise attack. At nine that morning, Cross led 816 men and officers out of camp to the cheers of the brigade. They marched four miles toward the enemy and took a position along Edsall's Hill; the Rebels were believed to be only five miles away. "One night here a captain saw a rebel near one of his posts, who, challenged, gave no answer," Livermore wrote. "The captain collected a squad and approached the immovable enemy, a shot was fired, I think, and it was demonstrated to be a stump." Another night two civilians wandered into the line, saying they had had enough of the rebel cause. Colonel Cross invited them to dinner and then ordered them taken to headquarters, believing they might be spies. Small parties were dispatched on patrol, Livermore said, the men "listening anxiously for the barking of dogs, which our book told us was a sign of moving men, or the noises of a camp, or straining our eyes to see the light of the enemy's camp-fires; but with no result but emptiness or an encounter with adventurous New Jersey soldiers who held the line to the right of us."

Most of the real action while on picket occurred within the Fifth's lines. Major Cook got drunk again, and berated one confused squad for failing to shoulder arms on his command when in fact the men had complied immediately and continued to throughout his tirade. When a sutler's wagon approached the Fifth's camp, bearing pies, cheese, and other delicacies, off-duty soldiers crowded eagerly around the wagon. They ignored a sergeant's order calling them away, so an incensed Cross raced to the wagon and dispersed the crowd, waving his sword in all directions. "To all appearances," Livermore wrote, he "did not distinguish between the back and the edge of it." When the regiment finally returned to Camp California, the entire brigade was promptly ordered to Edsall's Hill under Cross's command, to meet what proved to be an imagined threat. The next day, halfway back to camp again, the men were sent to the hill one more time. The only apparent result of the maneuver was to deny the men food or drinkable water, leaving those with a dark outlook to chew on their dissatisfactions. "Our marching back and forth did not amount to anything," Private Peabody wrote home on December 14.

"Our living that we get now is not fit for the hogs to live on. Our bread is old and sour and our chief cook is sick and the other don't know how to cook. The soup that they make will give a man the shits if he looks at it. Our Colenel does not prove as good as was expected. He is very quick tempered." Not everyone shared that view—"Our Colonel is very popular, though very strict," another soldier wrote on December 17—and Cross remained his regiment's biggest booster. "The Fifth Regiment is hard to beat," he boasted to Henry Kent in a letter written the same day.

Cross was much less tolerant of powers and forces beyond his control. He complained that the Sanitary Commission was slow to provide comforts to men in the field. "I say it & I say it boldly," he wrote Kent, "the Sanitary Committee as at present managed is a gigantic humbug. Do say so, & caution our people not to send anything to it." He was angered by the influence of radical Republicans in Washington, who seemed intent on pressing their anti-slavery crusade no matter what the consequences. "This attempt to make an abolition war is going to make trouble if not stopped," he told Kent. "A little more attention to soldiers and less to negroes is what is wanted. If not we shall get whipped." He remained bitter over the War Department's refusal to issue his men the superior Springfield rifle, lighter and more durable than the Enfields the regiment carried instead. "Enfields are a swindle, locks break, rammers bend and the bayonets are as brittle as sealing wax," he wrote in an overstated campaign to enlist Governor Berry's assistance. In another letter he added: "Seventy-four of my Enfields are worthless. It's enough to make a parson swear."

What outraged Cross most was any effort to interfere directly with his command. Congressman Thomas Edwards did just that when he arranged to have Private Oratus Verry discharged from the regiment. Verry was underage and did not like army life, so his parents asked Edwards for help. Cross resisted the congressman's intervention nearly to the point of insubordination. "Dear Sir," he wrote Edwards angrily. "Private Oratus J. Verry, Company F, will be discharged according to orders; but allow me to say that his discharge is an outrage against military custom, against law, and cannot fail to have a bad example. The young man is strong, able bodied, and if *he* is discharged, with equal reason might one-half of our army be discharged. I shall see that Oratus Verry is prosecuted for obtaining money and clothes from the United States under false pretenses. It seems to me, *Sir*, with all due respect, that at this crisis of our National affairs, Members of Congress would do better service by attending to public business, retrenching expenses, punishing corrupt officers, and providing means to pay those who are enduring the hardships and dangers of the field, than to spend time and energy in getting able-bodied men discharged from service. Such, Sir, is the opinion of Your obedient servant, Edward E. Cross." The colonel's scathing letter soon found its way into print. "On inquiry we learned that Mr. Edwards had done no more than any one would have done," the *Keene Sentinel* wrote, "that he justly owed to one of his constituents, the father of the young man, who was a minor, and was enlisted against the consent of both his parents, and under very improper influences." The War Department was no more sympathetic than the Republican press back home: "Your persistence in regarding him a deserter after the renewed order of the secretary is an assumption of authority and disobedience of orders, without excuse," one warning to Cross read.

On the whole, however, life at Camp California was pleasant enough, and most men realized it. When the regiment finally came back from Edsall's Hill, Lieutenant Moore wrote that his men were as pleased "as if we had returned to palaces." For Moore, returning to camp meant resuming his social life. "Tuesday evening, our Captain, Lieut. Cross and myself, visited the Misses Howard, who live just above our camp," he told his sister. "Though rather inclined towards the South, we find it pleasant to visit there." Paymasters came to camp more regularly than they would when the army was in the field. In mid-December, the Thanksgiving feast from Amherst finally reached camp, too. "At last the long-looked-for box has come," a soldier told the *Farmer's Cabinet*, "and right welcome is it in our little but well-filled parlor, and such a rush to see its contents! They were in much better condition than we had expected, after 19 days of travel. The meats were all spoiled, but the other articles were good. We talk of burying the pig under arms!" The delivery was one among many reasons for this soldier's spirited outlook. "We are faring better now than we have done—getting part soft bread in our rations," he continued. "The weather for the last ten days has been like your August, but the nights are chilly. We have made our supper of doughnuts, cakes and pies, soft bread and Stewart's butter, and I am now finishing with one of Mrs. Hardy's cigars. We have plenty of wood and water, and the railroad from Washington to Springfield is but half a mile from us, and is to be re-opened soon." On December 24, Private Charles Scott wrote to a friend in the same buoyant tone. "I am as fat as a possom and you would not know me if you should see me," he wrote. "I think that the war is most done and i dont think that england will turn in and fite against the north, no way nor no shape. This afternoon i have been Chopping and driving two horses, drawing wood for the Cooks to Cook for the Company. Tomorrow is Christmas and we are goin to have a little funn."

The colonel had in mind more than a little fun, and he delivered it, resurrecting the regimental celebration originally planned for Thanksgiving. Drill was canceled for Christmas Day, and Cross ordered athletic entertainment in its place. It was the regiment's first day off duty since gathering in Concord. At ten o'clock, there was a five-hundred-yard footrace, with a first prize of four dollars and a second of two. A wrestling match followed, with prizes of its own. Dinner was oysters and bread, followed by a visit from the Fourth Rhode Island, which produced a contest, too. "The R.I. Regiment gave us a treat of fun in the shape of a 'Race in a Bag,'" Lieutenant Moore wrote his father. "Five men from each wing of their Regiment were placed in a large bag which was made fast around their necks. — Taking their places in line, they started for the goal. Some went to the ground, 'heels over head,' to the amusement of all present. Only two reached the goal and were declared worthy of prizes." At three o'clock, the Fifth formed for the day's main event: the chase for a greased pig, provided by the colonel himself. "We formed in a square," wrote Private John McCrillis, "and poor piggy was let loose. After a few minutes he was seized by Pat Rowen, but escaped. Soon he was seized and carried away by a member of Company I." A jumping contest concluded the day. It was difficult to be so far from home on a holiday—"Oh how I should like to be with you tonight," Lieutenant Larkin wrote his wife Jenny —but this was a Christmas that drew the Fifth together. Moore approved because the men never got out of hand. "There were no drunken broils or fights so common among a large concourse of men," he wrote home. The regiment's camp song would be dated to this Christmas Day, twenty verses long and sung to the tune of "Camptown Races." One verse went like this:

> Our Colonel, he's a perfect brick, du da, du da,
> And with him the boys are bound to stick, du da, du da day
> Our Major, too, his name is Cook, du da, du da,
> Is a first-rate man with an ugly look, du da, du da day
>
> We're bound to march all night,
> We're bound to march all day,
> We're the boys from the Granite State,
> Some hundred miles away.

Beginning on the day after Christmas, Cross curtailed drilling so the regiment could prepare true winter quarters. The men felled pine trees, cut them in four-foot lengths, and then split the logs. These were placed on end in a trench matching the circular base of each Sibley tent, with an opening for a doorway. Gaps between the logs were filled with mud, and the tent was erected again on top of its new wooden base, creating a much more spacious home. The stove was placed in the middle of the tent, with a chimney made of mud and stones or even barrels. The men made flooring of evergreen boughs, broken-down hardtack boxes, or tree bark. Some used saplings or branches to erect bed frames on which they placed their woolen blankets; others filled sacks called "ticks" with straw for homemade mattresses. For a pillow, shoes or a knapsack might do. By January 4, when the first snow of the season fell, the men had transformed their camp into a semipermanent village. "I wish you could take a peep at us to-night in our snug, cosy quarters," one soldier wrote to the *Farmer's Cabinet*. "We are a merry set of fellows, and living in fair clover, having all the necessaries of life, and some of its *luxuries*. We draw half our bread rations in flour, and have biscuits and doughnuts as we want. Our biscuits are not quite as solid as a brick, nor quite as heavy as *two*, but they are *good*."

Making life still more comfortable were generous packages from home. The women of Claremont knitted mittens for the men of Company G, earning a thank-you note and a request from Captain Long: "The forefinger should be separate," he said, "as no one could wear the old fashioned kind and use a rifle." Three bountiful shipments arrived for the men of Company C. The women of Bethlehem sent twenty-one nightcaps, four bed ticks, four pairs of flannel drawers, four pairs of mittens, three pillowcases, and two quilts; the ladies of Littleton sent one quilt, three ticks, one blanket, and a bundle specially for Private Theron Farr from his mother; and the Soldiers Aid Society added nine ticks, fifteen pairs of mittens, seven pairs of socks, and seven nightcaps. In Company A, Lieutenant Larkin shared a box from his wife Jenny, containing strawberry preserves, pies, doughnuts, stockings, tobacco, whiskey, and more. "I have just been eating a good supper that tasts like home," he wrote on January 5, "and everything came in good shape. The Boys all wished they wer married." Larkin's tent, too, was more homelike than others, featuring a wooden door with a latch that had been removed from an abandoned home nearby. The lieutenant had time to indulge his interest in photography, taking eighteen pictures in one day alone at a cost of fifty cents each. He also adopted a puppy, named it Dixie, declared it "smart as a cricket," and planned to send it home for his daughter Belle at winter's end.

One officer, Doctor John Bucknam, became the object of widespread envy when he was joined in the field by his wife, Anna, who took a room in the home of a "very nice family" near the Fifth's camp. The doctor visited his wife when duty allowed. She passed the rest of her time sewing and talking with another boarder, the wife of a captain from the Eighty-first Pennsylvania. To live in Virginia was to live among slaves, and some time passed before Anna

Bucknam "became quite accustomed to the black faces around me," as she put it to her sister-in-law. "At first, I wanted to laugh sometimes—especially at the table. One of the waiters was such a comical looking 'object,' but there is 'nothing like getting used to a thing' you know, and soon Beachy's grinning teeth and rolled up eyes became a settled institution. . . . I like the southern people, some of them very much indeed."

All in all, the men pronounced themselves so comfortable that it led to murmuring back home, particularly on the subject of pay. The *People's Journal* in Littleton printed a reminder that a soldier's family was as dependent on his wages as ever. "Many of the soldiers," it said, "as well as officers, are now in receipt of better wages than they have ever had before, and far better than multitudes of mechanics and laborers are receiving in this war time. The soldier, under army rule has, or should have, while in health, few and inexpensive wants to be supplied, and it is not right the money should go to the sutler which wives and children so much need at home." In fact most money did go home, as the men were at some pains to note. In January, Cross wrote, $23,000 of the $36,000 in pay drawn by the regiment was sent to New Hampshire. When Company G was chided in the pages of the *National Eagle*, Captain Long rose to his men's defense. "I think the amount sent home by this Company cannot fall short of $2000 this payment," he wrote. "I think no Company in the Regiment has come up to this sum. The men of Company G think of friends at home, and many of them keep but very little money for their own use."

Such was the intimacy between the men and their communities that gossip traveled between camp and home as easily as the mail. One victim of this phenomenon was Captain Barton, who learned that he had become the subject of unflattering conversation among the ladies of the Soldiers Aid Society in his hometown of Newport. Barton asked his father, Levi, to investigate. "A word about the scandal you refered to," Levi answered not long after. "I will tell you what I have heard on the condition that you keep perfectly quiet and say nothing to any one here. Do you promise? Well then I will begin." The father said that some considered Barton lazy and others a drunk, blaming him for the failure of their packages to reach the men of his company. "You can imagine how a man of my temperament would be likely to stand such stuff," Levi wrote. "I was bound not to rest easy so when the society met yesterday I was present in their midst." The guilty party appeared to be a Mrs. Adams, who sought out Levi to explain herself. "She said she never said what had been laid to her but said she had *heard* it mentioned by others a number of times but gave no names. I think she perhaps has a little of the hateful quallity so prevalent in the world which takes delight in pulling down rather than building up. But say nothing and let it work. If you conduct prudently and wisely it can do you no harm." Some in the Fifth chose to combat such rumors directly. One officer wrote the *Granite State Free Press* in defense of Surgeon Luther Knight, saying no one should think him responsible for the prevalence of disease in camp. A soldier who signed himself "Iago" rebutted a series of tales in the same paper: "There has been some stories about in New Hampshire that ought to be corrected," he wrote. "Such stories as that the letters were opened by the Chaplain, and the money taken out, and that the Commissary had sold rations that belonged to the men, probably are not credited, and they ought not to be. And I learn that another story has been going the rounds that touches a little nearer home: that is, that the Chief Bugler has been drunk, cashiered and reduced to the ranks, which are all alike utterly false, as he remains in good grace yet. And still another one, too, I will correct: Letters written to soldiers *are not* opened and read in Washington."

On January 14, the regiment was ordered back to Edsall's Hill for its second stint of picket duty—and with it an assignment more substantial than fending off gossip. The weather was the most wintry yet, with three inches of snow on the ground and freezing rain in the air. "We were all covered with ice and shone like new bayonets," a soldier who signed himself "Private" wrote to the *Farmer's Cabinet*. The men made wigwams from fence boards, logs, and hay taken from farmer Edsall's fields. Cornstalks or hay, laid on the muddy ground, sufficed for bedding. "Trees being plenty, we did not suffer for a fire," the *Cabinet*'s correspondent added. "Boys would chop them to see them fall. We felled four acres of nice timber in four days, more for fun than for fuel." Duty on the picket line was cold and disagreeable, but in the makeshift camp, Sergeant Livermore wrote, the men were "quite cozy. We played cards, slept, ate, and drank when not on duty." On the seventeenth, however, came orders that stirred the camp: a detachment of forty men was to be sent several miles beyond Union lines to apprehend a rebel sympathizer named Marshall, believed to be responsible for the capture of ten Yankees not long before.

The men left at half past two in the morning on the eighteenth. Captain Barton was given command of what was to be the Fifth's first foray into harm's way. Colonel Cross put his brother, Lieutenant Richard Cross, in charge of the rear guard. "We worked our way along very carefully, for the first few miles," the anonymous "Private" told the *Cabinet*, "our courage increasing as we advanced, for at first the hop of a rabbit would stop the company." The men encountered no rebel soldiers and only one white man, whom they brought along for security's sake. When they drew within a mile of Marshall's house at Burke's Station, they halted. Barton hesitated, apparently uncertain of his next step—a flinch that did not escape notice. "The commanding officer seemed rather loath to approach his invisible enemy," wrote Sergeant Livermore, who was among several soldiers who volunteered to scout ahead. As bold as he was young, the seventeen-year-old Livermore walked to Marshall's house with a comrade and knocked on the door. He was pleased to find Marshall there—along with his sister and two "good-looking daughters." The sergeant announced that he was from a Louisiana regiment, out searching for Yankee pickets. When one of the daughters asked why his belt buckle said "U.S.," Livermore answered that theirs was called the Under the Sun Regiment. It seemed to work. They were given fresh milk and a promise that dinner would be waiting when they returned. As the scouts made their way back to Barton, however, they heard three shots fired in what seemed a signal to nearby Rebels. "Our officers were not very pleased that they had shown themselves," "Private" wrote, "but concluded to proceed double quick." The men descended on Marshall's home, arresting him, ten cows, sixteen chickens and ducks, one horse, and two colts. They left six beehives and the honey within on the veranda for fear of getting stung, and hurried off before rebel pickets could arrive. It was two in the afternoon before the detachment returned to camp, twelve hours after setting out. "All the boys are feeling very well over their success," "Private" wrote, "except Joseph W. He swears that he will not eat any of the chickens, nor drink any of the milk. He thinks it was the meanest scrape that he was ever in, and it was rather tough to witness the old man's parting with his sister and children, on their knees, imploring us to return him soon. Of all places in this world, deliver me from a situation between the two armies." In fact Joseph Wetherbee was not alone in his misgivings. "I call it no better than stealing," wrote Lieutenant Larkin, who hoped that General Howard would order the animals returned. The last word in the matter actually came from Colonel Cross, who credited the successful mission to his brother, not Barton. "Dick went out with 40 men the other night & brought in one rebel & 10 *cows* prisoners," Cross wrote to Kent on January 20. "The cows we shall eat—blessed by God—soon." Cross's letter mentioned the continued prevalence of measles in camp, hinted at a romantic interest ("I sent Miss H the 'picter'"), and concluded with a vague but ominous promise. "I have yet made no changes," it said. "But there will be changes soon." It would be almost a month before Cross's meaning became clear.

In the meantime, the regiment settled into the routines of its winter life—which is not to say that the passing weeks were uneventful. Lieutenant Welcome Crafts returned from an extended trip home with a batch of recruits. ("Crafts . . . has been absent in New Hampshire long enough to enlist a whole regiment," Captain Sturtevant grumbled to a friend.) Drills grew more elaborate as the men grew more skilled; one day seven regiments joined in maneuvers, the men firing blanks in a satisfying and smoky show of force. "The mumps got hold of the regiment," Livermore wrote, "and I was a victim." Governor Berry and the secretary of state visited Camp California on February 2; by mid-February, rumors of an impending campaign were rampant. "The Colonel says that we are to march through Manassas Gap, unless the rebels whip two hundred thousand of us," one soldier wrote to the *Farmer's Cabinet*. "The boys are so excited to-night over the news that we are to march soon, that I can't *hear myself think*, much less retain an idea long enough to write it." When Jenny sent Lieutenant Larkin a picture of their infant daughter Belle, it deepened his longing for home. "I could leave but what would every body say of me," he wrote. "And the Regiment I should leave would call me a coward and a sneak. I want to see this war settled and I want to help settle it and I hope to retire at the close with honor to myself and family. I know it is hard for you but is it not hearder for me that can neather see you or my children." On February 12, the regiment lost its first member to a gunshot wound: Private John Merrill of Company D, who was on guard when a boy approached with a loaded pistol. As the men examined the gun it went off, the ball striking Merrill in the chest. "Two surgeons were there in less than ten minutes, and everything was done for him that could be," a comrade told the *Cabinet*. "He had his senses until the last. He called for 'Andrew,' a number of times, his messmate, who was standing over him all the time. — His last call was for his wife, whose miniature was held before him, but he could not see it, his eyes were fixed, and he died without a struggle." On February 19, the mumbly Private Peabody got a letter from his parents that brightened his mood. "I received yours to day and was glad to hear from home once more, for I had began to think that you had forgotten me," he wrote. "I have not had a letter since the 10 of Jan. and had written four. My health is very good. We have some very fine weather now which is drying up the road quite fast. We are spoiling for a fight here, and we begin to think that the galant 5 reg. will not have a chance to give the rebels a thrashing before the war is over." Corporal Walter Drew decided that nearby homes lacked the "neat, tidy appearance of the New England cottage" because their owners relied on reluctant slaves who worked only out of fear. "The more one becomes acquainted with the institution of slavery," Drew wrote, "the more he abhors and detests it." On the twenty-second, the regiment was celebrating George Washington's birthday when a New Hampshire artillery outfit galloped into camp. Each man in the Fifth was issued fourteen blank rounds and the artillerists 150. "We burned them all," one soldier wrote, "making quite an interesting drill and a good deal of smoke."

On February 23, Colonel Cross made matters more interesting still. During dress parade, he announced the "changes" he had hinted at to his friend a month before. Two captains and two lieutenants were dismissed; one of those rewarded with promotions was his brother, named captain of Company K in place of the inept Captain Welch. Lieutenant J. B. David of Company K was also swept away, causing Sergeant Livermore to fear that his company's poor standing would cost him any chance of advancement. "The consternation of our two officers was exceeding," Livermore wrote, "and their calamity must have weighed very heavily." The four who were dismissed had failed competency exams required of officers—but the circumstances were suspect. Cross had ordered only those he wished to dismiss to take the exams. The change in Company K was immediate and bracing—particularly for its first sergeant, Livermore. "At inspections now," he wrote, "every button must be in place and buttoned, every bit of metal polished bright, every gun as clean clear to the bottom of the bore as it could be made, every stitch sewed, every particle of dust absent, every strap in place, every man clean, every one's hair short and combed, every shoe blacked clear around the heels, every knapsack packed with a clean change of underclothes, and every cartridge, cap, and primer in its place. And if any of these were found wrong, a scowl or reprimand cast at the first sergeant let him know that *he* had been remiss."

Welch and David did not surrender to their fate but instead raced to Washington, where Welch hoped to trade on political connections with the state's all-Republican congressional delegation. Having set wheels spinning in the capital, the two officers returned to the vicinity of Camp California to await the results. What followed was a confrontation with Cross that they reported in a subsequent letter to Governor Berry, replete with what they hoped to be damaging references to the colonel's political views. "About 6 o'clock P.M. Col Cross entered and ordered us out of the house," Welch and David wrote, "said we were God dam fools and no use to try and get back in the Regt. Gov Berry and the whole delegation could not reinstate us. Did not care a God dm for the whole delegation." With that, the officers wrote, the colonel drew his sword and said he would settle the matter himself. Seeing that they were unarmed, Cross set down the sword and renewed his challenge. "David replied he did not come there to fight. [Cross] said you God dam scoundrels, leave here before dark, and abused us shamefully." With that the colonel left—but before long reinforcements arrived. "In came Major W. W. Cook drunk and ordered us out of the house, took Lieut David by the coat and threw him on the floor, scratched him in the face, drove us out, and we was obliged to flee for safety. He calls us a dam cult of Black Republicans. He knows we are strong friends of the party and have always abused us by words when he had occasion so to do. He with Lieut R. S. Cross, Capt. Murray, Band Master and the sutler remained in the house till nearly morn drinking and Gambling." The colonel prevailed in the political skirmish with his ousted officers, despite a delay in processing the promotions that left him fuming. "Why, O why don't you send the commissions! You are certainly in possession of all the dates," he wrote the secretary of state weeks later. "Welch and David can *never* come back, as they are *trying* to do. I won't have either of them, and they cannot be forced on me. I have *blocked* the game in Washington."

Although such friction must have caused Governor Berry to wonder about his appointment of Colonel Cross, in fact the colonel had enjoyed a successful winter. His regiment was now ready for war, more disciplined and better trained than most, fearful of its colonel but appreciative of him, too. "We need nothing to complete our satisfaction but a little active service," one soldier wrote the *Cabinet*. On the night of March 9, the regiment received orders to prepare for a march the next morning. Each man was to carry sixty rounds of ammunition and three days of cooked rations, "where or for what," Lieutenant Larkin wrote that night, "nobody seems to know." Larkin could see that the time had come to part with his well-appointed tent, his photography pastime, and his little dog, Dixie. He arranged to send the dog home with Private Thomas Bruce of Franklin, who had been discharged due to lameness. "Give him som supper and keep him all night if he will stay and give him 2 dollars for me if the dog gets there safe," he wrote Jenny. "I shall write you again before we go into a fight. Untill then good by. Don't be worried about me for I am all right and expect to come out so if I can." At seven the next morning the Fifth was on the march, the men having left many dear possessions at Camp California, never to be recovered.

Anna Bucknam, the doctor's wife, watched as a wing of the army passed by the house where she had been boarding. "For hours the road was black with Infantry, Cavalry, and Artillery crowding by," she wrote. "Now and then a band would stop and play for us a few minutes—beautifully." Her excitement over the spectacle was tempered by concern for her husband, John, on the move with the Fifth. "I am so anxious about him," she wrote, "but the 'Rebels' have retreated from Manassas, you know, without fighting. I am so glad. John writes every opportunity and seems in good health and spirits." The time had come for Anna Bucknam to go home. The Army of the Potomac was stretching its muscles in preparation for a campaign intended to crush the rebellion.

On to Richmond

"I fear we shall always be the bloodless
Fifth."
—Sergeant George Gove,
Yorktown, May 7, 1862

IN FIVE MONTHS UNDER ARMS, COLONEL CROSS HAD transformed the Fifth New Hampshire from a gang of eager but inexperienced volunteers into a disciplined infantry regiment. The men now understood what it took to be soldiers. In Cross, they knew they had an exacting commander who would not brook disobedience, disorder, or dishonor. They had experienced hardships and losses and learned the value of close comrades and competent line officers. For all these gains, the men knew the final test of veterans still awaited them: they had yet to come under infantry fire. Now, as spring approached and word of a real campaign blossomed in the warmth around their campfires, their chance to prove themselves seemed near. "The moment of action has arrived," their commanding general, George McClellan, wrote them in a circular dated March 14, 1862.

Just hours before the general's press rolled out this message, a struggle at the highest levels of government over the direction of the Army of the Potomac had reached its resolution. Eager to see his eastern army move, President Lincoln had approved McClellan's plan to attack Richmond. By land, the Confederate capital lay little more than sixty miles south of Camp California and the army's supply base. There were obstacles in this path—rivers, swamps, wilderness, and an enemy army—but McClellan's reasons for rejecting the direct route had less to do with these than with his infatuation with grand military designs. He planned to mass his army at the wharves of Alexandria, load the men onto ships, and send them out the Potomac River and down the Chesapeake Bay to Virginia's lower peninsula. At the tip of the peninsula, near Hampton Roads, lay Fortress Monroe. McClellan's march on Richmond, seventy-five miles inland, would begin there.

As these plans took shape, the Fifth New Hampshire headed west into Virginia, away from Alexandria, on a trial run. McClellan wanted to break up winter camp, give the men a long march, rid them of excess baggage, and have them fight if the occasion arose. For three weeks beginning early the morning of March 10, the Fifth and other units of the Army of the Potomac chased the Rebels with little to show for it but brief encounters with artillery and cavalry. During one artillery duel the regiment came in range of the enemy. "The cannon balls flew over our heads at a great rate, fortunately hitting no one," Private Miles Peabody wrote his parents. "There was one ball that went over my head so close that I made a polite bow to it as it passed." McClellan's aim of giving the men a taste of campaigning succeeded with Peabody, who found the excursion trying and uncomfortable. The Federals had destroyed any bridges that the Rebels did not, and it rained often. "I never knew what it was to undergo hardships before," Peabody wrote, "but I think I know something about it now. If anyone wants to know what it is to be a soldier let him learn to go without eating, then wade all the brooks that he can find, with 30 or 40 lbs. on his back, without a chance to dry his feet till night, then take and roll up in a blanket, lay down on the ground, then go to sleep if he can. And like as not you will have an officer swearing at you half the time."

The first of April found the men hurrying back toward Alexandria, living as they went off livestock from local farms. At one halt Sergeant Thomas Livermore saw a soldier shoot a pig. He joined the mob slashing and jousting for a slice of pork, speared the pig's liver on a stick, gave it a few turns over a pile of burning fence rails, and gulped it down. At Manassas Junction, the retreating rebel army had left hundreds of dead animals to rot. The men slept amid the stench of the carcasses and "ran in peril of drinking their essence in the streams," Livermore wrote. The next morning, the men boarded open-platform cars and, "packed like herring between each other's knees," rode to Alexandria. Cross camped the men in a field and spent the night settling them in and preparing for departure.

By the time the Fifth set sail, the toil and excitement of moving an army of 100,000 men, cannons, wagons, livestock, and supplies had enlivened Alexandria for days. At nine o'clock on the morning of April 4, Cross, six of the regiment's ten companies, and the regimental cornet band boarded the *Donaldson*. The steamer, part of a motley armada carrying McClellan's army to Fortress Monroe, towed two schooners of Pennsylvania cavalry. Lieutenant Colonel Samuel Langley and the Fifth's other four companies embarked on the *Croton*. Adopting a style to suit the occasion, Cross wrote Henry Kent: "After a month of hard service, night & day in front of the enemy, without tents & only 4 wagons to a Regiment, our Brigade embarked yesterday to join the thousands of brave & good fellows that have 'gone before' toward Richmond by water." Early in their voyage, the men aboard the *Donaldson* heard a sermon. Chaplain Elijah Wilkins, a printer by profession, exhibited little Christian charity toward the Rebels. He struck one listener in the regiment as "an iron-headed Cromwellian Puritan," a man who "preached a good sermon on Sunday and well oiled his Sharp's rifle and Colt's pistol on Monday."

Fine spring weather made for smooth sailing. "We have had a good passage but slow & sure, as no axident has yet happened," Lieutenant James Larkin wrote his wife after the *Donaldson* dropped anchor in sight of Fortress Monroe. From the upper deck on a clear day, Larkin saw warships and ocean steamers in nearly every direction. The ironclad *Monitor* was nearby, with "steam up all the time ready for the *Merrimack* when she shall again see fit to attact her." The fort was a low, sprawling outpost in the shape of a seven-pointed star. Begun in the 1820s, it was named after President James Monroe. Around its stone walls and sturdy earthworks ran a wide moat. Inside, Larkin saw one of Professor Thaddeus Lowe's balloons inflated and ready to ascend on a reconnaissance mission. Lowe, a New Hampshireman, had been assigned to assess the Confederate defenses at Yorktown, McClellan's first objective, but the balloon flight produced little useful intelligence.

The Fifth's destination was twelve miles up the York River at Ship Point, but the weather turned before all the men had reached it. After the *Donaldson* steamed ahead, storms detained the *Croton* near Fortress Monroe for five days. This caused discomfort for the men aboard the smaller steamer, most of whom had only their rubber blankets to pitch on the wet deck. Livermore pulled three hardtack crates together to make a bed. On its thirty-inch width he and Corporal Daniel Harrington rolled up together in a rubber blanket to sleep. Livermore blessed his good fortune that his bunkmate was clean. Harrington, a tall Irishman, asked Livermore hopefully if he had ever heard of an illiterate corporal being promoted to sergeant. Livermore assured him he had. This generous feeling toward Harrington was not universal; many soldiers resented even his corporal's stripes. "We have had a promotion in our company which took us by surprise," Private Peabody wrote home. "A great bull headed Irishman has been appointed Corporal. He cannot read nor write which is a disgrace to the Company for there are fifty in the company that are better fited for it than he was."

Finally, on April 11, the *Croton* steamed to Ship Point, and the Fifth was reunited five miles southeast of Yorktown on a sandy campground within earshot of lapping waves. The camp was named for Winfield Scott, the old Mexican War hero who had retired six months earlier as the army's general in chief. Private Henry Holt wrote his grandfather from Camp Scott that the

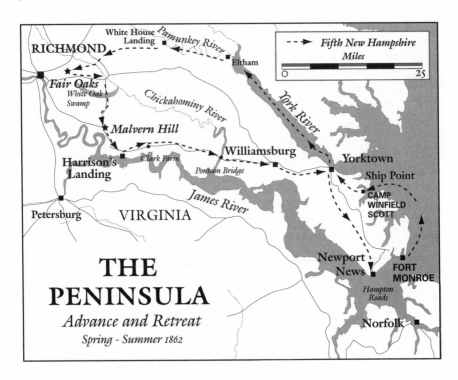

White House
Landing
RICHMOND
Pamunkey River
Eltham

- - - ► *Fifth New Hampshire*
Miles
0   25

Fair Oaks
White Oak
Swamp

Chickahominy River

★ *Malvern Hill*

York River

Harrison's
Landing
Clark Farm
Williamsburg
Yorktown
Ship Point
Pontoon Bridge

CAMP
WINFIELD
SCOTT

James River

Petersburg   VIRGINIA

Newport
News
FORT
MONROE
Hampton
Roads

THE
PENINSULA
Advance and Retreat
Spring - Summer 1862

Norfolk

"peach and pear trees are in full blossom and things look like spring." For the
first time in more than a month, the men had tents. They built an oven of Virginia mud, but they had to cover the beans they baked in it to keep flakes of
clay from spoiling the food. Colonel Cross ordered the regimental band to
practice an hour a day and to play three pieces each night beginning at seven
o'clock. In their spare time, some of the band members, including Lieutenant
Larkin's younger brother Albert, waded into a creek to rake oysters. "I have
had several good meals of them," James Larkin wrote home. "They are large
nice flavored oysters."

As pleasant as these surroundings were, the thrill of arrival soon gave way
to mortal fears and a longing for home. Illness struck with a vengeance. Peninsula fevers killed eleven members of the Fifth during April alone, including
Albert Larkin. In the same letter in which he touted the oysters, James Larkin
wrote that his brother's illness was "nothing serious." Albert died less than a
week later, strengthening Lieutenant Larkin's resolve to come home to Jenny
and their children. "If I am alive I will come home by the 4th of July whether
the war is ended or not," he wrote. "You may set that down as so." Private
Peabody pined for spring in Antrim. "I wish I could stop in at home about

this time and go to the cubbord," he wrote his parents. "I think that I would have something good to eat." As for the campaign, his thoughts swirled in an odd brew of bravado and avoidance. The Fifth was far behind the front lines, he wrote, and would not be called upon unless absolutely needed. He had heard a rumor that Congress had ordered the discharge of two hundred thousand men, and "if so we shall be some of them." But if it did come to a fight, Peabody wrote, "I have no doubt that we shall kick them at evry place that they chose to make a stand." Colonel Cross knew his regiment was ready and expected a battle any day. He wrote Kent with a sense of foreboding: "Somehow I have the idea that this god abandoned spot is to be my future residence. For thousands of us the end of our lives is at hand. The men do not seem to realize it, but I do because I have seen this thing before."

General McClellan shared neither the colonel's melancholy state of mind nor his eagerness for battle. He accepted as gospel inflated estimates of enemy strength, believing that he was greatly outnumbered when the opposite was true. He decided to besiege rather than attack Yorktown. His army appreciated McClellan's concerns for its safety, but at Yorktown his reluctance to risk his men's lives stopped him from committing his army when he should have. In fact, McClellan excelled in just the sort of operation he now ordered: the careful massing of troops, fortifying of positions, and placing of siege guns.

Sent to join the Engineers' Brigade, the Fifth helped mount the siege. One detail built a hundred-foot observation tower of logs. Others manufactured the tall sturdy baskets used to shore up parapets and gun positions. Lieutenant Larkin said his men preferred this light factory work to "digging entrenchments & going on picket. It is business of the Engineer corpse. They say we make them as well as they do." As the men worked one rainy day, several of Livermore's soldiers spied a sutler's wagon and forced the sutler to stop. They drank as they worked, and when they returned to camp carrying the baskets they had made, the sergeant worried that Captain Richard Cross would detect the wobble in their step. Livermore's detail survived this test, but at inspection that night the captain pulled a drunken man from the ranks and humiliated him in front of the company.

Abruptly, on May 4, the Fifth was ordered to leave behind its labors and prepare to move. Larkin discounted rumors that the Confederate army had deserted Yorktown, but for once the rumors were true. He saw Professor Lowe's balloon ascend once more, and Lowe's passenger, Brigadier General Samuel Heintzelman, shouted down that the Rebels were gone. With the band playing and the drums beating on a Sunday morning, Larkin began his letter home with these exultant words: "Once more our army is victorious without a battle. The Rebels have fled before us as usual and the national flag waves over Yorktown." Though he discredited rumors of the collapse of the enemy and mass surrenders at McClellan's feet, his swollen confidence caused him to write: "I hardly think the rebs will make a stand in Virginia." Another soldier of the Fifth, writing as "Serepta," reveled in the historical precedent of the regiment's latest advance. He described to newspaper readers back home how the Fifth had entered Yorktown and "encamped on the ground where Cornwallis surrendered, and almost under the same tree, which stands in all its glory as of old." The Rebels had left behind crude land mines "made of large shells, loaded and set in the ground enough to cover them," Serepta wrote. These "torpedoes" were "fixed with a percussion cap, causing them to explode when stepped upon, but they were discovered in season to prevent the terrible results that the rebels expected would follow our occupation of this place." Rebel prisoners were ordered to find and remove the explosives.

Not all the men of the Fifth shared in the triumphant mood of Captain Larkin and Serepta. Corporal Benjamin Chase, a homesick eighteen-year-old in Larkin's company, had a hard time joining in the celebratory spirit. In a letter home, he tried to reassure his mother about his future, but he could not help speculating about his own death. Bennie sent Nancy Chase photographs for her parlor of Colonel Cross and Elmer Ellsworth, the first Union martyr of the war, and passed along news of the rebel abandonment of Yorktown. "It says in the paper that the rebels have got tired and sick of the war and want it ended," he wrote. His mother should not worry for "we shall soon be at home if we don't get killed, and I don't think that we shall get killed. I hant ben a mite afraid of getting killed."

McClellan's triumph at Yorktown was an illusion. His siege preparations had been for naught, and the Confederates under General Joseph Johnston had used the time to build up their forces. Now they fell back toward Richmond with McClellan's army in pursuit. The armies clashed at Williamsburg on May 5, but the Fifth only heard the guns. At dusk that day the regiment was ordered to lead Brigadier General Israel Richardson's division on the march in a cold soaking rain toward the field of battle. "We blundered on, the mud perfectly awful, and mixed up with tree tops, logs, brushwood, with now and then a deep hole full of water," Colonel Cross wrote. "Through this state of things we toiled along, officers and men covered with dirt and wet to the skin." Sergeant Livermore slipped and belly flopped, barely managing to keep his rifle out of "the liquid mess." At two in the morning on May 6, as the Fifth neared the battlefield at Williamsburg, the men were told they were not needed. They fell into a cornfield to pass what was left of the night, "the most tired and miserable of men," Cross wrote. With a comrade the good-natured Private George Spalding "shared five fence rails for a bed to keep us from the wet ground—not a very comfortable bed, I assure you, but much better then none. As one must endure some hardships (especially if he goes for a soldier) we did not complain but were thankful for so good a bed even as that." At daybreak the regiment marched the fourteen miles back to Yorktown. Morale sagged. "I fear we shall always be the bloodless Fifth," Sergeant George Gove wrote in his diary. Larkin's joy over the rebel departure from Yorktown turned to frustration. "It seems we are the tail of everything," he wrote. "We march and counter march & seeming to no purpois. We have done more hard marching & as little fighting as any portion of the Army of the Potomac." Any day, the men expected to move from Yorktown toward the Confederate capital, but the way things were going, the Fifth would be the last to have that honor. "I dont expect to find any rebs in Richmond when we get there if we ever go," Larkin wrote.

The men had little time to dwell on their misfortune. They were ordered aboard the *Cornelius Vanderbilt*, a large riverboat, and steamed up the York and Pamunkey Rivers to a landing called Eltham. From there they set out upon a westward march of twenty-three miles over rolling and verdant land. Their mood changed as they marched. They were headed toward the Confederate capital now, and renewed thoughts of the rebel retreat from Yorktown restored their confidence. "We are about 16 miles from Richmond and I am in hopes we shall be in there before Saturday night," Private Thomas Law wrote his sister from the banks of the Pamunkey. "If they stand before our R., we will whip them out so there will not be so much left of them as a greese spot. I hope it will be the closing up of this horrid war." Law expected to be home by August 1 if not sooner. Private Spalding wrote to his cousin: "Whethere there are any rebels between here and Richmond I do not know. We expected to have a fight, and a hard one, too, at Yorktown, but the rebels run so we got disappointed. Whethere they will run away from Richmond remains to be seen." Spalding suspected he would not be home in time for haying, but the crop he would really miss had already been gathered. "It is pretty certain I shall not get any of Miss Brooks maple sugar this spring, but I hope to next," he wrote. Though it did nothing to satisfy a sweet tooth, the march held some rewards. Colonel Cross painted a romantic picture of a campground along the way at St. Peter's Church. The men of Richardson's division lay "all around on the crests and sides of the sloping hills, with trains parked in a vast and beautiful amphitheatre below," he wrote. Cross saw the army's campfires being lit one after another and heard the many distant voices as one low murmur. At evening parade he gazed across to the highest hills and the camp of "the 'red artillery,' their parti-colored guidons fluttering in the breeze—the grim cannon frowning on the host beneath. On each hill the different Regiments under arms, music playing, colors waving and the bright arms glittering in the declining sunbeams." On May 21, the regiment crossed the Richmond and York River Railroad and headed for the Chickahominy River. Richmond was almost in sight.

Even as rumors of battle redoubled, disease remained the most immediate and persistent enemy. With the sick rolls growing, the army began issuing a daily whiskey ration: two ounces in the morning, two at night. Even the regiment's fifteen-year-old drummer boy joined the line of men with tin cups to receive their doses. Cross's order conveying this popular prescription warned the men that "there will be no sharing or hoarding." The colonel took other measures to see to his regiment's health. "There is an abundance of soap for issue," he reminded the men. He advised them to put ashes in the wash water to clean the grease out of the haversacks in which they carried their rations. "Officers and men should remember that nothing is so unhealthy in a hot climate as grease, fried bread and half-boiled meat," he wrote. Among those overcome by fever and sent home was Captain Charles Long of the Claremont company. The *Northern Advocate* of Claremont reported Long's presence at home in an article that began with a rosy assessment of the war's progress. "Victory after victory has crowned the union arms, and . . . everything appears to foreshadow a speedy winding up of the rebellion," wrote editor Joseph Weber. "At least so it looks to us."

The colonel's attention to his men's health was just one reflection of a presence that only grew with time. On the march, he cut a fine figure riding Jack, a large red horse with a black mane and tail. In camp, nothing seemed to escape his gaze. Corporal Charles Hale was a member of the color guard, an honor that, to his thinking, came with a cost: he always had to pitch his tent near the colonel's. This gave him more of an opportunity than he wanted to watch Cross "stalking up and down in his restless way, stroking that tawney beard and looking seventeen different ways out of his eyes for Sunday." Hale was just twenty years old and, in his own words, "a diffident, shrinking sort of a customer." By contrast, he found Cross "fiery, impulsive and fearless" and often wished that he was in some other regiment so that he could admire the colonel from a safe distance.

Cross was at his fiercest in handling disciplinary matters. A private's pay was thirteen dollars a month, and many men sent home the greater part of it to support their families, which the war had deprived of their labor. Sometimes the men sent home so much money, or frittered so much away, that they ran short. When Cross caught one of his officers lending money to his men at a high interest rate, he meted out swift justice. It did not help the offender, Lieutenant Welcome Crafts, that he came from Cross's home county. The colonel ordered Crafts arrested, made him return any interest, and told his debtors they owed him only the principal of their loans. Crafts's punishment was public humiliation. Stripped of his sword, he was made to stand in the middle of a square on dress parade while the men listened to the order reprimanding him in scathing terms. Crafts got his sword back and returned to duty the next day, but Cross's message was lost on no one. "If I had subjected myself to such disgrace," wrote Livermore, "I should have tried hard to leave my bones on the next battle-field." Such a field at last lay close by, the battle not a week into the future.

The two commanding generals plotted their strategies. McClellan intended to mount another siege. He sent two corps south of the Chickahominy River and three north and began to deploy them in a crescent facing Richmond. But the rebel army had burned several bridges as it retreated to concentrate around its capital, putting McClellan at risk of isolating the thirty-three thousand Union soldiers south of the river. On the north bank, Brigadier General Bull Sumner's Second Corps, including the Fifth New Hampshire, had no bridges immediately before it. Thus the Chickahominy divided the Army of the Potomac. Johnston, the rebel commander, meant to exploit this weakness. The approach of the Yankees had created panic in Richmond, and he knew he had to act. He devised a superb plan to surprise McClellan's army before it dug in. Johnston would march his army along three roads and send it in a coordinated attack against the Federals south of the river. With the rest of McClellan's men stranded north of the Chickahominy, the Rebels would enjoy a five-to-three advantage in manpower. Recognizing this threat, McClellan moved to reconnect his divided army.

At daybreak on May 28, Sumner set Richardson's division to the task of building the bridges that would allow reinforcements to cross. Richardson ordered the Fifth New Hampshire to build one bridge; a mile downriver, he assigned the Eighty-first Pennsylvania, also of Brigadier General Oliver O. Howard's brigade, to build another. Sumner's corps was to cross first to meet any enemy threat, and the bridges needed the strength to support infantry, artillery, and supply trains. The task was daunting. The land along the Chickahominy was swampy, the insects noisome, the air thick and damp. There was nothing grand about the river—"contemptible" and "insignificant" were among the adjectives the Fifth's official historian chose for it. It was only a hundred feet wide, but its banks were marshy and insubstantial. The expanse to be bridged was a quarter mile. To determine a route for the bridge, Cross mounted Jack and, accompanied by a lieutenant, rode into the swamp "at the imminent risk of our horses' lives and our own." "All through the swamp," Cross wrote, "the dark, almost thick water was from two to six feet deep.

The swamp itself was a mass of dank vegetation, huge trees, saplings, bushes, grape vines and creeping plants. Beneath the water lay a bed of rich, soft earth about the consistency of mortar." Building a bridge here, Cross decided, "seemed impossible." The First Minnesota had found it so, laying a temporary bridge over the stream itself but abandoning the job of constructing the long approaches.

Cross organized his men into work gangs and assigned each to a task: chopping wood, hauling it to the bank or floating it downriver, and placing the bridge. The good swimmers guided the larger logs a half mile or more downstream. Several gangs built ten-foot cribs of heavy logs, notching and securing them in log-house fashion. Sometimes working up to their armpits in the river, the men sank the cribs at intervals of twenty-five feet from one end of the bridge to the other. In some places, the cribs were set on relatively solid ground, but where the water was deepest, they had to be tall and sturdy enough to rise above the surface and support the weight of the advancing army. Upon these cribs, the men laid thick stringers fifteen feet apart. For the roadbed they used logs rather than planks, as none of the timber was sawn. The tallest trees they laid along a row of double-size cribs in the main stream. The men used grapevine to lash these trees to the supports and, once the road was in, to strap on curbs to prevent wagons and artillery pieces from straying into the river. Sumner gave the bridge its name—the Grapevine Bridge—because of these bindings. On the second day of the job, four hundred men from the Sixty-fourth New York and the Irish Brigade joined Cross's detail. A barrel of whiskey appeared on the bridge at about noon, "the head knocked in and the boys allowed a liberal ration," Private William Weston wrote. Cross and another officer presided over the doling of the whiskey into tin cups. From that time forward, Cross wrote, "the labor pushed on with renewed vigor until at sundown I had the happiness of sending word to Gen. Howard that the bridge was ready for inspection." The colonel mounted Jack and galloped across to the south bank. The job, he wrote, was "solid and well done."

Whether the bridge could support the weight of a large portion of the Army of the Potomac remained to be seen, and nature upped the odds. The bridge was completed on May 29, a Thursday. Late the next afternoon, a huge thunderstorm blew up. A member of the Fifth Regiment was one of many in both armies who called the storm the worst they had ever seen. He wrote: "The lightning was blinding and incessant, the thunder one continual roar, and the rain fell in torrents, turning the gentle incline on which we were encamped into one complete sheet of water, which ran like a river. The storm lasted far into the night, turning every brook, rivulet and river into a raging torrent far above its natural level." The lazy Chickahominy suddenly became "one wide sea of swift-rushing, muddy waters." Colonel Cross slept fitfully, fearing that the river would wash away his bridge. He rose early on May 31 and once again rode across, this time with his adjutant, Charles Dodd. "Found the Bridge all safe," he wrote, "and so reported to Gen. Sumner."

General Johnston welcomed the storm but lacked the skill to take full advantage of it. He had ordered his army to attack the Union corps south of the river the very morning Cross took his anxious ride across the Grapevine Bridge. Johnston aimed to divide and conquer; he believed the swollen river would prevent Federal reinforcements from crossing once his attack began. There was nothing wrong with Johnston's plan, but the hindrances on his side were far greater than on McClellan's, and he had created most of them. He had issued no written orders to Major General James Longstreet, who was to lead the attack. Worse, he had failed to coordinate his three-column attack. Longstreet took the wrong road, and the commander of another column, Major General Benjamin Huger, overslept. Johnston's orders called for an attack at eight in the morning, but it was five hours later before the shooting began. In the confusion, few of the soldiers available to Johnston reached the fight. These errors spared McClellan a disaster. Nevertheless, when the Confederate assault did begin, the Rebels quickly overran Brigadier General Silas Casey's forward positions and drove his division back at Seven Pines, near Fair Oaks Station. Hours passed before Casey and Major General Erasmus Keyes, his corps commander, informed McClellan's headquarters of the attack.

On the other side of the river, the Fifth's corps commander, Bull Sumner, needed no instructions. At the sound of musketry, he ordered his command up to the bridges. Adjutant Dodd wrote that some of the men "were preparing for a nap, some were washing, some gathering cedar boughs for soft beds, and some were diligently engaged in that soldierly pastime—with shirt and pants off—hunting vermin, when suddenly we heard one gun and another and another in quick succession." Colonel Cross anticipated Sumner's order and had his men roll their blankets and prepare to move out. "For once I felt that we were wanted," he wrote. The colonel rode along the lines telling his men that the moment they had been waiting for had arrived and that they must keep their places as they marched to the fight. The men cheered. Sumner ordered one division, under Brigadier General John Sedgwick, to cross the Grapevine Bridge and the other, under Richardson and including the Fifth, to cross a mile downstream on the bridge built by the Eighty-first Pennsylvania. Sedgwick's men made it across, but the flood had swept away portions of the Pennsylvanians' bridge. Once Richardson saw that he could not cross his division there, he marched his men more than a mile around to the Grapevine Bridge, where at last they prepared to move out toward Seven Pines.

Five minutes before the Fifth crossed, Lieutenant Larkin arranged to send an extraordinary letter he had written four days earlier to his wife Jenny and their children. At the bottom of the last page he found room for a short note. He told his wife that the battle had begun and that a friend had promised to forward the letter if Larkin did not survive. "Good by Dear ones. Yours in Death & Life," he signed it. The letter attempted to justify to Jenny, Bubby, and Belle his having gone to war. Its contradiction was transparent: he expressed confidence about coming through, but his message was a last will and testament.

"As the contending armies seem now to be on the eve of a fierce battle, and many a brave form will be layed silent in Death, and Thousands of homes will be called to mourn for loved ones slayen," he began, "it is not unreasonable to suppose that I may be among the number who shall fall on that day. Still I have no fears. On the contrary I feel I shall come out safe & be restored to your loving imbraces once more. But if it is ordered otherwise I feel that I should leave some advise and a consoling word for I am not unmindful of the greate responsibility which rests upon you in bringing up those Darling little ones. Many is the hour I have lain and thought of these things in the stillness of night before and since I left you. It was a greate sacrifice for me to leave you, & you thought it could not be possible I could do it, thinking so much of my children as I did. But that greate love I bore them, & you, was one of the principal reasons which led me to leave you. For in connection with the duty I felt I owed my country I felt I owed as greate a duty to my family. Times were hard. I thought if I could save a few hundred dollars to enjoy with my family hereafter, benefit my health, & at the same time serve my country, I should be discharging a solemn duty to my family and my country. But you will say you would prefer poverty with me, to riches without me. But I am to proud to see you and my children want for anything which I could possably get.

"If I fall you will come in possession of ($1500) fifteen hundred dollars by my life insurance, & with what other property you have will with carefull use & investing it at good advantage enable you to suport yourself & Children & educate them respectably. But above all things Dear Jenny be watchful of their moral training that there may never be a blot on their dear name or character. Oh with what ceaseless vigilance should you watch over little Bell that she may grow up to womanhood as spotless & pure as she is now. I can see her now, the same little pure Angle that she was the first time I pressed my lips to her sweet mouth. You may think I am partial to her, but I love darling buby just as well. But a boy can make his way through the world easier than a girl. But I would not have you be less careful with his morals. The little dears will never know their Father, but Jenny, if such a thing is possable, after leaving this earth I shall ever be with you & them to assist your trying and lonley journy through this short life until we meet where partings will be no more."

For others, crossing the river was a hardship, but one that offered promise, not peril. Ten years Larkin's junior, Sergeant Livermore was eager to march toward the sound of enemy guns. He had no wife and children back home and gave no thought to his future beyond the war. His problem was that he had been sick for three days. Some men were glad to stay behind with illness, but Livermore wanted his commission as a lieutenant and thought the coming battle might be the Fifth's only one. No illness could keep him from crossing the Grapevine Bridge, even though "the swollen current already hid some of the timbers and threatened to lift them from their places." Another stout-hearted soldier, Private Weston, remembered wading "half-way to our knees in places, and artillery sank half-way to the muzzles in water, but a firm footing was secured by all."

As had happened at Williamsburg, however, the Fifth came up too late to fight. On the Richmond side of the Chickahominy, the regiment paused by a wheatfield as the division closed up. The men reached the battlefield after an hour's march, passing through Sedgwick's division, which had arrived in time to join the fight. The pleading of wounded men all across the field had replaced the sounds of battle. The chill of the night seemed severe after the heat of their exertion. "Oh, is there not one among you who has a blanket for a freezing man?" a soldier beseeched Lieutenant William Moore. Colonel Cross, astride Jack, heard one man say: "Don't tread on me, sir. I am badly wounded and very cold." A Mississippian, shot through both legs, begged for water. "We passed a good many dead & dying, but it was so dark we could not tell whether they wer friends or foes," wrote Larkin. For the first time, Livermore "smelled here the damp, mouldy odor which I have attributed to blood on other battle-fields." He heard men in his company grumble that the battle was over. "This regiment never will get into a fight," said Private Rufus Watson. It was a sentiment Livermore shared. "I cared for nothing but battle," he wrote.

Preparing for the resumption of fighting on Sunday morning, Richardson ordered the Fifth into camp at the front line — so close to the Rebels that "we could throw crackers to each other," as Moore heard one man put it. The general "told us as we passed not to return until we wer whiped," Larkin wrote. Cross posted two companies in an advance position across the railroad tracks just east of Fair Oaks Station. Captain James Perry, the farmer who commanded one of them, noted that his pickets had the sounds of rebel voices to keep them awake. The Rebels occupied the former campsite of

Union General Casey's troops. "They appeared to enjoy themselves much, eating the provisions and drinking the coffee left by Casey's commissary department," Perry wrote. "The coffee appeared to be a great treat to them, but in the morning they were obliged to think of something else, as Yankee bullets occasionally flew a little too near them." Cross deployed his other eight companies in line of battle, and they lay on the wet earth with their loaded rifles at their sides. Sentinels guarded the approach to each company's position. Cross asked his officers to stay awake through the night. At eleven o'clock, when all was in order, he spread his cloak on the ground and lay down, "but not to close my eyes. My regiment was the alarm clock of the army. I had no desire to sleep." Twice before dawn the officers woke the men and told them to prepare for a fight, but no enemy appeared. Cross talked quietly with the regimental surgeon, Luther Knight, about the coming battle.

But these were not idle hours. The ground before the regiment was dense forest, and as he talked with Knight, Cross saw torches bobbing among the trees a few hundred yards from where his men slept. He woke Major William Cook and sent him forward with several men to see whether the lights were from rebel camps. Without waiting for Cook to report back, the colonel set out on his own, walking through a field of tree stumps and dead and wounded men. Suddenly he heard the click of a rifle lock. A Southern voice said: "Who comes there!" Thinking fast, Cross answered: "Wounded man of the Fifth Texas. Who are you?" The voice replied: "Pickets of the Second Alabama." Cross asked for directions to a doctor. The guard obliged him, and the colonel slipped back to the camp of the Fifth New Hampshire. Captain Edward Sturtevant, commanding one of the two advance companies, took three men with him and actually entered a rebel camp. Before taking his leave, he exchanged pleasantries with the enemy soldiers and warned them "to keep a good lookout." Larkin, Sturtevant's first lieutenant, was lying twenty yards in front of the company when he saw a man wander toward him. The man carried a large backpack, and a saber clattered at his side. "I allowed him to get between me and the company," Larkin wrote, then "I arose and took hold of his arm & asked him where he was going." The man answered that he had his colonel's permission to come out and make a bed in the woods. When he identified himself as a member of a Texas regiment, Larkin seized him and stripped him of his pack and saber. Colonel Cross, using intelligence gained from these encounters, shifted his front slightly to face the enemy squarely and avoid a rebel flanking attack. He sent word back to the division's brigade commanders in his rear advising them to do the same.

With dawn approaching, Cross was eager to engage the enemy. He asked to send his regiment to attack the rebel pickets, but Richardson denied his

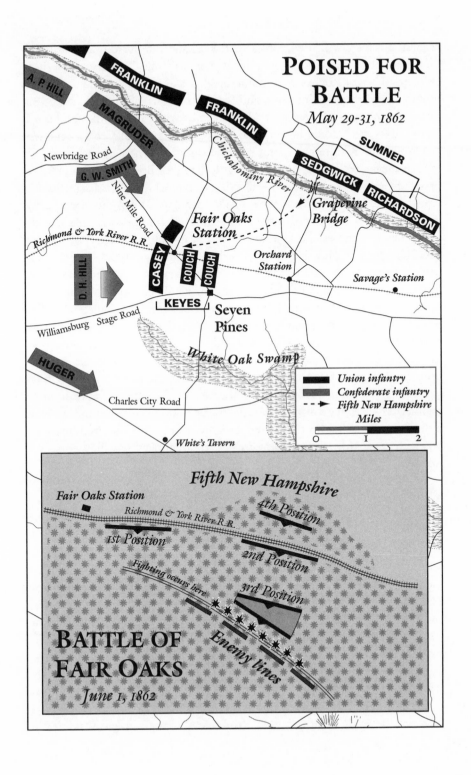

POISED FOR BATTLE
May 29-31, 1862

A. P. HILL
FRANKLIN
FRANKLIN
MAGRUDER
G. W. SMITH
SUMNER
SEDGWICK
RICHARDSON
Newbridge Road
Nine Mile Road
Chickahominy River
Grapevine Bridge
Richmond & York River R.R.
Fair Oaks Station
CASEY
COUCH
COUCH
Orchard Station
Savage's Station
D. H. HILL
KEYES
Seven Pines
Williamsburg Stage Road
White Oak Swamp
HUGER
Charles City Road

Union infantry
Confederate infantry
Fifth New Hampshire
Miles
0   1   2

White's Tavern

Fifth New Hampshire
Fair Oaks Station
Richmond & York River R.R.
4th Position
1st Position
2nd Position
Fighting occurs here
3rd Position
BATTLE OF FAIR OAKS
June 1, 1862
Enemy lines

request and the enemy fled. Cross sent skirmishers in pursuit, and although they met with some success, two of his men were hit. The first was Private Stephen Avery of Rochester. A minié ball—a slug as big around as a man's thumb—tore through his lung, and his companions left him for dead. But Avery rose under his own power and walked back to camp. Although his soldiering days were done, he survived the wound. Most of Cross's regiment still lay in line of battle, the colors not yet unfurled, when an enemy orderly rode in among them. The horseman was looking for Brigadier General Roger Pryor of General Longstreet's Right Wing of the Army of Northern Virginia. Cross walked up and asked for the man's dispatches. When the man reached into his jacket, Cross grabbed the bridle and took him prisoner. He sent the dispatches to Sumner and kept the rider's beautiful black mare for himself, later shipping it to New Hampshire by train. By daylight rebel sharpshooters had deployed. One put a ball through Cross's coat, and another ball passed near his nose. This being the first time the men had been so near infantry fire, Sergeant Livermore recorded the sounds with care. The bullets that flew overhead passed with a piping tone; others "sounded like a very small circular saw cutting through thin strips of wood, and sometimes great blue flies." Livermore was also in earshot when Sumner rode up to Cross and said in a deep, loud voice: "If they come out here, give 'em the bayonet! Give 'em the bayonet! They can't stand that." Still the men of the Fifth remained in place, their anxiety—a "harrowing curiosity," Livermore called it—rising. In eight months, sickness and death had reduced the rolls by one hundred fifty men, but with more than eight hundred rifles, the regiment was the strongest it would ever be for a fight.

As Cross waited to lead the Fifth to battle, he watched his brigade commander, General Howard, send in other regiments. The Eighty-first Pennsylvania attacked first, but Cross reported that these men broke at the first fire and left their colonel dead on the field. He attributed their failure in part to the regiment's composition: "partly Irish & partly American." Howard himself led two more regiments into the woods across the tracks and to the left of the Fifth's line. As he cheered the men forward, two balls struck his right arm. The second one, Cross reported, "shattered the bone in a shocking manner," and Howard left the field. "The regts. in his brigade are not sorry," Sergeant Charles Phelps wrote home. "Glad to get read of him." Surgeon Knight assisted in the amputation of the general's arm.

As the senior colonel in the brigade, Cross took command. Seeing that "the three other regiments of the brigade had been some time in action and severely handled," he ordered them to re-form behind the Irish Brigade. He marched the Fifth a half mile down the tracks away from Fair Oaks Station and toward the main rebel line. "We went down the rail road where the lead was plenty," wrote Sergeant Phelps. "They was in the woods about fifty rods." Cross wanted to send his men right in, but two incidents delayed him. The first occurred on the far left of his own battle line, which stretched three hundred yards along the tracks. A captain on Howard's staff called out to Cross's left company commander, Captain Ira Barton, to come to him, and Barton marched his men away. Cross ordered him to return, but not before at least one of Barton's men was shot. Elements of the Irish Brigade caused the second delay. In Cross's words, these men came up "in a perfect mob." The colonel had written the day before that Brigadier General Thomas Francis Meagher, commander of the Irish, was drunk on the march to battle and "behaved in a very disgraceful style, shouting and riding about in a manner highly unbecoming an officer and a gentleman, especially on such an occasion." Meagher's binges were legendary, reports of his being drunk on the field numerous. Now, as the battle loomed, Meagher was nowhere to be seen and his brigade's "whole movement was a farce."

Cross, by contrast, was in position to give his men precisely what many of them thought they wanted: an order to march straight toward the enemy. It was around eleven o'clock when the colonel shouted, "Charge them like hell, boys! Show 'em you are damned Yankees." Down the railroad embankment and into the woods they went. "They entered in full line of battle, the colors marching proudly in front, the blue flag of the State and the stars and stripes almost blending together in the breeze," one observer wrote. The men heard a volley from their rear. This was the Sixty-ninth New York of the Irish Brigade; Cross and some of his men believed the Irish had panicked and fired into their backs as they advanced. Two officers, Major Cook and the colonel's brother, Captain Richard Cross, fell at this time and later blamed the Irish for their wounds. Like others in the Fifth, Larkin resented the favorable notices the Irish Brigade consistently won in the New York and Boston papers, but he heard afterward that the New Yorkers had fired not into the Fifth's backs but to the right of the regiment, to ward off a flank attack. Larkin wasn't sure what to believe.

As the Fifth marched to battle, the men fixed their gaze on what lay ahead of them, not behind. The Confederates, men of General George Pickett's brigade, waited three hundred yards from where the Fifth had begun its advance. "The Confederates wore white bands around their hats—so that they were easily distinguished from our men," Cross wrote. Livermore's company had a cart path to travel, and along the way he saw a soldier sitting against a tree facing the advancing regiment. "He bore a ghastly wound upon his head [and] could not speak, for he motioned with a hand over his shoulder constantly, evidently, gallant fellow, telling us that our enemy was there." About fifty feet from the Confederate line, Colonel Cross ordered his men to open fire. It was the moment of truth for the Fifth New Hampshire. Corporal Charles Hale, who described Cross as "a holy terror" that day, marched in the center of the line as part of the color guard. As he paused on the field, the right companies of the regiment engaged the enemy first; then the left swung forward and joined the fight. "The whole line was soon firing by file—no volleys," Hale wrote. A crescendo of gunfire rose in the warm spring air. "They had the first fire at us, but we stood up and let them have it," Sergeant Phelps wrote. Cross "could hear the balls strike with a tearing sound into the close ranks of the rebels." The Fifth held its ground. "Bullets flew in myriads around us, humming deadly songs, hitting our men," Livermore wrote. Balls smashed into trees, and bits of wood flew into Livermore's face. The smell of burning powder "inspirited me a little," he wrote. "I never shall forget how we made those woods ring with our firing." George Spalding, a private in Livermore's company, found that "we did not think of the danger we were in" but of "little else then to load and fire as fast as possible."

On the far left, where Corporal Hale had noticed the regiment's slight delay in engaging the enemy, Captain Barton was having trouble again. "It was a dense swamp, mud, vines and underbrush," he wrote. "It was very hard for me to keep my company in any line through it." When his company did shoot, its target proved to be not the enemy but members of the Sixty-fourth New York, another regiment in the brigade. Lieutenant Rodney Crowley of the Sixty-fourth was moving his company out of the woods when he heard the command to open fire. He saw the aimed rifles before him and hit the ground. "As soon as this volley passed over me I rose and went directly forward to the center of the Fifth New Hampshire," he wrote. There, behind the color company, he saw Cross stalking back and forth waving his pistol and "using emphatic language about the men keeping in line." Crowley shouted to Cross that the Sixty-fourth was in front of the Fifth's far left. Barton had already caused the colonel one headache by marching his company away just before the charge; now Cross had to order Barton to change directions and get his men back in line. This proved to be no easy task for the captain, whose company fired on Union troops a second time before he finally got it right. "On the Regiment 'lummuxed,'" Barton wrote, "and soon commenced to fire—were ordered to cease as we were firing on friends—moved forward—made a half right wheel which brought us into line as well as nearer the enemy—opened again—ceased again as before—moved up again and pitched in in good earnest."

Once Barton's company found the enemy, it took heavy casualties. One of his privates, a former schoolteacher from Croydon named Alonzo Allen, described the carnage. Allen's townsman, Lloyd Forehand, was shot in the thigh. Two other Croydon men, Frank Hersey and a young farmer named Henry Stockwell, were among the company's six dead. "Hersey was shot through the head and died instantly," Allen wrote his mother in a letter that the local newspaper published shortly after the battle. "The bullet entered his eye and passed through, the blood spirting in jets. Henry Stockwell was also shot through the head and lived a day or two—even after his brains partly run out."

Farther up the Fifth's battle line, Captain James Perry's company, mostly Lebanon men, withstood the opening volley from the Rebels. "They expected, without doubt, that we should fall back in confusion, like the British at Bunker Hill, because they had seen the whites of our eyes," Perry wrote. "But they were mistaken then, for although many of our men fell at this fire, yet the rest of them stood firm as their own granite hills." The return fire was murderous. The Rebels "were just rising from cover, and it cut them down like grass, and they concluded to leave," Perry wrote. This single exchange killed four of Perry's men outright and felled sixteen others, three of whom would die from their wounds.

The closeness of the two lines moved many participants to vivid description. Lieutenant Jacob Keller, the Prussian immigrant who led the Claremont company, told a friend back home: "We fought so close that if a little nearer the powder of the one would have burned the faces of the other." Larkin wrote his wife: "We advanced in line & went nearly to the muzles of their guns before they fired or we could see them but they got ours soon after in fine stile." Balls whizzed past Larkin's head, and the man right in front of him was shot. "Men that will stand under such a fire will stand anywhere," Larkin wrote. Livermore, whose job was to keep his men from falling back, was surprised at how little fear he felt in the face of fire. "I was far more indifferent to everything than I could have supposed before," he wrote. Captain Barton observed a similar coolness in the soldiers who fought for him. Not thirty feet from the Rebels, "they picked their men as a hunter would his game. Not a man flinched." Private Allen, fighting under Barton, put it this way: "After the first volley I had not the least fear, but rather an eagerness to get up to the rebels." For the Claremont company, as for Barton's company, this first instance of courage under fire proved lethal. A single volley killed four of the Claremonters.

The soldiers learned at the first roar of the rebel muskets what all battle veterans already knew: whether a man lived or died was a matter of chance. Corporal Benjamin Chase was in a thick wood within thirty yards of the enemy when the first volley came. "It was a wonder that I dident get killed as I was right among them all," he wrote his mother. "The boys that got killed and wounded stood right beside of me." One aspect of the experience troubled him deeply. He had been "awfull luckey in not getting wounded," he wrote, but "it was a hard sight to see the dead and wounded lay on the battle ground." Private Spalding wrote his cousin Mary: "I was'nt scared, not much—at least I didn't tremble any. One man was shot while standing but a few feet from me. He was shot through the head and lived but a short time, but I had got so use to seeing men killed that I thought nothing of it."

The Confederate line fell back, and on Cross's orders, the Fifth again advanced and fired at close range. "Our officers to a man rallied our brave boys to the work of death," said Lieutenant Moore. "So severe was the rebel's fire, that it seemed as if all our men would go down." Cross wrote that his regiment behaved nobly, "only two or three showing the white feather." Seeing that some men were being hit with buckshot, he ordered a third advance. As he shouted "Forward in line!" a minié ball pierced his left thigh and passed cleanly through. The colonel kept his feet for a few moments then sagged to the ground. During the battle he "raged like a lion," his men told a correspondent from the *Cincinnati Commercial,* and "when his long body fell he went down like a pine tree." Cross propped himself up and continued to give commands. A spray of buckshot stung him in the right temple, "a ball passed through my hat, and one through the sleeve of my blouse—in all seven balls struck my person," he wrote. Moore saw Cross sitting against a tree, his face covered with blood. Men were trying to help him, but Cross gestured wildly, ordering them to fight on. "Go back!" Moore heard him cry. "Forward! Forward! Charge the devils! Charge them!" Finally, Corporal Matthew Towne and Lieutenant James Parks helped the colonel back to the railroad tracks near Fair Oaks Station.

By this time, the battle was nearly done. Barton's company remained in the thick of it to the end. As the firing slackened, a shot tore into the lower back of Private Allen, the Croydon man who had seen so many of his fellow soldiers hit. The shot knocked Allen to the ground. He struggled to his feet and asked Barton if he might retire. With the captain's permission, Allen managed in great pain to leave the field and begin the walk to the hospital. At about the same time the captain saw a favorite corporal—his namesake Thomas Barton —echo Cross's last cry of "Forward!" and fall dead before his comrades as he obeyed his own command. With Cross out of action, Lieutenant Colonel Langley took charge of the Fifth, but the regiment had moved so far forward without support that it was in danger of being flanked. Langley led the men out of the woods. Lieutenant Keller asked for volunteers to remain and bring out the Claremont company's wounded. Nineteen-year-old Private Robert Henry Chase stepped forward to lead the mission, and three others joined him. To their surprise, the enemy had not all fallen back. Private George Hacket was shot in the leg while tending to a wounded man, and rebel soldiers jumped Chase and took him prisoner. He spent six months in prison camps before he was exchanged.

In the immediate aftermath of the battle, most of the survivors experienced relief and euphoria. Since it was not yet eleven o'clock in the morning and the fighting was over for the day, they had time to reflect. The battle had taken forty minutes, but "it did not seem as though we were in ten minutes," Private Spalding wrote. It had been a time of extreme clarity, and now its meaning came clear, too. The men of the Fifth had upheld their honor. They had at last "seen the elephant" and would henceforth be looked upon by their fellow battle veterans as worthy comrades. They counted their losses and wondered why they had survived and how they had managed to fight on without pause after seeing their comrades fall. Certain they had dealt the Confederates a severe blow, they named their grounds near Fair Oaks "Camp Victory." "The people of Richmond came out to see us whipped," wrote Private George Smith, "but they had to go back without seeing that, but they saw their men run home to their mothers, I think." Unlike Smith, Lieutenant Larkin had gained new respect for the enemy. He wrote to his wife and children on stationery embossed with a drawing of a curbside newsboy holding up a sheet that read: "EXTRA . . . Glorious News! Total defeat of the Rebels!" He expressed a longing to "press you all to my heart tonight," but he was confident his homecoming was nigh. He believed McClellan's army was on the verge of crushing "the rebel hosts now in front of Richmond. I think the greate hope of the rebellion is gone." Nevertheless, having seen "the flower of the Rebel army," he had "got decidedly a better opinion of their soldiers than I had before."

The wounded Colonel Cross took time and care in assessing the Fifth's performance, his prose positively glowing in both his journal and his official report to Governor Nathaniel Berry. "When the regiment entered the woods," he wrote in the journal, "it was an anxious moment for me. I did not know whether they would stand or not. But they did stand in the most heroic style, never faltering & firing with a rapidity which astonished the rebels, making them give way." To Berry, Cross wrote: "The Fifth fired the first and last shot in the great battle of June 1, and alone met and drove back a strong column of the enemy—fighting them at thirty yards range and, although outflanked by greatly superior numbers of the Rebels, causing them to break and retire. Our loss was severe, but we had the satisfaction of having performed our duty without flinching and added another enduring laurel to the glory of our State."

On June 2, the day after the battle, some of the officers and men visited the wounded in the hospital and also saw to the burial of the dead. Captain Barton buried five men from his company in one grave, "the spot marked by a single pine." The very thought of it made him resent how glibly politicians and editors demanded the sacking of the rebel capital. "Let me have a few of those 'On-to-Richmond'-through-blood fellows out here—I would like to have them put through," he wrote. Barton found the emotion of the moment overwhelming, writing: "A heartless heart would bleed to see what I have seen." The soldiers in the burial details had the closest view of the human residue of battle. "It was sadding to see those with whome we had been so long associated rolled up in their blankets and burried far from home and away from friends who were anxiously waiting their return," wrote Private Spalding. Private Smith cringed at the sight of head wounds and "legs shot off and in their boots." It fell to him to bury some of the Confederate dead after his company's grave digging was done, and "that was not very pleasant to do for they had laid in the hot sun and smelt very bad." Even men not assigned to the burial details were curious about the bodies. When he learned that the Rebels had withdrawn, Sergeant Phelps "went out to see the dead. Such a sight I never saw before and never want to again. [I] could not turn my head without seeing fifteen or twenty dead bodys. They have been busy covring them up, but yet there is a large number left." In Lieutenant Keller's Claremont company, the four men who had gone down mortally wounded in a single volley were laid to rest in a single grave. Three had died instantly, the fourth, Sergeant Charles Wetherbee, the next morning. Back home in Claremont, in its report of the deaths, the *National Eagle* reminded its readers that "the tall form of Wetherbee" had stood out ten months earlier when he marched in the first rank of the company's daily parades on the town common. Twenty-four hours after the battle, Keller had a detail dig the grave not far from where the four had fallen. "The place we fought presents an awful spectacle," he wrote. "Friend and foe lay mingled together." His visit to the hospital was even more disturbing. One man he saw, Private Damon Hunter of Claremont, had lost both an arm and a leg, and Keller correctly predicted that Hunter could not live. "I would give much not to have been there," Keller wrote of the hospital. "Our wounded are badly off, and die rapidly. Hundreds lay around holes, in which they have to rest from their earthly labors, after being pushed in. What makes men such devils?"

The experience of Private Alonzo Allen, who had been shot in the back, confirmed Keller's misgivings about the field hospital. Allen's wound hurt so much that he could barely hobble the two miles from the battlefield to the "great mansion house" that had been converted to a hospital. Not half the wounded could find a place inside the farmhouse or its several outbuildings. One who did, Livermore's sometime tentmate Sergeant George Gove, lay in a hen coop nursing the gunshot wound to his left arm. When at last a surgeon examined Private Allen's back, "he dared not probe such a wound or dig out the shot. He said that I should get up quicker to keep it wet in cold water and let nature do its work." In fact, this was good advice: the wet and cold stopped the bleeding, and by keeping a surgeon's tool out of the wound, Allen avoided the bacteria that caused many a mortal infection. On the Sunday night of the battle, Allen went to lie on the ground in the front yard amid the wounded and dying. There he remained through the next day, and the next, and the next, and the next. Nightly rains kept his blankets and clothing soaked. Heedful of the surgeon's advice, Allen wrote that the weather "served to cool our wounds." But he had no food and "came very near starving to death." Allen was fortunate in one way: he had the company of a man from home. He and another severely wounded private from Croydon, Albert Miner, had found one another and lay talking on the lawn. Early in their ordeal, the emotion-wracked Captain Barton visited them. "He very feelingly took our hands in his and anxiously inquired the nature and extent of our wounds," Allen wrote. "He cried like a child when we asked about the rest of the boys, trying to look stern as a rock all the time. He said, 'We have no company now—they are nearly all dead or wounded.'" Barton's company had lost twenty-four dead and wounded, a quarter of its original strength and the most casualties of any company in the regiment. On Wednesday, three days after the battle, Allen's younger brother Oscar, a private in the company, found him and gave him and Miner two ounces of whiskey each, "which greatly revived us." Finally, on Thursday night, four days after they had gone out to lie on the lawn, Miner and Alonzo Allen were loaded into large wicker baskets and carried to a train. The train, packed with wounded men, took them from Fair Oaks Station to White House Landing. They boarded the steamer *Louisiana* and, one week after the battle, reached Fortress Monroe, where they had caught their first glimpse of the Peninsula two months before. Bad weather detained them until the eleventh, when at last they steamed up Chesapeake Bay toward Philadelphia and its large military hospital. "Here we have the best of care from the attendants, who are ladies and gentlemen," Allen wrote his sister. "Some of the ladies are young and very pretty. My wound has weakened my back and knees so that I can walk but a few rods at a time. But I think I may be able to join my regiment in a few weeks." In fact, his fighting days were done.

Wounded Rebels who had fallen into Union hands were also treated at the field hospital near Fair Oaks. When Livermore visited to look after wounded men from his company, he saw a long row of Confederate dead being buried side by side in a trench and watched the surgeons amputate limbs "with the most businesslike air." They gave a Confederate soldier chloroform and cut off a limb, and the man, in a stupor, blurted out, "I wish I had a cabbage!" Laughter filled the room. Private Lloyd Forehand, who had been shot in the thigh, estimated that a hundred Rebels lay near him, "some with their arms off, others with their legs greening." He heard a man mutter, "Damn the Yankees!"

Forehand, who had joined the regiment at sixteen, saw Colonel Cross carried into the hospital. He was smoking a cigar and laughing, and he shouted: "Hello, Forehand! Did a damn cuss hit you?" Forehand responded that yes, he had been a marked man. Eventually, Forehand took the same train and boat trip as Private Allen, and they wound up in the same hospital ward in Philadelphia. From there Forehand wrote his mother a letter that, though no doubt welcome, might also have both insulted and alarmed her. "I am better of[f] than I should be at home," he wrote. "We have everything we want and could not ask for better care. We have nice comfortable beds and plenty to eat." He informed her that the "little accident I met with the first day of June" had caused "a bulett hole through my leg above the knee through the thick flesh." The doctor had told him it would take longer to heal than a knife wound because the "ball is poison to the flesh."

Cross left the Peninsula several days before Privates Allen and Forehand, but his departure was not without its trials. On the day of the battle, he was carried to the farmhouse, where a surgeon dressed his wounds, then taken outside to sleep under the trees. The next morning, Cross and other officers were loaded into ambulances for the ride to Savage's Station, farther down the railroad line. Four officers traveled prone in each ambulance, some with their wounded limbs strapped to wagon bows to limit jostling during transport. Once Cross was aboard, he watched as the young officer next to him, a Pennsylvanian named Francis Adams Donaldson, had his left arm tied down. "Now there, youngster," Cross said to him when the job was done, "as long as you are so secure, just be kind enough to help me keep steady with your free arm." As they bumped along toward the station, Donaldson wrote, Cross "used some strong adjectives by way of easing his pain, as he put it." To the same end, the colonel thirsted for strong drink. At quarter-mile intervals along the road to the station, volunteers from the Christian Commission had set up "A" tents where they served lemonade, claret punch, and liquors to the wounded officers. At each stop, Donaldson asked for and received claret punch, but Cross got lemonade, "much to his disgust. He always asked for stimulant but was always refused." Cross was pallid from loss of blood, and he seemed feverish; hence the doctors believed alcohol would worsen rather than relieve his condition. At Savage's Station the officers were "put in box cars filled to their utmost" and taken to White House Landing.

The landing on the Pamunkey River was a collection point for wounded men, including rebel captives, who were to be transported to northern hospitals. Orderlies helped Cross and the others from the train to a paddleboat whose decks were already covered with horribly wounded men. The paddleboat carried the wounded out to the point of the Peninsula, where Cross had landed with his regiment two months before. There, he was loaded onto the *R. S. Spaulding*, an ocean steamer converted to a hospital ship. As each man was hoisted over the rail and onto the *Spaulding*, a crewman hollered out the nature of the wound so that the litter bearers would know on which side of the ship to place the patient. With an almost comic cadence, the shouts tolled the sad cost of battle: "Right stump! Left stump! Right fracture! Left fracture!" The *Spaulding* carried fifteen hundred wounded men on the six-day voyage to Philadelphia. Cross's traveling companions included his own major, William Cook, and General Howard. The general, a Mainer, would return, but not Cook. He had been shot in the right hip; the ball had lodged near the sciatic nerve, where it remained for the rest of his life.

Aboard the *Spaulding*, one amenity in particular pleased the men: the presence of female nurses. Cross was no exception, if only because it gave him a chance to tease, flirt, and be difficult. Once their patients were aboard, the nurses washed them and dressed their wounds. From the perspective of Harriet Whitten, a volunteer nurse from New Hampshire, the spirits of the wounded officers and soldiers ranged from the buoyant to the pathetic. She wrote home that the officers were "a great deal more trouble than the men. As most of them were but slightly wounded they ate like pigs, and were sending their orderlies for all sorts of things not in the Hospital diet. Col. Cross' demands for eggs were so unreasonable that I almost wished myself a hen that I might satisfy him." Because of Cross's height, "a coop had to be nailed at the end of his bunk to receive his feet," Whitten wrote. Across from the colonel lay a rebel lieutenant, "a handsome dark youth. They used to talk over the war and discuss the different points in an amicable & gentlemanly way." Whitten felt sorry for the rebel private in a bunk above the two officers. The man "cried whenever he spoke," she wrote. He was "a simple country fellow, forced into the army only four or five weeks ago—his whole heart with his wife and 'those two sweet little boys.' One morning when I asked him how he was, he burst into tears, 'Oh, last night I was in my own barn.' Poor fellow, his brother was killed by his side when he was wounded."

The good nature that Harriet Whitten observed in the colonel reflected in part his pride in the Fifth's performance at Fair Oaks. Writing from the *Spaulding*, he expressed this to Henry Kent in New Hampshire: "The regiment did nobly, more than nobly, gloriously." He wanted Kent to ask the Legislature to take formal note of the Fifth's success, and his friend obliged him. On June 10, Kent called for a resolution of thanks to the Fifth. A committee amended the measure to include two other New Hampshire infantry regiments and a cavalry battalion. The Fifth, the resolution said, "bore the brunt of the fight before Richmond" and "only changed its position to carry the glorious stars and stripes and the flag of the State nearer to the enemy."

No legislative proclamation or inflated rhetoric could transform the battle of Fair Oaks into the decisive victory the men of the Fifth believed they had won. The battle changed nothing, and the casualty figures that morning had been roughly equal: 1,132 on the rebel side, 1,203 on the Union side. The Fifth had lost 41 dead or mortally wounded and 129 wounded. Of the wounded, 53 would never return to duty, including Jeremiah Young, a forty-five-year-old private who had lost an eye to a rebel ball. Back home in Wolfeboro one day that fall, his daughter noticed that Young had disappeared from his yard. Finding the barn locked from the inside, she peered "through a crack in the door, saw her father suspended from the girt, his knees resting on the floor. She immediately gave the alarm, but life was extinct." The newspaper reported that although Young had seemed to be recovering from his war wound, "he had expressed a fear that he should become insane."

Shortly after the shooting stopped at Fair Oaks, the two armies paused as their commanders considered their next moves. General McClellan, who was suffering from malaria, visited the battlefield to the cheers of his soldiers. "He said he never herd such musketry firing in all the fights he was in as when the 5th marched," Sergeant Phelps wrote. McClellan issued a circular reporting that the Rebels were "now at bay in front of their Capital. The final and decisive battle is at hand." In truth, he still believed his army was outnumbered. He ordered more bridges built across the Chickahominy to improve his mobility and supply lines. His strategy combined a siege of Richmond with calculated advances out of his army's entrenchments. On the Confederate side, President Jefferson Davis chose General Robert E. Lee to succeed the wounded Johnston as commander of the Army of Northern Virginia. Lee quickly plotted an offensive strategy. He ordered his troops to dig in where they were and sent Brigadier General J. E. B. Stuart's cavalry on a reconnaissance mission. Stuart and his brigade circled McClellan's entire army. Lee sent "deserters" into the Union lines with false reports of his intentions. He ordered Stonewall Jackson and his army to move east from the Shenandoah Valley, which Jackson did with surprising stealth. Once Jackson arrived, Lee had more than 92,000 soldiers under his command to McClellan's 100,000. Finally, the Confederate commander put together a plan to disrupt McClellan's siege, bring the Union army to battle, and chase it from the gates of Richmond.

The men of the Fifth were oblivious to all this. Although they had suffered heavy losses, they believed the prize was within reach. A mere six miles away, the spires of the Confederate capital were visible from the treetops. During the march to the Chickahominy, several of them had wagered that they would be back in New Hampshire by the Fourth of July. Now, as they basked in their success at Fair Oaks and awaited orders for the climactic march, the odds favored the bet. On June 4, the regiment's tents and gear were still north of the river. To write to his sister, Sergeant Phelps had to scrounge a "dirty sheet" of stationery from a camp the Fifth had recaptured from the Rebels. McClellan's army "was going to make an advance this morning, but it rained all night and all the forenoon," he wrote. In Phelps's view, the weather had only postponed the inevitable. As he informed Sophia Phelps back in Amherst, "Richmond will have to fall soon."

Retreat

"What a day and what marching—16
miles through clouds of dust, which
was so thick and heavy that it was impossable to see the man in front. . . .
It was a sad contrast, that long line
of dust covered soldiers, to that quiet
throng that wound its way to church in
each New England village at the call of
the sabbath bell."
—Lieutenant William Moore,
August 24, 1862

A S THE MEN OF THE FIFTH NEW HAMPSHIRE SET UP
camp near Fair Oaks Station, General McClellan's boast that Richmond would soon be theirs kept them on the alert. "We are expecting another battle here every minute," Private Theron Farr wrote his sister on
June 9, eight days after the Fair Oaks fight. "We have had to sleep with our
equipment on every night since the battle and we are alarmed about every
night by the pickets firing at each other." In fact, a battle might have been
better for their spirits than the cautious approach McClellan adopted. Each
passing day eroded the hope of a quick and decisive victory. McClellan told
confidants, as well as the War Department in Washington, that he faced an
army of 200,000, more than twice its actual size. He made unreasonable demands for reinforcements, then blamed Washington for denying them. Just
eighteen days after Fair Oaks, he decided to retreat from the vicinity of Richmond, a movement he would portray as a daring sweep south to a new stronghold on the James River. For the time being, he kept this intention to himself,
leaving his army in an edgy standoff throughout most of June with a rebel
force backed up to its capital.

During this time the Fifth camped near the railroad tracks, only a few hundred yards from the Fair Oaks battleground. The weather was fairly dry, Private Farr wrote, but "we have showers here once in awhile that will make our eyeballs jingle I tell you." Farr, a farmer, informed his family of the early start of fruits that back home in New Hampshire's North Country ripened only in late summer or fall. "The apples and peaches are as big as robins' eggs," he wrote. Private Miles Peabody, ever obsessed with food, had already seen green peas and ripe cherries and strawberries. A frugal man, he declined to pay the twenty-cent going rate for a quart of berries. Peabody also saw McClellan for the first time. The general rode along the line with his staff one day, "a great stout robust looking officer with an eye keen as a brier." His description was larger than life, but Peabody read the general's mind. There might be a battle, he wrote home, but a siege seemed more likely. "I should not be supprised [if] they played the same game here that [they] did at Yorktown."

The Fifth strengthened its position against an enemy force that, like McClellan's, seemed content to stay put and defend its ground. The men cleared an area one hundred yards wide between their bivouac and the woods where the Rebels had dug in. They erected a barricade five feet high between their tents and the cleared field. Because they were so close to the rebel lines, picket duty was dangerous. The pickets had to cross the open ground and move quietly through the woods to a line about two hundred yards from the enemy. "The pickets do a goodeel of firing at one another," Peabody observed. "They have to keep hid behind trees on both sides and if a man pops his head out he is shure to get a ball through it." The newly promoted Lieutenant Thomas Livermore wrote that "the crack of the rifle was heard day and night, and the scattering shots often swelled into a rolling fusilade, to be followed by the roar of shells whirling over the crouching pickets. The time was full of alarms." Through some mistake, Livermore's men once endured thirty-six hours on the picket line without relief. When a man fell asleep lying behind a tree, Captain Richard Cross punished him by making him move forward to a stump that barely shielded him. "He won't sleep much there," Cross joked to Livermore, and Cross was right. Each time the man moved, a shot from the enemy picket line struck near him. When Lieutenant William Moore took his men up to the picket line on June 10, he found the soldiers on duty there "skirmishing with the enemy. As soon as they got their trouble settled I relieved them." A sharpshooter hit one of his men in the neck and another in the head. At 10:30 that night, Moore himself was wounded, but he was more embarrassed than hurt. "I very unfortunately accidently discharged my pistol," he wrote, "the shot taking effect in my left hand."

If minor accidents and rebel fire were not trouble enough, the men had their own artillery to worry about. Livermore saw a soldier brought in from picket with his back ripped open by a Union shell that had been fired too low. Moore wrote home that the enemy had had by far the worst of an exchange of fire on June 18. The Rebels moved a large force forward, quickly pushing back the Fifth's picket line. Brigadier General Israel Richardson ordered up artillery fire, which drove off the attackers and caused them heavy losses. The next day, "they hung out a large flag of truce to bury their dead and carry off their wounded, as of course we were not going to do the work of burying since we had prepared them for their last resting place." The only problem, Moore wrote, was that during the shelling a round of Union canister had landed in Lieutenant James Larkin's company. It wounded four men, one mortally and another so badly that he never returned to duty.

Letters home about these dangers, not to mention the local newspapers' printing of the casualty lists from the Fair Oaks battle, caused dread in many households. Benjamin Chase, a corporal in Larkin's company, heard from his younger sister that their mother worried about him constantly. He was one of eleven children, three of whom were in the army. His father, Madison Chase, a farmer, had injured himself before the war, and the family depended on—and received—nearly all of Bennie's pay. "I can make as much money out hear as I can at home," Corporal Chase wrote his father, "but it is the hardest way of making money I ever see. I hope and prey that I shall get home a live. I never want to be in another battle, but if we have to fight, I shall fight again." Chase tried to ease his mother's mind, but he lacked the writer's art. "We are in a good deal of danger now, liable to go into battle at eny minute," he wrote. "You must not worry about me. I may live to get home again and may not. If I get killed out hear it will be the last of me, but I have a great mind of getting home again. This battle up hear to Richmond they all [say] will end the war. Oh how I do hope it will. The next battle will be soon, I think. Mother, I shant get home in July but may get home in August or September. Oh how I only do wish I could be at home by July so as to get some good green peas to eat. You know, mother, how I do like them. A piece of brown bread would taste like honey to me out hear. We hant had eny since we left Concord. I shall know what hard living is if I ever get home. If I was at home now I should never enlist again. I am tired of the war and all the boys are, too. It's a nasty muddy swamp whare we are now—awfull unhealthy place."

As Chase's description suggested, illness preyed on men and morale. Larkin wrote his wife that he was feeling unwell—news that must have alarmed Jenny Larkin, whose brother-in-law had died on the Peninsula less than two months before. Disease had killed twenty-five members of the Fifth since the regiment's arrival at Fortress Monroe and had sent forty men home for good in May alone. Usually these men went on sick call one day and were never seen again; occasionally, as in the case of Private George Webb of the Claremont company, a fatal malady paid a visit right in camp. The forty-six-year-old Webb had enlisted back in September with one of his three sons. At Fair Oaks, he became ill but not ill enough to go to a hospital. On June 15, he suddenly fell into a speechless fit and died. He was buried nearby. Larkin assured his wife that his own queasiness would soon pass, but he longed to come home on leave. In fact, he was so frustrated at the rejection of his furlough requests that he tried in vain to resign. A package in the mail only fed his homesickness. The box contained early strawberries and sardines as well as doughnuts and pies "all safe and nice & as fresh as tho just baked. It made tears start for a moment."

Private James Daniels of Salmon Falls, a faithful but sparing diarist, captured in his entries for June 1862 the ennui and anxiety of an army waiting for something to happen to it. He wrote every day, usually just one sentence, sometimes just a sentence fragment. His account of the Fair Oaks battle had been thirty-two words long. "Fair Oaks swamp; a terrible battle was fought," it opened. "The Fifth New Hampshire Volunteers were engaged." The other seventeen words recorded casualty figures for the five companies in his half of the line of battle. After being assigned to both the burial detail and the lumberjacking crew that cleared the land between the camp and the woods, Daniels recorded three weeks of picket duty and watchful waiting. "Expectations of a fight," he wrote on the eighth. And the next day: "Still waiting for the enemy to advance, but they did not." On June 11, a celestial event warranted a further phrase: "Still in front of the enemy, waiting for them to come; turned out to-night; the moon was in eclipse." On the fourteenth: "In camp; went on duty; lay in the intrenchments." On the twentieth: "Received my tobacco from home; the rebels fired a few shells over our camp." On the twenty-second and again on the twenty-fourth: "Nothing important."

On June 25, McClellan tested the strength of the enemy in what seemed to be the start of the campaign his army had been waiting for. The men of the Fifth moved up to the line to witness a Union attack to their left. To their cheers, two brigades sent out by Brigadier General Joseph Hooker quickly drove the rebel pickets before them. The fighting that day at Oak Grove ended with a short advance, heavy casualties, and a retreat. This was only the first of a series of fights that exposed McClellan's want of boldness and decided the fate of his campaign. The Union commander had already resolved to move his army; he called the movement a "change of base" before an enemy superior in number. He had chosen the destination and the route. By attacking the Union right north of the Chickahominy the next day, General

Lee chose the time. Lee's objectives were to drive McClellan away from Richmond and destroy his army. The week in which the two generals set out to achieve their aims became known as the Seven Days. They consisted of a rapid withdrawal to the James River by McClellan's army and a series of ill-planned and disorganized attacks by Lee's pursuing Rebels.

To the men of the Fifth, the second and third days of the seven brought the sound of battle but no contact with the enemy. They heard artillery and musketry across the river on their far right, as Lee's army attacked at Mechanicsville and then Gaines's Mill. The latter was the deadliest battle in the East to this point of the war. At dusk, some of the men of the Fifth climbed trees and watched the fire bursts from the cannons. Rumors circulated that the final assault on Richmond had begun. "I think Richmond will be ours by the Fourth of July," Sergeant Charles Phelps wrote to his sister Sophia on June 27, the day of the Gaines's Mill battle. He told her of the firing that had kept the men on alert for three days. "We have to sleep with guns in one hand and grub in the other and turn out three or four times a night," Phelps wrote. "We have got used to it and can sleep on a stone as well as anywhere." Phelps and many of his fellow soldiers initally believed that Union Brigadier General Fitz John Porter had driven back the enemy. In truth, Porter's corps fought defensively at Gaines's Mill, in keeping with McClellan's delusion that Lee had him vastly outnumbered. McClellan lost eight thousand men in the battle, including nearly three thousand captured. Lee lost more—almost twice as many dead and wounded—but his army nearly drove Union forces into the Chickahominy.

McClellan's retreat was a huge enterprise: he had to move an army of nearly 100,000 men, more than three hundred cannons and siege guns, thirty-eight hundred wagons and ambulances, and a herd of twenty-five hundred cattle. The new Union base would be across the Peninsula on the James River, at Harrison's Landing. Gunboats had already steamed up the James to fortify the spot.

The men of the Fifth knew nothing of McClellan's design. The night of the Gaines's Mill battle, they struck their tents, but the alarm proved false and they pitched them again. All that night and all day June 28, the Union forces that had fought north of the Chickahominy crossed the bridges and streamed past on their way to Harrison's Landing. This parade of defeated men confirmed the suspicion that the battle had been lost, and the Fifth stood ready to leave. At three o'clock on June 29, a humid Sunday morning, the regiment joined the flow and marched away. Some men guessed they were in full retreat, but they saw no order that spelled it out. All they knew was that they were on the move and that the move was away from Richmond. They were

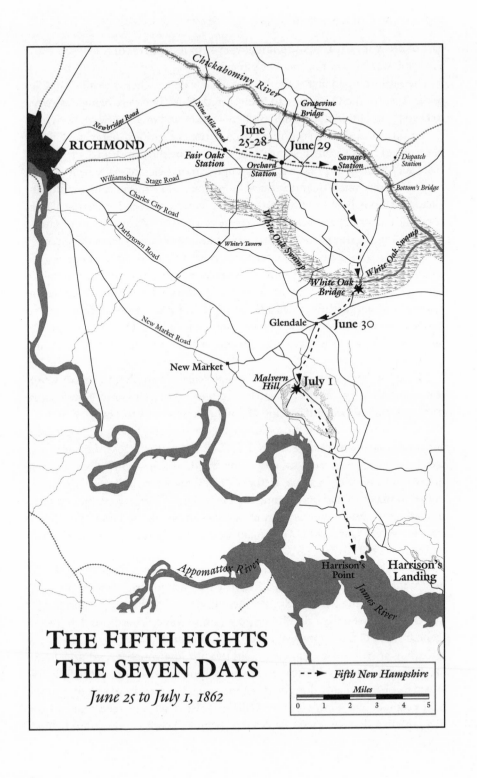

Chickahominy River

Newbridge Road

RICHMOND

Nine Mile Road

June 25-28

Grapevine Bridge

June 29

Savage's Station

Dispatch Station

Fair Oaks Station

Orchard Station

Bottom's Bridge

Williamsburg Stage Road

Charles City Road

White Oak Swamp

Darbytown Road

White's Tavern

White Oak Swamp

White Oak Bridge

Glendale

June 30

New Market Road

New Market

Malvern Hill

July 1

Appomattox River

Harrison's Point

Harrison's Landing

James River

THE FIFTH FIGHTS
THE SEVEN DAYS

June 25 to July 1, 1862

- - - ► *Fifth New Hampshire*

Miles

0   1   2   3   4   5

part of the rear guard, an assignment they kept for the rest of the Seven Days. Their job was to slow the enemy's pursuit.

The Fifth stopped first at Orchard Station, a depot where the food supplies of the Army of the Potomac had been stored. Now they were being destroyed to keep them out of rebel hands. Spilled whiskey and molasses formed rivulets in the dirt, and flames consumed huge stores of rations. Sergeant Charles Hale found it "a frightful sight to see such a destruction of property, especially such articles as potatoes, dried apples, molasses, &c., of which we had received but a small quantity for a long time." Livermore and Lieutenant Charles Ballou shared a different reaction as they watched towering flames consume a stack of hardtack boxes as large as a house. "We had a sort of savage joy in seeing the destruction which would keep our rations from the enemy," Livermore wrote. The two lieutenants decided to hold out as long as they could against the advancing Rebels. When at last they ordered their detail to fall back, one man, Private John Bickford, whom Livermore described as "a quiet boy and faithful, unclean, but good to have," was too frightened to budge from behind the bread box where he was hiding. The Rebels captured him, and after seven weeks at the prison on Belle Isle, he died of fever and malnutrition.

McClellan had given Brigadier General William Franklin, the Sixth Corps commander, charge of the rear-guard fighting. While the Fifth New Hampshire was still at Orchard Station, Franklin rode ahead to Savage's Station. There, long rows of white hospital tents, each housing fifteen or twenty sick and wounded men, lined a cleared field north of the tracks. South of the tracks lay another clearing of about one hundred acres. The hills along one side would provide good cover for a defending force, and Franklin determined to make a stand here to impede Lee's army. "The day was hot and sultry and wore away slowly as we waited either to be attacked or at nightfall to start for White Oak Bridge," Franklin wrote. The bridge lay six miles south on the route of retreat.

The Fifth took up its position near the tracks at Savage's Station. As the men waited for battle, Captain Richard Cross feared that some in his company were suffering from sunstroke. He sent a detail to find ice, but no sooner had the ice arrived than the Rebels came on in force. Livermore described a scene from hell: the oppressive heat, the humid air filled with the dust of the retreating army, smoke billowing from the burning supplies, and now heavy fire from the enemy. When the rear guard pulled out after nightfall, it followed its orders to abandon the three thousand wounded and sick men at the field hospital. The Fifth's Private William LeBosquet, nineteen-year-old son of a preacher, had contracted typhoid fever and was among those left behind.

A comrade in his company, Private Peabody, wrote home that ambulances had carried LeBosquet and two others to the station, then "left them on the ground to the tender mercies of the rebels. That such things should be done is a shame and a disgrace to the army."

Peabody also expressed his hostility toward freed slaves, who were plentiful on the Peninsula. "On the retreat I saw sick and wounded soldiers who could jest crall along on foot, while there was any number of robust negroes who could get plenty of chances to ride," Peabody wrote. "I would like to know if the negroes have got to be treated better than our sick and wounded soldiers. If they have, it is high time that this war was brought to a close. The negroes that I have seen here are a very lazy disgusting set of human beings as I ever saw. There are a number employed as servents for the Officers, but I would not have one of them about me for all they could do."

It was midnight by the time the Fifth followed the rest of McClellan's army onto the road through White Oak Swamp. The swamp took its name from a narrow stream, a tributary of the Chickahominy. Although there were marshes in the lowlands, the road to the bridge wound through hills and valleys. The Fifth rounded the final curve before the bridge just before daylight. The bridge had become a bottleneck, and Richardson, the crusty division commander, stood near it swearing and shouting to hasten his men across. After all had reached the other side, the Fifth was detailed to help destroy the bridge, which a New York regiment had rebuilt just the day before. By the time the men had dismantled it, the sun and the heat of the new day were rising. The men moved back to higher ground, stuck their bayonets in the earth, and attached their blankets to the locks of their rifles for shelter. Beneath these makeshift roofs, they lay down to sleep.

The sleep was sweaty and restless, the awakening abrupt. "Not a note was heard from the rebels till two o'clock, when all of a sudden they opened with a perfect torrent of shell," wrote Sergeant Hale. "Our batteries soon got the range, and then there was music I assure you." The Rebels had come down the same road as McClellan's army. The last curve before the White Oak Bridge skirts a hill some fifty feet high, and on that hill General Stonewall Jackson placed thirty guns. Trees on the hill gave the artillery cover. Across White Oak Swamp, on the hillside where the men of the Fifth were sleeping, the land had been cleared, making the men an open target. "They had us in a rather tight fix this time," Hale wrote. In the chaos of confused soldiers, galloping horses, and frantic mule trains, a New York regiment fled in disorder toward the Fifth's position. Brigadier General John Caldwell rode up and shouted, "Fifth New Hampshire, rise up!" The men stood with fixed bayonets pointed at the New Yorkers, arresting their flight.

There was reason to run. Of all the federal troops left to slow the Rebels at White Oak crossing, only Caldwell's brigade was on ground exposed to shelling. Ordered to support Captain George Hazzard's artillery battery, the men lay flat perhaps 150 yards to the rear, "ready to spring up and rush forward in case the infantry or cavalry charge up to capture the guns," as Sergeant Hale put it. When the fire was heavy, as it was here, this position was "the most trying to be in of any I have seen," Hale wrote. "I would much rather hear the venomous buzz of the bullet than the screech of a shot or solid shell." This fear was widely shared, and it made the behavior of Charles Fullerton all the more remarkable. Fullerton, a boy of ten or eleven from Concord who had come along with the regiment and acted as a valet to some of the junior officers, lay on the line among the men. While the shells rained in, he calmly played with his pet squirrel.

The Confederate gunners found the brigade's range. Shells burst repeatedly between Hazzard's battery and the Fifth's position, and solid shot landed among the men. "The shot hit some of our men and scattered their vitals and brains upon the ground, and we hugged the earth to escape this horrible fate," wrote Lieutenant Livermore. He saw a shell strike in the nearby Second Delaware and blow a man's head twenty feet into the air. "I do not know that I have ever feared artillery as I feared it then," Livermore wrote. In the dry heat, clouds of dust flew up each time a shell hit the ground. "What we most dreaded were the six pound shot, a little larger than one's fist, and the railroad iron," wrote Hale. The shot "would strike the ground and bound several times. They would inflict a terrible wound, even at their last bound." The balls could be seen in flight. Lieutenant Jacob Keller sat on a knapsack in front of the regiment warning the men when the rounds were coming and where they were likely to land. Keller's effort could not protect the entire regiment. A cannonball struck Corporal Edward Howe of Lebanon and "cut off his right leg near the body, also his left heel," Captain James Perry wrote. The same ball ripped off the right arm of another man, Private George Percival. Lieutenant Nathan Randlett did his best under the circumstances, buckling a strap around Howe's leg to stanch the flow of blood, but with such severe wounds the two men needed medical treatment. Their fellow soldiers bore them up and carried them to a field hospital. Both were presumed dead and left behind when the surgeons had to abandon the hospital.

As Livermore lay clutching the earth, he heard someone shout his name. Lieutenant Colonel Samuel Langley, the regimental commander in Colonel Cross's absence, wanted Livermore to run to Caldwell and seek permission to move the Fifth to safer ground. Caldwell was in a wood a quarter mile away, and Lieutenant John Ricker and a sergeant beside him laid bets on how far

Livermore would make it before he was hit. Livermore alternately walked and ran, dodging and ducking to the sounds of the shells. At last he reached Caldwell. Informed of the situation, the brigade commander said: "Tell the colonel to move where he pleases if he don't go off the field." Livermore made it back across the open ground to deliver this message.

For two other men, the order to move came too late. Just as Livermore's company stood to depart, a cannon shot went past him and struck Privates James Nichols and George Tebbetts. The shot left Nichols's arm dangling by a strip of flesh, and he came to Captain Cross holding the severed arm in his good hand. "Captain, I am wounded and want to go to the rear," Nichols said. The men had been told not to leave the line without permission, but Livermore was amazed nevertheless at a man so badly wounded following orders. He came to see Nichols's request as the ultimate example of the discipline of the Fifth New Hampshire. As obedient as Nichols might have been, Private Peabody had mixed feelings about him. Nichols was "the biggest theif in the Company," Peabody wrote. "He would steal everything he could lay his hands on. But peace to his ashes, he died a soldier's death." In fact, Nichols survived. Tebbetts, who did not have to be in the fight at all, was not so fortunate. Because his fine penmanship and sharp mind had earned him the job of company clerk, Tebbetts had been given the option the night before of going ahead with the regimental wagon train. But he wanted to carry a rifle with his comrades. Now some of them gathered his bloody body in a blanket and carried him away. He died later that day and was buried on the field.

After the Fifth moved out of harm's way, Richardson ordered two of his brigades, Caldwell's and the Irish, to rush to the aid of Union troops at Glendale, four miles southwest of the White Oak Bridge. "We thought it was rather hard to stand what we had all afternoon, and then be rushed off into another division and into another fight," wrote Sergeant Hale. Confederate Major General James Longstreet had attacked at Glendale in an attempt to split McClellan's army in half. The men of the Fifth reached the fight at nightfall and were put in reserve. As they waited, balls struck trees and shells came crashing through. No order came to attack, but when darkness set in and the firing died away, the Fifth moved to the most advanced position Union forces had gained. The men lay at the edge of a wood with the field of battle before them. They saw the torches of enemy rescue parties searching the field and heard wounded men call out their regimental identifications in hope of being taken in. Some searchers "came within a few rods of where we lay, and we could hear all their conversation," Hale wrote. "The ground around us was covered with our dead and wounded." The wounded "begged piteously for water." Almost no one in the regiment had any. Hale had filled his canteen in the morning but emptied it before noon. "In more than one instance I heard as high as a dollar offered for a drink of water, by some one almost overpowered by heat," he wrote.

Because they had not had a good night's rest in four days and had been fighting and marching all afternoon, the men had trouble staying awake. Hale dozed off beside a stump but was jostled back to consciousness. "I started up and found a man on his knees beside me, clutching my canteen, which he shook with the frenzy of a dying man. 'What do you want,' said I. He made a motion for a drink of water. I looked at him closely and saw he had received a terrible wound. A bullet had struck him in the cheek, carrying away nearly the whole lower part of his face and most of the nose." At two o'clock in the morning, when the order came to withdraw, officers had to crouch and creep among the men to rouse them. Several found themselves trying to wake corpses. No one woke Lieutenant Welcome Crafts, who had slipped away and fallen asleep. The Rebels captured Crafts and took him to Libby prison.

In the night, the Fifth marched away from Glendale and back toward McClellan's route of retreat. The men had miles to go and still no water. Hale snatched a cupful from a brook that crossed the road; it was half mud, and hundreds of horses and men had passed through the brook, but he was too thirsty to care. Many of the men were asleep on their feet. As they tramped along, Lieutenant Charles Ballou watched Livermore drift off out of the ranks. Ballou woke his friend from his stupor and guided him back to his place. At last they climbed a hill—Malvern Hill—and lay down. Livermore ate crackers for breakfast while the surgeon amputated the finger of the man beside him without chloroform. The patient did not cry out.

In line of battle on a scorching July 1, the men of the Fifth once more found themselves a target of Confederate artillery and once more cheered the order to march toward battle. That morning, Captain Edward Sturtevant, the ranking company commander, had taken command of the regiment from Lieutenant Colonel Langley, who had fallen ill with a bronchial condition. The soldiers liked Sturtevant's nature; he was, in Livermore's opinion, "honest and brave, but a little wanting in decision." To Livermore's relief, Sturtevant did decide to get his men off the open ground. He sent them across a field to support a battery. As Livermore ran, his curiosity got the better of him and he looked to his left to watch a rebel gun crew in action. "I saw one pull the string, saw the flash of the piece, heard the roar, and the whiz of the shell, heard it burst, heard the humming of the fragments, and wondered if I was to be hit, and quicker than a flash something stung my leg on the calf, and I limped out of the ranks, a wounded man." To leave the field seemed more perilous to him than to struggle on, and before long he reached the regiment again. His wound, a painful, ugly bruise, began to swell. Sturtevant ordered him to a hospital, and Livermore hobbled off. Along the way the lieutenant found "a good-looking negro man" named Charles. Charles had been servant to a captain but the captain was dead, and Charles was looking for a job. Livermore hired him on the spot.

McClellan's troops held the high ground and a well-fortified position on Malvern Hill, and they made the most of it. The Union artillery behind which the Fifth was deployed sat on a ridgeline facing down the hill's gentle northern slope. Rebel infantry had to cross a mile of open ground to reach that line, and thousands died trying. Union forces killed or wounded 5,620 Rebels. Their own casualties were half that. This result so heartened General Porter, whose corps had been retreating since Gaines's Mill, that he asked McClellan for reinforcements and permission to renew the fight in the morning. But the day's success failed to shake McClellan's conviction that the retreat must resume. Before dawn on July 2, the Army of the Potomac embarked on the march south to the destination McClellan had chosen for it, Harrison's Landing. On Malvern Hill, Sturtevant awaited orders to bring the Fifth into the line of march. No orders arrived, and when the captain at last gave them on his own, his men formed the last regiment to leave the hill. They marched off in a heavy, dispiriting rain, following the rest of the army over ten miles of muddy road.

This was a gloomy time for the men of the Fifth, as it was for the entire army. It was a time to wonder why they had retreated from a victorious field, to curse the elements, to seek the sleep of the exhausted, and to count their losses. In three days of fighting at Orchard Station, Savage's Station, White Oak Swamp, and Malvern Hill, the Fifth had lost 10 dead and 42 wounded. From Fair Oaks on June 1 through Malvern Hill on July 1, the loss had been 54 killed or mortally wounded and 172 wounded. More than one man in four who had been fit for battle when June began had suffered at least a wound by the time it ended.

McClellan had glowing praise for the men, but they did not take his words at face value. He wrote in a message to his troops that in the last ten days they had "illustrated the valor and endurance of the American soldier. Attacked by superior forces, without hope of reenforcements, you have succeeded in changing your base of operations by a flank movement, always regarded as the most hazardous of military expedients. The enemy may at any moment attack you. Let them come, and we will convert their repulse into a final defeat." Private Henry Holden believed what he had seen, not what his general told him. "We have just fell back from Richmond about twenty miles to draw the rebels out and did we draw them out," he wrote his brother. "They came after us like wolves." Holden credited higher forces with watching over him during the Seven Days, writing: "I suppose you would like to hear about how I escaped the bullets. I do not know unless it was the hand of the Lord that shielded me from them." McClellan's grand locutions failed to influence Private Peabody's thinking in the least. He wrote home that the retreat had been more disastrous than the rout at Bull Run the previous summer. "I suppose that we have got to fight our way back again if ever we get to Richmond, which is very doubtfull to me," Peabody wrote. Illness—"a slow billious fever"—had kept Lieutenant Larkin out of the battles, but he was as much a realist as Peabody. Avoiding the fate of the sick and wounded who were abandoned to enemy hands, Larkin had been carried in an ambulance from Fair Oaks Station to the James River. "It was very fortunate for I got red of a terribal hard march and a severe storm that drenched the soldiers to the skin and evry one exposed," Larkin wrote. He hoped never to see another retreat, but he also knew that "the Rebs. were terrably slaughtered" during the Seven Days fighting. Larkin rejected the idea that the retreat had been voluntary. "A good many pretended the move was stratedgy, but a man with half an eye could easly see we wer forced to it," he wrote. Now that his health was "first rate," he had rejoined the regiment. "To see the tiard and jagged worn out men makes me think I could never complain for myself," he wrote. "Those men that got wounded at Fair Oaks and got home are fortunate men for they have got clear of more hardships than the pain of wounds." The day before he wrote—the day of McClellan's congratulatory message—had been Independence Day. There was "not much enthusiasm, but we fired a salute by the way of keeping up appearances," Larkin wrote.

The army's new base was a square tract on the north bank of the James River at Harrison Point. The principal camp lay on the lawn of a great plantation with an illustrious history. The father of a signer of the Declaration of Independence, Benjamin Harrison, had built the plantation house in 1726. The nation's ninth president, William Henry Harrison, had been born in the house, and every president from George Washington to John Tyler, a neighbor, had been entertained there. Now McClellan set up his headquarters on the second floor. Behind the house, a broad, tiered lawn ran a quarter mile down to the James. McClellan ordered his army to set up camp on this lawn and the adjacent fields. Richardson's division, including the Fifth New Hampshire, pitched its tents near the river along a slight bend just east of the landing itself. After the men had made camp, each brigade sent large details to help build a long line of forts, redoubts, and rifle pits to protect the army's position. The fortifications ran more than two miles on each side, enclosing a square with the river as the south side. To the men of the Fifth the duty seemed a repeat of their work of a month earlier near Fair Oaks. The weather was even hotter and the daylight at its longest, so the men toiled from four to eight in the morning, rested during the heat of day, then resumed work from four to nine in the evening.

Once this labor was done and they grew accustomed to the humidity and the low, languid rattle of the cicadas, some of the men began to enjoy their new surroundings. They made platforms so they could sleep eighteen inches above the ground. Corporal Benjamin Chase explained why in a letter home: vermin. "Some call them ground lice and body lice. They crall up from the ground on to us and up off the wood, too. They are hateful things." The men swam in the James and settled into a routine of drill and inspection. These were "good easy times," Larkin told his wife. "I don't wear anything over my lungs, my shirt boosom thrown open, and never take the slightest cold. I lay down on my bed of poles and sleep as sound as a nut without any thing over me, the tent open and the air circulating freely." The officers' cuisine had also improved: cod, mackerel, beef, pork, potatoes, applesauce, lemons, milk, and cheese. "It is nice soldiering when you have no marching or hard duty to do," Larkin wrote. "If I could only have you and Darlings near me, I should like it well. I have got your faces here before me. Wish they were real. I should be happy."

In the relative peace of midsummer on the James, commerce, some of it illicit, enriched camp life. Harrison's Landing was safe enough for sutlers, and soldiers who had U.S. Treasury notes could improve their diet by buying from them. Private Henry Holt asked his grandfather to send money. He liked hardtack well enough if he had nothing else to eat, as had been the case at Fair Oaks, but things were different now. "I have not been where I could spend any money till now and living on hard bread all the time does not go first rate when soft bread is for sale in camp," he wrote. Since water for drinking was scarce, some men of the Fifth dug deep wells and tried to profit from them by selling to other regiments. This "bartering of Nature's freest gift" hurt the Fifth's reputation, and Livermore, for one, speculated that Colonel Cross would have stopped it had he been there. The men prized articles and food from New Hampshire. Lieutenant William Moore wrote to thank "the good, kind and motherly ladies at home" for a box of handmade apparel. Lieutenant Samuel Quinn was ill with fever and could not write himself, but Moore assured Mrs. J. H. Kendrick that Quinn appreciated "the comfortable slippers, which I suppose your willing hands made." Another thank-you letter lamented that some gifts sent by the ladies "have been sold out to the soldiers," a reference to the underground market in the camp. Corporal Chase had seen several comrades receive boxes, and he sent his father detailed instructions for one of his own. He wanted a wide-brimmed hat to keep off the sun, but his most explicit order was for food. "I want a lot of gingerbread and sweat cakes," he wrote. "If the bluberies are ripe tell the children to pick some and put some in the cakes. You need not be afraid that it will make me sick to eat such rich stuff for it wont." Besides, Chase did not plan to eat all the home-baked goods he received. He named several members of his company who were turning a profit on their food supplies. Private Mike Morris was selling ginger cakes. "He bys them by the barrell and makes 6 or 7 dollars on a barrell," Chase wrote. As usual, Chase promised to share his profits with his family, although he needed a dollar and half for another piece of business. "I guess I will get my picture taken and send it home so if I should get killed out hear you could have it to look at," the corporal wrote.

As always, the men speculated about whether the Rebels would attack. "If they do there will be such a battle as when Greek meets Greek," Moore predicted in a letter home. "There will be no danger of their superior force [in number] flanking us; they will have to give us a direct front attack and they know we can whip them then though they fight like devils." Even the usually dour Private Peabody was confident. "If the rebels should chose to attack us here, they will have warm work," he wrote his parents. Lee had no intention of attacking; the Federals occupied a fortified position with added support from gunboats on the James. A detail of the Fifth joined a patrol toward Malvern Hill but made no contact with the enemy. Corporal Chase saw a few rebel shells fall harmlessly in the river. "Our folks fired at them and stoped them," he wrote. "Our gunboats are all strung along up the river and down."

McClellan later claimed that his intention had been to rest his army here for a few days before renewing his offensive on Richmond. He blamed interference from Washington for staying his hand and used a presidential visit to press his case for reinforcements. He also told Lincoln that the institution of slavery must be maintained and private property protected within the rebel states. "A declaration of radical views, especially on slavery, will rapidly disintegrate our present Armies" and make recruitment "almost hopeless," McClellan wrote. The men were curious to see Lincoln. When he reviewed the troops on July 8, Lieutenant Livermore described his expression as "anxious but kind." McClellan, whose statements had done nothing to ease the president's anxiety, wrote his wife that Lincoln "really seems quite incapable of rising to the height of the merits of the question & the magnitude of the crisis."

Democratic editors took the party line on the crumbling of the Peninsula campaign. In his July 9 edition, William Butterfield of the *New Hampshire Patriot* in Concord wrote: "It is doubtful which is the most prominent sentiment in the minds of all patriotic men, admiration of the masterly generalship of Gen. McClellan and the heroic conduct of his troops in their late conflicts before Richmond, or execration of the dastardly conduct of those who have so long and successfully labored to bring upon that army the late disasters. To the minds of loyal and patriotic men, the authors of this mischief are guilty of ten thousand murders; the blood shed in those battles is upon their heads, and history will record them as the vilest traitors and most heartless wretches that ever controlled the destiny of a nation. Let the hundreds of people in New Hampshire whose sons, fathers and brothers have been murdered to further the political schemes of abolition traitors reflect upon the conduct of these men and the deplorable results of this conduct."

War news and politics dominated the papers, but the most anxiously read columns reported the fate of individual soldiers. In the late spring and early summer of 1862, there were heavy new burdens for the citizenry to bear. As McClellan's hopes before Richmond dwindled, it didn't matter where one laid the blame: a huge effort to defeat the rebellion had failed at high human cost. Rochester, near the state's short seacoast, had contributed several soldiers to a Fifth New Hampshire company under the respected Mexican War veteran John Murray. In June, four wounded men, including two recruits to the Fifth from Captain Murray's company, returned home. One of the four had had a thumb shot off; another had lost his right index finger. The two soldiers from the Fifth were Stephen Avery, who had seemed to rise from the dead after being shot through a lung at the start of the Fair Oaks battle, and Charles Bliss, who was hit twice at Fair Oaks, in the breast and in the thigh. "Every such return helped to stimulate and confirm the determination of the people," wrote Franklin McDuffee, a town official. This determination did not make it any easier for cities and towns to raise recruits. No longer were ten-dollar bonuses of any use; the amounts were climbing into the hundreds of dollars. There was little fervor for sending more sons and husbands to join in what had revealed itself as a long, terrible struggle.

Letters home from the field did not aid the recruiting effort. In mid-July, Private Peabody wrote to ask if his father thought New Hampshire could fill its quota of Lincoln's new call for troops without a draft. Peabody's advice for his nineteen-year-old brother George was "by all means to stay at home. If I was at home nothing would temp me to enlist again. It must be fatal for many of the northerners to come out here at this time of year. For example look at this regt. that came out here at [the] best time of year 1000 strong and now cannot turn out 200 for duty. I think that this retreat will prolong this war a year at least." Private George Spalding advised a young man back home that if he joined a regiment then forming in Concord, he would find "a harder life to lead than he expects." As for himself, Spalding wrote to his sister, "I am thankfull that I have escaped uninjured thus far, and am more fortunate then many other poor fellows have been, but it may be my turn next. There is no knowing when one is safe here."

The only consolation for the thinned ranks of the Fifth was the opportunity many officers and men saw to improve their lot through promotion. With the three top officers gone, Captain Sturtevant remained in command of the regiment. Colonel Cross was convalescing in New Hampshire, illness had forced Lieutenant Colonel Langley to take an extended furlough, and Major Cook had resigned because of his Fair Oaks wound. Sturtevant wanted Cook's job. In a letter marked "Confidential," he made his case to Anthony Colby, the state's adjutant general. Sturtevant pointed out that he had been the first man to enlist in New Hampshire, had never missed a day of duty, and had commanded the regiment during the battle of Malvern Hill. "[I] have been under fire in eight different engagements," he wrote, "and am not conscious of ever yet 'flinching' or sherking my duty. I am sober, temperate and call myself good pluck in a tight place." He told Colby that he would not be asking for his support if he were not "satisfied that there are many who are 'cheeky' enough to ask for place and power who are no more (if as much) deserving of it than I am." Sturtevant added this postscript: "The weather is hot—our men are now resting from their late fatigue and will soon be all right again." Although Lieutenant Larkin aspired to higher rank, his fondest hope was for a furlough. He had not been to New Hampshire since the Fifth's departure from Concord and was willing to play any angle that might bring him home. Sturtevant was Larkin's company commander, and despite the captain's worries about rank-jumpers, everyone in the regiment knew he would soon succeed Cook as major. Larkin was in line for the promotion to captain and Sturtevant's place, but he hoped he would not take formal command of the company quite yet. He had heard that the governor was soon to appoint two recruiters to return home and work at filling the Fifth's ranks. Larkin coveted this assignment and hoped Sturtevant would select him for it. In the meantime his desire to see his children tortured him. "I had a splendid Dream last night," he wrote his wife. "Oh it was happiness. I saw little Bell & Buby & kissed them times & times again. Oh it did seem a reality their little mouths to mine as in days gone by. Oh that it could be a reality. What pleasure and bliss when I can enfold you again in my heart." Events deferred his dream. On July 31, the day Sturtevant became a major, Larkin's promotion came through. Other officers were chosen for the recruiting mission.

As had happened in the weeks after Fair Oaks, the army's sedentary life at Harrison's Landing eroded manpower and confidence. In mid-July, the Fifth was called out in anticipation of being paid for May and June. "Our Regiment presented quite a different appearance at this muster to the one at Camp Winfield Scott" three months before, Lieutenant William Moore observed. Some companies could turn out only twenty men. The men had done what they could to create a healthy camp, but malaria and other diseases preyed on them. "This beats all the places I ever saw for flies," wrote Private Peabody. "They torment one most to death in the day time." At Harrison's Landing, illness killed twenty men and removed thirty more from the regiment's ranks for good. Sergeant Charles Phelps wrote to his sister in Amherst of two deaths in his company, adding that the only good that had come the soldiers' way in the last few days was an improvement in the menu. "We get soft bread now," he wrote. "About time, I should think." Like many other men pinned down on the Peninsula, Phelps resented the criticism of the army that he heard from home. He wished the men who remained behind in Amherst could be forced to live on hardtack for a month. "They would not say soldiers live well and have an easy time," he wrote. By general order the Fifth lost its cornet band on August 8. A few of the Fifth's musicians took up rifles and joined the ranks, but most gladly returned home.

Back in New Hampshire, Colonel Cross's wounds were healing. He had spent four weeks in the Philadelphia hospital before returning home to Lancaster in early July. Carrying a cane and wearing his military cap and coat, he joined Henry Kent and several other friends from Lancaster on a tour of the White Mountains. His war horse, Jack, was one of two that pulled the party's red wagon from Brabrook's White Mountain House to the Crawford House and up the eight-mile carriage road to the summit of Mount Washington. Cross amused his companions by imitating bugle calls, and each time he did, Jack's ears pricked up. The horse "would give a sort of deprecating look backward as if to modestly suggest that the present was mighty mean business for a soldier's horse to be engaged in," Kent wrote. On August 4, Cross attended a war meeting in the capital with Walter Harriman and General Howard. Harriman, a leading politician and newspaperman from Warner, was the colonel of a New Hampshire infantry regiment just then forming, the Eleventh. Howard, whose home was in neighboring Maine, had commanded the Fifth's brigade before losing an arm at Fair Oaks. The purpose of the meeting, and Cross's chief concern, was recruitment. The colonel was grateful that a large draft had been ordered, believing—without grounds, as it turned out—that he would soon receive 350 recruits for his regiment. The *Patriot*, Butterfield's Democratic weekly, described the meeting as spirited, but the editor was not entirely satisfied with Howard's speech. The general had advocated the formation of black regiments. "The speeches were able and eloquent, and the sentiments uttered were generally correct, patriotic and appropriate," Butterfield informed his readers. "The chief exception was the evident preference of Gen. Howard for the policy of Gen. Hunter, whose negro projects he commended."

By early August, the Army of the Potomac's stay at Harrison's Landing was coming to a close. There would be no battle here. Lincoln had lost patience with McClellan, who continued to clamor for reinforcements, asserting that the Confederate army was twice its actual size. The president appointed Henry Halleck as his general in chief, and Halleck decided that Major General John Pope should lead a new campaign on the Rappahannock. Halleck ordered Mc-Clellan, whose army had been stalled on the James for six weeks, to join Pope and his new Army of Virginia. The Fifth's Private Peabody correctly guessed the army's destination and ridiculed the movement as the second phase of a retreat from Richmond. "I suppose that you will be surprised to hear of another skedaddle of the Army of the Potomac, but such is the case," he wrote home on August 15. "The stores and siege guns are being loaded on the transports. By the time that you get this, you will hear of another grand strategic movement, a new base of operation." Private Henry Holt wrote to his grandfather that he and his compatriots had been ordered "to keep three days cooked rations on hand and twenty rounds of extra cartridges and hold ourselves in readiness to march at a moments notice." Captain Larkin informed his wife: "My trunk is packed & gone and we have had rations cooked & in our Haversacks until it has got to be an old story." Sumner's corps was the last to leave the camp on the James. The wagon train had carried off the tents and blankets, and the men of the Fifth lay several days without them before the order to depart finally came.

The hot and dusty march from Harrison's Landing to Newport News provided the final ignominy of McClellan's lost campaign. The first day, August 16, the men covered just five miles before camping on the plantation of a man named C. C. Clark, whom Lieutenant Moore described as "an open Secesh." An aide to McClellan asked Clark how much grain he had, and Clark responded that he had 15 barrels of corn and 15 bushels of oats. In fact, Clark's stores amounted to 215 barrels of corn and 500 bushels of oats. "Our animals did not suffer for a want of a plenty of grain," Moore wrote, and the teamsters filled their bags against the future. The next morning, a Sunday, the drums and bugles sounded an hour before sunrise, and by five o'clock Sumner's corps had hit the road. The army's route paralleled the James, passing several more riverfront plantations, including that of another Virginian who had been president, John Tyler. But this was no Sunday stroll along the river. "What a day and what marching—16 miles through clouds of dust, which was so thick and heavy that it was impossable to see the man in front," Moore wrote home several days later. "From early day till 10 o'cl P.M. we toiled on, tired and weary, covered from head to foot with dust and dirt, without ration and almost without water." What water some of them did have, Lieutenant Janvrin Graves remembered, "was gathered from the prints of the feet of the mules that had gone along." Moore put the unhappy march in perspective for his family: "It was a sad contrast, that long line of dust covered soldiers, to that quiet throng that wound its way to church in each New England village at the call of the sabbath bell." Near the end of the day's march, the men crossed a two-thousand-foot pontoon bridge across the Chickahominy River above Williamsburg. They no doubt recalled the bridge they themselves had built across the same river two and a half months before. Events had transformed the pride and optimism of that earlier moment into the dust and exhaustion of this day.

Other reminders of the failed campaign awaited the men as the long files of Sumner's corps resumed their march the next morning. The Fifth passed through Williamsburg, where in early May it had arrived too late for the fight, marching to the battlefield at night in the rain and mud, never firing a shot, then marching back. As the regiment passed the battlefield, Moore noted the damage done the trees by balls, shot, and shell. On August 20, the men reached Yorktown again, and Captain Larkin reflected on the emptiness he felt. "I am surprised at myself when I think that after months of hard service on the Peninsula I am again at this place without having accomplished any thing," he wrote. "It makes me sad when I think of the graves we have made & the number of brave men who have given their lives to their country & it realy has amounted to nothing so far." The men hoped they would embark by water from Yorktown and leave these troubles behind. They were, as Lieutenant Moore wrote, "sadly disappointed." Moore and his men were sent out on picket duty.

Then, at one o'clock in the morning, General Caldwell told his brigade to prepare to march again in four hours. The Fifth stepped off with little sleep and covered the seven miles to Warwick Court House before stopping for a rest. A court house, Moore explained to his family, "in the south is an institution as much as the negro, and it is here the whole population of the county gather to hear and be heard, drink whiskey and run horses." Sumner's corps marched eight more miles that afternoon and reached Newport News in a heavy rain the next morning. This was the Army of the Potomac's final destination on the Peninsula. The men had covered fifty-two miles on foot since their departure from Harrison's Landing. When the weather cleared in the afternoon, Moore wrote, "more than a thousand men were in the river bathing and fishing for oysters, happy as school boys just let lose from school for a short vacation."

Two days later, Colonel Cross rejoined the regiment with sixty-eight recruits and the Fifth's new assistant surgeon, William Child of Bath, a twenty-eight-year-old Dartmouth College man. Child had received his commission in Concord on August 13, then rushed to join Cross and the recruits, who were waiting for him on the train. A telegram had been sent ahead to Manchester, seventeen miles downriver, summoning a justice to the station. The justice swore in Child to state service through the train window. On the way to New York, one of the Fifth's recruits got drunk and fell off the train. The engineer halted. Child walked back in darkness and found the soldier lying still on his stomach. Child turned him over and, not knowing what else to do, began to massage the body. Suddenly the recruit thrust out his hands, blinked, looked around him, and said matter-of-factly, "What station's thish?" An incident the next night had a more sobering outcome. Just after the party's ship left New York for Fortress Monroe, a man jumped from the deck into the Atlantic. Child would never forget "the strange, unearthly scream as he went down into the dark, black waters."

Upon his arrival at Newport News, Child's first priority was to find his fellow townsmen and report all their news to his wife. Bath was a prosperous town in far northern New Hampshire. The doctor had promised the father of Alfred Balch that he would try to visit the young private's grave, but that proved to be impossible. Balch had been buried where he had fallen at Fair Oaks on June 1. Another Bath man, Ned Carleton, told Child that Balch had been "brave as a lion." The same was true of Billy Weston. "Carleton says he never saw such a man. He was first wounded in the leg and was coolly stooping to examine the wound when he was hit in the arm." Weston was recovering and would soon rejoin the regiment. The doctor's romantic expectation of war ran aground at Newport News. In its place there emerged the picture of a forlorn army: "The frying pan, and the bean hole; the greasy haversack, and the flattened knapsack; the barefooted boys, the sallow men, the threadbare officers and seedy generals; the diarrhoea and dysentery, the yellow eyes and malarious faces; the beds upon the bare earth in the mud; the mist and rain, with a cold wind chilling the weakened bodies; the braying mules, the swearing drivers and the howling wagon-masters."

The men welcomed Colonel Cross, who returned their good wishes but was dismayed by the scene Child described and especially by the look of his own regiment. "I found everything in a very disorganized state—discipline broken, and a general confusion," he wrote in his journal. He "commenced reforms" within ten minutes of his arrival and soon brought the Fifth back under his exacting hand. Ever loyal to McClellan, Cross wrote to Kent blaming others for calling off the campaign. The effects of the retreat were "disastrous," he wrote. "A great battle would not have damaged us more—the officers dispirited, the men tired and homesick & the whole army shattered & disgusted. All McClellans generals opposed the movement & Mc himself offered to advance on Richmond at a day's notice. But Pope was in danger! Washington exposed, and off we are trundled to the old war path of the Rappahannock."

Cross distributed the recruits to his companies by county. Five were from Milford, Lieutenant Livermore's hometown. The lieutenant was just eighteen years old, and the thought of giving orders to these older neighbors caused him a tinge of self-doubt. "I then had to pursue the difficult path of an officer over those whom I had always known as men while I was a boy," he wrote. To his relief, he found he could easily balance the two facets of this relationship, "maintaining my character as an officer and evincing my friendship for them." Thirteen recruits went into the Concord company under the newly promoted Captain Larkin, and he was pleased to get them.

Larkin was less pleased with the days that followed. The night of August 25, the regiment steamed out of Newport News on the *America*, bound for Aquia Creek, the Union landing and supply depot south of Washington. Larkin used his knee as a desk to write to his wife, who had sent him pictures of their children. "I should not have known bubby if any one else had shone it me for their child & Bell has altered," he wrote. "She looks as important as a Queen." His children had grown while the Union's prospects had declined. Larkin believed the Army of the Potomac was on the defensive and the Rebels were stronger than ever. He wondered who from home had been drafted. "Now is the time that every man must come up if they expect to save the government," he wrote. As the *America* moved slowly up the Potomac, Larkin had only to look around him for evidence of the urgency he sensed about his country's future. The Fifth was a testament to the army's reverses. Five months before, the New Hampshiremen had traveled the same river in the opposite direction, a regiment of more than nine hundred rifles untested in battle but certain of victory.

"Richardson's Foot Cavalry"

"From appearances the Gen. has
great confidence in the 5th NH."
—Doctor William Child,
September 16, 1862

THE MEN OF THE FIFTH WERE A GRIM SET WHEN they disembarked from their steamship at the Union supply base at Aquia Creek, their army's retreat having left them ill disposed toward the world in general. The men marched inland several miles and established camp as the sun set. Just as they settled, however, they were ordered to pack, return to the landing, and board another ship. At this unhappy moment a civilian appeared on the fringes of camp, hopeful of profiting from the regiment's presence. Lieutenant Janvrin Graves regarded the man with the eyes of a hungry dog.

"What have you got?" Graves said.

"I have got three bottles of whiskey."

"What do you ask for them?"

"Five dollars."

Graves had neither the time nor the inclination to bargain, and his counteroffer reflected the circumstances: a dollar for all the whiskey or arrest. "I took it," he wrote, "knocked the head off [a] bottle and gave the boys a drink, and then we started."

The Fifth's change in orders was part of General George McClellan's reluctant response to the plight of another Union army threatened by Rebels outside Washington. Within days, the regiment would join a belated, exhausting, and unsuccessful rescue effort. This new defeat, close to the capital and humiliating, threw Washington into a frenzy of fear and recrimination. Before long, however, the Rebels would press their luck and their attack, providing the army a chance at redemption. For Colonel Cross and the Fifth, the result would be a march of hurrahs and plenty, capped by a bright morning of glory.

On the night of August 27, however, such dreams were far from mind as the Fifth trudged back to the landing. The men boarded a new ship and quickly fell asleep as it steamed up the Potomac River. After breakfast—which Lieutenant Thomas Livermore supplemented with a bottle of claret—the soldiers disembarked and, to their delight, marched over familiar ground to their old winter home at Camp California. But their second stay was far briefer than the first. The next day, August 29, the regiment was ordered north again, to Arlington Heights outside Washington. Cross did what he could to raise the spirits of his men. "It was a pleasant tramp," Livermore wrote, "for the colonel put on a jolly air, whether he felt it or not, and led in songs and cheers."

The march carried the Fifth near the camp of the Ninth New Hampshire, a fresh regiment just four days removed from Concord. The newcomers, resplendent in fresh uniforms and shiny gear, were astonished by the condition of the passing veterans in Bull Sumner's Second Corps. "They looked weather-beaten, worn out, and ragged," one diarist said. "Some are almost destitute of shoes. They are in the lightest marching order possible, not one in a hundred having a knapsack." To see the Fifth—"plodding along, bronzed, dirty, and grim," one onlooker wrote, and vastly reduced in numbers—was to glimpse the Ninth's own uncertain future. The newcomers were struck by the self-reliant and determined attitude of the veterans, many of whom were derisive in return. There was growling in the Fifth about the reluctance of "bounty men" to get their uniforms dirty; the men of the Ninth, Graves wrote, "said they did not see what we were so nasty for." A gracious Cross paid the new men a visit, and the Ninth's band serenaded him in return. Major Edward Sturtevant was also a celebrated guest in the Ninth's camp; he was known by a few who had served with him in the First New Hampshire, and admired by many as the state's first war volunteer. The Ninth would be a hardened regiment too before long, but for the moment its members were left acutely aware of their subordinate status to the Fifth. "My God!" one member of the Ninth said. "Shall we ever look like that?"

The regiments did not remain neighbors for long, because trouble was close at hand. Having driven McClellan's men away from Richmond, Lee had promptly turned his attention to the new Union army under Major General John Pope, not thirty miles from Washington. Pope, a braggart who had won success in the West, was overmatched. President Lincoln had pushed McClellan to help—and McClellan had resisted, saying his army needed rest and suggesting that a better course might be to leave Pope "to get out of his scrape." At midday on August 30, however, the men of the Fifth heard distant firing. The order to move toward it came at two in the afternoon, provoking a new round of grumbling from the veterans, who wondered why they and not the newcomers were being sent forward to help. "Lee was said to be surrounded and probably there would be a great surrender of the whole rebel army," Graves wrote. "Orders were given that any men not able to march should stay behind, and in about ten minutes' time [we] were on the march." The fight was on the same ground as the war's first great battle, at Bull Run, and it was Pope, not Lee, who was in danger. Three days had passed since McClellan was first ordered to assist Pope. The soldiers he was sending would arrive too late.

The sad truth became clear as the Fifth approached Centreville, beyond which lay the battlefield. It was raining, the time just before midnight; the regiment had marched twenty-three miles since afternoon. The rain was of little concern to the tired men, who focused instead on the flow of discouraged, disabled, and disorganized soldiers—Pope's army—streaming past them to the rear. "There were indications of a great battle," Cross wrote. "We found, however, that General Pope had been badly whipped, and his army badly scarred." Because McClellan considered Pope a rival, his men did too, and some taunted the defeated soldiers as they staggered past in the dark.

In the morning, the Fifth was pushed forward through light rain and Pope's dissolving army to help form a shield covering the Union retreat. It was the same trying role the regiment had filled during the retreat from the Peninsula. "The day was cold and uncomfortable," Livermore wrote, "and we passed a dreary time, somewhat relieved of dullness by the expectation of seeing at any moment the advancing enemy." Because the men had left their baggage behind, they were without tents, blankets, or overcoats. About twenty lacked shoes. Livermore had the good fortune to have carried a quilt on the march; with night, he and his tentmate pulled their sodden prize tight around them and slept. Cross worried that his regiment was being pushed past its limit. "The men, greatly worn by long hardships on the Peninsula, had not the strength for such efforts," he wrote.

The next day both discomfort and anxiety grew. The Fifth was among a handful of regiments left in the front line, a thin defense in the face of an entire rebel army, nearby but motionless in the heavy rain. With darkness, the men were ordered forward into a thicket that clawed at their damp clothes— "a perfect jungle," Cross called it. The men stumbled about for hours in a vain effort to connect with other Union troops on their flank. They spent a chilling night, passing hushed, anxious talk along the line as they gazed at low clouds reddened by rebel campfires. Cross remembered the night for its cold, Livermore for its "most profound darkness." Just before dawn came the

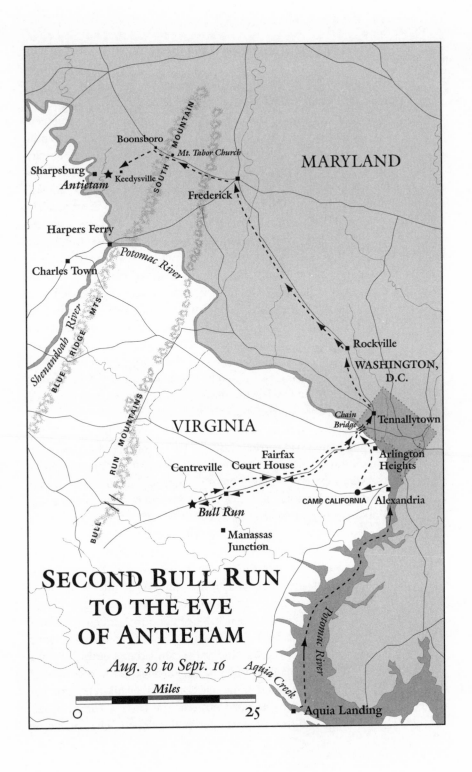

MARYLAND

Boonsboro

SOUTH MOUNTAIN

Mt. Tabor Church

Sharpsburg
Antietam
Keedysville

Frederick

Harpers Ferry

Potomac River

Charles Town

Shenandoah River

BLUE RIDGE MTS.

Rockville

WASHINGTON, D.C.

VIRGINIA

Chain Bridge

Tennallytown

BULL RUN MOUNTAINS

Fairfax
Court House

Centreville

Arlington
Heights

CAMP CALIFORNIA

Alexandria

Bull Run

Manassas
Junction

SECOND BULL RUN
TO THE EVE
OF ANTIETAM

Aug. 30 to Sept. 16

Aquia Creek

Potomac River

Miles

0   25

Aquia Landing

order to withdraw, one which the sleepless and shaken regiment obeyed with gratitude.

The Fifth's march back toward Washington carried it into the chaos of Pope's retreat. At Fairfax Court House the tangle of wagons, artillery, and swearing, milling men proved impassable. After an hour's rest the regiment made its way around the clot and continued toward Washington, marching deep into the night before collapsing in a peach orchard outside the city. Exhausted as they were, the men had covered twenty-six miles that day. Colonel Cross fell asleep on his feet and tumbled to the ground not once but several times along the march. "Oh but we had a hard time of it," he wrote. The catastrophe plunged Washington into its deepest despair; a rebel attack seemed imminent and defeat likely. The government ordered bars closed and guns issued to civilian workers as the city swirled with questions. Who was to blame for the disaster, the incompetent Pope or the dallying McClellan? Where would the daring Lee strike next? Did the Union army have any fight left in it?

In the case of the Fifth, the immediate answer was no. The men didn't stir until late the next day, September 3. They finally rose to strip the orchard, stew the peaches, and, in late afternoon, cross the Chain Bridge to Tennallytown. That night hunger led Lieutenant Graves into the nearby camp of the Irish Brigade. He returned bearing twenty-eight loaves of soft bread in arms so burdened they ached. Graves tried to whisper his men awake, but there was no keeping fresh food a secret from the rest of the regiment. Once found out, Graves said approvingly, his men "were very liberal with their bread."

The exhausting march had carried the Fifth back inside Washington's formidable defenses and within reach of supplies; their effect was bracing, and it took hold the very next day. The regiment's baggage train arrived in camp. Army wagons delivered rations, clothing, even some shoes. Also welcome was word that Pope had been relieved and McClellan put in overall command. The men rejoiced in what Livermore called "the assurance that all was safe." They took comfort in the prospect of an extended rest; as the Peninsula campaign had shown, McClellan was a general who looked after his men—and not someone who went anywhere in a hurry. When Captain Larkin sat to describe the debacle to his wife Jenny, his spirits were rising already. "I have come through all safe and sound but it has been about as much as I could stand," wrote Larkin, who was still weak from malaria contracted on the Peninsula. "We crossed over here yesterday and are encamped in a beautiful place. We shall have our tents and blankets today & shall probily stay here for several days if not weeks. I wish you could come out & bring the children if you had someone to come with you." She need not fear the enemy, Larkin added: "If the Rebs attack Washington they will get badly whiped. They may cross the river into Maryland above here but I think it doubtfull. If they do they will get anihilated—we have an immense army yet and how it could ever be defeated I can't see." The next afternoon, September 5, Lieutenant Livermore slipped into Tennallytown for a dinner worthy of the name. He found one, and was savoring it as only a hungry soldier can. "But alas for human calculations in war," he wrote, "I had not reached my dessert when my astonished and erect ears announced to my bewildered mind that the 'General' was being sounded on the bugles of my regiment." Reluctant but obedient to the call, Livermore rushed back to camp. Within a half hour the regiment packed, fell in, and set off on the march.

Lee had again made his move, bringing a rebel army of forty-five thousand across the Potomac and into Maryland. In so doing he carried the war into the North for the first time—and left McClellan no choice but to pursue him. Official Washington's faith in McClellan was thin, but he was leading eighty-seven thousand believers. They had won their share of battles on the Peninsula, despite losing the campaign. They laid the blame for the Second Battle of Bull Run at Pope's feet. Though worn and weary, they were ready to follow McClellan's lead. The Rebels, having defied the Union, had now invaded it, striking the men close to home. "Full of hope and confidence we set out," Cross wrote. "No one in the army doubted the result." Uncertain of Lee's target, however, McClellan moved cautiously.

For the Fifth, the result was a slow march through rolling country with much to offer. On its first night the regiment camped near Rockville, Maryland, with rifles ready. But there were no Rebels in its front, only a flock of sheep. The army was under strict orders against foraging, but anxious farmers didn't stray far from their animals. "My men had longed for an opportunity for some time," Livermore wrote, "when Colonel Cross called me to his presence and said, 'Mr. Livermore, don't you on any account let two of your men go out and get one of those sheep for supper.' 'No, sir!' said I; and I went back and directed two stout and willing privates to go out and get a sheep. They took the opportunity when the owners were chasing some men of another regiment, and grasping each his sheep sped into our line with them over their shoulders, and then into a piece of woods behind." Livermore sent iron kettles into the woods. They came back filled with mutton and covered with leaves. "I sent one kettle to the colonel with my compliments, telling him that it contained rations I had drawn. He returned his thanks and caution against leaving any part of them in sight." As the days passed the delights kept coming: green fields, clean streams, pigs, grapes, turnips, "luckless, headless chickens," and rich, fresh milk. "Sometimes we were so fortunate as to find a still," Livermore wrote, "and could replenish our canteens with the warm beverage which they produced." Had anyone questioned the morality of the march, Livermore would have dismissed them so: "The people here and elsewhere we foraged were not generally very loyal, our rations were dry, we were marching to repel an enemy who would have stripped them, and we were hungry."

Refreshing as it may have been, the march was no frolic. "A good portion of the boys were barefooted," wrote Corporal Lewis Fernald. "The nights were remarkably cold, and we suffered a good deal." One of the shoeless soldiers was nineteen-year-old Private Jonathan Bronson, not long out of the hospital. Cross spotted him shivering one damp morning, dug money from his own purse, and bought the private a pair of shoes. Even a plodding pace proved too much for Captain Larkin, who was detached for an errand in Rockville but fell sick again and did not return. As the days passed, the Fifth's officers debated when the colonel would take notice of Larkin's absence and how violently he would react. Charles Bean's interest in this question was more than a sporting one. Larkin was his mentor and had advocated Bean's promotion to second lieutenant; on September 10 the promotion came through, but Larkin was not there to share in Bean's joy. At last Bean heard from the captain, who wrote that he was hospitalized and would rejoin the regiment as soon as he was able. "For three days after your departure I was all anxiety," Bean responded, "for fear something ill had happened to you and knowing Col Cross as I did—truly I thought no excuse would suffice for your delay—though he said nothing in regard to your non appearance." Bean told his patron of his fresh promotion; he confessed to using Larkin's sword in his absence and closed with thanks for his support. "Cap, your kindness to *me* is engraved upon my memory and will never be forgotten—and for which I am truly *thankful* to you. I can stop to write no more as we ready to commence operations."

On September 13 the Union Second Corps approached Frederick, Maryland, which had disappointed the Rebels with a polite but restrained response during an occupation that ended just a few days before. It delighted the Federals by embracing them as valiant liberators. Like other units before it, the Fifth straightened its columns, unfurled its colors, and paraded into a scene certain to quicken a soldier's pulse, if not his step. The town was filled with music, the air with flags and bunting. There seemed to be a woman in every window, each with a broad smile and a bright handkerchief. "It seemed more like a review than the march on the war path," Livermore wrote. There had been no moment as splendid since the men left New Hampshire, and the encouragement was well timed. Smoke rising from Catoctin Mountain, six miles beyond Frederick, marked a clash between Union skirmishers and a rebel rear guard. Before stopping on the far side of town, the regiment passed McClellan at a cross street and Major General Ambrose Burnside as well—"looking very gallant and warlike," Livermore wrote, "in his blue frock and side whiskers."

September 13 was a banner day for McClellan, too, thanks to two Indiana soldiers who discovered an envelope in a field outside Frederick. In it they found a treasure—three cigars—and the biggest intelligence coup of the war: a copy of Lee's plans, which showed that he had divided his army into four parts. In fact, as events had evolved, the four parts had become five. One was not fifteen miles west, on the far side of South Mountain, a second ten miles north of that, in Hagerstown. The rest were converging on a federal force of twelve thousand in Harpers Ferry, about twenty miles southwest of Frederick. Handed the plans in late morning, McClellan was exultant: "Now I know what to do!" he said. If the Federals moved quickly, they could crush each finger of the rebel army before Lee drew them back into a fist. But McClellan remained captive to his debilitating habit: he imagined rebel forces as being far bigger than his own. And so on the thirteenth he didn't move; he planned.

The next morning, the fourteenth, federal troops attacked at two mountain passes that separated them from a climactic battle. Lee's general on South Mountain, D. H. Hill, had never seen a more picturesque threat than the long columns of blue soldiers coming his way. His outnumbered Rebels, stretched through woods and fields, suffered heavy losses but held until night. The Fifth spent the day in reserve; with evening, the regiment moved toward the long mountain ridge, which rose from the farmland like a wall. As they marched, the men gazed at dead and wounded soldiers and abandoned guns and gear. Union stragglers were everywhere, and dust raised by advancing troops hung in the air. Lieutenant Graves led a detail that "got together a good number of the rebel dead" and covered them with blankets. Their sense of mortality as pointed as a bayonet, the men marched into the yard of the Mount Tabor Church for the night. "Halting," Livermore wrote, "we cooked our frugal suppers, and lay down to sleep expecting to march to bloody work in the morning." Dawn only deepened that expectation. The regiment was deployed in a battle line through foggy woods and ordered up the mountain. A half hour climb over rugged ground left hearts pounding—as did the prospect of facing Lee's soldiers somewhere in the mist. "I saw seventeen dead in one awful group," Cross wrote.

But as the regiment approached the contested pass, the men discovered what Union troops who had fought there the day before already knew: the Rebels had fled down the far side during the night. The news was a tonic to the army, eager to see its formidable enemy on the run. "A lot of gray clothes, old knapsacks and equipments thrown down by the road showed us how precipitate had been the retreat of the rebels," Livermore wrote, "which made us feel all the better."

Major General Israel Richardson's division formed in a column on the National Road to pursue the Rebels. The Irish Brigade was in the lead, the Fifth New Hampshire in the rear. Rebel horsemen, serving as a rear guard, were evident as the division began to descend on the village of Boonsboro, at the foot of the mountain two miles away. Richardson was a regular army man and an old Indian fighter, hard and popular; though the army's approach to South Mountain had been deliberate, he was determined to speed its descent. He halted the column and called for the Fifth New Hampshire, on the double.

Though the men of the Fifth did not know Richardson's purpose, they recognized his order for the compliment it was. They erupted in a cheer as troops ahead began shuffling right to let them pass. Veterans always preferred the front of a column to the rear, because it meant others choked on your dust instead of you choking on theirs; in pursuit of the enemy the lead position was also one of danger—and distinction. "There goes the Fighting Fifth! Give 'em hell, boys!" soldiers shouted in a cheer that ran along the column with the regiment. The trot forward—ten minutes, maybe less—was a passage that surpassed even the parade through Frederick, because it saw the Fifth celebrated not by unknowing civilians but by tested comrades. The men jogged past Colonel Francis Barlow's tough New Yorkers, the Eighty-first Pennsylvania, the Seventh New York, the Second Delaware, and on past four regiments more until—most glorious of all—the Fifth passed the Irish Brigade itself, boisterous and proud. "We went down with our canteens and traps rattling like a mule train," Livermore wrote. "We learned that the honor of leading the advance had been given us in preference to the leading brigade, to their chagrin and our pride, and we took it with elated hearts." Richardson greeted Cross with word that he had no cavalry to lead the skirmishers or artillery to support them. "Your regiment must act as both," he said. "Deploy and sweep both sides of the road."

It was a moment Cross might have dreamed of, an opportunity earned by months of hard service, one coming at the expense of the Irish and their flamboyant general, Thomas Francis Meagher. The Fifth would determine the pace of the long column behind it, and be the first to know its future. Cross sent four companies to the left of the road, four to the right, and kept two in the middle, forming a skirmish line nearly a half mile wide. Bugles pealing, the regiment surged forward, leading McClellan's army off the mountain. In Boonsboro, the men found a small bridge in flames and saved it. Wounded

Rebels emerged from fields and houses to surrender, while frightened residents strained to see without showing themselves in their windows. Their bolder neighbors stepped outside to offer water and fruit to Cross's men. Union cavalry had clashed with Rebels in town before moving off in a different direction. "Blood was yet fresh upon the pavement," Livermore wrote.

The Fifth pushed beyond Boonsboro, through fields and wood lots, across streams tucked into the rumpled land, and over fences and low hills for several miles toward Keedysville. "Rebel camp-fires were still burning in the fields and woods as our columns advanced, and their van-guard skirmishers covered the hill tops in front, and occasionally sent back a shot," wrote A. D. Richardson, a correspondent for the *New York Tribune* who accompanied the advance. In Keedysville, the correspondent wrote, "the Rebel pickets were at the end of the street as the head of Richardson's column reached the center of town. Col. Cross's skirmishers went straight forward, and they fell back at once." Once secure, the sweating men of the Fifth pulled off their shirts, pausing to pick at body lice energized by their exertions. The regiment had caught many Rebels who were stragglers, not skirmishers, too tired or too hungry to keep up with the withdrawal. These weary foes seemed little more dangerous than the lice; most appreciated were those who had taken but not yet eaten bread, honey, and other nourishment from the houses they passed. The food liberated from prisoners did not last long.

Refreshed, the regiment swept over two miles more toward Sharpsburg, a quiet town sustained by productive farms and jobs flowing from the Chesapeake and Ohio Canal. The setting was familiar to some in the Fifth, who had camped outside town the year before as members of the First New Hampshire. It was just short of two in the afternoon when the Fifth encountered its first real resistance from a thin line of rebel skirmishers in a thicket. The Rebels fired a volley but fled as the Fifth returned it and then pushed on. The regiment's pursuit led up an open hill, and as the men reached its crest they looked down toward a creek lined by trees and crossed by an arched stone bridge. Beyond was a large barn, a house, and a small orchard.

On the ridge high beyond that, just outside Sharpsburg, perhaps a mile away, was Lee's army, moving off the road and into a battle line that spread into the distance. The Rebels were not in retreat; they were preparing to fight, on ground of their choosing. "At last," A. D. Richardson wrote, "it seemed as if there were to be a great battle on open ground." It was a rare sight—officers on horseback, flags waving over the men, cannon barrels bright in the sun—but there was no time to admire it. "A puff of smoke among their batteries was followed by the shriek of a shell," Livermore wrote. It burst overhead, and a fragment hit Private John Melendy, who had joined the regiment just over a month before. Shaken, he got up and went on, the first casualty of a battle that would be known throughout the North by the name of the creek in front of the Fifth: Antietam. A second explosion nearly made Livermore the battle's second casualty. "I was suddenly blind and deaf, rushing winds whirled about my head, and I seemed to be oblivious to the field, the line, the enemy," he wrote. Knocked to the ground, he rolled toward cover, collected his wits, and selected a safer-looking spot on the line.

Soon the rebel artillery shifted its attention to the column of Union troops following the Fifth, leaving the regiment to concentrate on the skirmishers. Janvrin Graves's company dueled with Rebels who darted from behind the barn across the creek to fire, then disappeared behind it again to reload. One made the mistake of sitting and watching; Graves shot him. Colonel Cross climbed a knoll for a better view, and a sharpshooter's bullet nicked his left shoulder strap. The colonel climbed down. Lieutenant Ira Bronson, whose younger brother owed his shoes to Cross, became the target of another Rebel behind a bush on the near side of the creek. The Rebel's first shot just missed and Bronson scuttled toward him, shouting for help. The skirmisher got off a second shot and then a third before Bronson's men spotted him and fired. The Rebel rushed to the bridge, pulled off his hat, and waved it at the Fifth. The men cheered him for his gallantry as he turned and ran.

By three o'clock, McClellan was on the scene. He decided the rebel line was too strong and the hour too late for an attack, and he turned to deploying his army along its side of the creek. That decision was in itself a victory for Lee, whose bristling line was a bluff. More than half of his soldiers were still seventeen miles away at Harpers Ferry, where the federal garrison had surrendered early in the morning. The Fifth held its position until nine that night, when the regiment pulled back a half mile to sleep in a roadside ravine.

Despite the prospect of battle, the Fifth's was a satisfied camp. By Cross's count, the regiment had killed a dozen Rebels and captured sixty; only three in its own ranks were wounded. The men liked the fit of a new nickname — "Richardson's foot cavalry" — and reveled in a story that, true or not, made the rounds like good whiskey. It poked at the Irish Brigade's General Meagher who, the tale went, protested Richardson's decision to put the Fifth in front because it denied his men their moment of glory. Richardson's response fanned the regiment's pride: "If I was going to take Hell," the general said, "I should want the Fifth New Hampshire for skirmishers." The comment was fitting, because the Fifth had acquitted itself well. And soon it would have another chance at distinction, as the two armies plunged into a hell of their own making.

Antietam

"They struck the wrong crowd when
they ran against my brave men."
—Colonel Edward Cross to
Henry Kent, September 20, 1862

O N SEPTEMBER 16, THE DAY AFTER THE FIFTH RACED from South Mountain to the bank of Antietam Creek, both armies coiled for the strike to come. It seemed certain to be venomous, even decisive. The men of the Fifth huddled in a grassy hollow behind an artillery battalion from New York, whose sixteen heavy guns thundered from a hilltop at the rebel lines a mile away. The Rebels fired back, stray shots screeching over the guns and smashing to earth near the Fifth, showering the men with dirt. It was not a day of rest, not with the sounds and smells of battle already in the air. Some in the regiment were sent again to drive rebel skirmishers from the creek. Others tried unsuccessfully to destroy a stone mill dam, so the creek would be easier to ford. Two fled, including Private John Whitney, a thirty-one-year-old shoemaker who had joined the regiment a year before to the day. Many just kept their heads down and watched as Union troops under Major General Ambrose Burnside marched by on their way to positions to the south.

Doctor William Child, in the hollow with the regiment, pulled out pen and paper. "My Dear Wife," he began. "I have just read yours dated Sept. 7th. I am as well as ever in my life." That may have been true, but barely so, because the doctor was fresh from a terrifying errand. He had been sent to the regiment's wagon train, crowded into another hollow nearby, for supplies. As he approached, a rebel cannonball slammed into a mule, killing it and a second mule at its side. The wagons rushed away, and Child did too. It was the most threatening moment the doctor had faced during his month with the Fifth, time during which he had tended the sick and wounded but seen no battle firsthand. Child was an insecure man whose large features crowded a thin face. The doctor had educated tastes, being fond of theater and chess, but a homeward spirit; he had written his first letter, full of longing, on the very day he departed. There was much to miss: his wife, Carrie, who was pregnant, their home and his practice in Bath, and two children, Clinton, age three, and Kate, who would turn two on September 22. "Yesterday passed over a battle-field—how terrible—awful," Child's letter continued, as if in conversation. "Yes—What more I was about to write above I have forgotten for just then bang-whizz came the shells & balls from a rebel battery." Child told Carrie about the mules and the cannonball, and offered assurances. His footsore days were over; he had bought a horse for forty dollars and would ride rather than march tomorrow. The shelling had wounded a few Union soldiers, but none in the Fifth. As he wrote, a shaggy black dog ran past, its snout red and ravaged. It had been pawing at a shell in the ground when it exploded. Child mentioned it, coolly—"Just now along comes a dog with his upper jaw shot off"—and then closed: "Now write to me soon—and often—whether I write or not. If I am sick I will write anyway. When I do not write you may know that I am well."

The veterans of the Fifth might have told Child that, horse or no horse, he wouldn't be riding anywhere anytime soon. At midday General McClellan had decided to fight Robert E. Lee's Rebels; deliberate as ever, though, McClellan had also decided not to attack until the following day. At four in the afternoon, Union troops under Major General Joseph Hooker moved across Antietam Creek far to the right of the Fifth. Their purpose was positioning themselves to attack the next morning at the northern end of the rebel line, now four miles long. But they clashed with rebel troops as night fell, tipping Lee to McClellan's intentions. The day had also tipped the odds: though the Federals still outnumbered him heavily, Lee now had six of his nine divisions on the field, with two more on the way.

With evening each man in the Fifth drew eighty rounds of ammunition, a heavy load that foretold a hard fight. The men packed forty rounds into their cartridge boxes, stuffed their haversacks and pockets with the rest, and, as rain began, settled in—though not for long. During the night Richardson's division was awakened and ordered closer to McClellan's headquarters, outside a fine brick farmhouse overlooking Antietam Creek. Colonel Cross was disgusted; he wanted no part of guard duty. "I feared it would deprive us of our share in the battle," he wrote. Lieutenant Thomas Livermore wrestled with fears of a different sort. He was up before dawn to swallow a breakfast of coffee and crackers. As night weakened, he looked anxiously over the fields and farmhouses below. Atop a ridge on the other side of the creek, he could see rebel

MARYLAND

Mercerville

Fifth New Hampshire
Feet
0   5,000

UNION LINES

Miller's Cornfield
and Dunker Church

POTOMAC

Hagerstown Pike

CONFEDERATE LINES

Pry Farm

UNION LINES

The
Sunken
Lane

RIVER

Sharpsburg

Burnside
Bridge

Antietam Creek

VIRGINIA

BATTLE OF ANTIETAM

Morning of Sept. 17
With sites of day's major conflicts

gunners moving among their cannons. Smoke rose from a farmhouse in front of the guns; Confederates had torched it to deny shelter to Yankee sharpshooters. Livermore had been eager for battle on the Peninsula, but now his mind fluttered with questions. A fight was coming—but when? Where? How long would it last? Would federal troops attack, or be attacked? Who would win? Would he die? How? And how long did it take a dead man to reach heaven? "While we waited in the twilight, time flew with slow wings," Livermore wrote, "and the quicker I was in it and through it, alive or dead, the better I thought it would be."

The battle began with daylight, just after five, when Hooker's First Corps surged from woods at the northern end of the Yankee line. Only the crows had a better view of the battlefield than the men of the Fifth, in reserve high on the headquarters hill. Still, they didn't see the battle open; they heard it.

First came the crackle of muskets as skirmishers leading the Union advance encountered rebel pickets. Within minutes, Livermore wrote, "the rattling 'file firing' of a brigade began, then another joined, and another, until the woods roared with the musketry of thousands." Deeper was the thud of cannons on the field and the crunch of exploding shells. The heavy guns on the headquarters hill with the Fifth added their voices, too. Gun smoke rose in lines over the soldiers below, and then spread.

Cross was invited into McClellan's presence and introduced to the general he so admired. McClellan had commandeered the home of the prosperous Philip Pry, and the farmer's parlor chairs were arrayed on the grass for McClellan's staff. Stakes jabbed in the ground offered support for telescopes. Cross found the general "in good spirits, though thin and care-worn." A messenger delivered a report from the field. "All goes well," McClellan said. "Hooker is driving them." It certainly appeared to be true; Cross was drawn to his men by their exuberant shouts and found that the fight had spilled into view. "We could see the enemy retreating with Hooker's men in fast pursuit," Cross wrote. "Thousands of scattered rebels were seen breaking from the woods and scudding across the plowed fields now and then turning to fire." Pressing them were "long, dark lines" of Union troops. "Then we cheered like mad," Livermore wrote, "and Colonel Cross frantically shouted to our artillery on the bluff nearby to put the shells into them." But the success was short; a rebel counterattack drove the Federals back. The Union Twelfth Corps, under Major General Joseph Mansfield, joined the fight but was unable to break the rebel line. Hooker was wounded, Mansfield was killed, and their men were dead, hurt, or too spent to continue.

McClellan ordered the Second Corps into the fight at twenty past seven. Major General Bull Sumner had three divisions under his command, but McClellan held Richardson's division on the headquarters hill until troops coming from the rear could take its place. The corps's other two divisions, under John Sedgwick and William French, advanced down the hill and across Antietam Creek immediately. Sumner rode at the front of Sedgwick's division, which was its misfortune, because the general marched his men into disaster. Hidden by trees and terrain, rebel troops attacked on three sides and mauled the unsuspecting Yankees. Left to make his own way into action, French led his division farther south, toward a sunken road that formed the center of the rebel line. The farmers who traveled it called it Hog Trough Lane. It was a shortcut carved into the earth by wagon wheels and plodding horses, running through the fields and down toward a mill on Antietam Creek. Filling the lane and the ground behind were eight thousand Rebels, twenty-five hundred of them in a quarter-mile stretch of the road that was the heart of the Confederate defense. In succession each of French's three brigades charged over a ridge and at the road. Two of the attacks were made with fixed bayonets, but all met with failure. As each attack faltered, the Federals fell back to the ridge, lay down just behind its crest, and opened fire on the Rebels in the road.

At 9:20 came the order Richardson had been waiting for: advance. Finally his men too marched away from headquarters, with its parlor chairs and telescopes, and down the grassy slope toward Antietam Creek. Within ten minutes, the division began splashing across at a ford, the water no more than thigh deep. "The day was fair," Livermore wrote, "and nothing seemed to interfere with our fighting in comfort." The delay had seen the Fifth's ranks grow by one. Ned Stinson, a seventeen-year-old private who had been wounded at Fair Oaks and hospitalized since, had rejoined his mates in Company I as the regiment waited to go into battle. His officers told him he didn't have to fight that day, but Stinson grabbed a rifle, filled his pockets with cartridges, and fell in.

Once off the high ground the men lost sight of the battle but were impressed anew by its sound, a thundering convergence of cannon and musketry. Emerging on the far bank, they headed left along the creek before turning away from the water and up through rolling fields of stubble. They stopped at the base of a steep hill, beneath a cornfield owned by a farmer named William Roulette. A half mile away, hidden from view, was their objective: the sunken road, now the focal point of the fighting. Richardson placed his men in lines of battle under the shelter of the hill, with General John Caldwell's brigade, which included the Fifth, on the left, General Meagher's Irish Brigade on the right, and Colonel John Brooke's brigade in the rear. Richardson ordered the men to shed their blankets, knapsacks, and other camp items so they would be unencumbered in a charge. It was an unpopular command, because it meant men would lose valued possessions to confusion or thievery even if they survived the battle. Rather than part with a spare blue shirt from his mother, Corporal Benjamin Chase defied the order and kept his blanket, in which the shirt was rolled.

When the lines were ready, Richardson decided to send the Irish in first, relying on what Meagher fashioned "the impetuosity and recklessness of Irish soldiers in a charge." They climbed the hill and disappeared into the head-high corn. The men of the Fifth strained to hear as the Irish emerged on the far side, out of sight, gave a cheer for McClellan, another for the Army of the Potomac, and then threw themselves into the attack on the sunken road. Cross had his officers call the roll; 301 riflemen and eighteen officers responded, not counting the chaplain, Milo Ransom, and the three surgeons.

The order to follow the Irish Brigade into action was not long in coming.

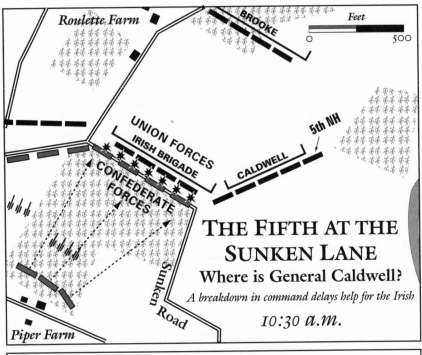

Roulette Farm

BROOKE

Feet

0   500

UNION FORCES

IRISH BRIGADE

5th NH

CALDWELL

CONFEDERATE FORCES

Sunken Road

Piper Farm

THE FIFTH AT THE SUNKEN LANE
Where is General Caldwell?

A breakdown in command delays help for the Irish

10:30 a.m.

Composed under fire

By companies:

- ■ The Fifth
- □ Irish (88th N.Y.)
- --▶ The Fifth's maneuvers

REBELS IN LANE

Moving as smartly as if on drill, the regiment replaces the 88th N.Y. and presses the attack

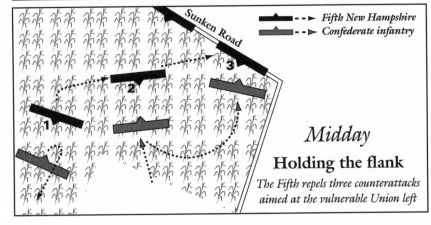

Sunken Road

■--▶ Fifth New Hampshire
■--▶ Confederate infantry

1

2

3

Midday
Holding the flank

The Fifth repels three counterattacks aimed at the vulnerable Union left

The Fifth was on the left of Caldwell's line as it marched up the hill and into the corn, the men rustling through the stalks and wondering what horrors the next stride or two or two dozen might reveal. They emerged into pasture and broke into a run; the ground fell away before them, then rose again. At last, in the smoke along that green rise, the Fifth could see the men of the Irish Brigade, crouching or lying flat as they fired into the sunken road beyond. Now Cross coaxed his men on; they had a fair field, he told them, and ought to whip the enemy. Wounded soldiers crawled, limped, or staggered their way. Riderless horses galloped aimlessly. Bullets whizzed by, some kicking up dirt at the Fifth's feet, a few striking unlucky marchers. One ball hit Private James Card under the right ear as he ran at Livermore's left elbow. "He fell as if struck by an axe," the lieutenant wrote, "and I said, 'There goes poor Card,' and never slackened my trot." Sergeant Amos Lawrence fell, too; overcome by fear, he feigned a wound and tumbled to the ground as his comrades rushed forward. The hard run made Corporal Chase rethink his decision to keep his blanket; he tugged it over his head and dropped it, his precious home-made shirt still inside. The Fifth's surgeons stopped in a sheltered spot and prepared for bloody work.

Richardson sent Caldwell's brigade to the left of the Irish, extending the federal line by five hundred yards with the Fifth at its far end. The maneuver put the brigade in a position to outflank the rebel line, by swinging like a door across the sunken road and slamming into the Rebels from the side. But no attack developed. For fifteen minutes the men waited in a field that sloped away from the action, sheltering them while the Irish and the Rebels shouted and swore and slew each other nearby in a fight so desperate it could not con-tinue long. Cross paced up, down, and up again before the Fifth's line, his agitation at once familiar and contagious. Fearful that the delay might weaken his regiment's resolve, Cross offered harsh encouragement. "Men, you are about to engage in battle," he shouted. "You have never disgraced your state; I hope you won't this time. If any man runs I want the file closers to shoot him; if they don't, I shall myself. That's all I have to say."

At last Richardson approached Caldwell's brigade, sword drawn and face dark. Cross called for three cheers for Richardson; the men gave them, and then three more for Cross. "Where's General Caldwell?" Richardson yelled. Many in the Fifth had seen him drop back on their way into line. "In the rear," Cross said. "Behind the haystack!" shouted others—an indictment in an army that measured leaders by how they faced danger. "God damn the field offi-cers!" Richardson cried, and then shouted toward the haystack: "General Caldwell, come up here, sir, and take command of your brigade."

But the Irish Brigade was spent, so Richardson could not wait. Instead he took over, ordering the brigade to march behind the Irish and replace them for yet another direct assault on the sunken road. The Fifth would take the place of the Eighty-eighth New York at the left of the Irish Brigade's line. "Go on, colonel," Richardson said to Cross, "and do all you can—relieve that regiment." As the general hurried off, Cross was hit by the tiny, searing iron fragments of a shell burst; they shredded his hat, spinning it to the ground, and cut him twice on the left cheek, once over the right eye. Blood streaked his face, but the wounds were not serious. Cross tied a red bandanna around his head and carried on.

The Irish had suffered heavily and were low on ammunition, though not on spirit. A private in a red shirt mounted a stray horse and cantered along the line, an inspiring sight—and perfect target—who went untouched as he urged the men on. Sergeant Charles Hale of the Fifth spotted Irish Molly, "a big muscular woman who had followed her husband in all the campaigns, and he a private soldier in the ranks. She was a little to the left of their line, apparently indifferent to the flying bullets, and was jumping up and down swinging her sun-bonnet around her head, as she cheered the Paddy's on." Hale filled with admiration: "The glimpse I got of that heroic woman in the drifting powder-smoke stiffened my back-bone immensely." One of Livermore's men showed his steel, too. The lieutenant was startled when Private Card appeared at his side, a lump big as an egg under his ear. The bullet that had struck him on the way into battle was spent; it had stunned him but did not even break his skin.

The Fifth's first challenge was just getting into position. The regiment—indeed, the entire brigade—had to change places with the Irish while under fire. If bungled, the switch would tangle the two brigades, threatening the control of officers and jeopardizing the attack. Sheltered for a few final moments by higher ground, the Fifth deployed in a line of battle about one hundred yards behind the Eighty-eighth New York. "The field was dotted with dead and wounded men," Livermore wrote, "and humming bullets gave warning that every step to the front was a step toward death." The formation was as familiar as a year of repetition could make it: the men grouped by companies, touching at the elbows, facing forward in a line 150 men long and two ranks deep, with lieutenants and sergeants forming a third rank in the rear. Cross ordered a rail fence in the Fifth's front knocked down, and the regiment began its advance. "By the right of companies to the front!" Cross cried. "By the right flank! March!" His order set in motion a complex maneuver that was beyond some troops on a parade ground, let alone a battlefield. The regiment broke from a long line into ten short columns, each made up of a company and marching straight toward the enemy. The battered Irish fell

Edward E. Cross, a sharp-edged journalist and relentless traveler, in a pre-war photograph. M. Faith Kent.

(Bottom left) Even as a young man, Cross lacked neither courage nor convictions. Lancaster Historical Society.

(Bottom right) Henry Kent, who stayed home in Lancaster, remained Cross's closest friend. Lancaster Historical Society.

Edward E. Sturtevant, a night constable in Concord, arose early one morning to become New Hampshire's first Civil War volunteer. Mike Pride.

Eleven of Amherst's first volunteers pose for a photographer a week after Fort Sumter. Four would go on to serve in the Fifth: George Washington George, Daniel A. Peabody, Charles H. Phelps, and James B. David. One would be cast from the regiment by Colonel Cross; one would lose his foot in battle; one would be discharged due to disability; and one would die after avenging the death of another. Edward D. Boylston, *Amherst in the Great Civil Conflict of 1861–65* (Amherst, N.H., 1893).

1. Alfred L. Boor.   6. Wm. W. Sawtelle.
2. Geo. W. Russell.   7. Daniel A. Peabody.
3. Rod. W. Burdick.   8. Charles H. Phelps.
4. Geo. W. George.   9. Henry S. Ober.
5. New. T. Hartshorn. 10. James B. David.
               11. Geo. W. Griswold.

The Fifth's first camp in the field, at Bladensburg, Maryland, is depicted in this 1861 lithograph by E. Sachse & Co. The conical tents at right are those of the Fifth; the tents at left are those of the Fourth Rhode Island. Library of Congress.

Though a colonel at only 29, Cross easily assumed a martial pose. Mike Pride.

The precocious Thomas Livermore enlisted underage and became a lieutenant at 18. U.S. Army Military History Institute.

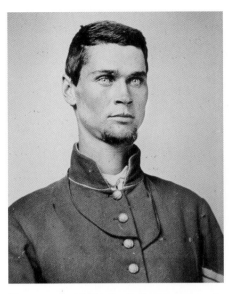

The strapping Miles Peabody was a natural soldier in two respects: his taste for food and his fondness for grumbling. Michael P. Hurt.

The hope of securing his young family's finances helped draw James Larkin away from home and into the army. U.S. Army Military History Institute.

Major William Cook was thought a brave man, but he was best known for his heavy drinking. Massachusetts Commandery, Military Order of the Loyal Legion, and U.S. Army Military History Institute.

Captain Charles Long thanked the ladies of Claremont for sending mittens, but asked that the forefingers be made separate so the men could fire their rifles. Lancaster Historical Society.

Colonel Cross's first winter in the field was controversial but productive. Shown here in a heavy greatcoat, he also made sure his men were well provisioned.

Captain Welcome Crafts's practice of lending money to enlisted men at high interest ran afoul of Cross's ethics.
Lancaster Historical Society.

Colonel Cross (with cane, foreground center) and Henry Kent (holding hat, seated behind Cross's left shoulder) during an outing atop Mount Washington. At the time, Cross was recovering from wounds suffered at Fair Oaks.
A. N. Somers, *The History of Lancaster, New Hampshire* (Concord, N.H., 1899).

Among the sights Doctor William Child witnessed as one battle drew near: a shaggy black dog with its jaw shot off. U.S. Army Military History Institute.

Burial parties had removed most of the rebel dead from Antietam's Bloody Lane when this photograph was taken. The Fifth fought at the far end of the lane, in the extreme distance of this photo. Massachusetts Commandery, Military Order of the Loyal Legion, and U.S. Army Military History Institute.

Richard Cross found himself at the center of a dispute between his brother, Colonel Cross, and two of the regiment's best officers. Massachusetts Commandery, Military Order of the Loyal Legion, and U.S. Army Military History Institute.

In its assault at Fredericksburg, the Fifth crossed a canal ditch (the dark line running across the center of the photo); formed beneath the bluff just beyond; and then charged toward Marye's Heights in the distance. Some men took shelter behind the Stratton house, the two-story brick building at right center. Massachusetts Commandery, Military Order of the Loyal Legion, and U.S. Army Military History Institute.

Captain John Murray was a veteran of the war with Mexico. New Hampshire
Veterans Association.

Having gone west in the Gold Rush before the war, Charles Ballou learned
Spanish so well that he became an interpreter. New Hampshire Veterans Association.

Captain James Perry, like Cross, was a Mason. This fraternal bond led the two to rescue a pair of wounded Rebels, fellow Masons both, following the battle of Antietam. New Hampshire Veterans Association.

(*Bottom left*) Steady and pious, Charles Hapgood was on good terms with both Cross and those who disliked the colonel. U.S. Army Military History Institute.

(*Bottom right*) George Gove's persistence in returning to the ranks after recovering from wounds led Colonel Cross to nominate him for the Medal of Honor. New Hampshire Veterans Association.

(Top) Doctor John Bucknam celebrated July 4, 1863, at the operating table. Lancaster Historical Society.

(Right) So loud were the cannons at Chancellorsville that John McCrillis lost his hearing. Massachusetts Commandery, Military Order of the Loyal Legion, and U.S. Army Military History Institute.

(Left) To Charles Hale, Colonel Cross in battle seemed to stand ten feet tall. U.S. Army Military History Institute.

(Right) Sergeant Charles Phelps was devoted both to the regiment, to which he returned despite wounds, and to his family, to whom he sent much of his pay. Edward D. Boylston, *Amherst in the Great Civil Conflict of 1861–65* (Amherst, N.H., 1893).

Three veterans of the Fifth stand on hallowed ground. They are, from left, Charles Hapgood, Isaac Hammond, and Augustus Sanborn. Robert Corrette.

Veterans of the Fifth and their families pose at the regimental monument at Gettysburg. The date was likely July 2, 1886; the occasion, the twenty-third anniversary of the Fifth's engagement on the very spot. Robert Corrette.

back between the advancing columns; as the men passed, the Irish gave a loud cheer. Once in the front, the companies of the Fifth swung back into a battle line, face-to-face with the Rebels.

In an instant the air itself was danger. "I shall never forget the scene," Livermore wrote. "We stood nearly on the edge of the sunken road which ran along the border of an extensive cornfield, behind us the greensward for a hundred yards was dotted with the dead and wounded, and far away across the creek our great guns were hurling shells over the valley and above our heads at the enemy. In the corn the gray lines of the enemy dotted with flags advanced, retreated, fired and yelled, and their arms glittered through the smoke which at times almost obscured the field." The men of the Fifth raised their muskets, fired the first of their eighty rounds, and dug into their cartridge boxes to load the next. A shell slammed into the ground near Livermore's feet "and tearing a trench sped on like something irresistible." A bullet struck Private Thomas Law in the forehead and dropped him. "Heaven! Heaven!" he muttered as friends knelt at his side. Blood was everywhere but his skull seemed whole, so his comrades shared a sense of hope as they sent him to the rear.

The Federals didn't know it, but the Confederates were close to collapse. One of Meagher's regiments, the Twenty-ninth Massachusetts, had made one last charge before withdrawing, and it sent scattered clusters of Rebels running. Three Confederate commanders were dead or badly wounded; rebel reinforcements emerging from the battered corn behind the sunken road mingled in confusion with men in line or hung back under cover. At the far end of the rebel line, an order to reposition one regiment was misunderstood and two regiments pulled back in retreat. Alert and aggressive, Colonel Francis Barlow pushed his New Yorkers into the gap, a position that enabled them to fire down the sunken road. With that, a line that had stood for two hours gave way in minutes; the Rebels turned and fled into the corn. The Federals surged forward with a yell. Richardson grabbed every man, every unit he could find and sent them forward, too. Ahead was the farm of Henry Piper, more than a quarter mile beyond the sunken road. If the Yanks could seize it, they would break the center of the rebel line and the back of Lee's army.

The men of the Fifth climbed over the rail fencing that the Rebels had piled in front of the sunken road, then scrambled down into the road itself. It was still filled with men—dead, disfigured, alive but too broken to move. A wounded Reb jabbed at Sergeant Hale with his bayonet; Hale decided the man was too far gone to fear and moved on. The regiment hurried across the road and climbed up, out, and into the cornfield on its far side. A Rebel killed while fleeing over a rail fence remained wedged in place, his body a torn and bloody mess. "Through mistake or rage," Livermore wrote, "our men had shot or bayoneted him many times." Private Charley Spencer collapsed in the corn just ahead of Hale; the sergeant would long remember his terrible dying cry.

Hundreds of Rebels stood before the Federals, but without time to reorganize, reload, and recover, they were done for. Whether they would get that time depended on rebel artillery, and the gunners knew it—as did Major General James Longstreet and his staff officers, who hurried to assist the cannoneers. As many as twenty cannons opened on the advancing Federals, shredding the corn with canister and case shot and gouging the soil at their feet. "That was my dread," Hale wrote. "I could endure rifle bullets, but when the big iron bullets went swishing through the air with a sound as though there were bushels of them, it made me wish that I was at home." A single shell burst killed one man and wounded seven in Company G, the Claremont company, while nearly ripping the regiment's state colors in two.

As the men pushed forward into the corn, undulations in the ground in turn sheltered them from cannon fire and exposed them to it. Two hundred weary Rebels, hastily assembled by General D. H. Hill, appeared in a line above them and charged down toward the Fifth. The Rebels lowered their heads as they advanced, as if to look away from their fate. This suggested they would not press hard for long, and the Fifth ripped the attackers with musketry. "Before they got to the foot of the slope there was no semblance of a line," Livermore wrote.

The Fifth had drawn apart from the advancing Yankee line, so Cross ordered the regiment to the right and rear to close the gap. He was standing in the middle of the Fifth's line, his focus on the enemy in his front, when Lieutenant George Gay appeared breathless at his side. Gay, promoted from the ranks by Cross just days before, grabbed the colonel's arm.

"Colonel," he said. "The enemy are outflanking us."

"Impossible," said Cross.

"They are—come and see, quick."

Cross ran to the left of the Fifth's line and looked to the rear. On the far side of a rise, about two hundred yards away, he could see several officers on horseback and five rebel battle flags bobbing over the corn. The flags suggested a large force; in fact, it was about two hundred men, a second force pulled together in desperation by General Hill and sent to strike the Union line at its most vulnerable spot: the end, occupied by the Fifth. "In an instant the gray-backs raised their well-known battle yell and came on," Cross wrote. With a cry of his own, Cross set the Fifth in motion, moving it to the left and rear without breaking from its battle line. He caught Hale's eye and beckoned him to his side. "Sergeant," he said, "run and find the general and tell him that the enemy is on our left flank." Hale balanced his rifle over his right shoulder and dashed through the corn to the rear. Captain Richard Cross, the colonel's brother, thinking Hale a coward and not a messenger, aimed a revolver at his back and pulled the trigger. It misfired.

The rise between the two forces was valuable ground. The first to reach it would have the advantage, and both raced upward through the corn. Hale had crossed back over the sunken road and climbed the grassy slope on its far side; he couldn't find General Caldwell, so he turned to watch the Fifth's fight unfold. "Some little distance to the left of where I knew our line must be," he wrote, "I saw two rebel battle flags moving above the corn tassels; down among the corn there was a tremendous commotion and shouting, and some sharp firing, indicating that something serious was going on; it was the Fifth New Hampshire changing front."

The Fifth won the contest for the high ground and, at a distance of about thirty paces, the men leveled their rifles and fired. The Rebels staggered and fell back. "It was beautiful to see how the devils piled up," Cross wrote. But it wasn't over yet; the Confederates gathered themselves, shifted farther to the Fifth's left, and tried again.

Cross moved the regiment to the edge of the cornfield to face the threat, placing his line in the sunken road itself. "In this road there lay so many dead rebels that they formed a line which one might have walked upon as far as I could see," Livermore wrote. "It was on this ghastly flooring that we kneeled for the last struggle." Hale gave up his hunt for Caldwell and ran back to the regiment. He spotted the Rebel who had threatened him his first time across the road. "Say Yank," the Johnny said, the belligerence drained from his eyes. "For the love of God lift that dead man off my hurt leg." Hale shoved the corpse away with the butt of his rifle and hurried on to report. "Sir, I could not find the general," he told Cross. "Go to your company!" the colonel shouted.

The Fifth was ready when the Rebels struck, but this time the attackers were not easily thrown back. Lieutenant Charles Bean, promoted on his way to the battlefield, fell with a minié ball in his thigh. Lieutenant Gay was also hit; hand to his head, he turned and walked to the rear, where he would remain lost from his comrades until nightfall. Captain Charles Long was shot in the left arm, the bullet breaking one bone and displacing another. Corporal George Nettleton had been staggered by a shell fragment that struck his head, but he fought on. So did Lieutenant Graves, who was hit in the arm. "Our regiment was alone," one soldier wrote, "and it seemed as if we should be swept away."

With the fight at its peak, some men down and others beginning to waver, Colonel Cross was seized by an inspiration born of his past. "Put on the war paint!" he cried. As men nearby looked toward him, Cross smeared his bloody face with gunpowder from the torn cartridge papers at his feet. The soldiers bent to do the same. "Give 'em the war whoop!" Cross shouted. The moment exemplified Cross's fierceness under fire—and its effect on his men. Western war cries ran up and down the New Hampshire line, loud enough to rise over the rattle of gunfire, with the colonel, one soldier said, "giving us the example by shouting the Indian yell terrifically. We all took it up, and if the confederates never heard the colonel's 'Wild Indian' before, they heard it then." Perhaps, Livermore wrote, "this devilish-looking line of faces" and their "horrid whoop" helped repel the enemy; "at any rate, it reanimated us and let him know we were unterrified."

Without orders but alert to trouble, Major Harry Boyd McKeen of the Eighty-first Pennsylvania led his regiment into line beside the Fifth. Even those who couldn't see the fresh troops arrive felt the surge in firepower. Improbably, the Rebels drew closer still; emotions carried men on both sides into a rare and inexplicable frenzy. "Fire! Fire! Fire faster!" men in the Fifth shouted, cursing and whooping. A rebel color-bearer came within fifteen feet of the Yankee line and held his blue flag high. "He went down in a twinkling," wrote Livermore. Just as quick was Corporal Nettleton's reaction; at great risk, he ran forward, grabbed the flag, and raced back to the Fifth's line. Livermore knelt on a dead Rebel; noticing that his musket was cocked, the lieutenant picked it up and fired. He liked the feel of it and looked among the corpses for another weapon. But an officer's job was directing his men, not hunting for rifles. Cross—"omnipresent, omniscient and omnipotent," Livermore wrote—brought him up short. "Mister Livermore!" the colonel yelled. "Tend to your company!"

For ten minutes the two sides locked in a fight of supreme intensity, unthinking and, it seemed, unending. At last, the Rebels fell back. Fresh troops under Colonel Brooke passed the Fifth and advanced toward Piper's farm; Sergeant Hale and a few others in the Fifth got lost in the smoky confusion and found themselves charging with Brooke into another fight. Cross pulled the Fifth back from the sunken road to a spot where his exhausted men could rest in the trampled grass without being exposed to cannon fire.

For the second time that day, the colonel ordered a roll call. One hundred twenty-five men and ten officers were missing, more than one out of every three men who had gone into battle. Among the wounded was Private Stinson, who had rejoined the regiment just that morning. His luck did not match his courage, and he was shot through the right lung. Among the more fortunate was bugler David Roys, who found that a minié ball had broken his belt plate and passed through two thicknesses of his leather belt, then his clothing—but left him with only a bruise. There was Card, too, his jaw aching from the ball that had struck him under the ear on the way into battle; he had fought as well as anyone, Livermore decided, but would not eat much for days.

While his comrades rested in the grass, Hale hunted for someone in Brooke's brigade who would permit him and his men to leave the battlefield and rejoin the Fifth. "I found the major of the left regiment and reported the circumstances to him," Hale wrote, "saying that I was afraid that my colonel would be displeased at my getting lost, and that I would lose my rank. 'Put your men on the left of my line and I will stand by you,' he said, and so we had a second dose of it, for it was simply awful the way the canister was tearing up the ground, and making kindleing-wood of the fences around Piper's buildings." As the firing diminished, Hale tried again; this time the major approved. Hale's relief mixed with fear as he found the Fifth—and Colonel Cross. "He looked to me to be about ten feet high as we marched up," Hale wrote. "I explained the circumstances, and to my great relief and satisfaction saw that he was pleased." Cross, Major Edward Sturtevant, and Hale's company commander, Captain James Perry, joined in marveling at their wayward men's appetite for battle. "They chaffed us a good bit," Hale wrote, and then Cross dismissed them crisply. "The next time, you look sharp for your own colors," he said. "That is all I have to say; go to your companies."

The rebel counterattack that fell on the Fifth had succeeded in blunting the Union charge, and soon a single shell burst would stop it altogether. Just before one in the afternoon, Richardson concluded his men could gain no more without support from cannons to counter the rebel artillery. He pulled his infantry back across the sunken road to regroup and set out to commandeer and position Yankee guns. Richardson approached a Union battery dueling with the Rebels and told its commander to prepare for an advance. As they spoke, a rebel shell exploded nearby and a fragment slammed into Richardson's chest. The general's pale face was enough for Child to make a diagnosis as the ambulance wagon hurried by. "Death was upon him," the surgeon wrote. Not long after Richardson was wounded, a brigadier general rode toward the Fifth and spoke to Colonel Cross. Even from a distance the newcomer had a commanding presence; lying in the grass, the men speculated on his identity and his purpose. "We learned to our great satisfaction that it was General Winfield S. Hancock," Livermore wrote.

Hancock, who was to replace Richardson, carried a fighting reputation that stirred the men. He also carried orders not to press the attack; McClellan wanted him to hold his ground. There was one more rebel charge that after-noon, met in part by skirmishers from the Fifth, and the artillery persisted in a deafening exchange that discouraged ambition on both sides. The focus of the fighting shifted south, where General Burnside's troops battled for hours to cross a bridge over the Antietam. They finally broke through, threatening to separate Lee's men from their line of retreat, and—for the third time that day —putting the Union army on the verge of triumph. But the hours lost in cross-ing the bridge proved decisive; the last of Lee's troops arrived from Harpers Ferry just in time to smash Burnside's attack and end the day's fighting.

With dark the guns at last fell silent, but rest did not come easily. "In place of the din of arms," Cross wrote, "we now heard a perfect chorus of groans and cries of pain and distress from the thousands of wounded that covered the ground in front of our lines." The day had been the bloodiest of the war. Three thousand Yankees had fallen in the fight for the sunken road alone, as had 2,600 Rebels. Lieutenant Graves called it Death's Road, but the name that would stick was Bloody Lane. The Fifth had been more fortunate than regiments engaged longer in the lane. Only eight of its members were dead, although 116 were wounded. In total, Union casualties for the day exceeded 12,000 dead, wounded, or missing. Lee lost 10,300, a quarter of his army.

Staggering as the numbers were, the officers of the Fifth found themselves focused on a single casualty. After nightfall, word reached Livermore that a "Corporal Gay" of the Fifth lay wounded near another regiment's line. The lieutenant sent several men to fetch him; they returned bearing a heavy load. A shell had blown off the top of Lieutenant Gay's skull. Somehow, he had walked some distance to the rear; somehow, he was still alive. Union troops had stolen the helpless officer's watch and sword. "The poor boy," Livermore wrote, "insensible to the world and wounded beyond all hope, was laid down beside us, his old comrades, to die, and all that night, amidst the alarms of the battle-field, we watched him as he chafed the earth with his foot." Cross knelt at his side and held his hand; hours before, it had been Gay who alerted him to the flanking attack repulsed by the Fifth. "Poor Gay," Cross wrote, "only four days a lieutenant, a young gentleman of extraordinary talent, cheerful, diligent, beloved by his entire circle of acquaintances." Gay never regained consciousness, and died the next day.

With morning, soldiers on both sides expected the battle to resume. The Fifth remained near the sunken road and sent a skirmish line into the corn where the regiment had fought the day before. A wounded rebel officer, lying amid the stalks, drew one of the Fifth's skirmishers to his side with whispered pleas. He handed the soldier a message scrawled in blood on a slip of paper and begged him to take it to a member of the Masons, a fraternal organization steeped in secrecy and pledged to mutual support. The soldier made his way back through the corn and found Cross. The colonel was a Mason but could not decipher the message; he summoned Captain Perry, who recognized it as a call for help. Cross, Perry, and two other Masons crawled into the corn seeking yesterday's enemy, now a brother. They found their man, lifted him onto a blanket, and dragged him out. He was Lieutenant John Edon of the Tenth Alabama, wounded in the thigh and chest, and he alerted his rescuers to another wounded Mason, Lieutenant Colonel Nesbit of the Thirtieth Georgia. Both were taken to the barn serving as the Fifth's field hospital and put under the care of Child and Chaplain Ransom, who were Masons themselves. Cross visited the hospital at about ten in the morning; suffering men were everywhere, inside and out. The barn was filled with twenty-eight men, all but four of them from the Fifth. "Some one asked him [Cross] why the ball had not been opened," wrote Lieutenant Graves, who had spent the night in the barn. "Oh, it is some of McClellan's tactics," Cross said. "Give the enemy a day to bury their dead, and then they are all in our hands." Nesbit, the Georgian, burst out in relief: "Thank God for that!" he said, fearing the Rebels were lost if forced to fight again that day. "It is the salvation of our army."

For the surgeons, no rest was possible. Adding a note to his latest letter home, Doctor Child barely had time for punctuation. "We had a hard fight yesterday expect another today—am well," it said. "Write soon." The barn was filthy and alive with flies; the doctors considered it an unhealthy setting for the wounded men. Child ventured onto the battlefield and collected dozens of tents and blankets. The doctors pitched them in a haphazard array, using boards, sticks, and rifles for poles, then moved the broken soldiers outside and into the fresh air.

Cross also made the most of the battlefield. The morning brought a group of twenty-seven recruits from home, and the colonel introduced himself with a grim but practical order, telling them to equip themselves from the dead. They had been enlisted by Hilas Davis, who had been promised a lieutenant's rank in the Ninth New Hampshire before a falling-out led him to the Fifth instead. Davis arrived on the battlefield wearing an officer's uniform, but Cross told him to discard it and find a private's. Davis would have to earn an officer's rank in the Fifth. Having thus welcomed the regiment's newest members, the colonel acted on an old frustration. He had long wanted to replace the Fifth's Enfield rifles with the superior Springfield model. The debris of battle presented Cross with an opportunity to bypass army bureaucrats, and he seized it. "All night long we carried off rebel wounded and the next day picked up over 400 rifles," Cross wrote to Henry Kent. "I changed all my Enfields for Springfield Rifles in the field."

Some in the Fifth drew burial detail, an ugly assignment but safer than the skirmish line, where the recruits were soon placed. "Everybody expected an instant attack," Cross wrote. "The skirmishers were firing constantly." One squad from the Fifth crouched behind a fence in the corn; for company it had a soldier from another regiment who sat upright against the rails, shot through the head the day before. One of the recruits was forty-four-year-old Nelson Whittemore of New Haven, Connecticut, who had been hired as a substitute for another man, John Walker of Claremont, editor of the *National Eagle*. A year and a half of war had made volunteers harder to come by. "Whitmore will make a tough, keen soldier," Walker assured his readers.

As the hours passed, the fear of attack receded. Curiosity drew Livermore to the carnage in the sunken road, where he found a battle line of corpses that stretched for a quarter mile. Thieves had slit almost every pocket. "Some of them had died instantly while at their meal," Livermore wrote, "with their plates before them, and their crackers in their mouths or being carried to them." At the hospital, Chaplain Ransom paused in his labors long enough for a report to the *People's Journal* in Littleton. "I understand that the Rebels are trying this morning to escape," he wrote, "but they have but little chance left." He related the Fifth's exploits of the day before, crediting Cross with saving an entire division from capture. "If they are not honored by their friends at home," Ransom wrote of the Fifth, "it will be because they cannot appreciate noble deeds." He noted too that Cross had possession of the rebel flag captured by Nettleton. A regiment's flag was a precious symbol, tying men to their cause and the people back home who had presented it. No blow could hit harder than to lose a flag in battle; no success could be sweeter than to take one. The Fifth's trophy was made of dark blue silk with two women painted in its center, one holding a pod of unripe cotton, the other a staff and scroll reading "The Constitution of North Carolina" and, below that, "4th Regiment, North Carolina." The colonel gave a piece of it to Nettleton, who mailed it to his wife in Claremont along with assurances that the Lord was with him and the Rebels were in retreat. Some of Nettleton's admiring comrades suspected that faith and courage could not entirely explain his remarkable act. "It was said that when he was wounded on the head," Livermore wrote, "he was made crazy by the blow."

Near day's end Cross decided that Gay should be buried with full honors in a more peaceful setting. He sent Livermore after General Caldwell for permission to take a burial party across Antietam Creek. The general said no; orders to move were imminent. So the officers of the Fifth gathered outside the field hospital where Gay's body had been taken. It was Child who captured the scene: "The young man—a mere lad," he wrote, "his soldier's garb, the powder begrimed officers and soldiers; the muffled drums and wailing fife; the slow, solemn march and the unusual sorrow on every face; the firing on the front lines; the groans of the wounded and the white, ashen faces of the dying; the slow, careful moving of the stretchers and the ambulances; the hushed, earnest, busy labors of the surgeons at the operating tables; the loving tenderness of clergymen, and the solemn ministrations of the priests, and the occasional rush and roar of a shot or shell was the last filling in and completion of this awful picture of war." Gay's friends lowered his body into a shallow grave and mounded it with soil. They returned to camp in time for the march, which carried them to the woods at the northern end of the battlefield, where they bivouacked for the night.

During the darkness Lee pulled his troops off the battlefield, across the Potomac, and back into Virginia. His retreat elated McClellan—and Cross too. "This has been for the Rebels a Waterloo defeat," Cross wrote to Kent on September 20. The Rebels had fought desperately, and many prisoners considered the outcome "the ruin of their cause." Cross celebrated McClellan's role: "I hope this great victory of the favorite General of the Army, will put to shame the envious cowardly sneaks who stay at home & abuse him." He related the Fifth's clash in the corn as proudly as Ransom had. "My boys brought down their rifles as cool as on parade, & our volley tore them into fragments," he wrote. "They struck the wrong crowd when they ran against my brave men."

Cross harbored darker thoughts, too. General Meagher, he wrote in his journal, had been drunk during the battle, as usual. "Gen. Caldwell did not show himself either brave or skillful," he added, "and he lost the confidence of his soldiers." Cross was not entirely discreet; some officers heard him call Caldwell "a damned coward." If Caldwell considered Cross a doubter, however, he showed no sign of it in his official report. "The Fifth New Hampshire Volunteers, commanded by Colonel Cross, formed the extreme left of my line, and behaved with the greatest gallantry," Caldwell wrote, praising as well the skill and quickness of Cross, "ever on the alert."

Though McClellan and his allies thought Antietam a triumph, President Lincoln did not. McClellan had been satisfied to drive Lee from the North; Lincoln wanted his general to destroy Lee's army, and he worried more about its continued existence than its location. Still, Lincoln seized on McClellan's success, however limited: on September 22, he issued the Emancipation Proclamation, declaring all slaves in rebel states to be free as of the new year. What many had viewed as a political struggle was now unavoidably a moral one.

On the morning of the twenty-second, the Fifth packed for the march to Bolivar Heights, overlooking Harpers Ferry, which Lee had held briefly just days before. Child, weary and suffering from a severe cold, remained on the battlefield with the wounded. He watched the regiment go, then sat to write home. "My Dear Wife," he began. "Day before yesterday I dressed the wounds of 64 different men—some having two or three each. Yesterday I was at work from daylight till dark—today I am completely exhausted—but shall soon be able to go at it again." He enclosed a bit of gold lace from Lieutenant Edon's rebel uniform as well as a sobering glimpse of Antietam's most tangible outcome. "The days after the battle are a thousand times worse than the day of the battle," he wrote. "The dead appear sickening but they suffer no pain. But the poor wounded soldiers that yet have life and sensation make a most horrid picture. Great indeed must have been our sins if such is our punishment."

Eleven members of the Fifth wounded during the great battle succumbed in its aftermath, bringing the regiment's death toll to nineteen. One such casualty was Private Law, whose head wound at the sunken road had not seemed mortal; he died in a hospital in New York City on October 11. Another victim was the freshly promoted Lieutenant Bean, who died of his leg wound on September 19. His mentor, Captain Larkin, had missed the promotion and the battle due to sickness, so he never had the opportunity to congratulate Bean. Instead, he carefully preserved the exuberant letter Bean wrote him on the way to Antietam. An item in a Manchester newspaper suggested Bean died because his comrades were slow to get him aid, leading to two sharp letters from the field in rebuttal. More fortunate than Bean was George Washington George, shot in the leg during the fight. He lost his left foot but not his life, was discharged the following April, and was welcomed with dark humor in the hometown *Farmer's Cabinet*. "All honor to the returned *defooted*, but brave and *undefeated* defender of our liberties," it said. Corporal Benjamin Chase, who had escaped the battle unwounded, would have given almost anything to be heading home, too. "I don't hardly know what to say to you, dear mother," he wrote on September 28. "I hate this foolish war more and more every day I live." There was no talk of the Fifth's brave stand in Chase's letter, and there were no flashes of humor either. "It looked sad to me to see so many dead bodys that I see the other day lying on the battlefield," he wrote. "I thought to myself if thear mothers could only see them they would be crasy."

Child stayed at Antietam for weeks. He grew very sick, and recovered; with time, he wrote less about stench and exhaustion and more about his comfortable quarters and bountiful diet. But like Chase he was pained by the battle's outcome. It had caused so much suffering, and settled so little. On October 19, a farmer brought his wife and three children to the hospital bearing bread, pies, ginger cakes, butter, apples, and peach sauce. As Child showed the family through the wards, an amputee motioned to the farmer's young boy; tears rolling down his sunburned face, the soldier took the child by the hand and held on in silence.

That night Child addressed a letter to his three-year-old son, Clinton. He wrote simply and at length, describing where he slept, what he ate, and what he did. "Papa sees many sick folks here," he wrote. "They have many sores. Sometimes papa makes much blood. Out here men try to make other men 'all dead,' but they will not hurt papa. Papa has seen much dead folk. It made Papa sick to see them." Child told the boy about what he missed most—the pig and the corn, his horse and wagon, the kitchen and sitting room, family members and neighbors. "Papa must wait much time before he can see his things," he wrote. "It makes papa cry when he thinks about it. But Papa will come home sometime. Papa wants Clint and Kate to put each one a flower into the next letter mama writes. Papa knows that Clint loves the flowers." Back home in Bath the trees would soon be bare, marking the hard turn toward winter. "You must tell papa whether the birds sing now in the trees or if they are all gone," Child closed. "The birds will come back, and I hope papa will come back with them."

Autumn Tempest

"In a very excited manner [Colonel
Cross] cried out to them to halt and
fix bayonets. He told them to file to
the rear and bayonet any man that fell
out of the ranks or did not keep up
with his company."

—Captain William Moore

THE FALL OF 1862 BEGAN WITH A CHANCE FOR THE
Fifth New Hampshire to recuperate in the mountains, but the easy
times there soon dissolved in turmoil. During the narrow victory at
Antietam the men of the Fifth had again distinguished themselves in battle.
Rather than push his army to pursue the Rebels, as President Lincoln wanted
him to do, General McClellan rewarded the men with a long rest in a strong
defensive position. This brought on a clash of wills between the president and
his field commander. Devoted to McClellan and suspicious of the administration, Colonel Cross had no doubt about which side to take in this debate.
Before autumn was done, Cross's loyalty to McClellan, coupled with his ex-
plosive temper and autocratic ways, would send him into a fury that threatened his command of his regiment.

On September 22, the Fifth marched the fourteen miles from Sharpsburg
to Harpers Ferry. The army had seized the old arsenal town, and McClellan
ordered the regiments arriving there to set up camp in the nearby hills to
await supplies, equipment, recruits, and orders. The hills were known as Bolivar Heights, and a more secure or healthier campground would have been
hard to imagine. Bolivar Heights was a mile-long tongue of land seventy-five
yards wide at its broadest expanse and several hundred feet above the Shenandoah Valley. The river whispered past on its way to the Potomac less than a
mile away. In the cool of those early autumn dawns, the mist rising from the

Shenandoah and the Potomac formed long feathers of fog that obscured the bases of the higher ridges across the way. Harpers Ferry, the town at the confluence of the rivers, was in ruins. The Union army had burned its arsenal there the day after Virginia seceded in 1861, and the Confederate army had torched the town's factories and B&O railroad bridge soon after. Two days before Antietam, in one of the great Union embarrassments of the war, General Stonewall Jackson had captured the entire federal garrison at Harpers Ferry. Now that Union troops had retaken the town, McClellan intended to sit tight. "The army is not now in condition to undertake another campaign nor bring on another battle," he wrote Henry Halleck, Lincoln's general in chief. McClellan wanted to rebuild the old regiments and, when that was done, to bring the Army of the Potomac back to the Peninsula for another campaign against Richmond. In the meantime, duty was routine. For the Fifth New Hampshire, the days began with reveille at six; breakfast was at seven, company drill at nine, battalion drill at three, dress parade at half past five, tattoo at eight, and taps at nine. In their off hours the men set to work building a brick oven big enough to bake bread for the entire regiment.

While awaiting this luxury, the men supplemented their diets with food from the sutlers—sometimes with comic results. Several officers, including Captain Jacob Keller, a Prussian immigrant who had come to Claremont just a dozen years earlier, bought tins of preserved pigeon meat. The other officers opened their tins, gagged at the first whiff, and returned the spoiled meat to the sutler. That night, as the officers drank hot toddies and told stories around a campfire, one of them related how he had gone into Keller's tent and seen empty pigeon cans there. He asked Keller if he had eaten the pigeons, and Keller acknowledged he had. "Why, Keller!" the officer said. "They were bad. Didn't you know it?" Keller replied, "Fy, no. I tought dey was a little fwild." The officers around the campfire burst into laughter.

The men had ample time to write home, and Lieutenant William Moore was one of the regiment's most eloquent correspondents. Sometimes the local paper printed his letters to his family. Moore was a superb drill officer, having learned the art while serving in Abram Duryee's Fifth New York Regiment, a Zouave outfit, before joining the Fifth New Hampshire. He had flourished under Cross; just twenty years old, he was on the verge of taking command of a company. Like Cross, Moore came from a town in the far north of the state and was proud of his Revolutionary lineage. The firstborn son of a doctor in Littleton, he was named for a grandfather who had left home at eighteen to fight with General John Stark at Bennington. Moore's maternal great-grandfather, Littleton's founder, had fought at Bunker Hill. Shortly after Fort Sumter, one of the lieutenant's four sisters, Elizabeth, had collected eighty dollars from the ladies of Littleton to equip each of the town's recruits with a pistol. When she learned that the government would supply the soldiers with "carnal weapons," her mind turned to fortifying their spirits, and she spent the money on Bibles. From Bolivar Heights, with his usual flair for detail, William described for Lizzie Moore the one break in routine during the Fifth's nearly six weeks there—"a reconnaisance in force" that the regiment made with its division on October 16.

Brigadier General Winfield Scott Hancock had replaced the fallen Israel Richardson as the Fifth's division commander, and McClellan ordered Hancock to take the division and fifteen hundred additional men on a march to Charles Town. The objective was to determine the strength of Confederate forces in the Shenandoah Valley farther south. As Moore described it, the men awoke at dawn to the roll of kettledrums and the call of the bugle. It was a spectacular day—warm and bright, with the leaves turning. Hancock's men marched down from Bolivar Heights at seven o'clock. In Halltown, halfway to Charles Town, they met resistance from rebel artillery and cavalry. Major Edward Sturtevant, whom Moore regarded as "one of our best officers," took the Fifth out as skirmishers to the right of the turnpike. An artillery duel commenced. The cannon boomed up and down the turnpike and through the woods, but "instead of disturbing our men in the least they would look on with all the calmness that a school boy would watch a game of ball," Moore wrote. "The ball is opened!" one man shouted. "I see where that shell burst," said another. Caught up in the immediacy of his narrative, Moore slipped into present tense: "Now comes a missile that hums & whistles louder than the rest; that's the rail road iron, say the men." Over fences and across fields, the Fifth advanced to support a battery on the right of the road. The artillerists fired, reloaded in an instant, and aimed anew, and the gun "again sends her compliments to the enemy." A solid shot struck one of the Union guns, killing one man and wounding five, but before long the Federals drove the Rebels back.

The Fifth marched to the outskirts of Charles Town with colors flying, but the regiment's welcome was cool. Three years before, John Brown had been hanged in Charles Town, and the town remained "one of the hot beds of secession," Moore wrote. He counted only one or two Union families there, a circumstance that eased the consciences of the men of the Fifth as they procured lunch. They halted near a farm where "hens and chickens were plenty. The men immediately deployed as skirmishers around the yard and in one short half hour made prisoners of every one, from the cock of the roost down, so when we marched through town most every man had a brace of barnyard fowls in his hand." Colonel Cross chuckled and said in jest that he would have no chicken thieves in his regiment. Moments later, as the Fifth crossed a fence, a chicken escaped and flew cackling into the air. "Who let that hen go?" Cross shouted. "The idea of letting a hen go out of this regiment!" The men laughed raucously. As they ate their chicken dinner, they could see rebel cavalry a half mile distant. Shortly their own top generals, McClellan, Darius Couch, and Hancock, rode up to share this view of the enemy. As the three men conferred, a woman in her seventies with a long wooden cane suddenly appeared and hobbled up to take McClellan's measure. She circled him with an inquisitive look and at last stopped and gazed up at him. "General, I have heard so much of you," she said. "I desire to have the pleasure of speaking to you." With a bemused smile McClellan tipped his hat to the woman, and she tottered back to her little house, saying as she passed Lieutenant Moore, "He is a real solid man—I know."

The next day, several officers enjoyed an old-fashioned New England boiled dinner compliments of a Charles Town farmer. Lieutenant Thomas Livermore and other officers found a cauldron and cooked part of a fresh pig, some salted meat, and a large quantity of vegetables harvested from a nearby garden. Livermore went to the farmhouse to borrow silverware. The woman of the house, whose sons were serving in the Confederate army, only reluctantly lent the utensils. The officers and three New York newspaper correspondents sat together on an India rubber blanket as Colonel Cross presided over the meal. Afterward, they returned the silverware.

Despite this happy excursion, Cross had begun to stew over his prospects for promotion to brigadier general. He believed he had earned the rank and saw officers with lesser credentials being promoted ahead of him. When the detail returned to Bolivar Heights, he shared his frustrations with Henry Kent back in New Hampshire. "I begin to believe that hard work, hard times & danger don't amount to anything," he wrote. Several generals had recommended him for promotion; he had three commendations for bravery under fire and battlefield experience as a general, having been in command of a brigade at Fair Oaks. "If they don't give me the place it is an act of gross injustice," he wrote. Many factors blocked Cross's promotion, most of them self-created. He was blunt, and he aired his suspicions openly, leaving no slack for the diplomacy that might have served his ends. His loyalty to McClellan in all things military and political alienated New Hampshire's Republican congressional delegation and Secretary of War Edwin Stanton. Cross was smart enough to understand these dynamics but too bullheaded to work within them. He continued to hope that military merit alone would win him a star; in the meantime he blustered about what he would do if he didn't get it. "Let me tell you I can get along without the service better than the service can without me!" he wrote Kent. "If we mean to whip the South we must keep our old officers & old troops. If I am not appointed I shall quit the Service & go back to the Land of the Hidalgos."

However much Kent sympathized with Cross's frustrations, the colonel's letter found him in a brighter frame of mind. Having worked since the war's outbreak to organize the state's recruiting efforts, Kent had been rewarded with command of the newly created Seventeenth New Hampshire. Cross applauded Kent's good fortune, if not his term of service—"I am glad you have a Regiment, but it should have been a three years instead of 9 mos. militia"—and, as always, was full of paternalistic advice for his boyhood friend. "Leave all your prejudices at home," Cross wrote, without a trace of irony. "Do just, & strive to preserve discipline among officers and men or you are a *goner*." As for old Lancaster friends, Cross wrote, "Do not take many people from Coos. They will all watch you like cats & be the first to find fault—Mark my word." In response to Kent's inquiries, he offered unvarnished thoughts on two former officers of the Fifth who were seeking senior positions in the Seventeenth. "In Long you have a good & brave soldier," Cross wrote. "I have been trying for a long time to secure his appointment. *Barton* is *nowhere*, compared to Long." For all his pride in the regiment he led, Cross professed to be ready to share the burdens and the glory of war. "I hope & trust that you nine months men will have the front of the battle & let the old Rg'ts rest," he closed.

In late October Cross wrote Governor Nathaniel Berry a long assessment of the Fifth New Hampshire's first year under arms. He filled this report with florid prose and superlatives. He described long, hard marches, saying of one of them: "No more severe march has been made by any regiment in the Army of the Potomac." He wrote that on one terrible campground his men had made "the neatest and most comfortable quarters in the division." Alluding to the regiment's hardships and want of supplies, he told of his men sleeping many wet nights without tents and of men with no shoes, no coats, no blankets. He recounted the building of the Grapevine Bridge. Despite much illness, he reported, "at no time up to the Battle of Fair Oaks did the regiment fail to turn out more men for duty than any other in the entire division." Of that battle, he wrote with the "proud satisfaction of having done our duty without flinching" and of adding "another enduring laurel to the military glory of our state." He described for the governor two moments fresh in his memory: the day General Richardson summoned the Fifth to the head of the column on the road to Antietam and the capture forty-eight hours later of the state colors of the Fourth North Carolina. Cross closed his one-year briefing with eloquence and passion: "In whatever position placed, in battle or on the march, enduring hunger, cold or heat, the regiment has never faltered, never failed to do its duty. A sense of obligation to my officers and men for their patience, courage and fortitude, constrains me to bear this testimony to their worth and their character as brave soldiers. It is my earnest wish that those who are left of us may live to see the skies of our country no longer darkened with the clouds of war, but radiant and glorious in the sunshine of peace; and I can but feel confident that our native state will honor and cherish the names of those gallant soldiers who have so nobly sustained her military renown."

Two days after Cross composed this report, the Fifth received marching orders. The men, who had just finished building their oven, would have no chance to bake in it. During the march south along the slopes of the Blue Ridge, Sergeant George Gove paused to note the anniversary of the Fifth's departure from Concord. His journal entry, with only slight overstatement, was a numerical footnote to Cross's more colorful assay: "The Fifth New Hampshire Regiment left Concord one year ago to-day. We then had more than one thousand men. Now we can muster for duty but two hundred." Captain James Larkin wrote his wife that several new regiments from New Hampshire were on the march with the Fifth. He expected a hard campaign. "I think these times will give them a good initiation and make them think of New Hampshire with tears in their eyes," he wrote. Larkin believed the rebel army must be wanting for shoes and clothing, and the size of the Army of the Potomac filled him with confidence. "If this army dont take Richmond they had better hang up their fiddle," he wrote.

As abruptly as this new march down into Virginia had begun, it was in fact leisurely and pleasant, providing more opportunities to sample the local live-stock and the year's harvest. Private Miles Peabody took pride in the Fifth's harvesting ingenuity and appreciated Colonel Cross's encouragement of it. "Our Regt. has got to be the greatest sett of theives that there is in Uncle Sams servise," he wrote to his parents. "Every thing that they can lay their hands on in the way of pigs, poultry or potatoes or apples—in fact, every thing they want—they take posession of. The Colonel says to go in boys but be careful and not get caught." The only obstacle to the Fifth's appetite for fresh provisions was Hancock, the new division commander. Hancock dis-couraged foraging, engaging in a futile but persistent and annoying effort to uphold the army's general order against the practice. He was, in Livermore's words, "far too severe and exacting." In other ways, the men of the Fifth could not help but admire their new division commander. He was a profes-sional soldier, a thirty-eight-year-old West Point man from Pennsylvania who cut a fine figure in the saddle and managed somehow to wear a crisp white shirt on most occasions. He had much in common with Cross: a harsh, pro-fane tongue, fearlessness in battle, and Democratic politics. A junior officer

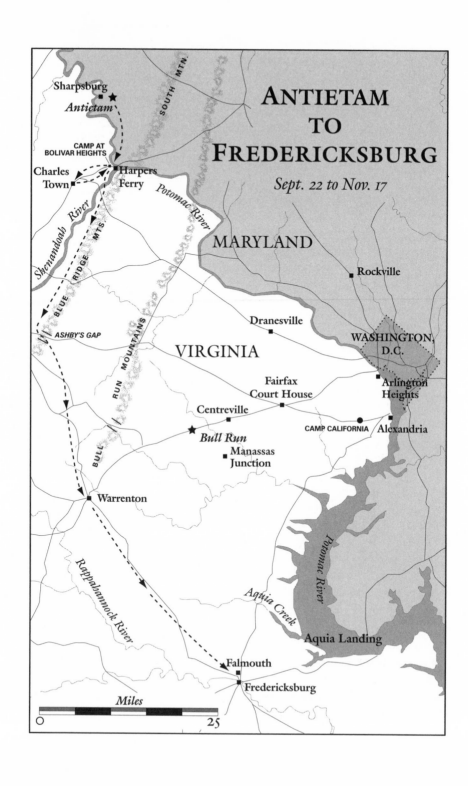

Sharpsburg
Antietam

CAMP AT
BOLIVAR HEIGHTS

SOUTH MTN.

Charles
Town

Harpers
Ferry

Potomac River

ANTIETAM
TO
FREDERICKSBURG

Sept. 22 to Nov. 17

Shenandoah River

BLUE RIDGE MTS.

MARYLAND

Rockville

ASHBY'S GAP

BULL RUN MOUNTAINS

Dranesville

VIRGINIA

WASHINGTON,
D.C.

Fairfax
Court House

Arlington
Heights

Centreville

CAMP CALIFORNIA

Alexandria

★ *Bull Run*
Manassas
Junction

BULL

Warrenton

Rappahannock River

Potomac River

Aquia Creek

Aquia Landing

Falmouth

Fredericksburg

Miles

0   25

once described him as the "tallest and most shapely, and in many respects the best looking officer of them all. I think if he were in citizens clothes, and should give commands in the army to those who do not know him, he would be likely to be obeyed at once, and without any question." Nevertheless, Hancock's anti-foraging obsession collided with reality almost from the moment the men left Bolivar Heights.

The trouble for the Fifth began the first night out. The regiment crossed the Potomac and Shenandoah Rivers, stopped late and camped along the Blue Ridge. The men headed into the cornfields to gather stalks, which they began stuffing into ticking sacks to make mattresses. When Hancock rode up to ask Cross if his men had been stripping the fields, Cross denied it; when Hancock rode on, the men returned to their task. Further proof that Hancock was fighting a battle as hopeless as it was unpopular came in a letter in which Lieutenant Moore described to his father the paradise the army was traversing. The valley, he wrote, "abounded with produce of all kinds, the sheep that fed on the hillsides were the fatest I ever saw, the pigs roved the woods in droves, and poultry fat and plump, fit for the Thanksgiving table were everywhere found. Milk new and fresh, and white honey could be had at every house. Of all these each soldier procured his share." In Ashby's Gap, the men hunted sheep at a local plantation. They butchered their quarry and disposed of the pelts and innards behind the camp of the Seventh New York. Early the next morning, the plantation's owner complained to Cross about his heavy losses, but the colonel gave him no satisfaction. The man returned with Hancock, who ordered the Fifth to stand inspection. Cross had forewarned the men, however, and their haversacks and frying pans contained no trace of fresh mutton. When Hancock departed, the men went to their tents, retrieved the meat from its hiding places within their bedding, and ate it for breakfast.

The Fifth soon had a more serious issue to digest. Just as the regiment turned east from the Blue Ridge gaps toward the Rappahannock, Lincoln finally acted on his frustration with McClellan's "slows." The president relieved his general and put Major General Ambrose Burnside in his place. Word of McClellan's sacking raced through the Army of the Potomac on November 8. Lieutenant Livermore understood that "the extremely leisurely marches" of the previous week had been the last straw. Still, McClellan's ouster was shocking and for the most part unpopular. "None believed, none wished it," Lieutenant Moore wrote to his father. Colonel Cross seethed, suggesting that McClellan had been on the verge of a climactic engagement with the Rebels when connivers in Washington persuaded Lincoln to relieve him. "He carried the hearts of the army with him," Cross wrote. Sergeant Gove, a spare writer but a discerning observer, sounded a different note: "I do not care; have lost confidence in Mac. Hope Burnside will do things up brown."

For the Fifth New Hampshire, the shock of McClellan's dismissal proved to be only a warning tremor. On the night of November 8, the regiment was assigned to guard a wagon train on the march to Warrenton. A wet snow from the previous night had melted, and the army had churned the road into a quagmire. No moon shone, making it difficult for the men to see and avoid the mud holes. These conditions had forced the wagon train to halt several times. After one stop, Captain James Perry's company marched up to the edge of a huge mud hole that had detained the wagons before it. Perry called his men to a halt and groped in the darkness for the easiest way past the obstacle. "No order was given by the colonel to march over the mud hole with any particular dispatch," Perry recalled. Nevertheless, by now it was no secret to any officer or man of the Fifth that Cross was a perfectionist in all things. "The regiment got strung out a good deal," Perry said, and word of the problem reached the head of the column. Already in a foul mood over McClellan's ouster, Colonel Cross rode back to investigate what was holding up the companies in the rear. From the moment he set out, "he was cursing and God-damning us," Perry said. Cross's anger soon turned to rage. "Close up, you God-damned hounds!" he shouted. "Your company officers are not worth a damn." By the time he reached his brother Richard's company, he had decided to take extreme measures. As the colonel rode up, Charles Ballou, one of Richard Cross's lieutenants, heard him hiss that "it was a damn pretty state of things that the regiment could not keep up." Lieutenant Moore, who was watching from nearby, described what the colonel said next to the men of his brother's Company K: "In a very excited manner he cried out to them to halt and fix bayonets. He told them to file to the rear and bayonet any man that fell out of the ranks or did not keep up with his company."

To some of the company commanders, the night march through the mud was hardship enough without having to bear a tirade from Colonel Cross. But this was more than a tirade. His order to his brother's company enraged the captains who heard it, and two of them decided to act on their anger. In earshot of several other officers, Captain Larkin spoke of pulling his company out of the column, and he and Perry both proposed giving up their swords, the symbols of their command. They preferred being placed under arrest, they said, to marching under such vindictive orders. A few minutes later, Lieutenant Moore approached Perry and asked him if he really meant to wheel his company out of line. "By no means," Perry said. On reflection he had realized that this would constitute mutiny, he told Moore. But he added that if the other company commanders would join him, he would gladly give up his sword. "I just don't like to march at the point of a bayonet and be called a damn lazy hound," Perry said. If the others would not relinquish their commands, he told Moore, he might prefer charges against Cross for conduct unbecoming an officer and a gentleman. Larkin was less circumspect than Perry. Once Lieutenant Ballou had agreed with him that Cross's order was "a pretty hard thing," Larkin suggested to him that all of the companies should halt and refuse to take another step until Richard Cross's company had unfixed bayonets and returned to its proper place in the column. Larkin told Moore that he would take his company out of line if the rest of the captains would follow his lead.

The talk of defying the colonel's orders and causing a scene quickly faded that night. Perry and Larkin were seasoned veterans and prudent men who had tolerated their colonel's temper for more than a year. The idea of filing charges against Cross struck both of them as the proper recourse. "I ordered my company to move forward in four ranks and not leave their places on any conditions but to march straight through mud or anything else that came in their way," Perry said. Larkin did the same. The regiment picked up its pace, halting only on orders from Cross to take in and push forward sick men who had lingered by the roadside. In subsequent days, even the notion of filing charges against Cross died away. Fellow officers, especially those who disliked the colonel in the first place, commiserated with Larkin and Perry, reminding them of earlier incidents in which Cross's behavior had been offensive or outrageous. But in his regular letters to his wife, with whom he was always candid and forthright, Larkin did not even mention the angry confrontation of November 8.

The Army of the Potomac paused at Warrenton to bid McClellan farewell. In a hasty letter to his wife, Larkin assessed the change. "It comes unexpected to the army and seems to cast a gloom over it, for as far as I can judge he is loved by the men," he wrote. "The polliticians, I supose, have caused it." The day of McClellan's grand review had been beautiful, with fine marching on good roads. "There is miles of troops in all directions," Larkin wrote Jenny. Lieutenant Moore described to his father the Fifth's part in the farewell. The men lined up "in full dress, with our torn banners flying, drawn up in a line facing the pike. A salute of 16 guns announced the approach of the Gen. He rode a fine stallion a few paces in advance of his staff. He never looked better, more calm than usual. The smile that so often greeted his troops was not seen, but he was never greeted with a more hearty huzza than went up to him that morn. The drums beat and the flags waved, in short everything showed that the army was still his. Old soldiers strove in vain to repress their tears as they looked upon their beloved Gen. for the last time. They believed in him and trusted him."

The men resumed their march, but not before the colonel acted on their complaints about sore feet. This was a persistent problem, and the colonel thought he had solved it with the issue of new shoes three weeks earlier at Bolivar Heights. He assigned three officers, including Larkin, to survey the men about the shoes. The regiment had marched forty miles since then, and the men's croaking had been constant. The three officers reported back that 50 of the 250 pairs of shoes were worthless and the rest nearly so. Cross concurred with the recommendation that the price of shoes be reduced to fifty cents a pair so that most of the men could afford new ones again.

In Burnside's reorganized army, the Fifth was part of Major General Bull Sumner's Right Grand Division. As Sumner's men marched toward the Rappahannock River, both the weather and the terrain changed. The undulating, fertile ground of central Virginia lay behind the men, and as they traversed the flatter woodlands, bleak November rains began. On November 17, Sumner's pickets drove a small Confederate force across the river into Fredericksburg. On high ground near Falmouth, the Fifth set up camp near a pine wood. "I have herd it said that six Army corps's were to mass here," Larkin wrote his wife. "Then I supose it will be on to Richmond. The rebs are on the other side of the river, but not in very strong force."

The disciplinarian in Cross asserted itself as soon as the Fifth began to settle into its camp, which many of the men assumed would be their winter quarters. Private Patrick Shaw, charged with straggling twice within the sound of enemy guns, forfeited a month's pay. For six hours Shaw was compelled to wear over his shoulders a bread box with the word "Straggler" written in large letters on its side. When Lieutenant Albert Cummings and his party of thirteen officers and men returned late from a pass, Cross prohibited any further leaves for six weeks. "The Col. regrets very much that officers should not set a better example and think more of their words as gentlemen," his order read. "If officers and soldiers cannot keep their promises, they can have no privileges." A few days later, Cross rescinded this order, writing: "The Col. does not wish to be unjust to the good soldiers of the regiment." One man caught in between the two orders was Private Benjamin Cook, who was denied a leave to return home to Concord even though his wife had just died there.

By far the severest and most unsettling action Cross took in the days after his regiment's arrival near Falmouth was against Larkin and Perry. While the two captains might be willing to chalk up Cross's November 8 outburst to experience, Cross lacked such a pliable nature when he believed his authority had been questioned. Who had informed him of what was said that night is impossible to know, but the colonel convinced himself that both captains — Larkin in particular — were set against him. Word of their intention to charge him with conduct unbecoming an officer had rippled through the regiment. Perhaps Cross reasoned that if he acted against them first, any charges they filed against him would be discounted as mere retaliation. On November 21, thirteen days after the incident, Cross sent identical notes to Perry and Larkin. The notes read: "On the night of Nov. 8, 1862, while the Fifth Regt. was under urgent orders, and acting as guard to a valuable train, you endeavored to excite a mutiny in the Regt. in violation of the 7th Article of War. You will within one hour from the receipt of this note make a proper apology in writing or you will be arrested and sent before the Military Commission for trial."

Neither company commander saw fit to apologize, and Cross had them arrested. Larkin remained defiant and confident, writing to his wife: "You kneed borrow no trouble on that account for I am glad of it. Charges have gone in against him and if he has a trial he will be Dismissed. I firmly believe he is cutting a big swath just now but he may get humbled. If he gets his deserts, he will. The general is all right on our side and says the charge against us would not hurt a chicken." Larkin even saw a silver lining in the arrests. He wrote Jenny that Colonel Cross "took our Swords and we have no command while under arrest. Consequently if there should be a Battle we should be deprived of the pleasure of going in it." This was no idle consideration. The meager rebel force the Fifth had observed in Fredericksburg was growing by the day. "The Rebs are gathering in strong force on the opposite bank of the river throwing up woorks and getting guns in position while we have some 150 guns to open on them from this side," Larkin wrote. "I expect they will open in the morning as the wagon trains have all gone to the rear and the people who live in range of the guns have skedadaled back." On December 5, Larkin wrote Jenny: "Capt. Perry is having his trial now on our so-called mutiny. I presume they will have me over the coals next, but it wont amount to anything, only for the Colonel to show his A—— and he has done that so many times we are all use to it."

The two officers filed countercharges against Cross. With help from others, Larkin prepared them. The charges, most of which were petty, centered on the colonel's harsh language and extreme behavior on the night of November 8, especially the order to bayonet stragglers, but it included additional specifications. These played to Cross's immediate superiors, Brigadier General John Caldwell, the brigade commander, and Hancock, the division commander. For Caldwell's benefit, Larkin revived an accusation that had made the rounds after Antietam. Cross and others believed that in the heat of battle Caldwell had hidden behind a haystack, and Larkin wrote that Cross had called Caldwell "a damned coward" on account of this. With General Hancock's admonitions against foraging in mind, the captain charged that Cross had sent

Private Henry McMurphy out to steal chickens and, on another occasion, had told his servant and the regimental musicians in a low voice to "Deploy and catch those turkeys." In both cases, Larkin wrote, Cross feasted on the pilfered poultry. The final specification was for berating the officers in front of the regiment with these words: "Your men are fools to take rails or corn stalks and other things right before the Generals. They should know enough to be more sly about it and wait till some other regiment had begun to take them."

News of the showdown between Cross and his two captains soon reached New Hampshire. Ira Barton, a former company commander in the Fifth, followed the story through correspondence with his friends in the regiment. Barton had resigned in early September, to the colonel's satisfaction. Barton's air of privilege had long irritated Cross, who also considered him a malingerer. Then Barton had mishandled his company at Fair Oaks, firing on the Sixty-fourth New York. Now, back home in Newport, he was establishing himself as an agent for war claims, petitioning the government on behalf of widows, parents, and former soldiers. His challenges were to put the best face on his premature return home, especially stories about his excessive drinking, and to press for another military appointment. His doting father Levi, the county solicitor and a prominent Republican, overwhelmed him with advice, hectoring him to pull strings and to prove that he was no drunkard. But in his quest for a new command, Ira Barton lacked the support of the one man he needed most: Colonel Cross.

Barton had several sources of information in keeping up with news of the Fifth. His chief informant was his cousin, Lieutenant Sumner Hurd, who was still with the regiment, but Barton also corresponded with Captain Charles Hapgood, who had landed a long-term assignment as the Fifth's recruiter in New Hampshire. Barton urged Hapgood to resign rather than return to the field. Hapgood was straightforward in response: "About my going back to the Reg't., I do not feel as you do about it. The Col seems to be very friendly. I get letters from him every week. I like him. I can't help it. You may call it infatuation or what you like. I am alive to his faults and am no apologist for them, but since the Reg't. left Concord, I have had no reason to complain." Hapgood did not want his respect for the colonel to poison his relations with Barton and the other disaffected officers. "Am I not in a very unfortunate position?" he wrote. "For myself I can find no fault, but my friends (you chiefly) in the Reg't. have been treated differently, and were I in their places I might do as they have done."

Cross's efforts to purge unwanted underlings went beyond Perry and Larkin. After accusing Captain Horace Pierce of "tardiness in sending a detail for guard," the colonel asked for his resignation—and got it. Cross also settled the matter of Lieutenant Colonel Samuel Langley, who had become ill and left the regiment abruptly during the Seven Days fighting. In a letter conveying regimental gossip to Barton, Hapgood wrote that "the sweetest of all is that Col. Langley has been reported for discharge for being absent 80 days without leave." It was assumed that Major Edward Sturtevant would succeed Langley, but if that happened, the major's job was up for grabs. Cross wanted Captain John Murray, a Mexican War veteran, for major, but some of the men had another idea. "There has been a paper circulated in the Regt. for Perry," Hapgood wrote. There was yet a third possibility: Hapgood had learned that if the regiment's line officers had their way, he would be the choice for major.

Back at Falmouth, Major Sturtevant found himself in the same predicament as Hapgood, hoping for promotion and caught between his admiration for Cross and his respect for the other officers. "I doubt not I shall get all I deserve," he wrote to John Wilson, a former congressman who had been his boss during his days as a printer in Concord. If Sturtevant did get the promotion to lieutenant colonel, as he expected, he knew whom he wanted to succeed him as major. Whatever might have happened on the road from Bolivar Heights to the Rappahannock—and whatever Cross might think—Sturtevant wrote that Captain Perry "has richly earned meritorious consideration."

This high opinion of Perry indicated just how internecine—and even partial—the courts-martial of Perry and Larkin were likely to be. The man assigned to preside at both trials was none other than Sturtevant himself. In Perry's case, because two officers of the court were ill, only six sat in judgment; two of them, Captain Welcome Crafts, a company commander in the Fifth, and Sturtevant, were colleagues of the defendant. Adding to the awkwardness of the situation, on the night of the alleged offenses, Colonel Cross had ordered his own brother's company to fix bayonets and enforce his will. In neither trial did the colonel either testify or make any case beyond a brief statement of charges. Probably he intended by his absence to limit the scope of the testimony. Had he come forward as a witness, Perry and Larkin would have had the right to question him. The other obstacle to a vigorous and impartial examination of the facts was that Cross was looking over the shoulder of everyone involved. Every witness was an officer of the Fifth, and they all knew the colonel would find out what they said. The court understood this, too. Witnesses testified with differing degrees of reluctance, but in no case did the court or the judge advocate, a lieutenant from the Irish Brigade, push any witness beyond what he wished to say.

The courts-martial were held on successive days. Sturtevant called Perry's to order on the morning of December 5. The first witness was Captain Jacob Keller, whose company had been marching second to last in the column when

Cross ordered his brother's regiment to replace the rear guard and fix bayonets. Keller testified that he had heard nothing, spoken to no one, and had no relevant testimony to give. Next in the witness chair was Captain Richard Cross. Although his skills as a military engineer and an expert with the bayonet impressed the men, the younger Cross was not the soldier his brother was. He drank too much and was sometimes a bully and a boor, and his kinship with the colonel raised eyebrows. He was chagrined to be called as a witness, especially when the word around camp was that the colonel had ordered "a favorite company" to fix bayonets. Though seldom known to hold his tongue, Captain Cross said nothing before the court, and no one pressed him. Perry, who questioned several witnesses himself, did not even ask Captain Cross about his brother's order to bayonet stragglers. Charles Ballou, Richard Cross's first lieutenant, testified that he had heard the colonel's instructions to fix bayonets but not the order to use them on stragglers. Ballou also told the court that all the officers believed they were doing their duty on the night in question and that the colonel's tantrum therefore came as a shock. In both cases, Captain William Moore, a favorite of the colonel who had been promoted to a company command just weeks before the trial, presented the fullest and most persuasive account of the dispute. He had heard Cross's excited orders to his brother's company, including the command to bayonet the first straggler, and he repeated them in court. He had also spoken to both Perry and Larkin that night. Each briefly considered acts of disobedience, Moore testified, but each quickly cooled down and changed his mind. They decided on the spot that their proper course was to file charges against the colonel. The last word in the courts-martial went to the defendants, and each made a statement denying mutinous intentions. Larkin's trial ended the afternoon of December 6, a Saturday, and he and Perry remained under arrest, awaiting the verdict.

Regardless of the outcome, Larkin's court-martial seemed to be only the beginning of his troubles with Cross. The captain remained confident of acquittal. "I don't feel any trouble about the result," he wrote his wife three days after the case ended. "Charges have been preferred against Col. C—— and he will be tried if we stay here. I have prefered charges against him that wil fetch him, I think, without any doubt." What Cross expected from Major Sturtevant's panel is unknown, as he never mentioned the incident or the courts-martial in his journal. Toward Larkin, however, he continued to display his temper. Cross did not believe Larkin's assertion that an illness had caused him to miss the Maryland campaign and the battle of Antietam. "He has been down on me like a thousand of brick since I came back," Larkin wrote his wife, "and since we have been here he has been worse than ever."

The paymaster, whom the regiment had been awaiting for months, arrived the day after the trials ended, and Larkin went to collect his due. Cross ordered the paymaster to withhold Larkin's pay, saying the captain had been absent without leave at Antietam. Larkin challenged Cross. "I told him some truths in a mild maner when he got mad [and] farely boiled over," Larkin wrote his wife. "He called me every thing he could lay his tongue to and then offered to tear up his commission and throw off his rank and go out and give me satisfaction (fight he meant). But I kept perfectly cool and let him boil. I knew he was making himself ridiculas to every one there, and was cutting his own throat, and I prefered to get my redress through the propper authorities rather than fight with him." Whether Larkin was hiding behind the military justice code or honestly feared dismissal from the service if he fought Cross, he believed that it was Cross who now risked being cashiered. "Take things all together I cant see much chance for his highness to stay long in the service," he wrote his wife. "I have nearly every officer and man in the regiment on my side and if the Generals do not bring him to trial after a reasonable length of time, I will not serve under him anyway." Officers who had witnessed the confrontation approached Larkin to tell him he had done the right thing. "I did not speak a disrespectfull woord to him, or give him any cause to use such language to me and there is where I shall have him when it comes to trial," Larkin wrote. "It was hard woork to take it but I knew he was my superior officer and it was my best course." At least one other witness to these events sided with Larkin: two days later, the paymaster sent for him and paid him.

As caught up as he was in his own case, Larkin kept a close ear to camp talk about General Burnside's immediate plans. The rumors conflicted: some men were certain the new general intended to attack, but others thought it unlikely. Winter was coming, and the men, accustomed to the pace of McClellan, had cut pines from a nearby wood and, along streets laid out by company, built low log huts with canvas tents for roofs. Before many days the place had the look and feel of winter quarters, with smoke billowing from makeshift chimneys on chilly nights. The portable pontoon bridges on which Burnside intended that his men cross the river were due any day, but, being veterans, the men knew that in the army tomorrow was often a long time coming. Larkin did not credit the rumors of a move forward. In the same December 9 letter in which he detailed the confrontation with Cross in the paymaster's tent, he wrote to Jenny: "I can't see how it would be possible to moove an army in this cold wether. It would be terrable for the poor soldier. The people of the north who are howling for a foreward moovement ought to come out and lay out for a few weeks on the cold ground and march through the mud."

The next day, the court issued its verdicts. It found Larkin and Perry not guilty of mutinous behavior. Their swords at their sides, they resumed their commands. If Burnside indeed intended to attack the rebel force that had been building up across the river for four weeks, Larkin and Perry would lead their companies to battle once again — and their charges against Colonel Cross would have to wait.

10 | Fredericksburg

"We went right up into the blaze of the
enemy's fire and fought them until
we were most all cut down."
— Corporal Luther M. Chase,
December 19, 1862

FIFTEEN MONTHS OF SOLDIERING WITH THE FIFTH
New Hampshire had sharpened the opinions of twenty-two-year-old
Private Miles Peabody. "All the bread we get is nine crackers a day
and ½ lb. meat, nothing to bye, and nothing to bye with," he wrote his parents from the Fifth's camp at Falmouth on December 1. "We have been looking for the paymaster for three months but we have given that up in dispair.
They owe us five months pay. If we do not get it before long I hope the army
will lay down its arms and refuse to do duty till they do get it." For Thanksgiving, Peabody had eaten "four hard crackers and water" while envying the
bounteous meal he imagined his family enjoying back in Antrim. It was not
only meager meals and meager pay that caused him to tell his family he would
quit soldiering immediately if he could do so honorably. In his eyes, the
Rebels had proved themselves the equal of the Union army, and they had superior leaders. "I don't think we can ever conquer them, and if this war is carried on to the end of three years we shall have to acknowledge their independance after all," Peabody wrote. "Would it not be far better to settle it now?
There has been a good eel of talk of union feeling at the South. That is sheer
humbug, for they are far better united here than at the North." As the Fifth
settled in across the Rappahannock River from Fredericksburg, Private
Peabody fastened on the camp rumor of a thirty-day armistice during which
the two sides would negotiate an end to the war. He also had an opinion of
the current prospects of General Burnside's army. When the Fifth arrived opposite Fredericksburg in mid-November, "the enemy had only a small force in

the City and we could have taken it very easy," he wrote, "but it was not done and now the enemy have a large force there and if we take the place, it will be after a hard fight. I cannot see why we did not occupy the city at once."

Private Peabody's view was a common one in the Army of the Potomac. From their camps across the Rappahannock, men of all ranks observed with dismay the buildup of rebel troops on the hills above Fredericksburg. If they wanted confirmation of what their eyes told them, they could get it themselves from enemy soldiers. All they had to do was approach the river's edge, where they could banter with the Rebels on the other side. The newly promoted Captain William Moore described to his sister one such encounter with the Fifth's "grayback friends."

"Why don't Burnside come over here and settle this goddam war? We're sick of it," a Rebel shouted.

"He is coming one of these days and you had better leave damned sudden," a Federal replied.

One Rebel was wearing a blue uniform that he said he had acquired during a previous battle from which the Bluebellies "skedaddled." Why, he asked, had the Federals left the Peninsula in such a hurry? A soldier of the Fifth responded with a taunt about Lee's retreat from Antietam Creek. The conversation turned to the *Monitor* and the *Merrimack*, the two ironclads that had fought an indecisive battle the previous March. A short time later, the *Virginia*, as the Confederates had renamed the *Merrimack*, had been scuttled and sunk by her own captain. Now, looking upriver, a Rebel asked, "Where is your *Monitor*?"

"On the water," came the reply. "Where is your *Merrimack*?"

"In the water," a Rebel answered.

At this, the men laughed together and, despite the November chill, waded to midstream and exchanged knives, newspapers, and tobacco. When they returned to their respective riverbanks, the chiding began anew, but its tenor soon changed. They "lost their good feelings and called each other some pretty hard names," Moore wrote.

Had Burnside had his way, his army would indeed have crossed the river in mid-November. He saw the Rappahannock and Fredericksburg as minor obstacles in his army's rapid march on Richmond. The river flows through Fredericksburg, and the Fifth was in one of the two corps under Major General Bull Sumner that reached the bank opposite the city on November 17. The river was shallow enough that Sumner's forty thousand men could have waded across and seized the city, easily chasing off the small Confederate force there. But the rest of Burnside's army was not yet up, and sending Sumner's grand division into the city would have risked dividing his army. Because late autumn rains had begun, the river might rise, preventing Burnside from supplying Sumner's men. He decided to await pontoon bridges so his army could cross as one. Burnside's boss, General Henry Halleck, cool to Burnside's plan for a rapid advance in the first place, dallied in getting the pontoons south.

General Lee, meanwhile, hurried his forces to Fredericksburg. He knew why McClellan had been sacked and believed Burnside would feel compelled to be aggressive. Once he had confirmed that Burnside was concentrating his army on the Rappahannock with the intention of crossing at Fredericksburg and marching on Richmond, Lee began fortifying a line in the hills above the city. On Marye's Heights, an estate overlooking the town a half mile from the river, General Longstreet's wing of the Army of Northern Virginia began to dig in on November 20. The Telegraph Road, a sunken road twenty-five feet wide, ran along the base of the heights, and a four-foot stone wall skirted the road, facing toward town. It required little labor or ingenuity to convert this position into what one Union colonel called "the most perfect infantry parapet conceivable." The stone wall would shield infantrymen from frontal fire. The ground beneath their feet was solid, and the width of the road gave them room to maneuver as they loaded and fired. The heights rose steeply behind the road. Sharpshooters placed in rifle pits in this embankment and the guns of the rebel artillery could easily fire into any assaulting force without endangering their own infantry arrayed before them.

As the two armies gathered, Murat Halstead, a correspondent and editor of the *Cincinnati Commercial*, persuaded the War Office in Washington to issue him a pass to the front. Halstead knew Colonel Cross from Cross's days at the *Cincinnati Times*. When Halstead reached the army's camp on the Rappahannock on December 10, he went looking for his old friend. The smell of coffee and bacon sweetened the air, and Halstead heard a soldier say, "We'll whip them this time sure." Sumner himself directed Halstead to Cross's tent, which was less than a quarter mile from the general's headquarters. Halstead found Cross writing instructions for his possessions in the event he was killed in the coming battle. His men had stood a close inspection and been issued rations and ammunition. Cross's quarters were the typical hut made of thin pines with a shelter tent for a roof. He had a large brick chimney, and when Halstead arrived, the fire was burning. Pinned on one wall was a cartoon from *Vanity Fair* of General McClellan sitting by the roadside awaiting the praise his country owed him. Cross told Halstead that the old regiments, including the Fifth, were confident McClellan was destined to return to lead them once more.

No doubt relieved to have the trials of Captains James Larkin and James

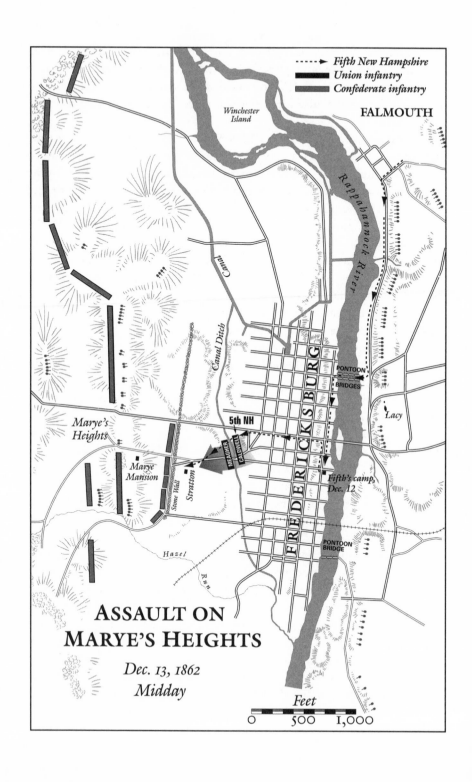

Fifth New Hampshire
Union infantry
Confederate infantry

FALMOUTH

Winchester
Island

Rappahannock River

Canal

Canal Ditch

PONTOON
BRIDGES

Lacy

5th NH

Marye's
Heights

Marye
Mansion

MEAGHER
CALDWELL

Stone Wall

Stratton

Fifth's camp,
Dec. 12

PONTOON
BRIDGE

Hazel

Run

FREDERICKSBURG

ASSAULT ON
MARYE'S HEIGHTS

Dec. 13, 1862
Midday

Feet

0   500   1,000

Perry behind him, Cross's brother Richard planned a party that night in the fifteen-by-twenty-foot log hut his company had built for him. The colonel invited Halstead to come along. The occasion for the party—a soiree, the participants styled it—was the promotion of several officers, including Captain Moore, who acted as master of ceremonies, but the men knew a hard battle lay just ahead. Lieutenant Thomas Livermore called it "a rough wassail" with the mood of a last reunion. All but one of the colonels of the First Brigade joined twenty-five other officers in drinking whiskey punch and singing of home and flag. When the singers reached the line in "E Pluribus Unum" asserting that the nation will fall when the flag trails in the dust, several men shouted, "Never! Never!" Another song began "Unfurl the glorious banner," and Halstead noted the rich, solemn voices of Lieutenant George Nettleton, who had been promoted from corporal for his bravery at Antietam, and Captains Perry and John Murray. The officers sang another favorite— "McClellan Is Our Leader, So March Along"—and raised their glasses and their voices to Little Mac.

Halstead and Cross returned to the colonel's quarters at midnight, but neither man slept. Shortly after they retired, the First Brigade's commander, Brigadier General John Caldwell, summoned his colonels to give them instructions. The pontoon bridges were to be laid in the morning, and Sumner's Right Grand Division was to cross the river and take part in a frontal assault on Marye's Heights. Halstead lay in Cross's hut reflecting on the magnitude of what he was about to witness. He listened for hours to the rumble of artillery trains and the staccato of horses' hooves as aides bustled about the camp.

Before dawn the regiment heard two reports from heavy cannon near the river and intermittent bursts of musketry. Major Edward Sturtevant welcomed the sound. "As for myself, the sooner the battle comes the better," he had just written to an old friend in Washington. At half past five, Larkin found time to scribble a note to his wife. He told her he had been mistaken in his belief that his court-martial would keep him out of action. "We are going across the river and shall have a hard fight," he wrote. In case he didn't have the chance himself, Larkin asked a sick officer who was staying behind to send Jenny the letter and two hundred dollars. The men packed, struck their tents, and ate breakfast. At the bugle's call, they gathered their haversacks, ammunition, and rifles and joined their division in the silent march of battle-wise veterans toward the sound of the guns on the Rappahannock.

Then, just below the crest of a bluff before the river, they stopped and waited. They heard but could not see the rebel resistance to the laying of the pontoon bridges. Brigadier General William Barksdale's Mississippi sharpshooters manned the buildings of the city, and neither musket nor artillery fire from the opposite bank could keep them from picking off the troops sent out to assemble the bridges. Murat Halstead left the Fifth and moved to the crest of the bluff with a view of Fredericksburg. At first he saw only the spires protruding from the smoky fog, but before day's end he had climbed down to the riverside to examine for himself the bridge-layers' bloody, ball-scarred boats. He also witnessed the ineffectual work of the Union artillery, which fired so rapidly he could not count the explosions. At last, the Seventh Michigan crossed the river, and an infantry assault drove off Barksdale's men. As advance units secured the town, the Fifth remained on the other side of the river, camping uncomfortably on a hillside. The men had no tents to shelter them from the cold drizzle. The buildings of Fredericksburg were mainly of brick, and those ignited during the artillery barrage burned slowly. At dusk the sky turned a deep, gaudy purple. Grimy smoke rose from the town and bent northward, in Halstead's words, "a plume bowed in the wind."

Just after daybreak the next morning, December 12, the Fifth joined the rowdy occupying force. The men double-quicked to the river's edge, crossed a pontoon bridge, and entered the acrid air of the smoldering city. Fog obscured their movement, but later the sun warmed the day into the fifties. Furniture, books, bedding, mirrors, and other household goods littered the streets, and many soldiers joined in the foraging and looting that had begun the night before. Lieutenant Livermore and others raided a beehive, then Livermore entered the handsome house nearby and helped himself to apples and, having no spoon, a handful of fruit preserves. Exploring a steamboat wharf near the Fifth's camp on Sophia Street, the street nearest the Rappahannock, the men discovered many long boxes of tobacco submerged in the river. They assumed the Rebels had dumped the tobacco to prevent their taking it. Yet the tobacco was so tightly packed that it remained dry, and the men lay on the wharf for hours fishing it out with oyster tongs. Colonel Cross approved this operation on the condition that the men collecting the tobacco share it freely with their comrades. When an officer from another regiment said he intended to peddle tobacco to his men, Cross exploded. He threatened the man with court-martial, then took matters into his own hands. As the Fifth hooted and jeered the officer, Cross literally kicked him off the wharf. One man estimated that the Fifth rescued more than a ton of tobacco. The men filled their pockets and knapsacks, and some even stuffed tobacco inside their shirts as padding against enemy missiles. They had seen the Confederate lines above town, and they could guess what awaited them. Their fatalism put them on edge, leading to a noisy and destructive bivouac. As a fitting accompaniment to the chaos of a hostile army come to town, men banged on pianos that had been dragged into the streets. These rough symphonies sometimes ended with the musicians crushing the keys with the butts of their muskets. Some men shaved in mirrors in the streets, then smashed them. Others flaunted women's clothing they had stolen from shops and closets.

The men awoke to a foggy, freezing Saturday morning, December 13, and immediately busied themselves with details. As quartermaster, Livermore would be staying behind when the regiment marched to battle. He made himself flapjacks at a local house and took away four china saucers and plates for his mess table. After breakfast, Corporal John McCrillis entrusted to Livermore a piece of blue velvet he had looted from a shop. Livermore thought this a trifling prize but could not refuse McCrillis; he put the velvet under his saddle to conceal it from the guard posted at the bridges with orders to confiscate plunder. McCrillis and Private A. Morrison George struck a deal: if one of them did not return from battle, the other would search the field for him. Colonel Cross, joined by his adjutant, Charles Dodd, and Major Sturtevant, had slept in a house. "Early in the morning I was among my brave boys," he wrote. "I found them cheerful and full of hope." The colonel felt dizzy and weak. "Still I kept as brave a front as my physical condition admitted—thank God my soul was strong and bright," he wrote. He had finished revising his will, the task Halstead had interrupted two nights before, and he gave the key to his trunk to the chaplain.

With the battle looming, there were decisions to make about the assignments of some of the line officers. Lieutenant Sumner Hurd was ill, or so he claimed. On the Peninsula, Hurd had developed the reputation of a malingerer, and for that Cross disliked him. Now Hurd told Nettleton, his second lieutenant, that his illness might force him to fall out during the march; he asked Nettleton to take his place. Hurd promised that if he could not keep up, he would serve as a file closer, prodding potential stragglers back into formation. Nettleton was glad to oblige. Lieutenant Samuel B. Little of the Claremont company had been wounded in the thigh at Antietam and sent home to recuperate. On December 8, ignoring doctor's orders, he started back south. When he appeared for duty on the morning of the battle, he was still weak, and Cross told him to remain in town. Little wouldn't hear of it. Two days before, a sharpshooter had killed one of his five brothers, Moses, as he laid a pontoon bridge across the river. Nothing could keep Little from joining the fight.

At 8:15, the Second Corps commander, Major General Darius Couch, received Burnside's order to move out "for the purpose of seizing the heights in the rear of the town." Unaware of these orders and heartened by the silence from the hills, the Union soldiers engaged in one last round of wishful thinking. Word spread that the Confederates had never really had a large force at

Fredericksburg, that whatever troops had been there had skedaddled, just as they had before, leaving Quaker guns—logs disguised as cannons—to cover their retreat. The sound of battle on the Union left, first artillery, then musketry, disrupted these musings. This was the opening of Burnside's attempt to turn the Confederate right, the first phase of his battle plan. His intention was for his troops on the left to break the rebel line and move into position to flank the infantry on Marye's Heights. He envisioned this flank attack occurring just as Sumner's Right Grand Division made its frontal assault. Ambiguous orders, poor communication, and lethargic field generalship doomed the assault on his left. There would be no flank attack on the Rebels behind the stone wall.

As the morning fog lifted, the first of Sumner's regiments emerged from the city and moved off toward Marye's Heights. These were Brigadier General William French's troops. At about half past eleven, the men of the Fifth heard the Confederate artillery open and knew the battle on their end of the field had commenced. Couch had ordered General Hancock, the Fifth's division commander, to send in his brigades at fifteen-minute intervals on the heels of French's troops. Hancock called together his regimental commanders. As Colonel Robert Nugent of the Sixty-ninth New York remembered it, Hancock instructed the colonels to leave behind their horses and lead on foot "as we were going to have a severe struggle [and] scarcely a pigeon could live through it." After the meeting Nugent shook hands with Colonel Cross and said: "Cross, we are going to have hot work today, but if you get into Richmond before I do, order dinner at the Spottswood Hotel and I will dine with you."

From Sophia Street, as they formed for attack, Hancock's men could not see the fighting below the heights; the buildings of town and nearly a half mile of open field separated them from French's assault. They heard musketry, however, and soon the odor of burning sulfur suffused the air. As the rifle fire died down, the cheers and taunts of the rebel infantrymen carried down into town, the men's first inkling of the result. The Irish Brigade was preparing to march ahead of Caldwell's brigade. Cross, circulating among his own men, overheard General Meagher speaking to one of his regiments. Meagher reminded his men that because they were Irish, the outside world would judge their behavior in battle critically, and because they were Americans now, it was their duty and privilege to give all to uphold the Union. Cross despised Meagher, describing him as "a consummate humbug, charlatan, imposter, pretending to be a soldier" and predicting that Meagher's drunkenness and incompetence would one day be exposed. He described Meagher's words to his men that morning as "one of those frothy, meaningless speeches peculiar to the man." Turning to his own regiment, Cross counted 249 rifles and nineteen officers present for battle. He told his men it would be a bloody fight and reminded them "to stand firm and fire low, to close on their colors and be steady." Each man carried sixty rounds of ammunition.

At around half past twelve, Hancock's division left the city. Four abreast, the Fifth marched with Caldwell's brigade behind the Irish along Sophia Street, then turned left toward Marye's Heights. At the sight of another Yankee division starting toward the plain below, the Confederate artillery intensified its fire. The noise was deafening. Shells shook the buildings and houses, and chunks of brick, plaster, and wood cascaded into the ranks. It was seven hundred yards from the last buildings of the city to the base of Marye's Heights. A third of the way across this expanse, a mill canal fifteen feet wide crossed the route to the slight hollow where the men were to form for their final assault. A narrow bridge crossed the canal, but most of its planks had been removed. Like the regiments that had gone before it, the Fifth faltered briefly here as men either crossed the bridge with difficulty or splashed through the shallow water. As they reached the other side, they scrambled to form a line of battle. Here a twenty-five-foot rise blocked the enemy's view of them, and despite their fears, they paused for a few minutes in relative safety.

In this ravine the Fifth waited to carry out a plan of attack as simple as it was deadly. General Hancock had told his colonels to form battle lines by brigade and storm the hill. This meant their regiments were to stretch across the field two ranks deep, ascend the slope before them, traverse a plateau of three hundred yards, and take the enemy's rifle pits. The Fifth's place was at the extreme right of the line, the farthest from the rifle pits but within easy range of cannon. The attackers would be in full view of the enemy. Fences blocked their route, and the terrain was rough and muddy. As Hancock waited to send Caldwell's brigade forward, he watched from his saddle as Meagher's charge collapsed. He rode back, turned to the soldiers awaiting his command, and said: "General Caldwell, you will forward your brigade at once. The Irish Brigade is suffering severely." Cross had a few final words for his men. He told them that anyone who stopped to help a wounded man would be court-martialed for desertion in the face of the enemy. "Every man is expected to do his duty today," he said. "If I fall, never mind me. Fix bayonets! No man to fire a shot until he is inside rebel lines." On command, the regiment "rose up as one man," in Cross's words, and started on the double-quick toward Marye's Heights, part of the sixth brigade of Sumner's Right Grand Division to embark on the same mission that day. Obeying Cross's command of "Trail arms!" the men gripped their rifles midbarrel, and off they went into a field already strewn with dead and dying.

By now the rebel defenders knew what to expect. A battery just to the left of the Marye house had trained its guns on the spot where the Union right emerged from the ravine. The Fifth had marched only a few yards into the open when the diagonal fire of this battery found its range. The first shell exploded in the center of the color company. Sergeant Ruel Austin, a thirty-year-old farmer who had been chosen to bear the regimental colors, was knocked to the ground, but the shell fragment that felled him first struck and shattered his pocket watch, this good fortune possibly saving his life. A comrade took up the colors and bore them forward, but before the day was done, every member of the regiment's color guard was either killed or wounded. Another shell from this initial barrage found an even more auspicious target — Colonel Cross. Captain Larkin saw it happen. "A shell exploded rite in his face," he wrote. "I saw him fall and thought he was all stove in pieces." A large fragment hit Cross in the chest; other pieces hit him in the mouth, forehead, and hand. He lay on his stomach, his mouth full of dirt and blood, two teeth gone. A piece of another shell struck his left leg. He collected himself and tried to crawl, but a ball hit his scabbard, splitting it open, and knocked him over again. Unable to right himself, he rolled onto his back, feet to the foe, to await death. To make matters even worse, at about the same time Cross was hit, a rebel shell hit the left rear of the regiment, killing Major Sturtevant, the Concord constable who had been New Hampshire's first volunteer after Fort Sumter. Sturtevant had served as Cross's right-hand man for nearly six months, running the regiment in the colonel's absence, cleaning up the messy courts-martial, and gaining the men's respect for his reliable, even-tempered leadership. Now Sturtevant simply disappeared; his body was never found. Command of the Fifth passed to Captain John Murray, who, in Cross's opinion, had "no superior in the service for bravery and capacity to command."

Somehow the regiment pressed on. Above the din, the men rallied to commands of "Close in on the colors!" and "Steady! Forward!" They were veterans, well drilled and well led, and for two hundred yards neither the carnage nor the chaos of their futile mission broke their will to stay in place. They scrunched their necks, ducked their heads, and hunched forward — anything to make themselves less conspicuous. To reach the enemy, the regiment had to swing to the middle of the field, actually moving toward the most concentrated of the rebel fire. As other regiments broke apart, the Fifth held its formation, eliciting a compliment from a soldier of the 118th Pennsylvania who witnessed the attack from a distance. He wrote of seeing a regiment that "maintained a most excellent alignement," only later learning that "the organization whose splendid line had attracted such universal admiration was the 5th New Hampshire."

Still more than a hundred yards from the stone fence, the Fifth approached the uneven line where rebel infantry fire had stopped previous attackers. Seeking shelter from firepower that only increased as they advanced, a few of the men lay on the ground with soldiers who had gone before them. They hoped to take advantage of a slight rise between them and the Rebels, but their position afforded poor cover. Many who sought refuge from peril instead found a ground where the sharpshooters behind the Confederate infantry could kill them at their pleasure. When a piece of shell knocked Private Rodney Ramsey to the ground, he lay a few moments to collect himself, became angry over being hit, and fired three times toward the enemy. A ball struck his canteen, spilling his water before tearing into his thigh. Two comrades shouted to Ramsey from a ditch, and he hastened to join them. One of those who had beckoned was killed before Ramsey reached the position. Realizing that sharpshooters had a clear line of fire on the ditch and that the two of them were surrounded by dead men, Ramsey and the other soldier rolled three corpses up as breastworks and hid behind them for the rest of the day.

As the Fifth moved into easy infantry range, its officers began to drop with frequency. A ball shattered the right arm of Captain Jacob Keller. Lieutenant Little, who had rejoined the regiment that morning, took command of the Claremont company. Marksmen found Little twice. A rifle ball entered his right shoulder and penetrated deeply, lodging near his left shoulder; a second passed through his left calf. He was carried to a field hospital. Grapeshot in the thigh and a minié ball in the abdomen killed Lieutenant Nettleton, who had written to his wife shortly before the battle: "I may fall, but ever remember it was at the post of duty, and in a noble cause." It was Nettleton who had replaced Lieutenant Hurd, his ill superior. Hurd's prophecy also proved accurate; he indeed fell behind. By his own account, he was trying to catch up to the regiment when a piece of shell hit him in the chest, forcing him to walk off the field. Farther along, a minié ball struck Captain Moore in the arm. Moore relinquished command of his company to his lieutenant, then turned toward town. He had gone but a few paces when he was hit again and pitched to the ground. Private A. Morrison George was shot in the thigh and himself set out to find medical help. Presently he looked down and saw a face he recognized, the face of Captain Moore. Moore was dead. George tried to remove the captain's sword to take it to the rear, but his own wound had weakened him and bullets hissed all around him. He soon gave up on salvaging the sword and staggered off.

Not every wound was as severe as those that brought down Little, Nettleton, and Moore. At least two men were wounded atop "a strong four-board fence." The men had to "crawl through, climb over or break down" the fence,

Lieutenant John Bean remembered. As Sergeant Charles Hale hoisted himself over, a shell struck the fence, throwing him to the ground and injuring his groin. Captain Welcome Crafts was shot below the left knee climbing the same fence. Private George Farnum, who had enlisted as a bugler, was marching with his company when he felt a "right smart blow" to his right shoulder. He thought a comrade had stumbled into him, and he glanced about seeking the offender. Farnum marched on, but soon his right arm went numb and he felt "something warm trickling down my side and arm." In his overcoat cape he noticed a quarter-size hole. He raised the cape, found a hole of the same size in the strap of his knapsack, and concluded that he was hit. He turned back into the city, where the assistant surgeon, John Bucknam, dressed his wound.

The regiment angled to its left and headed toward a square two-story brick structure known as the Stratton house. The house sat one hundred yards from the rebel infantry, and a high board fence behind it ran parallel to the rebel line. The Fifth turned the corner beyond the house and came face to face with the enemy. "The men were greeted with a terrific fusillade of musketry from behind the stone wall directly in their front, and the dead and wounded fell like ripe grain before the reaper's sickle," wrote Private John Crosby. The flash of fire fringed the top of the stone wall as the Confederate infantrymen, four deep along a quarter-mile stretch of the Telegraph Road, worked at fever pitch. Over the din and through the smoke, Crosby heard "a weird, awful chorus of hoarse cries, the death shrieks of strong men in mortal agony." Men of the Fifth fell with each step. In Crosby's opinion, not one member of the regiment who progressed beyond the Stratton house fence escaped unharmed. He heard "a fearful gasping groan" behind him and turned to see Lieutenant Charles Ballou collapse as blood gushed from a gaping hole in his neck. Just as Ballou fell dead on his face, Crosby felt a stinging sensation in his right elbow. He knew instantly that the bone was shattered. He clenched his right sleeve in his teeth and ran back to the Stratton house. He crawled through a hole in the fence and sat down beside an outhouse in the yard.

Lieutenant Janvrin Graves, who had taken over his company from Captain Moore, was also wounded beyond the Stratton house. Men seeking shelter had already filled the house, so Graves settled for a spot in the yard where the house protected him from enemy fire. As he peered back into the haze from which he had just escaped, he witnessed three deaths in rapid succession. He saw Captain Murray, the commander of the regiment after Cross and Sturtevant fell, shot through the head. He watched Corporal Jacob Davis go down carrying the American flag. And he saw Captain Perry seize the flag from Davis, start back, and take a minié ball. The ball struck Perry's shoulder and penetrated his chest. He staggered a few steps and tumbled right onto Lieutenant Graves. As he lay dying, Perry passed on a message for Captain Larkin, telling him "to have no hard feelings against the Col.," who just days before had court-martialed them both.

Like Graves and Crosby, many of the wounded sought refuge at the Stratton house, but that landmark also provided the takeoff point for the Fifth's final forward movement of the day. Sergeant George Gove saw the regiment's state colors on the ground beyond the board fence, and he and Corporal McCrillis knocked an opening in the fence with their rifle butts. Private Frank Swift dropped his rifle, scooted through the opening, grabbed the flag, and rushed forward. When Swift was wounded, Gove took up the flag and waved it. He, too, went down. McCrillis collected the New Hampshire colors and carried them back to the Stratton house. With that, the Fifth's attack was spent.

Wherever they were, the remnants of the regiment could only wait for rescue or for nightfall. The battle raged on, as other brigades tried in vain to reach the rebel stronghold. Late in the day, stretcher bearers found Luther A. Chase and Charles Hart, two young Claremont men who had fallen together during the artillery barrage early in the Fifth's march. A cannonball had severed Chase's leg. For hours Hart lay near him, bleeding but conscious. When the rescuers arrived with only one stretcher, Hart knew he was near death and told them to take Chase. Hart, who had survived a minié ball in the thigh at Fair Oaks, was right about his prospects; he was buried on the field. Chase died on the way to a hospital. Colonel Cross lay in the open for three hours expecting death at any moment. Fresh regiments marched up the hill past him and, moments later, ran over him on their retreat down the plain. He heard gasps, turned his head, and saw a disemboweled captain from French's division dying within a foot of him. When the fire above and around him came heaviest, Cross covered his face with both hands and counted rapidly to one hundred. He admired the coolness of the Confederates' work and scorned the cowardice of Union soldiers who ran from the field with counterfeit wounds. Finally, Dan Cross, a lieutenant from the Fifth serving on General Caldwell's staff, found the colonel and helped carry him from the field. Private Crosby waited out the battle in the yard of the Stratton house. A hospital flag had been raised over the house, which had been filled with wounded since early in the assault. The flag did little good, however, because "three half-crazed Irishmen" refused to give up the fight. "Running about amid the dead and wounded, they would fill their caps with ammunition from the cartridge boxes of their fallen comrades, and returning to the smoke-house they would begin firing away in the direction of the enemy safely entrenched behind the stone wall," Crosby wrote. "They might as well have fired at the moon." After nightfall, Crosby again took his right sleeve in his teeth and headed for town. He could not find the Fifth's camp and wound up in the field hospital of a Massachusetts regiment.

Under cover of darkness, Captain Larkin, the only officer who remained with the Fifth's broken line, "brought off all that were left who were able to walk." This came to about thirty men. Other members of the regiment made it back on their own and straggled into the Fifth's camp during the night. Larkin was the fifth man to command the regiment in its half hour of action, but there was little left to command. Fifty-seven officers and men had been killed or mortally wounded, and one hundred with lesser wounds had either left the field or remained upon it. Exhausted as they were, the survivors stayed awake to see who might straggle in. They compared notes, trying to determine who was dead for certain and where the missing had last been seen alive. Rodney Ramsey, the private who had lain most of the day in a ditch shielded by Union corpses, had an ulterior motive for checking the faces of those returning from the battlefield. In a letter to his father, he reported that twenty-seven of the thirty-five men in his company had been killed or wounded and declared, "We have no regiment now." Yet Ramsey gave thanks for the survival of one particular comrade: "The fellow that I lent five dollars to has come back so that is all right." One member of the Fifth straggled in and pulled from his clothing five pounds of tobacco fished from the river the day before. Within it he found three minié balls.

General Burnside resisted the verdict that the day had pronounced on his misguided plan. He had lost 12,600 dead or wounded, more than 8,000 of them on the plain between the town and Marye's Heights. Confederate casualties totaled 5,400. Yet the next morning Burnside planned to send 15,000 more infantrymen in the same direction to renew the frontal assault. Alarmed, Bull Sumner persuaded Burnside to call a council of war, and his generals talked him out of his plan. The order was rescinded. In spite of this sensible reversal, Murat Halstead had already formed the judgment about Fredericksburg that would soon sweep the land. In his December 17 dispatch, he called the fire into which the Union troops had walked "positively annihilating" and wrote: "We had, it appeared, made the attack at the strongest point of the enemy's lines, placed ourselves just as they wanted us, made a magnificent display of the devotion and discipline of our soldiers, in a manner that afforded the enemy the entertainment of looking upon the display without much danger to themselves, and of slaughtering us without stint." Halstead summed up the battle in one sentence: "It can hardly be in human nature for men to show more valor, or generals to manifest less judgment, than were perceptible on our side that day."

The next day, the survivors' task was to search for their dead, missing, and wounded. In this, the Fifth, like other regiments, faced many obstacles. The two armies called no truce to bury the dead, and the ground was still contested. The regiments that came up in relief after the battle lay behind a rise in the landscape, out of view of the rebel pickets; this allowed the Rebels, who needed shoes and clothing, to strip many of the Union bodies bare. Nor were Union soldiers reluctant to rifle the pockets of their dead comrades. The corpses had other uses as well. The temperature that night dipped into the low thirties, and "frozen men were placed for dumb sentries." Some of the regiments that came up in relief slept with neither overcoats nor blankets. Men pulled corpses close to them to keep off the wind, and some used the limbs of the dead for pillows.

Not until ten o'clock on the night after the battle did Corporal John Mc-Crillis mount a party to search for Private George, the man he had promised to find if he did not return. With two other men from his company, McCrillis retraced the route the Fifth had taken thirty hours before. To their surprise, the searchers found George alive but immobile in a pigpen. Nearby lay another wounded man from their company, Private Charles Corey. It was a dark night, and the searchers trod with care through the dead and wounded as they climbed with curiosity and trepidation toward Marye's Heights. They went near enough to the stone wall to hear the voices of rebel soldiers and the sounds of their picks and shovels. Then McCrillis and his rescue party headed back down, helping George, Corey, and a few others to town. George survived, but Corey had been hit in both arms and a leg and died shortly after the leg was amputated.

In at least one case, the Fifth had help in confirming a death. Major Charles Adams moved his regiment, the First Minnesota, onto the battlefield to relieve U.S. regular troops. The Minnesotans took up a position "in the very midst of the stiffened, mangled corpses of the noble slain." The next morning, just before the center of their line, Adams's men saw the body of a captain of infantry stripped of his sword, belt, boots, and pantaloons. The dead man's cap was resting between his shoulders, "as though placed there by some friendly hand." Rebel sharpshooters still controlled the area where the body rested, and it was not until the next night that it was buried. In the dead man's pockets, members of his burial detail found a knife, a memorandum book, and a letter, confirming the man's identity: it was Captain William Moore. Major Adams saw to it that Moore's personal effects reached the Fifth New Hampshire, and Captain Richard Cross later took them to Moore's father in New Hampshire.

Dozens of soldiers from the Fifth needed medical care. General Hancock had appointed their surgeon, Luther Knight, to lead his division medical staff. John Bucknam, Knight's senior assistant, had waited in the Fifth's camp in the streets to treat any wounded who made it back. William Child, the Fifth's second assistant surgeon, had just finished his work at Smoketown Hospital near Antietam Creek in early December, and he arrived in Fredericksburg during the battle. As Child sought a hospital where he might help, a cannonball from Marye's Heights came bounding down the street toward him. He stepped aside and continued on, more careful now as he crossed the streets perpendicular to the rebel line. When he found a church that had been converted to a hospital, wounded soldiers already covered the floor. Child and the other surgeons toiled into the night, but after a solid shot crashed against one wall, they doused the lights and tried to aid those who did not require surgery. The next morning, Child found the remnant of his regiment. He was soon detailed to assist the Irish Brigade's surgeon, who had turned a merchant's house near the railroad depot into a hospital. On December 15, the day the Fifth crossed the river to its old camp, Child accompanied an ambulance train carrying wounded men to the divisional tent hospital that Surgeon Knight had set up. The night was cold and wet, and most of those in the train died before morning. Child was assigned to direct the cooking and distribution of food. Other surgeons spent December 16 and 17 amputating, with piles of arms, legs, hands, and feet rising around their tables as they worked—a sight familiar to Child from Antietam. Making his rounds of the tents each morning, he found half the patients dead. The doctor confided in his wife, Carrie, an opinion he could not share with those under his care. "I should much rather be killed outright than linger in a hospital with a severe wound," he wrote.

Private Crosby, who had made it down from the Stratton house with his shattered elbow, crossed the river with the rest, but by then he was already recuperating from his treatment. Captain Cross, his company commander, had found him in the field hospital of the Twenty-eighth Massachusetts. The sociable Crosby had made several friends there. Nearly every other wounded man in the field hospital had been shot in the leg, and with confidence that none could walk, Crosby placed a dozen slabs of tobacco from the Fifth's river cache on a mantel near his bed. When he awoke the next morning, the tobacco was gone. Crosby puzzled about it for a few minutes until the man nearest the fireplace, whose severe wound would soon cost him his leg, confessed that he had speared the tobacco with a ramrod. The two men shared a laugh and a smoke. Captain Cross tried in vain to persuade Crosby that his arm would be all right and that he should report to the Fifth's surgeons. "Although I had suffered no serious loss of blood and was not in any serious pain at any time, I was satisfied that no surgical skill could save my arm," Crosby wrote. He stayed where he was, and the next day the surgeons amputated his arm above the elbow. Captain Cross sent stretcher bearers to carry Crosby back to the Fifth and eventually across the river to the tent hospital. There chaplains handed out religious tracts to the wounded, "but veracity compels me to say that they were generally received with scant courtesy by the men," Crosby wrote.

Back home in New Hampshire, the magnitude of what had happened to the Fifth at Fredericksburg was never fully apprehended. The news came in sketchy newspaper reports and letters from the field—or there was simply no news. Because the regiment had been recruited from all around the state, the grief on the home front was diffuse rather than concentrated in one particular city or county. Nevertheless, all around the state in that sad, anxious holiday season, the news kept getting worse. Two members of the Fifth succumbed to wounds each day for five consecutive days beginning December 23. A wounded soldier told Doctor Child of the death of Private Ned Carleton, an acquaintance of the doctor's from back home in Bath. The soldier had been marching toward Marye's Heights right next to Carleton when a shell hit them both. Carleton's "brains and blood flew all over him," Child wrote home. The papers carried notice that Major Sturtevant was "missing and supposed killed," but there was no further news of him. Five days passed before Janvrin Graves, who succeeded Captain Moore as a company commander, wrote an account of his death in a letter of condolence to his family. The wait was far longer for definitive news of twenty-two-year-old Sergeant George Greeley, who had been a printer for the *Granite State Free Press* in Lebanon before the war. An early report indicated Greeley had been wounded in the knee and helped off the field, but no one ever saw him again. The newspaper finally gave up hope and ran a tribute to Greeley six months later. "There is little room to doubt that he met the fate of too many, alas! of that gallant band," the *Free Press* reported on June 13, 1863, "but whether he died surrounded by friends or foes of the flag and the country he loved, may never be known on earth." The paper recounted Greeley's enlistment and his record of steady promotion. "We never heard his name mentioned but with respect, save by a cowardly few who stay at home and make a business of breathing foul calumny against men, the latchet of whose shoes they are not worthy to unloose." The *Free Press* lamented the anonymity of Greeley's death. "Had he fallen thus honorably alone, many millions would have known his virtue and cherished his memory," the paper concluded. "As it is, among the many thousands that likewise fall his memory will be confined to those who knew, and loved and honored him. In that circle, however, we claim a place."

Until Fredericksburg, some New Hampshire towns had been spared losing a son to the war. In Amherst, the Christmas Day edition of a local weekly reported the wounding of four men: J. Byron Fay, in the left breast; Charles Phelps, in the left side above the hip; and the Vose brothers, Edward in the arm and George in the leg. The newspaper said all these wounds were slight, but this report proved to be optimistic. Two days after the battle, a surgeon had amputated George Vose's leg, and he died the day the newspaper appeared. The New Year's Day edition reported that "this community will ever cherish his memory with grateful hearts."

Claremont, a much larger town, had become all too accustomed to burying its sons. During a funeral sermon three weeks before Fredericksburg, a local pastor had told his congregation that illness and enemy fire had already killed thirty soldiers from Claremont. The Fifth Regiment alone had lost three Claremont men in battle at Fair Oaks, a fourth at White Oak Swamp, and a fifth at Antietam. Now the company that Captain Long had recruited fifteen months earlier had suffered heavy losses at Fredericksburg. Nine men of the company were killed, seventeen wounded. Six of the dead were from Claremont, as was Lieutenant Ballou, who had died leading another company. As Editor Joseph Weber prepared the four-page edition of his *Northern Advocate* for December 30, he struggled to keep up with the bad news. On page one he ran a letter of condolence to Ballou's sister from Captain Cross. "As an officer he had no superior in the regiment, and as a companion there was none better," Cross wrote. By the time Weber assembled the type for page two, word of Lieutenant Samuel Little's death had reached him. On page three, under a large headline, LATEST NEWS, Weber reported that Lieutenant George Nettleton was gone, too. Nettleton's widow, it was soon reported, was intent on seeing the flag of the Fourth North Carolina, which her husband had captured at Antietam. She wrote to Governor Nathaniel Berry, and he arranged for Captain Long to deliver the flag, "a mere 'tattered remnant,'" for display at a Republican meeting at Claremont town hall.

The Claremont casualties at Fredericksburg were working men—farmers, mill workers, mechanics, a bookkeeper, even a bridge builder. Typical of them in background and devotion to duty was Lieutenant Little, who had returned to the regiment still suffering from a wound on December 13 but declined Colonel Cross's offer to take the day off. Little was thirty-four years old and had overcome a difficult childhood. His mother died seven months after he was born, and his father disappeared. The youngest of six brothers, Samuel lived in an orphanage until he was hired out to a farmer at age ten. As an adult, he became a house painter, moved to Claremont, and went into business with a brother. On Sundays, he taught at the Universalist Church. After he was shot, Little was carried to the hospital at Falmouth. He suffered greatly from his wounds but managed to write friends in the regiment, telling them the doctors were hedging about his chances of recovery. He died on Christmas eve. His body was brought to Claremont, where a large crowd gathered at town hall for his funeral. The pastor read from Revelation: "Blessed are the dead which lie in the Lord from henceforth: Yea, saith the Spirit, that they may rest from their labors; and their works do follow them." The Hiram Lodge of Free and Accepted Masons buried Brother Little.

Twenty miles north of Claremont, Captain Perry's body arrived home five days after the battle. A farmer before the war, he had become Lebanon's most esteemed citizen-soldier. Someone from the local newspaper had either seen Perry's corpse or coaxed a description of it from the undertaker. The paper reported that his "death was caused by a musket ball entering his left shoulder, passing down through the region of the heart, and stopping, in sight but without breaking the skin, in the right side." The newspaper also published a letter from Chaplain Milo Ransom to Perry's wife. The letter praised the captain for his patriotism and bravery but closed with a disheartening note: "Your husband was robbed of anything he had on his person of any value." His funeral was so large that hundreds of townspeople had to stand outside the local Universalist Church to pay their last respects.

Not all bodies came right home. Private Shepard Caldwell was shot in the leg and did not survive the amputation. His widowed mother in Alstead wanted his body returned to New Hampshire and wondered whether she was due his back pay and bounty money. A friend, Elisha Towne, contacted Ira Barton, the former Fifth New Hampshire captain who had once been Caldwell's company commander. "Shepard was the only son she could count on," Towne wrote. Barton contacted Lieutenant Hurd in the Fifth's camp to inquire about the body. Hurd responded that "poor Caldwell was burried in his Blankett in a grave with another body but a board markes his side of the grave." Whoever came to fetch the body would have to bring a zinc-lined coffin, Hurd wrote, promising to help if he could. Towne succeeded in bringing Caldwell's body home, but his request for the money owed him took longer. As Barton worked his way through the red tape, Towne wrote him that it was imperative to keep the matter secret from Mrs. Caldwell's other sons "as Charles is sponging all he can from her." It was seven months before Barton secured the money.

Although the battle had nearly destroyed his regiment, Colonel Cross was proud of his men and eager to put the troubles of the preceding weeks behind him. His own wounds were less severe than those he had suffered at Fair Oaks. "The end of my days was reserved for another and I hope more fortunate occasion," he wrote. "I pray that it may be with the cheers of victory in my ears." After spending the night of the battle in a makeshift hospital in the mayor's house, he crossed the river to the Fifth's camp. His first order of business was to make amends with Larkin. Perry had died a brave death, and Larkin had led the regiment out of battle in its darkest hour. Cross praised Larkin in his official report and sent him an apology for his abusive behavior in the paymaster's tent. He also invited the captain for a visit. Larkin was as forgiving as Cross was contrite. "The Col. shook me warmly by the hand and was much affected," Larkin wrote his wife. "The appoligy he made was gentlemanly and all I could ask." Cross had been "cool and brave" at Fredericksburg, and he "stands higher with the regiment now than he ever did before," Larkin wrote. The colonel promised to visit Jenny Larkin in Concord, and the captain instructed his wife to greet Cross warmly "and don't alude to any difaculty we may ever have had or as though you ever herd of it." Larkin harbored no hard feelings toward Cross, "for he has made me all the reperation I could ask." When Cross's wounds allowed him to travel, he left for Washington. He wrote his father a note from the capital. "I am not half as badly hurt as the papers say," he assured him. By the last day of 1862 Cross was in Concord, and on New Year's Day he spoke at a Republican assembly convened to nominate a candidate for governor. He brought along the tattered colors of his regiment and those of the Fourth North Carolina. The Republicans cheered Cross as he stepped to the rostrum. He told them their cheers were not for him but for the men he had led, "the shattered remnants of that regiment of men who were left after ten bloody battles. Those men have carried the flags you see there in front of you in almost every fight. They have never, on any field, moved except toward the enemy, and those flags have never been trailed in dishonor." Cross knew Fredericksburg had been a foolish waste of lives, but he shared this opinion neither in his public remarks nor in his official reports on the battle. Instead he used these occasions to speak to the glory of the deaths of the "brave boys" and to make the claim that soldiers of the Fifth had fallen closer to the stone wall at the base of Marye's Heights than soldiers of any other unit.

Over the years several other regiments claimed this distinction but none could prove it. The bodies nearest the wall were the first to be stripped not only of anything useful but also of souvenirs, including insignia, papers, and other possessions that might have identified them. A captain in the Irish Brigade wrote to a friend that as he regained consciousness near the wall on the night of the battle, he asked a sergeant nearby to identify the men all around them. The sergeant answered: "They are the dead and wounded of the Sixtyninth and Eighty-eighth New York, as well as the Fifth New Hampshire."

Confederate soldiers behind the wall also identified the Fifth as one of the three regiments that had come nearest to reaching them. Cross's view of the battle, by contrast, had been limited to what he could see lying on his back two hundred yards from the stone wall, but in the report he wrote two days after the battle, he was typically scathing in the conclusion he drew from what he had observed. "Allow me to state here the reason why the loss of my regiment was so heavy was, the men held their ground and endeavored to whip the enemy, instead of skulking or shamefully leaving the field, as many of the new regiments did."

The soldiers of the Fifth blamed their leaders for the carnage, but their dismay did not extend to Cross. Lieutenant Augustus Sanborn, a Franklin man who had been promoted from the ranks, wrote his widowed mother that he hoped she would see the colonel during Cross's New Hampshire sojourn. "I supose that he will be back here before a grate while but if I was in his shoes and had been hit so many times as he has I would never com back again unless they give me a hire place than Col. for if there is a man in this army that is worthy of it is Col. Cross." The very thought of Cross not returning moved Sanborn to add: "I don't know what we should do with out him to look out for us." Others also believed that Cross was at last destined for a brigadier general's star. Captain Charles Hapgood traveled from Rochester, where he had been recruiting for the Fifth, to visit Cross in Concord. Cross had recommended him to Governor Berry for lieutenant colonel, a recommendation that Berry soon acted on. Hapgood found the colonel looking well despite his wounds. In part because of his speech to the Republicans, he was the "Lion of Concord," Hapgood wrote. Cross told Hapgood he would leave the service if he did not get his star, and Hapgood believed the promotion would come shortly. General Hancock shared this high opinion of Cross and saw the Fifth New Hampshire as a reflection of its leader. "I do not believe there is a better regiment in the world," Hancock wrote to the state's two U.S. senators. "It now numbers but about 100 bayonets for duty, but these men are refined gold. I would trust that regiment now to hold a position that a new regiment of a thousand men would be driven from." Hancock concluded: "I consider that Col. Cross has made the regiment what it is. He should be promoted. One hundred men is too small a command for him."

Although the regimental roll still exceeded that number, its effective manpower back at Falmouth was less than a hundred, and for the most part their morale was sinking. "Could you see us now you would not know us," Lieutenant Hurd wrote to his cousin Barton. "You inquire for the 5th Regt—they will tell you here is what is left of it." When Cross filed his first report two days after the battle, he counted three officers and sixty-three men present for duty. One of those officers was Hurd, but the colonel mocked his claim that he had been wounded during the battle and told him he would never be promoted. Although he complained bitterly about Cross, Hurd eventually resigned "by reason of inability to command." Sergeant George Gove, whose wounds beyond the Stratton house had been too slight to earn him a furlough, wrote in his diary: "We have nothing to do now, for the very good reason we can do nothing. The Fifth New Hampshire is played out." Gove had been in the hospital at the Lacy house, "a large mansion splendidly furnished," and noted from his bed the arrival of more and more wounded. "This has been a great defeat and failure," he wrote. On December 16, Gove returned to the regiment. "Feel homesick and discontented; old comrades all gone," he wrote. "Don't know what will be done with the remainder of the regiment." Private Miles Peabody believed that the army was finished for the winter. "Since the fight the soldiers have lost what little confidence they ever had in Gen. Burnsides," he wrote home. "It would be almost impossible to get what is left of this Division into a fight. What is left of this Regt. say that they will never fight again if they can help it." Private Jonathan French, who had been home nursing a leg wound from Antietam, returned to his company at Christmastime. Still lame, he was assigned cooking duty. This was "not so hard for him as to do another duty for there is but a few to cook for in a Co.," a friend wrote home. Corporal James Daniels described in his journal days of light drill, occasional inspection, or picket duty and wet weather, with only a hint at the mood of the regiment. On New Year's Day 1863, he wrote: "In camp; very pleasant; the regiment in line; a few remarks from the chaplain. Plenty men drunk and fighting."

During the weeks after the battle, Captain Larkin's pleasure at being back in the colonel's good graces turned bittersweet. Cross left his brother Richard in charge of the five companies of the regiment's right wing and Larkin in charge of the left. Larkin's command totaled forty-two rifles. When the Fifth boarded the train in Concord in October 1861, his company alone had been larger than the entire regiment now. "Our regiment marched up in splendid stile under an awful fire of grape and canester shot and shell and rifle balls and they did not flinch until completely cut down," he wrote his wife. "I hope the howlers after McClelland have learned a lesson. Mc would never have sacrifised lives like that for no purpose." He blamed the slaughter on "the men of the north who are staying at home crying on to Richmond afrade the army will eat up a few dollars by making a shure thing." As for his own safety, he wrote: "I have come to the conclusion that there is a charm that keeps the bullets off me for they sung around me like a swarm of bees and not one tuched me." Once he was sure which men from his company were dead, he wrote to their next of kin. This sad duty, coupled with the furloughs granted to wounded officers, heightened Larkin's resentment at having been fourteen months in the field without leave. Writing to Jenny on their seventh wedding anniversary, he grew nostalgic: "You recollect what castles of happiness we built, little dreaming that our then happy country would be desolated by war and we should be parted for years." He yearned so deeply for her that he questioned the good fortune of having walked off the field at Frederickburg unscathed. "If I had been fortunate enough to have got a slight wound I should have come home," he wrote. He was eager to see his son and added this postscript to one letter: "Bubby, you need not cry for Papa had some soft bread & potatoes and mackerel today."

Not everyone was so homesick and downhearted. In its first issue of the new year, the *People's Journal* of Littleton carried letters from members of the Fifth that captured both the men's disgust over Fredericksburg and their resilience. "I must say I consider it nothing but an useless slaughter," an anonymous soldier wrote of the battle. "A total sacrifice of thousands of the noblest, bravest hearts that have ever espoused our country's cause." Just two columns to the right of this lament, there appeared a much different assessment of the regiment's frame of mind. Even in the shadow of Fredericksburg, Sergeant Luther M. Chase remained good-natured and optimistic. The Rebels had just killed Captain Perry, Chase's commanding officer, and seven soldiers from his company. Chase himself was among the wounded, as he had been at Fair Oaks and again at White Oak Swamp, where a shell fragment sliced off the end of his left big toe. This time, he had been shot twice, taking a minié ball in the right knee and another in the left leg just above the ankle. Chase knew the Army of the Potomac had been "severely whipped," storming the enemy stronghold again and again with nothing to show for it. "I wonder how any of us got out alive," he wrote. Yet Chase was ready for more. The wound in his left leg had caused "a pretty good gash," he wrote, "but I think if I have good luck I shall be able to go back to the Regiment in a few days. Except my wounds I never enjoyed better health in my life. I am enjoying my self very well, and have been soldiering it long enough to know that there is no use in being otherwise."

 | ## "Camp near Falmouth"

"A negro will be a nigger at all events."
—Doctor William Child

A S THE NEW YEAR TURNED, THE FIFTH NEW HAMPSHIRE
was a shattered regiment. Its colonel had returned to New Hampshire to recuperate from his wounds. Its lieutenant colonel had
gone on furlough and never returned. Its major and three of its ten company
commanders had been killed at Fredericksburg. The majority of the soldiers
who had marched up toward Marye's Heights lay in either graves or hospitals.
Although some of the men remained determined and optimistic, the mood of
those who marched back to the Army of the Potomac's camp near Falmouth
reflected the discouragement of the army as a whole. They had no faith in
General Burnside, and they had begun to doubt whether they could defeat
the Rebels. Many of them also realized that the cause for which they were
fighting had shifted beneath them.

The Emancipation Proclamation, which took effect on January 1, changed
the calculus of the war at home as well as in the field. President Lincoln's bold
stroke threatened the Republicans' grip on New Hampshire's political offices.
Election day was scheduled in March, and the result would be an early ref-
erendum on the president's policies. In the field, the proclamation had an
unsettling effect on the camp of Cross's regiment. Until now, the men of the
Fifth had shared a cause upon which nearly all of them could agree: to uphold the Revolutionary legacy of their grandfathers and great-grandfathers by
preventing the Union from fragmenting. The Emancipation Proclamation,
coupled with the poor generalship that had led the Army of the Potomac to
slaughter and humiliation in 1862, undermined the men's sense of a common
purpose. While they had always understood that slavery was somehow to blame
for the war, most of them saw abolitionists as dangerous extremists. They had
persuaded themselves that they were not fighting to interfere with states' rights
to establish institutions as they saw fit. Most had never seen a black person

before the war began; fewer than two hundred Negroes of voting age lived in New Hampshire, nearly all of them in or around Portsmouth. Partisan newspapers had conditioned the soldiers to see blacks as lazy, deceitful, and ignorant—an inferior race. The men's own experiences had seemed to confirm this prejudice. When Private Miles Peabody wrote during the Peninsula campaign that "the negroes that I have seen here are a very lazy disgusting set of human beings," he was expressing an opinion shared by many of his fellow soldiers. Yet now, it seemed, Lincoln would have his armies fight to free the slaves.

The men's closest exposure to Negroes came mainly in and around their camps. After the debacle at Fredericksburg, the Fifth crossed the Rappahannock and marched about two miles north to Falmouth and a camp that was as permanent as any the men inhabited during the war. Soldiers had stripped the area of vegetation and so often marched and drilled upon the ground that it was as hard as a floor. Of the earth upon which they camped, Lieutenant Livermore wrote: "So complete a change would not be wrought by a quarter of a century of peace." Around this canvas city, former slaves established a camp of their own. They had fled to the Army of the Potomac because they needed protection and had nowhere else to go. All sought freedom; few found work. Many of the Fifth's officers, like their counterparts throughout the army, had black servants to prepare their meals, sweep and tidy their shanties, and keep their equipment clean. But most of these freed slaves—contraband of war, in the official vernacular and often in the conversations of the soldiers—lived in squalor in ravines and woodlands on the borders of the camp near Falmouth.

Conditions in these squatter camps caused such concern in early 1863 that the army ordered a detail to investigate. Among those sent was William Child, the Fifth's assistant surgeon. Child described the Falmouth camp itself as "the picture of desolation." Dead horses and mules were drawn into piles around abandoned corrals. "Their bloated, decaying, festering bodies filled the air with an intolerable stench, and afforded a disgusting feast to the thousands of buzzards which gorged themselves until unable to fly or walk, and then spewed out the half digested, fluid filth," Child wrote. In the squatter camps he found thousands of black people living with scant food or shelter and no means of improving their lot. "Many of these sickened and died on account of exposure to cold, rain and snow, general neglect, and a personal lack of common sense in caring for themselves," he wrote. "They were absolutely without hope, worthless and utterly dejected in spirit, diseased in body and debased in soul." They were also, he decided, "a burden on the government."

Such encounters did little to arouse the sympathy or broaden the views of even educated men like Child, who saw Negroes less as people than as an alien and inferior species, a curiosity encountered on a journey far from home. A few months after his tour of the squatter camps, the doctor attended an entertainment at a large camp hall near Boston. Some officers brought in several contrabands and a banjo. This troupe "made right hideous with their thumping and singing," Child wrote to his wife. "A negro will be a nigger at all events. There was one little fat fellow that just filled my eye. He was black as night with thick projecting lips, large white rolling eyes and wide, open mouth full of shining teeth." The men asked the blacks to sing "The Linkum Gunboats Are Coming," and after a few moments of animated but feigned reluctance, they complied. "I thought the d——l was coming instead of the gunboats," Child wrote. The officers gave the performers whiskey. The result was "more awful singing, more vigorous dancing, broader grinning, more rolling of the eyes, more gravity of face and more of the nigger in general on the part of the contrabands and more mirth on the part of the officers. How they would 'go it.' One would alone sing a few words all the while thruming the banjo, then all hands would sing the chorus with upturned faces, half closed eyes and fully extended mouths—the banjo 'nigger' redoubling his efforts. Well, a negro will be a 'nigger.'"

Livermore, like Child an educated man, referred to Negroes as "little darkies" and sometimes projected the misdeeds or sloth of a servant onto the race as a whole. When he received a letter from home asking "how many of the 'dear negroes'" he had liberated, he found it amusing. "I was a complete believer in emancipation," he wrote, "but I had not grown to regard the negroes with great affection." To illustrate his feelings, he told the story of an old Negro servant whom the officers called "Gabriel." Lieutenant Charles Hale, Livermore's new tentmate, had brought Gabriel with him from his former company, where the man had cooked for Captain Perry until Perry's death at Fredericksburg. Gabriel slept in a small tent next to Livermore and Hale's. He cooked and washed all day, singing hymns all the while. To Livermore's chagrin, he learned that "the thrifty old saint was not content with his wages from us, but took in washing from the men." Livermore looked into Gabriel's tent one day and was alarmed to find it half filled with clothes. The clothes, some of which were inhabited by lice, were too near the food supply. Livermore tried to convince Gabriel to keep the dirty clothes away from the food but concluded that he was too stupid or too stubborn to listen, and they parted ways. Experiences like this one reinforced the racial prejudices ingrained in the men by the years of polarizing debate that had led the country to war.

When words turned to war, these prejudices did not prevent minds from changing on the larger issue of slavery. Quite the contrary. In Livermore's case, the change was from the abstract to the immediate. If his encounters with black people discouraged him about the prospects of that race, the experience of war cemented his belief that slavery's hour was passing. General McClellan had warned Lincoln at Harrison's Landing the previous summer that shifting the aim of the war from preserving the Union to freeing the slaves would cause a revolt in the ranks. Even though Edward Cross was a Democratic extremist and many in the Fifth shared their colonel's political sentiments, Livermore disagreed with McClellan's assertion. For him, "the negro question" was no longer philosophical but now practical: time and events had answered it. "When we enlisted and before we fought we declared, when we said anything about it, that we were not going to fight for abolition," Livermore wrote. Then the fighting began, and "the practical aspect which the question assumed soon convinced all earnest soldiers that when the negroes fled to us they ought to be free; they worked for rebels at home, served them in the army, and labored on their fortifications under the lash, while when they escaped they brought loyal hearts and willing hands, as well as valuable information, to us." In Livermore's thinking, this was the reason no protests boiled up from the ranks when it became known after Antietam that Lincoln proposed to free the slaves in the rebel states.

Practicality aside, where it did exist, opinion against the Emancipation Proclamation was sharp. The newly promoted Corporal Miles Peabody, who was an avid and politically attuned newspaper reader, wrote to his parents in January 1863 to dampen their optimism about the effects of Lincoln's limited freeing of slaves. The proclamation, he wrote, "is not worth the paper that it was wrote on for it cannot take efect only as the Slave States are conquered. And now mark my words, before six months more rolls by, the South will have acchieved their independance, and be recognized by Forign powers." Peabody's parents responded with surprise at what they saw as a souring of his political outlook. "You seem to think that I am getting a little secesh," he wrote back, asserting that he was far from alone. "You cannot find hardly a Republican in this Regt." In a letter to his brother and sister, Peabody was even blunter. "When I enlisted I supposed that I was to fight to restore the Constitution and the Laws," he wrote, "but I found out that I was mistaken for it has been all nigger nigger. As for me I did not come out here to shed my blood for the sake of raising the niggers on an equal footing with the whites, and if there be anyone left in your vicinity who want to fight for that purpose, jest send them out her and I will let them have my chance." Peabody's view of the Union army's prospects reinforced his discouragement over the shifting cause of the war. "The course that the Government has pursued toward the South has been such as to unite them to a man," he wrote. The Rebels were "now fighting for their homes and their properties and who can blame them for fighting for that? The way the war has been carried on for nearly two years plainly shows that we cannot conquer them. What then in the name of Heaven, I ask, is the use of wasting any more blood and treasure in so hopeless a task! Why not conclude some honorable peace with them, and let them go? Is not the soil of the South suffisantly drenched with the best blood of the North to satisfy even the raving fannatics of the North? There is not scarcely a man in this Regt. who, if he was at home, would vote to help carry this war on any longer."

Colonel Cross's views on slavery and the causes of the war differed only slightly from Corporal Peabody's. He would have loathed Peabody's defeatism, but he was scathing in his criticism of Union leadership. His long-held disdain for abolitionism figured prominently in his assessment. He believed that proponents of abolition determined who got ahead in the army, much to the detriment of the war effort. Cross was desperate for a promotion to brigadier general and followed with interest the appointments of new brigadiers. Writing to former president Franklin Pierce, now a Democratic patriarch in Concord, Cross noted that Lincoln had handed out several stars in early 1863, "and had the Army been searched for that purpose he could not have selected more unworthy men." While drunk and unfit radical Republicans became generals, he wrote, the abolitionist governor of Massachusetts, for one, succeeded in pushing political rivals out of the army. "Noble and well-tried officers" were ousted "through the spleen & malice of John A. Andrew & associates," Cross wrote. "Did anyone ever hear or know of anything equal to the malice of Niggerism!" The colonel informed Pierce that the Army of the Potomac was again "full of Abolition spies, under the guise of tract distributors, State Agents, chaplains, & Sanitary Commission agents. The correspondents of the Abolition papers are also among the worst and most malignant spies of the administration. Every opinion an officer privately expresses in social conversation is likely to appear against him when he least expects it. All the 2d & 3d rate officers, the sneaks, the malingerers, the cowards, have found this out, & cover their deficiencies by the cloak of Abolitionism. That is why so many of this sort are coming up to be Colonels, Generals, etc."

In fact, defeats on the battlefield and Lincoln's turn toward abolishing slavery had bolstered opposition prospects in the coming New Hampshire elections. Democratic rhetoric, both in the party organs and from the mouths of the candidates, influenced the harsh view expressed by the Fifth's Corporal Peabody and soldiers of like mind. The Democrats running for Congress said they preferred the downfall of the government to the enforcement of the Emancipation Proclamation. Writing of the proclamation in his *Patriot*, Concord editor William Butterfield accused Lincoln of "the greatest crime ever committed by a Chief Magistrate of a free people." The *Laconia Democrat* cried that "Now is the time to strike down the abolition traitors who have deluged the land in blood." After Congress passed the Conscription Act, granting the president drafting powers normally restricted to governors, the Laconia newspaper wrote: "Who would have thought that we were coming to this? . . . When he calls for one-third, or one-half, or even the whole of the enrolled militia, they must march! And all to free a set of nasty, thievish, lazy niggers."

New Hampshire Republicans knew that these views were gaining favor with the electorate. On January 1, the night they heard from Cross at their nominating convention, they praised Lincoln's "vigorous and decisive measures" to put down the rebellion but carefully avoided endorsing the Emancipation Proclamation. They nominated a railroad man, Joseph Gilmore of Concord, for governor. With the war effort stalled, however, Gilmore's election was in doubt. To hold the governor's office, the Republicans cooked up a scheme. Walter Harriman, editor of the *Manchester Union* and colonel of the Eleventh New Hampshire, had been Gilmore's chief challenger for the nomination. Party leaders persuaded Harriman to run as a War Democrat. The aim was to deny the real Democratic nominee, Ira Eastman, a majority of the popular vote, throwing the election into the Republican-controlled House. For insurance, the governor brought the Second New Hampshire home from the Army of the Potomac's camps to vote. The scheme succeeded, but barely. Eastman won 49 percent of the vote, Gilmore 43, and Harriman 7. The House elected Gilmore governor.

In Virginia, the soldiers of the Fifth New Hampshire followed these events through letters and newspapers from home, but their focus never strayed far from the prospects of the regiment and the army. As the weeks passed after the Fredericksburg disaster, many officers and soldiers returned to the regiment from furlough and convalescent leave with fresh accounts of events in New Hampshire and speculation about the regiment's future. There seemed to be a new rumor daily. One day the Fifth was going home, the next it was headed to Fort McHenry in Baltimore, the next to garrison duty in Washington. Word of Cross's desire to be assigned to Arizona reached the men, who fanned the rumor to their advantage. Cross "has been appointed military Gov. of the Teritory of Arizona and very likely we shall go with him and spend the rest of our time there," Corporal Peabody wrote to his parents. "I had rather do that than remain here for we shall not have so much fighting to do there and I think we have done our share of that." Peabody developed this thought further in a February 14 letter to his brother and sister. "I have often thought what a fool I was in coming out here," he wrote, "but then I don't think I should ever have satisfide myself until I had come and seen the elephant, but I have had a pretty good chance to see him and I am fully satisfide." So many of the regiment's officers were dead or departed that the camp buzzed about who would be promoted, but mainly the soldiers worried about the next battle. Fredericksburg had doused any faith they had in Burnside. Like Peabody, many now wondered if the South should not be left to go its own way. On the other hand, experience led them to believe that more bloodshed was certain — and probably imminent.

For two of the family men among the Fifth's officers, Captain Larkin and Doctor Child, pessimism ran deep during the weeks after Fredericksburg. Larkin remained homesick, longing to see his children's Christmas stockings hanging in their Concord home and to take his family for a sleigh ride. But he also shared with his wife Jenny his view of the war effort. "What a thought to contemplate, the vast army of cripples the country will have thrown back uppon it should the war end even now," he wrote. "Then to think it may yet last for years makes me heartsick. It may all be for the best, yet it is hard for us to see it." At about the same time, a beautiful night at the end of an unseasonably warm day drew Child into a contemplative mood. Through his open tent flap, he heard the music of a brigade band. "A thousand campfires all around us are dimly glimmering through their own smoke amid the pine and oak trees," Child wrote his wife. "The soldiers have gone to rest and to dream of home." He soon found himself reflecting on the future. "We must prepare for worse times than we have yet seen," he wrote. "Many homes both north and south are yet to be desolated. There are yet to be more widows and orphans — more childless fathers and mothers. . . . Death has not yet had a sufficient harvest, though one would think that he must be glutted." This dark thought led Child in subsequent days to more pointed doubts about the prospects of the Army of the Potomac. "We send out great expeditions which so far have resulted in nothing that tends to put out the rebellion. Our large army has met with defeat after defeat, and yet we are always boasting of superiority. When shall we see ourselves as we are?" Child could not discern how the tide might be turned. "Disaster so often comes when we are assured of success that all the army are becoming tired of the present state of affairs," he wrote. The only hope was bold new leadership. "The fact is we want the man — the great man who is able to combine and direct our strength and lead us on to victory," even "a slow but sure success. We have not yet seen the man. Is there one?"

Although Fredericksburg had confirmed General Burnside's own doubts about his fitness to lead the Army of the Potomac, he remained in command. Now, despite the obstacles presented by winter, he sought atonement for

Fredericksburg with a new campaign. Burnside's corps commanders, many of whom disparaged him privately and, in some cases, coveted his job, doubted the wisdom of a January attack. Burnside ignored their counsel, winning tepid support from Washington to send his army across the Rappahannock above Fredericksburg to drive Lee's army from its stronghold.

The Fifth New Hampshire scarcely had the command structure or the manpower to join the march, but the men expected to go nevertheless. On January 16, they were read marching orders during dress parade, but these were countermanded. The next day Burnside himself reviewed them. According to Private James Daniels, the regiment again received "orders to march at a moment's notice." The men were told to pack three days' rations and sixty rounds of ammunition and to prepare to leave their knapsacks behind. One man from each regiment was to stay and guard the camp. Corporal Peabody correctly guessed that Burnside intended to cross the river well above Fredericksburg, but he wondered how the army could ever take the Confederate positions on Marye's Heights and the other hills that rose above the town. "It does not seem possible that our Gens. think of attacking that place again after such a lesson as they rec. there before," he wrote. The word around camp was that Lee had sent many of his troops west or south, but Peabody feared "another trap." Captain Larkin was likewise gloomy. "I am fearful it will be a sorry job," he wrote his wife, "but time can only tell. I have not the courage that I had when we went over before. Neither have the men." The regiment had no staff officers, only two captains—Larkin and Richard Cross—and no colors. On January 20, Peabody wrote his parents that the corps of Generals William Franklin and Joseph Hooker had been passing by all morning and the men of the Fifth expected to leave at any time. "This Regt. feels rather downhearted at the prospect," he wrote. "Many of them say that they will not go into another fight, but I have never refused to fight and shall not now." Livermore stood in the rain and wind with others in his regiment to watch "various columns of troops filing by us up the river, and as the news spread about that another movement against the enemy was in progress, we waited with patient hearts for our orders to pack up."

Fortunately for the Fifth, the orders never came. The movement was a disaster. It rained for more than twenty-four hours, the army sank in the mud, and soon Burnside had to call it back. Child described the scene: "Such mud I never saw or imagined. It would average from six to twelve inches—and every few rods a pit that would swallow a wagon, six mules and all." Peabody wrote his parents that the army had spent three days trying to advance during the worst storm of the season. "No pen can portray what they suffered in that time," he wrote. "It is said that they were in a state of mutiny until they were ordered back. It is a most disasterous faliour, for a large No. of soldiers have perished in the storm. It was rumored that the night after the troops returned that Gen. Burnside had three balls shot through his tent, but I will not tell it for truth." Livermore, in whose care Colonel Cross had left his horses, rode out to watch the pioneers working knee-deep in mud to lay the corduroy roads upon which Burnside hoped his sunken and dispirited divisions might return to camp. "To get them back was the most difficult part of what was termed 'Burnside's Mud March,'" Livermore wrote. Child believed that if his neighbors in Bath could have witnessed the march, "they would then believe that experienced Generals here know as much as inexperienced fools in New England."

The debacle ended Burnside's short term at the head of the Army of the Potomac and left his army in despair deeper than the mud. Agitated by the late events, Child wrote to his wife: "Will fortune ever favor us? All are sick of the war and wish for peace. But shall we yield thus? No—call out every man at the North that can perform any kind of military duty. Pour them then down over the South. What the enemy cannot slay, camp fever and dysentery will." While scorning this pointless loss of life, Child resented those who did not take up arms. "Oh, Carrie," he wrote, "why don't those at home who have been so firey and furious against any compromise come out here and learn what it is to be a soldier? Let them come here away from wife and children and every thing that makes life sweet. Let them march through snow and rain, through mud and hot burning sun, the ground for a bed, the sky for a covering. . . . Where are those in N.H. who have talked so bravely? Let them walk up to the Fredericksburg batteries. We need all their aid."

Some of the sour feelings within the regiment reached the public directly. An unusual example was a maudlin essay from the chaplain, Milo Ransom, who had been with the Fifth since just before the regiment set sail from the Peninsula. Ransom wrote to the *Statesman* in Concord with the ostensible purpose of defending the army's surgeons against widespread accusations of incompetence. Newspaper correspondents in the field, Ransom wrote, "report for facts occurrences which have no foundation—mere inferences—which are perceived by the public as 'the truth and nothing but the truth.' Our army surgeons have been accused without mercy and without truth." As proof that the press's exaggerations had sunk in, Ransom cited a recent conversation he had had in Washington, D.C., with an unnamed man from New Hampshire. "Half our army surgeons ought to be shot," Ransom quoted the man as saying. The chaplain went on to praise the surgeons of the Fifth in particular, assuring the *Statesman*'s readers that when the army set up camp on Bolivar Heights after Antietam, the sick had received the best of care. "Wine, jelly, and soft bread and butter were given to them every day," he wrote, "and they were daily visited and prescribed for by one of the surgeons in charge." As chaplain, Ransom was stationed in the hospital and would naturally have taken criticism of the surgeons personally, but only toward the end of his missive did he disclose his ulterior motive for writing: a defense of his own profession. Many in the field and at home seemed to assume that chaplains were lazy in camp, cowards under fire, and prone to poor sermons. "The public have been misled, and some newspaper reporters seem to delight in slandering many noble Christian ministers," Ransom wrote. "Nothing is more conspicuous in newspapers than unjust attacks upon chaplains." For himself, Ransom accepted the cloak of martyrdom, writing: "It is 'no new thing under the sun' to have ministers of the Gospel serve as scape-goats, 'to bear off the sins of the man.' It is nothing strange to have them 'persecuted for righteousness' sake.'" He acknowledged that "a few army chaplains have yet to learn the rudiments of Christianity" but stressed the unfairness of judging the many by the few.

Captain Larkin's complaints remained more personal than either Child's or Ransom's. Larkin was pleased that the regiment had missed the mud march, but he brooded over his situation and the army's. His main complaint was that he still had had no leave, and until other officers returned he was unlikely to get one. His resentment led him to renew his bitter feelings toward Colonel Cross. It did not help that Cross was in Concord and had visited Jenny Larkin, whom the captain had not seen in more than fifteen months—or that she had found Cross engaging. The Larkins were romantics. Jenny Larkin sometimes sent verse to her husband, and the two of them shared a belief in spiritualism, the notion that the dead can be contacted through a medium. Before battle, if he had the opportunity, the captain always expressed his vision of the afterlife with his wife. In mid-January, when it appeared the regiment might again march on Fredericksburg, he told her not to worry. "If I should be wounded and live, I shall come home, and if I get killed, I should be sent home if possable." Even were the worst to happen, he wrote, "I know we will meet in that woorld where parting and Strife will never come." When Colonel Cross visited Jenny Larkin in Concord, he sang her husband's praises and engaged her spiritualist fancies. She wrote James Larkin to tell him of Cross's kindness and charm, and her husband responded playfully at first, then with a bitter edge. In a postscript to a mid-January letter, he wrote: "I was aware that Col. Cross was a spiritualist and a whiskey spiritualist and a good medium at it. I have seen its effects on many occasions. He is most anything for the occasion. I was in hopes he would be a Brigadeer." In Jenny's next letter, Larkin heard about Cross again. "You said the Col. told you he would get me ordered on recruiting," he responded. "I hope you know enough of him not to have believed it. You cant place any more confidence in his word than in the wind. He always has some fine story for every one, and that is the last of it." In addition to his longing for a furlough, Larkin resented being passed over for promotion. He was not the regiment's senior captain in terms of service, but he had been with the Fifth nearly every step of the way. Now, with Lieutenant Colonel Langley long gone and Major Sturtevant recently dead, Colonel Cross was promoting his brother Richard to major and Captain Charles Hapgood to lieutenant colonel. Hapgood had fallen ill on the Peninsula and returned to New Hampshire as a recruiter for seven months. He had missed the Fifth's fights at Antietam and Fredericksburg. This extended absence was not lost on Larkin, one of his rivals for promotion. "That is the way they do business in N.H.," Larkin wrote. "The ones that are at home the most get the best offices. Well, I don't care. I don't intend to stay with the regiment any longer than untill some of the officers get back. I suppose our Lieut Col. will be here soon if there is no danger of a fight."

The changes in command went all the way to the top. In addition to Burnside's downfall, two of his subordinates, William Franklin and the Fifth New Hampshire's corps commander, old Bull Sumner, left the Army of the Potomac, Sumner at his own request. In Burnside's place, Lincoln appointed Brigadier General Joseph Hooker, a West Pointer and Mexican War veteran from Massachusetts who had led one of the three Grand Divisions in Burnside's short-lived command. Both before and during the war, Hooker had regularly been involved in political scrapes. Lincoln knew he had been part of a cabal which had sought to undermine Burnside. But Lincoln's choices were limited, and Hooker's record on the Peninsula and at South Mountain and Antietam was admirable. Hooker had his work cut out for him. Poor leadership, slaughter and humiliation on the battlefield, bad food, and dreadful weather had sunk the Army of the Potomac's morale to a new low. Desertion was rampant, and cynicism ran high. As much as they welcomed Burnside's departure, the officers and men of the Fifth weren't sure what to think of Hooker. "Now [that] Joe Hooker has command you may expect to see something snap," the Fifth's Captain Frank Butler wrote home. "Some of us will get hurt. I wish he had been in command at Antietam and Fredericksburg." Less impressed, Captain Larkin wrote to Jenny: "The army has changed hands again, but no General has science enough to cope with Virginia mud."

Hooker's first order of business was to reorganize the Army of the Potomac and put into positions of responsibility men in whom he had faith. He improved the army's cavalry arm and its intelligence service. He swiftly cracked down on desertion, using soldiers in the field to stop men from fleeing and law enforcement officers all across the North to round up men who had disappeared from the ranks. He had incoming packages checked for civilian clothes. He also convinced Lincoln to sign an amnesty that brought deserters back to the ranks. Hooker liberalized furlough policies, heightening the anticipation of men like Larkin who had not been home since their regiments entered the field. He named a new medical director, and sounder sanitary practices soon curbed the level of sickness. He saw to it that the army received better food. And at the suggestion of Major General Dan Butterfield, his chief of staff, Hooker authorized the issuance of a distinctive badge to each corps. The badges were colored red, white, or blue to signify the first, second, or third division of a corps. In part, the purpose of the badges was to enhance order on the battlefield and discourage stragglers, but their chief result was to boost morale.

The men longed more than anything for leadership on the battlefield, but in the meantime, Hooker's "soft bread and onions" campaign won their approval. Like other soldiers, the men of the Fifth grew fond of their badge — a red trefoil, the trefoil the symbol of the Second Corps, under Major General Darius Couch, the red signifying the First Division, under Major General Winfield Scott Hancock. They wore their badges on their hats and painted them on their wagons, and the red trefoil soon became "a cherished token," Livermore wrote.

Before leaving New Hampshire to return to Falmouth, Cross visited Henry Kent at Camp Ethan Allen on the plains just east of Concord. There his old friend had taken command of the Seventeenth New Hampshire. Kent had encouraged his men to form a glee club, and Private Walter Binney became its star performer. For Cross, who loved music, Binney sang his signature solo, "Mother Magraw and Her Son." Cross also visited the former captain of his Claremont company, Charles Long, who had left the Fifth after being wounded at Antietam and was now Kent's lieutenant colonel. While campaigning with the Fifth in Virginia, Long had taken a black servant named George Saunders. Now Saunders was the Seventeenth's cook, mascot, and master of ceremonies. Saunders had a superstition that he was exposed to the devil's deeds each night between the time he uttered "amen" and the time he was safely in bed. It amused Kent and the other officers to watch him arrange his blankets so he could spring into them "before the debbel could ketch up with him." "George was a good boy," the Seventeenth's historian wrote, "but he had a white soul."

Cross left Concord on February 1, but his wounds had not sufficiently healed, and he lingered first in Boston, then in Washington. In the capital, he watched the conscription debate in the Senate and pursued his promotion. He remained doubtful about winning his brigadier's star, writing to Franklin

Pierce in Concord that Congressman Edward Rollins, a leading New Hampshire Republican, seemed to know "everything I said or done as a democrat." Rollins had endorsed the promotion in writing but without enthusiasm. To a note to Lincoln from other Cross supporters, he had appended a single sentence: "I hope that Col. Cross may be appointed Brig. Gen." By the colonel's own count, eleven generals had recommended him for promotion. But like Hancock, whose praise for Cross was effusive, nearly all the prominent civilians who wrote on Cross's behalf were Democrats. One was John Forney, the Philadelphia editor, whose letter to President Lincoln said Cross was "accomplished, loyal and full of the cause." Another was Robert Walker, who had served in President Polk's cabinet and been sent to Kansas as governor by President Buchanan. In early March, Cross himself wrote to Secretary of War Edwin Stanton to make his case. After enumerating his supporters and reminding Stanton that he had been "nine times wounded by balls during the present war," Cross could not resist showing his frustration and defensiveness at being passed over. "As an act of justice," he wrote Stanton, "I ask that my case be considered, and that I may be informed if there is anything against my character." Cross seemed resigned to remaining a colonel and inclined to stay in the army. "My senior officers oppose my resigning and my Regt is in great trouble about it," he wrote Pierce.

Newly promoted Lieutenant Colonel Hapgood reached the Fifth's camp near Falmouth on February 3 and, with Cross absent, assumed command. One of his first acts was to present to the regiment a "new and splendid sett of colors" that Cross had procured from the governor in Concord. "As the colors carried at the head of the Regt in former times . . . were never trailed in the dust, so these, while the gallant men of this Reg't live, shall never be dishonored but be returned to our State when Peace shall again spread its benign influence over our whole land," Hapgood wrote the governor. The men knew Hapgood as a solid and steady officer and a devout Christian. A man of thirty-two years, he had grown up in Shrewsbury, Massachusetts, and learned the gun-making trade at the shoulder of his father, Jacob. He married in 1854 and by the time war broke out had established himself as a merchant in Worcester, Massachusetts, and Amherst, New Hampshire. In September 1861, he disposed of the businesses and accepted a commission as a captain to command Company I of the Fifth New Hampshire. Hapgood was a resourceful man and a good judge of character who earned the respect of both his superiors and the men who served under him. Unlike Cross, he was neither hot-tempered nor opinionated, and as a result, he had good relationships with men on Cross's bad side as well as his good.

In his first report to Governor Berry, written from the Fifth's camp a week after his arrival, Hapgood put the best face on the regiment's situation. "I find the men in very comfortable quarters with plenty to eat and apparently in good spirits, tho' sadly reduced in numbers," he wrote. In fact, recruits and men returning from illness, wounds, and furlough had bolstered the numbers. Two hundred thirty-two officers and men were present for duty; 274 were listed as absent, although many of these were gone for good. Hapgood submitted a report to New Hampshire's adjutant general enumerating the Fifth's casualties to date. One hundred sixteen members of the Fifth had been killed or mortally wounded in battle, and 104 had died of "natural causes," he wrote. Perhaps his long absence from the field had made the problem seem more acute than it actually was, but Hapgood noticed an annoying practice in camp and took steps to stop it in his regiment. "The habit that prevails to an alarming extent in some reg'ts. of this Brigade of hooting and shouting to both officers and men it is hoped will not be indulged in this command and it will not be tolerated by anyone," he said in a February 11 order. He added that he did not mean to interfere with "a cheerful flow of spirits in any one but rather to encourage it." A mild case of smallpox interrupted Hapgood's first month of command. "Although I went into his tent and conversed with him, I did not take it," Lieutenant Livermore wrote.

In early March, there occurred an event that pulled the men's emotions in two directions. With the mail came many boxes that had been held up for months. Some of them were addressed to men who had been killed at Fredericksburg or had died of their wounds—a reminder of lost comrades and futile campaigns. On the other hand, the receipt of so much largesse from home was a "Grand Jubilee," in the words of Private James Daniels. The company commanders opened the boxes of the men who were no longer with the regiment and found that most of the food—"comprising almost everything prepared in New Hampshire kitchens," Livermore wrote—had spoiled. There were a few useful articles of clothing, but the real treasure was liquid. "Out of nearly every box there came a bottle, jug, or can of wine and other liquor, from the vilest to the best," Livermore wrote. The men received some of the drink, but the officers kept most of it for themselves. In Livermore's cabin, "the commanders of several companies indulged themselves on a liberal allowance." The homemade food in Corporal Miles Peabody's box was ruined except for some doughnuts and butter. Even these "tasted very strong of new leather." Peabody's palate tolerated the odd taste because of its source. The food had been packed weeks before with the new boots he had requested. These were "jest the fit and they are a noble pair. I have been offered $10 for them but would not sell them at any price," he wrote to his parents. Colonel Cross's frequent complaints to the governor and other higher-ups that the men wore out shoes in a matter of a few weeks' marching attested to the value of a good pair of boots.

Because it had lost so many officers at Fredericksburg and through resignation, the Fifth needed new lieutenants and captains. These company-level promotions reflected a veteran regiment that had seen fierce fighting. In an order dated March 16, Adjutant Charles Dodd listed four sergeants and a private to be elevated from the ranks to second lieutenant. Three of the five had been severely wounded, and the other two had been cited for meritorious conduct in battle. One, Ruel Austin, had been saved at Fredericksburg when the minié ball that felled him hit his pocket watch. Austin, Dodd's order said, "has carried the national colors in every battle in which the regiment has been engaged." The officers who moved up to company commands, including Thomas Livermore, had similar credentials. Cross appended a note to the order, ending with a sentence that became a motto for his command: "The Fifth New Hampshire Regiment never changed its position under fire, except towards the enemy."

Cross returned in mid-March and quickly dispelled any lingering clouds of despair over his regiment. With his flair for the dramatic, he asserted his authority by stripping a sergeant's chevron off his sleeve in front of the men. The disgraced man was Amos Lawrence, whom Cross had charged with feigning a wound and leaving the field during the march to battle at Antietam Creek. "The Col. takes this occasion to state that Serg't Lawrence was liable to be tried for his life, but it was not deemed expedient to tarnish the reputation of the Reg't by bringing one of its Serg'ts to trial for cowardice," Cross's order read. He shipped Lawrence to the ambulance corps with a copy of the order. Now that the Fifth's ranks were restored, the colonel saw to it that the men drilled hard. In Private James Daniel's terse diary, drill, inspection, and dress parade began to appear in nearly every entry. Cross embraced his veteran officers, letting them know that he reciprocated the respect they bore him for his courage and leadership. He clearly wanted to put the discord of late 1862 behind him. Captain Larkin, who had at last received his furlough and overstayed it, returned to find Cross showing affection for him. When the colonel assigned him to lead 290 men on the picket line, he lent Larkin his horse. Particularly to men like Larkin who had been with the regiment from the beginning, the colonel's iron hand and all-seeing eye were welcome. His absence had caused them to realize that their identity as a regiment was intertwined with Cross's sternness, decisiveness, and valor. They had seen him bloodied in three battles. They knew he wanted his brigadier general's star, and although they could guess that his own impetuosity and his politics kept him from getting it, they also knew he deserved it. They had heard him threaten again and again to return to the West, and yet here he was, a man they could follow with pride and confidence even if Hooker proved to be another loser. As a symbol of their admiration for Cross, the officers and soldiers took up a collection and bought him a saber and gold-plated spurs and ordered him a gold watch.

Hooker's attention to discipline, health, food, and cleanliness matched Cross's priorities in the Fifth's camp. As the case of Corporal Schribner Cates demonstrated, the premium on order applied to the lowest link in the chain of command. The order punishing Cates for failing to keep his men in line put all the Fifth's sergeants and corporals on notice "that they will be reduced to the ranks instantly if they fail to prevent quarreling, wrangling and loud talking in their quarters." Surgeon John Bucknam began inspecting each company's mess. His report one day praised the quality of the soup in six of the ten companies, criticized it as "slightly burned" in two others, and cited the final two for too much grease. The same day, a brigade inspector checked the Fifth's ranks for cleanliness and gave nine of the companies high marks. The inspection report noted that "the Col. himself desires particularly to speak of the neat appearance of Co. E and to express his opinion that Corp. J. Lynch of said Co. was by all odds the neatest appearing soldier in the regiment." Cross exempted the cleanest soldier of each company from one tour of picket duty. Company F, under Captain Albert Cummings, was the black sheep of the regiment on this day. The inspector rated the company inferior and named three of its privates as the regiment's most slovenly soldiers. All drew extra duty. The shaming was not lost on Captain Cummings. When the next inspection came eight days later, the inspector wrote: "Co. F is noted as one of the cleanest companies of the Reg't and particularly the company quarters."

As the Fifth rounded into fighting trim again, some of its visits to the drill field were anything but routine. On March 22, Private Daniels noted in his diary that the men were formed to hear that their former commander, Bull Sumner, had died the previous day at his home in New York, where he had stopped to rest before setting out for his new command in Missouri. Livermore offered faint praise for the general: "He was a noble-looking old man and an invincible fighter, but had not that genius which leads generals to fight their men to the best purpose." Two days later, as part of Hooker's campaign against desertion, the Fifth New Hampshire formed a line with its division of five thousand soldiers to watch three men drummed out of the service. The three had had half their scalps forcibly shaved from the forehead to the back of the neck. On their backs they bore large boards reading "COWARD." Guards stood six paces behind them with bayonets pointed at the men's heads. Behind the guards all the drummers, buglers, and fifers of the division—perhaps one hundred musicians—played the "Rogue's March." Prodded by their guards, the three cowards marched all around the line of soldiers. To men from a small state who valued their honor, the message was potent. It was "the most disgraceful thing that has come under my observation since being in the army," Child wrote home.

For Cross, Sumner's death had personal consequences. The general had intervened on Cross's behalf with the administration, asking not only that he be promoted to brigadier general but also that he be sent to the Arizona Territory. On April 14, Cross wrote to Franklin Pierce in Concord that Lincoln himself had promised him his star and that orders to Arizona "were in my hands when they were countermanded by the War Department on account of Gen. Sumner's death. Otherwise it would have been my future to join the destinies of a new territory. This hope kept me in the service—together with the natural reluctance which a commander feels to leave the tried, true & brave men of his command, who have so nobly acquitted themselves in this war." The colonel sensed that the promised promotion wasn't coming through either. He noted that Lincoln had already given several other colonels their stars and that the War Department seemed intent on forming recruits into new regiments rather than filling the depleted ranks of veteran regiments like the Fifth New Hampshire. In Cross's view, this was "one of the most *insane* and foolish ideas that could be entertained at this time. We should have another lot of armed *mobs* for the next year to secure defeat and disgrace." Nor could the colonel resist sharing with Pierce his real opinion of Hooker. He accused the commanding general of giving the chief sutler's job to a man whose "real business is to cheat the gov't—manage the newspaper correspondents—keep the *Hooker* sentiment up, by the aid of *whiskey* and *champagne*."

Meanwhile, all was not drill and discipline in the "Camp near Falmouth," as the men invariably described their winter quarters at the top of their letters home. When time allowed, the officers enjoyed the old camaraderie, socializing, singing, and playing cards. Captain Larkin and three lieutenants signed a self-improvement pact under which any of them caught swearing would be fined twenty-five cents per offense. The kitty, which was to pay for food, reached $1.25 the first day. "I think it will be a good thing and break us of the habit," Larkin wrote. During the wait for orders to move, the men amused themselves with a Saturday night dance—"Cotillions and Contra dances in the Company streets," Larkin informed his wife. Lest Jenny Larkin think he was stepping out on her, he quickly added: "We had no ladies but took turns in being ladies. I was lady for the Col. in one dance." Captain Livermore loved poker so much that he once played twenty-four straight hours. He lost a lot of money at it, too, but he didn't care. He was just nineteen years old.

Unlike many of the other officers, he had no wife and family at home depending on his pay. "The thought of what I should do after I left the army never stayed in my head long enough to fix a plan there, for I presumed it very likely that I should be killed before the war was over," he wrote. One night, several officers became rowdy while playing poker in a tent next to Colonel Cross's. Unable to sleep, Cross stewed until his anger boiled over, then crashed the poker game with a pair of handcuffs in one hand and a saber in the other. Silence reclaimed the night.

Cross employed pen as well as sword in his campaign to curb his officers' vices, warning them that when they gambled, their reputations back home were among the stakes. "To a game of cards, now and then at proper hours there is no objection," he told them in a circular. "But the practice of assembling evening after evening and day after day is very pernicious—especially when it becomes known to the enlisted men. They will be sure to follow the example of their superiors and will write home every fault they find against an officer to grieve his friends and gratify his enemies. Besides, gambling causes ill feeling, disappointment and trouble." As for cursing, the colonel advised, "Nothing so weakens the authority of officers over their men as rough vulgar language to one another. The men 'reason' if the officers do not respect each other why should we respect them?" As opposed to the saber-wielding terror of the wee hours, Cross conveyed this message "with cordial sentiments of friendship," writing: "Let us all remember that we have a character to preserve and that honor and chivalry are the true gems of a soldiers life."

While the Fifth took lessons in morale and morality, Confederate units lay just across the Rappahannock. The night Larkin rode the colonel's horse to lead the regiment on picket duty, he observed rebel soldiers fortifying their positions. "They seem to be very busy intrenching themselves," he wrote. "They have rifle pits through every street in Fredericksburgh and along the river banks for miles. I could see them drilling very plain." Sergeant Charles Phelps wrote his sister that the "Grey Backs" had managed to send "the Richmond papers and some tobaco across on a little boat and a note asking us to send them some coffee and a late paper." Phelps's companions complied with this request. Men of the two armies also bantered with one another. "One of them sung out for us to come over and take a drink and all go home," wrote Larkin. "I think they would be glad to do it."

By mid-April, Hooker had restored the Army of the Potomac and settled on a bold and imaginative plan of attack. The men of the Fifth did not know the plan, but as spring came to Virginia, they sensed a battle coming. Although Cross disparaged Hooker and longed for a return of McClellan to command the army, even he could see how well prepared the men were to fight. "No army in the world was ever better armed, clothed or equipped," he wrote in his journal. "All the vast resources of the nation—intellect, money, skill, and everything which could be suggested to make an army strong and confident, was lavished without stint." Larkin wrote home on April 13: "We don't heare anything about cumming home now and I don't think we shall come." The next day the men were ordered to pack eight days' rations and to be prepared to move by six in the evening. Hooker put a premium on mobility. The men sent their overcoats and other clothing unneeded for a spring campaign to Washington for storage. They packed only an extra shirt and pair of socks. They brought more rations than usual: sugar, coffee, bread, and salt for five days in their knapsacks, three days' full rations in their haversacks. Each man carried sixty rounds of ammunition. "This looks like woork, and hard woork," Larkin wrote his wife. But the captain didn't seem to mind. Whether it was the changes in the army since the dead of winter or more immediate pleasures—his recent leave, a package one of his lieutenants had just brought him from home, and the paymaster's impending visit—Larkin's outlook was once again sunny. "I think we shall clean out the rebs," he wrote. "Things look well and I think Hooker will either sink or swim, and I am glad something is to be done."

 Chancellorsville

"I think while I write they are trying to
flank us upon the right—the firing is
very rapid. Gen. Howard is there with
his corps and if they drive him they will
do well. The cannonading is terrible."
                    —Doctor John Bucknam,
                    May 2, 1863

FOR AN AGGRESSIVE REGIMENT LIKE THE FIFTH NEW
Hampshire, one of the rewards of survival was promotion. In October of 1861, Thomas Livermore had been mustered into the Fifth as his company's first sergeant at the age of seventeen. He was a handsome, bright, and serious soldier and, with two months in the disbanded First New Hampshire regiment on his record, an experienced one. The fearlessness of youth endeared soldiers like Livermore to Colonel Cross, who had been a brash and adventuresome young man himself not so many years before. When openings in command occurred through resignation or death, Cross liked to promote such men. They looked up to him for the right reasons, they stayed clear of the cabals his older officers sometimes engaged in, and they shared his taste for battle. Another such officer, twenty-year-old Captain William Moore, had been leading a company when he died at Fredericksburg, and now Livermore had a company of his own. A lieutenant since just after Fair Oaks, he welcomed the promotion to captain. But as the spring of 1863 came to Virginia and the army readied for a new campaign, Livermore wondered if he measured up to his new responsibilities. All indications were that he would soon find out.

By April, the Fifth had risen from a beaten remnant to a small but seasoned fighting force with a positive outlook. As the new commander of the Army of the Potomac, Joseph Hooker had yet to prove himself where it counted—on the battlefield—but the men owed their regiment's revival to his policies. Like their beloved McClellan, Hooker had allowed them to regain their strength while preparing them for battle. Desertion and death from sickness were almost unknown in the Fifth during those months. There were no new recruits, but men returning from the sick and wounded lists increased the regiment's rolls to more than two hundred. The Fifth regained its edge and yearned to settle the score with the Rebels.

Hooker's plan of attack made use of his vastly superior numbers—he had more than a hundred thousand men to about sixty thousand for Robert E. Lee—and it opened with a surprise. Lee's army was just across the Rappahannock, holding Marye's Heights in Fredericksburg in the center of a broken line that followed the river for twenty miles. Lee's left was near Chancellorsville, a crossroads in the Wilderness. While making displays elsewhere along Lee's line, Hooker planned to send the main body of his army—three corps comprising forty-two thousand infantrymen—to cross the Rappahannock far upriver, then circle back and fall on Lee's left flank. To the extent that Hooker could convince Lee that the Army of the Potomac's attention was focused on Fredericksburg, he could surprise him with a large concentration of forces at Chancellorsville. To aid in the deception, Hooker ordered ten thousand troops to a Rappahannock ford almost directly across from Chancellorsville. Their mission was to guard the main force's route to a ford farther upriver and to chase off rebel defenders. Once they had accomplished this task, they were to cross themselves, march the five miles to Chancellorsville, and join the rest of the army there.

Brigadier's star or no brigadier's star, Colonel Cross was to lead a temporary brigade on this assignment. Lieutenant Colonel Charles Hapgood had succeeded Cross in command of the Fifth, which joined the Eighty-first Pennsylvania and the Eighty-eighth New York to form Cross's brigade. The Pennsylvanians had served with the Fifth on the Peninsula, at Antietam, and at Fredericksburg. The Eighty-eighth New York came from the Irish Brigade, which had suffered so many casualties as to be near extinction. The Fifth had followed these men into battle at Antietam and Fredericksburg. Cross marched his old regiment and the Eighty-first Pennsylvania out at sunrise on April 28. "I am sure the Fifth Regiment was never in better fighting condition," he wrote. His brigade's destination was a stretch along the river up to United States Ford, a march of eight miles from its camp near Falmouth. The ford took its name from the abandoned United States Gold Mine nearby. The Fifth and the Eighty-first were assigned to occupy forty-one houses near the ford to prevent their inhabitants from informing Lee of the huge numbers of federal soldiers who were passing by on the twenty-five-mile march to Kelly's

Ford. The Fifth had charge of twenty-seven of the houses. These were rude but comfortable dwellings of wood and brick, many of them with chimneys at both ends. Their inhabitants were women, old men, children, and blacks.

The job of securing the houses proved to be a pleasant interlude. The spring weather was good, the duty leisurely and interesting. "We found the people very generally full of smothered rebellion, but quite civil," Cross wrote. On a small stream the men of the Fifth discovered an old gristmill. A man named Bradshaw had been the local miller until Union soldiers arrested him months before. An old black man had tried to take up the enterprise, but "the crazy old concern had got so much out of repair as to be useless." The Fifth's Sergeant Samuel Dolbear and a few other soldiers restored the mill to working order. During the next two days, the soldiers ran the mill, and local residents, under close guard, brought corn on their backs from distances of up to four miles. The soldiers made hoecakes, keeping some for themselves and giving the rest to their involuntary hosts. Although the soldiers had learned to appreciate if not enjoy the hardtack that was the staple of their diet, they were pleased to supplant it for a few days with something tasty and more digestible. There were other amusements as well. A resident told Doctor William Child, the assistant surgeon, about a buzzard's nest on the property of one of the houses the regiment was guarding. This, the man said, was an ill omen. The curious young doctor asked to see it, and the man obliged him. Child saw an adult buzzard move nervously but silently around the nest, which was situated in the hollow of a tree trunk; inside the nest he observed a young bird and an unhatched egg. "To the native these seemed to convey something of awe, but to the writer the only thing awful was the odor emanating from the nest and its surroundings," Child wrote.

Captain Livermore was in charge of guarding the dwellings in the center of the Fifth New Hampshire's position and had authorized the gristmill operation. With some other officers, he took over the first floor of a spacious and well-furnished house. Charlie Fullerton, a boy of about eleven from Concord, rounded up "a troop of little darkies" from the surrounding cabins to wait on Livermore and his lieutenant, Charles Hale. Charlie had acted as a valet ever since the regiment's formation, and the officers appreciated his efforts to provide them with sustenance and to keep their dwellings clean. After nights during which they caroused into the wee hours, they especially appreciated his habit of saving at least one bottle of whiskey for morning. Colonel Cross liked Charlie so much he gave him a pair of corporal's chevrons.

The easy duty of guarding houses lasted just two days. The order for the regiment to move out toward the river came at half past five on the afternoon of April 30. Hapgood, who had been staying in a comfortable farmhouse, finished his dinner of boiled mutton and called in the Fifth's sentries just in time to salute Hooker as the general rode past. Hooker's turning movement had succeeded. He had deployed the main body of his army across the river in a line threatening Lee's left. As the men of the Fifth prepared to march to join this vast army, there was only one discordant note. The lessons Hooker had tried to teach potential deserters had apparently not impressed Charles Hutchinson, a twenty-year-old private from Colonel Cross's hometown. When the roll was called, Hutchinson had disappeared. Cross fired off a letter to the *Statesman* in Concord purchasing advertisements in three successive editions giving the particulars of Hutchinson's desertion. "I want to catch Hutchinson and have him shot," Cross wrote. If presented with evidence that the private had been arrested and jailed in Concord, the colonel vowed, "I will pay fifty dollars in addition to the amount paid by the Government." Hutchinson managed to avoid his appointment with the firing squad, but Cross's bluster no doubt impressed others.

The Fifth marched off at dusk to join the main body of Hooker's army. The men soon reached the embankment leading down to United States Ford, where a pontoon bridge had been laid, and bivouacked near the river. At ten the next morning, on May 1, they crossed the bridge and scrambled up the steep wooded bank on the rebel side of the river. Wagon trains and artillery blocked the road, making for a laborious march. During one halt, an order from Hooker was read to the men informing them that the Eleventh and Twelfth Corps had crossed the river—"a brilliant success," the announcement called it. "The enemy now must come out of his trenches to fight us," the men were told. Captain Livermore recalled that the order "put everybody in good spirits, and we marched on with light hearts." Surgeon John Bucknam wrote home that the regiment "felt sure of a victory and an onward march to Richmond."

Five miles through the tangle of the Virginia Wilderness lay the Chancellorsville crossroads. This was the center of Hooker's line, and here the general had set up his headquarters in the large Chancellor house with its several outbuildings. As the Fifth started toward that point, Livermore heard the crash of artillery in the distance. "While my feet seemed willing to quicken their pace toward the field," he wrote, "I experienced a peculiar sinking sensation in the region of my heart, which, as nearly as I can analyze it, was rather the result of the instinctive dread of the unknown in battle, than the fear of death in battle. Something like the feeling which possesses one when in a dream he is falling from a great height, and yet not so near fear as that." Livermore found it odd that neither a charge on a battery nor the din of musketry in the heat of battle produced this effect on him. Rather it was "the sullen roar of these guns miles away, coming to us in the stillness and obscurity of the forest when we knew we were marching to encounter their fire." One factor that kept him going was his confidence that this new general—Hooker—at last had Lee where the Army of the Potomac wanted him. "I am not aware that I could have persuaded myself to turn back, with the prospect which we then believed lay before us."

The sounds Livermore heard came from a fight east of the Chancellorsville crossing. Hooker had sent two divisions and a corps toward Fredericksburg hoping to draw Lee's army into battle, and Lee had obliged him. Two miles out the Orange Turnpike, Brigadier General George Sykes's division of the Fifth Corps ran into a strong enemy force. Hooker ordered units from General Hancock's division to reinforce Sykes, but soon after they arrived and deployed on a ridge near the Newton house, he ordered them back. Hooker's idea was not to attack and destroy Lee's smaller army but to entice Lee to attack the Army of the Potomac in its strong defenses. The Newton house ridge was such a commanding position that Hooker's generals persuaded him to allow Hancock's men to remain there a while longer.

Cross's brigade, meanwhile, was still struggling through the clogged road from United States Ford to Chancellorsville. Upon reaching the crossroads, the men ate dinner to the sound of firing toward Fredericksburg. In midafternoon they marched out the Orange Turnpike toward the Newton house ridge. At the first halt, Livermore went to the surgeon and gave him his money, "which I did not wish to bequeath to any one who might cut my pocket out if I was killed." This worry proved premature. The Union troops were already pulling back in the face of an attack. The men of the Fifth encountered no enemy. "Thank God for the good fortune," Hapgood wrote in his diary.

The regiment returned to the Chancellor house, where Hooker instructed Hancock to face his division toward Fredericksburg. Hancock formed his men in three lines of battle, placing Cross's brigade in reserve. The men were ordered to dig in, but they had no tools. Hancock sent Cross eighty-nine shovels, fifty picks, and a dozen axes—a small supply for a unit of a thousand men. But with Cross standing over them, the men "completed one fortification in just forty minutes by the watch!" Within an hour they had dug a string of rifle pits six hundred yards long. They did not enjoy the protection of their handiwork for long. Ordered to move back, they marched off in moonlight so strong that they carried their weapons at trail arms lest the enemy pick up the glint of their barrels. The Fifth and Cross's other two regiments redeployed to form Hancock's extreme right, connecting with the division of Brigadier General John Geary from the Twelfth Corps. As they settled in for the night, the men were perfectly content to have avoided the fighting that day. "We for a wonder have escaped once," Sergeant George Gove wrote in his diary.

As always, the men were ignorant of the big picture. They certainly had no way of knowing that they were less than twenty-four hours from experiencing one of the most stunning movements of the war. During the night of May 1–2, as the Fifth changed position and tried to sleep, Lee and General Stonewall Jackson agreed on a daring plan. Hooker had put them in a tight spot, but they discovered a weakness in his army's position. The Rappahannock anchored Hooker's left flank, but the right flank of his four-mile line was exposed—"in the air," in the military vernacular. Because some of his army remained in Fredericksburg, Lee had only 41,000 soldiers available to him before Chancellorsville. Although this force was badly outnumbered, Jackson suggested that Lee split it, allowing Jackson to take 28,000 men on a march around Hooker's line without arousing the Federals' notice. Jackson proposed to march beyond Hooker's extreme right, reorient his forces in a battle line facing the exposed Union flank, and attack. Lee's part in this risky plan was to use the 13,000 men and twenty-four guns left to him to engage the enemy before him—the Union center, where Cross's brigade had just dug in. Lee's task was to avoid a full battle but to offer a serious enough challenge to occupy Hooker's attention while Jackson's men marched secretly around the Union flank.

The next day, the men of the Fifth took part in the fight against Lee's smaller force, not guessing it was a diversion. Confederate Major General Lafayette McLaws wrote that Lee had ordered his skirmish line to "make frequent demonstrations against the enemy in my front so as to create the impression that an assault was intended, but he did not wish me to really engage seriously, but rather to avoid doing so." Rebel artillery now occupied the Newton house ridge, where Hancock's division had been the day before. Shells fired from the ridge, coupled with demonstrative forays by Confederate units under McLaws and Major General Richard Anderson, kept Hancock's line occupied all day. Hapgood wrote that the rebel artillery fired old files and railroad iron on the Fifth beginning in early morning. In the afternoon he reported "a sharp fight" to the regiment's right, adding: "We appear to have the best of it." Cross sent a detachment under Captain John Ricker to join this infantry fight in the woods. The colonel reported that some nine-month men ran from this fight, but Hancock heard that the skedaddlers were from the Fifth New Hampshire. He sent word to Cross that some of his men had misbehaved. Cross could not brook for a moment the suggestion that soldiers from his old regiment had fled from enemy fire. With the fighting still in progress, he sent a messenger to the skirmish line to fetch Ricker. He took Ricker to

Hancock, and the captain assured the division commander that the men who had run were not from the Fifth.

The Fifth had no reason to view its endeavors of May 2 as anything more than an inconclusive battle that might precede a more serious one the next morning. The men were glad to have survived another day of fighting. As the sun set behind them, they broke out their rations. "We were resting easily with our arms beside us or stacked," Livermore wrote. "There seemed to us to have been nothing serious against us, and no one of us in the companies had reason to suppose we should be otherwise than successful." But the day was not done. "Our astonished ears were greeted with a sudden outburst of the most tremendous musketry" to the right and the rear, Livermore wrote. "We sprang to our feet and looked with anxious hearts across the plain."

For Bucknam, the Fifth's surgeon, the day had been one of waiting and trying to stay out of harm's way. A robust man who rode a fine black horse, Bucknam was a contemporary of Cross and had grown up with the colonel in Lancaster. He had been with the regiment from the beginning. On the morning of May 2, the rebel artillery fire had compelled Bucknam, Assistant Surgeon Child, and the other Second Corps doctors to move their hospital out of the Chancellor house clearing into the woods well behind the lines. They had used brush to fashion crude huts. For all their efforts, there were few casualties for the Fifth's surgeons to treat; the regiment had seen little action. Late in the afternoon Bucknam moved up to the line and found the men safely in their works and preparing to eat. He located a quiet spot and sat down to write in his diary. "It appears to be the object of Gen. Hooker to merely hold the place for the moment," he wrote. "Many rumors have been in circulation today—the principal one that the bridge is torn up between the Rebels and Richmond, and that they are completely surrounded. One thing is certain—they are very uneasy." The next sentence he put down in his diary marked the exact turning point in the battle. "I think while I write they are trying to flank us on the right—the firing is very rapid." But Bucknam had confidence in Brigadier General Oliver O. Howard, who had commanded the Fifth's brigade before being wounded at Fair Oaks and now led the Eleventh Corps on Hooker's extreme right. "Gen. Howard is there with his corps and if they drive him they will do well," Bucknam wrote. "The cannonading is terrible. I can hardly think."

Like Bucknam, Livermore was initially optimistic about the noise to the regiment's right and rear. Just nineteen years old and in command of an infantry company in battle for the first time, he thought the sound that suddenly filled the air was the Union cavalry riding in to attack Lee's rear. He shared this belief with those around him. He soon guessed the truth, but he kept up the

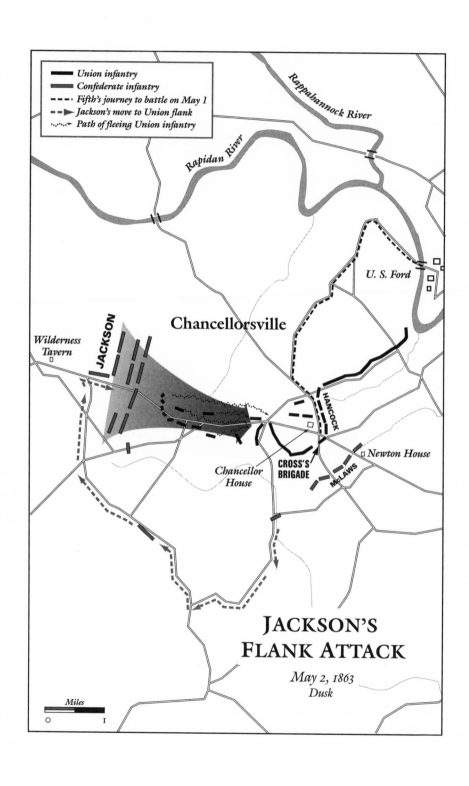

Union infantry
Confederate infantry
Fifth's journey to battle on May 1
Jackson's move to Union flank
Path of fleeing Union infantry

Rappahannock River

Rapidan River

U. S. Ford

Chancellorsville

JACKSON

Wilderness
Tavern

HANCOCK

Chancellor
House

CROSS'S
BRIGADE

Newton House

McLAWS

JACKSON'S
FLANK ATTACK

May 2, 1863
Dusk

Miles

0   1

appearance of being pleased. If he did otherwise, he worried, his men might join the panic—a needless fear, as it turned out. Before long, it became apparent to all that the increasing gunfire and furious clatter heralded bad news. Stonewall Jackson's men had achieved surprise, striking Hooker's right flank with superior force and speed. Many of the Union soldiers there were ill prepared. They saw themselves as having no choice but to run, be shot, or be captured. The effects of Jackson's blow reached the Fifth in a crescendo that became a stampede. Livermore described it thus: "Suddenly wagons, ambulances, men, artillery, and everything that makes an army, came rushing out of the woods on the north into the plain and across it and down the turnpike, and after a short interval a flying, confused, panic-stricken mass of soldiers in the direst condition, to the number of thousands, running for life, and alas! our own men."

Several of the regiments that were fleeing were Germans from Howard's Eleventh Corps—"Dutchmen," they were called. Even before the battle, most of the veterans had disparaged them because of their nationality and their newness to the Army of the Potomac. Hancock's challenge now was to stop the rout. "I had the rebels on my front, and the rebels and our stragglers on my rear," wrote Cross. Hancock swung Cross's brigade—the right of his line—to face the direction from which Howard's men were running. Cross ordered his men to fix bayonets and stop the flight of the Germans. Once the Fifth's company commanders had overseen the change of position, they stood behind their lines with swords drawn. It was an anxious time. A frantic artillery commander rushed up to Cross and asked, "What are you going to do?" "Stay here, sir!" the colonel replied. He tied his red silk handkerchief around his head and walked up and down the line shouting at the men to hold their position. They cheered in response. Livermore believed their resolve to stand their ground was buoyed "by their contempt for the Dutch who were running away." Cross was more direct. "The cowardice of the German troops was ludicrous," he wrote. "They hid in the woods, forced their way into our rifle-pit." The men saw Cross pursue an officer who tried to hide in a ditch. "Sare, you do nod know who I am!" the officer shouted. "I am a Prigadier General!" Cross replied: "No you're not. You're a damned coward." Doctor Bucknam, who had been writing in his diary when the rout began, hurried back to the corps hospital in the woods. When he had a chance to pick up his diary again, he wrote that Jackson's attack had created "a perfect panic" among Howard's men. The surgeons had had little to do during the day, but that quickly changed. "Hundreds and thousands came rushing back past our hospital," Bucknam wrote. "The wounded were brought in by the scores." Many of those who ran past the hospital escaped into the woods, but Cross estimated that his brigade turned back more than a thousand fleeing officers and men. The colonel called the rout "one of the most disgraceful scenes of the war."

The moonlight was bright again, and the mayhem lasted into the night. As the mad rush slowed to a trickle, the Fifth peered into the darkness for the rebel legions that had set Howard's men to flying. Livermore expected at any moment to order his men to stand against a charge, but "astonishing to relate the enemy did not advance across the plain." When the shooting died away, "an ominous silence prevailed," he wrote. In time, Livermore saw other Union troops move forward to check any further threat and marveled at the precision of their movement and at the sheet of flames that preceded the crash of their volley. After hours of fretful commotion, he and his men "slept a wakeful sleep."

The shock at what had happened did not diminish the regiment's confidence; the men had done their duty, and whatever the next day brought, they expected to do it just as well. Writing in his diary late that night, Lieutenant Colonel Hapgood described the evening's events in terms that, however terse, conveyed a veteran's calm about the turn the battle had taken. "At 6 p.m. very heavy firing at the extreme right," he wrote. "At $6\frac{3}{4}$ [we] are in again on the right. Howards corps broke & ran at the first fire, but by hard work we held the position & at 8 p.m. the 1st Corps came up and recovered the lost ground. 10 p.m. all quiet." Although the men could see and hear movement in the woods before them, they found only later that in the waning moments of the frenzy, Stonewall Jackson had become a casualty of his own success. He had pushed his men so hard and so fast, and so long into the night, that when he went out with a group of officers to scout ahead and see what the next day might bring, he exposed himself to confusion in the woods. A volley from one of his own units mortally wounded him.

After another night on edge, the Fifth New Hampshire awoke at five to the booming of Confederate batteries. Lee had seized the initiative with Jackson's flanking movement, and he did not intend to give it up. The shells falling on the Fifth's position foretold a long, discouraging morning. Forced back, they took a position in support of Captain Rufus Pettit's battery, but Confederate cannon soon found them again. The rebel guns "had come out of the woods and boldly taken a position on the plain and were firing on us and the Chancellorsville House at short range," Livermore wrote. Pettit's guns swung around to answer the new attack, putting the Fifth in a precarious spot. The men now lay in front of their own guns, where errant shells might land in their midst and the explosions of cannon fire assaulted their eardrums. The pounding cost Sergeant Major John McCrillis much of his hearing. But the real danger came from the rebel guns. "For about 40 minutes my command was under the heaviest fire it ever experienced," Cross wrote. To his chagrin, his brigade was again ordered back, as was General Geary's Twelfth Corps division, which fought beside the Fifth. Geary was a soldier after Cross's own heart, a six-foot five-inch Pennsylvanian who was blustery, opinionated, and ill-tempered—but a fighter. This made the order to fall back even more puzzling and galling. "I do not understand why Geary was not supported or re-enforced," Cross wrote. "The day was not lost if fresh troops and artillery had been thrown in. While lying under that awful fire my belief was that a fresh division and some artillery would soon be up to aid us, and I so stated to our men." All that kept Hooker's army from reversing the course of the battle was "a little vigorous action," Cross wrote.

The vigorous action Hooker ordered was in the wrong direction to suit Cross. The commanding general had had enough; he was withdrawing his army. As the Union line threatened to collapse around the Chancellorsville clearing, Hancock ordered Cross's brigade to turn. The Fifth's job now was to prevent a rebel attack on the retreating army. The Twelfth Corps marched out toward United States Ford, leaving Hancock's division to cover its departure. A shell set fire to the large Chancellor house, formerly Hooker's head-quarters but now a hospital. Some of Hancock's men helped the sick and wounded escape the flames. It occurred to Livermore that the Fifth New Hampshire was in a familiar position—acting as the rear guard, as it had during the retreat from the Peninsula and the second battle at Bull Run. "No one could fail to see that our field had been abandoned and that our brigade remained in its position only for the purpose of delaying the enemy until the rest had got well out of the way," Livermore wrote. "Nothing could be more uncomfortable and few positions more dangerous than ours." The Confederate artillery continued to pound away. "The air seemed full of bursting shells," Cross wrote. "From our rear, from the left, from the front, came a storm of missiles." Livermore saw a shell strike a stump behind which several men lay, hurling them and the stump into the dust. Three times Cross sent his aide, Lieutenant Byron Fay, to inform Hancock that the line was disintegrating. As Fay was returning from one trip, shrapnel tore into his knee. He delivered the general's message first, then informed Cross that he was wounded.

Before the Chancellorsville campaign, Livermore had made it a special project to get two of his soldiers to march with the company into battle. Both, he believed, had somehow managed to avoid every previous fight. Now, as the shells flew, one of these shirkers, Private Jared Davis, tried to hide behind an empty cracker box whose boards were less than a half inch thick. Livermore thought this was funnier than an ostrich hiding its head in the sand, but Cross was not amused. He charged over to Davis and kicked him. "You will disgrace my regiment," he said.

The colonel was everywhere. When Pettit's battery faltered, Cross approached an abandoned gun, sighted it, and fired it accurately into the Confederate infantry advancing on the plain. Doctor Child, who had lain in the trenches with the men during much of the fighting around the Chancellor house, wrote his wife that Cross fired the cannon three times. "He is perfectly cool in battle," Child wrote, "though he will 'dodge' shell as well as myself." Cross was about to dispatch the Fifth to man Pettit's guns when Hancock ordered his command to abandon the plateau. "We were under fire from three directions," Sergeant Gove wrote in his diary. "The Rebels drove us." Colonel Cross admitted that his men fell into "slight confusion" during their retreat across the clearing, but once they reached the woods, "we marched steadily, though our ranks were thinned and shattered by grape, canister and rifle balls," he wrote. "Had we delayed five minutes more we should have been taken prisoners or cut to pieces."

In their haste to leave, the Fifth and the other regiments abandoned any wounded man who could not walk. Doctor Bucknam, who had been working with several other surgeons at the hospital in the woods, could not remember a more desperate moment. "The shells and grapeshot of the enemy come flying over our hospital and have wounded four men severely here," he wrote. "We are obliged to move back again and leave our wounded, some 250 in number, in charge of four surgeons detailed to remain." Only a few of the wounded soldiers were from the Fifth, but hope was slight for men stranded under such conditions. Although they had nothing to fear from the veteran rebel regiments that moved forward into the old Union positions around the Chancellor house, Lee's army had no food or medical supplies to spare.

The Fifth's retreat, which occurred at about ten o'clock in the morning, covered little more than a half mile in the direction of United States Ford, but for young Captain Livermore, it was a test. The path led through a thick wood, and because the men were under artillery fire, Livermore's company stretched out. He stayed on the left, as he was supposed to, and shouted at his men to remain in their ranks, but the march was rapid and chaotic. Some men broke and ran. Just before they reached their new position, a shell scored a direct hit on George Frye, a corporal in Livermore's company. Frye simply disappeared, and his comrades found no trace of him. Livermore's attention was drawn elsewhere at that moment. A fragment, perhaps from the same shell that obliterated Frye, struck Private Davis, the man Livermore had coaxed into battle. The shrapnel nearly tore Davis's left arm off. "I seized him by his other arm and supported him," wrote Livermore. "I thought that as long as I had induced him to go into this battle I would help him out." The captain stayed with Davis until they found an ambulance. The arm was later amputated.

When the Fifth reached its new position in the woods, it turned to face the pursuing enemy. The men were barely in place when the rebel artillery opened on them again. Shells stripped the limbs from the trees, and shrapnel knocked down men sent to haul water. Working under fire, the men threw up breastworks all across their front. While supervising that work, Lieutenant Colonel Hapgood had reason to be thankful for the Bible he carried. "I got hit by a piece of canister in the breast & it should have killed me but for my 'book of Psalm' which Emma gave me," he wrote in his diary. "Thank God for the protection." The breastwork provided a more substantial shield against the rebel shells. At the outset of one short barrage, the general of a nearby brigade happened to be in the Fifth's position. Rather than return to his own brigade, "he ran down behind our works among our men," Livermore wrote. Cross saw the general and "was hardly restrained from driving him out of the trenches, as he considered his example pernicious to the men." In both Hapgood's and Cross's eyes, the Fifth was safe for the time being. "Can now hold our present position," Hapgood wrote before taking up duty as the officer of the picket for the night. Cross thought his brigade's line was too strong "to be successfully assailed by infantry."

Although they were fatigued from battle, march, and labor, many of the men had trouble sleeping, even behind their barricade. Reminders that danger was near were all around them. Doctor Child would remember two things about this night. One was that artillery shells ignited fires in the woods, and some of the wounded burned to death. The other was the noise from the woods: "Groans and cries were continually coming on the chilly night air, while whip-poor-wills caused a strange, woeful chorus hour after hour as they cried again and again." Even with an occasional shell coming in and with these sad sounds to haunt them, some of the men managed to fall asleep in the rifle pits they had so rapidly dug. A shell landed near Livermore without exploding, and he "trundled it along and hit the leg of one of them." The man awoke with a start, thinking that he had had a narrow escape.

The captain's practical joke was the act of a man yet in his teens, but he had a man-size problem to face, too. Because his company had become strung out during the rush from the Chancellorsville plateau, he was now missing several men. Soldiers in the regiment gave vivid accounts of the deaths of the absent men, and Livermore and other company commanders were initially inclined to report the missing as casualties. "But in the course of this and the next day," Livermore wrote, "a part of the reputed dead men came to the companies." Their excuse was that during the rapid retreat, other units had crossed the regiment's path, and in the confusion they had strayed off with these men. Several of Livermore's men were among nineteen members of the Fifth who were convicted after the battle of deserting their companies in the face of the enemy. These men lost a month's pay and drew thirty days' extra duty at the odious but necessary task of policing the camp. Private James Bias was singled out for additional humiliation. For six hours, he had to stand under guard wearing a board around his neck labeling him a coward and a straggler. Mc-Crillis, the regiment's sergeant major, was also among the missing who later returned to the regiment. He said a piece of shell had hit him, causing him to lose his way. This story failed to spare him a reduction to the ranks, and he was returned to Livermore's company. Although he was erratic and sometimes drank too much, McCrillis was a good enough soldier that Livermore sought and obtained permission to allow him a sergeant's rank. But the young captain fretted for his own reputation because of the straggling under his command. "I was very much chagrined that after going through the battle so well, I had in the first battle in which I commanded my company lost some men in this manner," Livermore wrote.

The men of the Fifth remained with the rest of the Army of the Potomac for more than two days waiting for Lee's infantry to attack. There were several alarms, but no attack ever came. "No signs of the enemy," Hapgood noted in his diary on May 5. Lee had accomplished his goal of repelling another Yankee initiative by another Yankee commander, and he saw no need of assaulting a well-positioned and much larger army. As the men waited behind their fortifications, Livermore had a conversation with Cross that struck him as a telling reflection of the colonel's character. The captain told Cross that since Hooker had called a retreat and seemed unwilling to move forward again, he wished the Army of the Potomac would just cross the Rappahannock and be done with the campaign. Cross bristled. "What do you want to go across the river for?" he asked Livermore. His tone told Livermore that he did not appreciate anyone suggesting a retreat, and Livermore struggled to find the words to answer Cross's question without upsetting him further. In retrospect, Livermore came to believe that Hooker's army could have attacked and beaten Lee's army at any time. Cross's instinct, Livermore believed, had been sound. "Although General Hooker rode along our lines looking rosy and gallant, yet his courage or judgment was insufficient for the occasion," he wrote. Instead of advancing, Hooker's army lay in its well protected rifle pits for more than two days, then "stole away before light."

It was 3:30 in the morning on May 6 when Hancock received orders to withdraw his division and move it back across the Rappahannock over the pontoon bridges at United States Ford. With a familiar sense of humiliation, the men of the Fifth joined the parade of defeat. The fine spring weather had ended, and a heavy rain slowed the dark three-mile march to the river. "The mud was half a leg deep most of the way," wrote Cross. "All along the forest were columns of troops looking dirty, fatigued and anxious." Less than a week before, the Fifth had crossed the same pontoon bridge in the other direction with its hopes as fresh as its new battle flags. Now, Cross wrote, his men were "weary, sad and almost discouraged." They did not stop until they had reached their old camp near Falmouth. By then, they were "a tired and hard-looking set," in the words of Doctor Bucknam. Sergeant Gove summed up their feelings in a brief diary entry: "The whole move has been a failure. Very tired."

Several officers in the regiment elaborated on Gove's dim view of the campaign. Cross was scathing, as usual. Hooker was "completely outgeneraled," the colonel wrote. "[He] has not the amount of brains necessary to handle a vast army." Still loyal to McClellan, Cross contended that he had known from the beginning that this latest pretender would fail. "Hooker's popularity lay chiefly in the soft bread, potatoes and onions he issued," Cross wrote. "The army never believed him to be a great commander—never. His failure was predicted by thousands of officers and soldiers, from the first day he started." Hapgood tried to be forward-looking and positive but found he could not. "What the next move of Gen. Hooker will be is of course impossible to tell," he wrote, "but I have no confidence in his ability to handle large bodies of men." Doctor Child wrote his wife: "A decided and immediate success is necessary or we shall never succeed in consequence of the anti-war feeling at the North." Captain James Larkin was one of many who mistakenly believed that alcohol had impaired the commanding general's judgment at Chancellorsville, but he did identify Hooker's most obvious mistake: the failure to take advantage of his superior numbers. It was the common opinion in camp that "we could have whiped the enemy and anihilated the army if Hooker had only put the men in," Larkin wrote. "There was not half the army that fought. I believe Hooker was drunk. I havent a bit of confidence in him. He should not be allowed to command the Army for another day."

For the Fifth there were more changes in leadership, but Cross remained a force in the men's lives. On May 21, General Hancock assumed command of the Second Corps and Brigadier General John Caldwell replaced Hancock at the head of the First Division. Cross was given Caldwell's old brigade—but no general's star. Although Hapgood retained nominal command of the Fifth, even off the battlefield Cross stayed involved with the details of running the regiment. The colonel feuded constantly with Major J. H. Whittlesey of the adjutant general's office in Concord over the fate of individual soldiers. It angered him when men he considered shirkers and even deserters overstayed their leaves and wheedled discharges out of state officials. He saw such events as insults to the men in the field who faced death, then bore the hardships of service only to face death again. Two cases in point were Privates Benjamin Blaisdell and Benjamin Bean. "Blaisdell is a notorious malingerer and I have now ascertained that he boasted that he would never rejoin the reg't.," Cross wrote Whittlesey in May. "It is very embarrassing to a Col. in the field to be constantly in receipt of letters notifying him of the discharge of his men without consulting him in reference to their character. In the case of Bean, Co. E, now at Concord, his comrades say he declaired his intention never to rejoin the reg't. He has been advertised as a deserter and should not be discharged." Not all of Cross's correspondence in this period dealt with problem soldiers. In response to an official request to nominate men for the Congressional Medal of Honor, he had no shortage of candidates. The three he chose were Sergeant Gove, who had been wounded near the stone wall at Fredericksburg but had still not missed a battle, and Privates Ned Stinson and Leonard Howard, both of whom had been wounded at Fair Oaks and Antietam. None of the men received the medal.

Life back in the camp near Falmouth soon returned to normal. The weather was warm, dry, and pleasant. "We have concerts here of our own getting up," Larkin wrote home ten days after the retreat. "We have a Banjo, Violin, Tambourine & Bones." There were the usual rumors about transfers and furloughs. Cross traveled to Washington, and word filtered down to the ranks that he had asked the president himself to send the regiment home for rest and recruitment, but nothing came of it. Captain Livermore's problems leading his company away from Chancellorsville had not undermined Cross's affection for him. The colonel invited the captain to dinner to try a new hardtack pudding he had concocted. Though skeptical of the colonel's recipe, Livermore was enchanted by a pair of sentinels posted outside Cross's tent. These were tortoises that Cross kept tied so he could observe their habits. He told Livermore they were his "monitors." Late May and early June provided a stretch of such "pleasant memories" for the captain and others. One came on June 1, the anniversary of the victory at Fair Oaks. General Howard, who had lost his arm in that battle, reviewed his old brigade and returned with Hapgood to the Fifth's camp. Hancock, Caldwell, and other generals joined in the celebration.

As the weeks passed, it became clear that the defeat at Chancellorsville had been frustrating but not disheartening in the way of the slaughter at Fredericksburg. The Fifth had lost five killed and twenty-eight wounded; the men were accustomed to much longer casualty lists. They also believed that if Hooker had given them the chance to win, they would have beaten Lee. And they had something to show for their defeat—Lee's loss of a general whose reputation had reached mythic proportions in both armies. On June 6, Corporal Miles Peabody suspended his chronic negativity in assessing the Fifth's future. "It may be that Lee is laing in some place to trap our army, but I think that old Hooker will be too much for him this time, for our troops have no 'Stonewall' to fear now," Peabody wrote. "Our armies in the South West are gaining immortal glories for themselves and it will be a pity if we cannot do something at this time to immortalize our selves." The next night, Hapgood noted in his diary that he had been in charge of the brigade that day—or, more precisely, a portion of it. "The Col. and 300 men of the Brigade have gone up to the river on a secret expidition," he wrote.

13 Gettysburg

"Colonel Cross, this day will bring you
a star."
— Major General Winfield Scott
Hancock, July 2, 1863

WITH HIS CHANCELLORSVILLE CAMPAIGN IN MAY of 1863, Union General Joseph Hooker briefly stole the initiative from Robert E. Lee. By early June, ever the aggressor, Lee had it back. Seeking to relieve Virginia farmers and force a decisive battle, Lee chose to invade the North again. He began by moving his army west from its victorious battlegrounds at Fredericksburg and Chancellorsville toward the Shenandoah Valley. This set in motion events that immediately involved Colonel Cross and his old regiment, and soon drew the entire Army of the Potomac toward a climactic clash with Lee and his troops. "I hope our Army may be fortunate against Lee," wrote Doctor John Bucknam of the Fifth as the campaign unfolded, "but have some fear."

The concentration of rebel cavalry preceding Lee's army attracted the attention of Hooker, who ordered Union horsemen supported by infantry to attack the Rebels near Culpeper Court House. Keeping pace with the cavalry was all-important, so the infantrymen were to be picked with care. "It is desired that the command selected should be well disciplined and drilled," Hooker's order read, "and capable of performing rapid marches, and that the officers should be drawn from those noted for energy and efficiency." General Hancock selected Colonel Cross from among his ten brigade commanders to lead the Second Corps detachment of three hundred men. Cross in turn drew on the soldiers he trusted most: the Fifth New Hampshire, from whose ranks he filled half of the detachment, leaving fewer than fifty members of the regiment in camp. Cross divided his detachment into two companies, placing Captain James Larkin in charge of one and Captain Thomas Livermore in command of the other—a measure of his feelings for both officers. "This was esteemed a great honor," Livermore wrote. "Leaving everything but blankets and arms and equipment in camp, we marched away to the north with lively curiosity and pleasure excited by the entirely unknown undertaking we were destined for." The troops were under the overall command of Brigadier General David Russell, a tough-minded veteran whose service dated to the Mexican War. It was not long before their mission came into focus—and in Livermore's case, clarity brought anxiety.

On the evening of June 8, after a march of twenty miles, Cross's detachment camped in a meadow near Kelly's Ford, the same Rappahannock River crossing Hooker's main force had used on its way to Chancellorsville. After supper, the colonel called his officers together. Their task, he explained, was to drive off Rebels holding the other side of the ford, thus enabling the Union cavalry to cross safely. Because the Union army had used the ford not long before, the Rebels were believed to have cannon guarding it now, so the attack would be made by surprise at night. Larkin was to command the first boatload of soldiers to cross—a "forlorn hope," Cross called it, a Napoleonic term for the first men to storm the walls of an enemy fort, men whose likely fate was death. "We shall move down to the river before light," Cross said. "You will see that the utmost silence is preserved in the ranks and that the men's dippers do not rattle against their bayonets, as we do not wish the enemy to know of our approach." The men were to capture the battery without firing a shot. "Your uncle will be there to lead you," Cross said of himself. "Now go back and go to bed, but do not expect to sleep more than a wink, for we shall move at two o'clock in the morning." Livermore saw no prospect for rest, not given such a briefing. "To meet death was our business," he wrote, "but this certain and accurately located battery to be stormed by us in so desperate a manner as to have been termed a forlorn hope, when it seemed inevitable that many of us would be killed, was a little startling." For Livermore any chance of sleep was lost when rations for the entire detachment arrived— in bulk. Livermore busied himself dividing the pork, coffee, sugar, and hardtack into portions to be distributed among the men.

It was four in the morning when the soldiers filed down the riverbank. Two wood-and-canvas boats were waiting, each capable of carrying about twenty men. As Larkin led the first men across, rebel pickets fired several stray shots from the far shore; every man tensed, but then all was quiet, save for the whisper of boats slipping through water. Livermore crossed on the boats' second trip, and the Union troops hurried up the bank and waited in the brush. As the sky brightened they could see a field before them about a half mile wide; on its far side were several rebel cavalrymen and a bank of red clay that

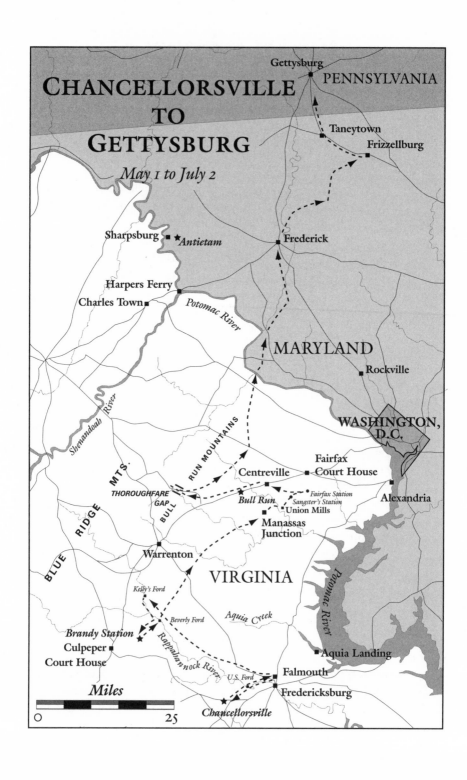

CHANCELLORSVILLE
TO
GETTYSBURG

May 1 to July 2

Gettysburg

PENNSYLVANIA

Taneytown
Frizzellburg

Sharpsburg ■ ★*Antietam*

Frederick

Harpers Ferry

Charles Town ■

Potomac River

MARYLAND

Rockville

Shenandoah River

WASHINGTON,
D.C.

BULL RUN MOUNTAINS

Fairfax
Court House

Centreville ■

*THOROUGHFARE
GAP*

BLUE RIDGE MTS.

Fairfax Station
Sangster's Station
■ Union Mills

Bull Run ★

Alexandria

BULL

Manassas
Junction

Warrenton ■

VIRGINIA

Potomac River

Kelly's Ford

Beverly Ford

Aquia Creek

Brandy Station ★
Culpeper ■
Court House

Rappahannock River

Aquia Landing

U.S. Ford

Falmouth

Fredericksburg

Miles

Chancellorsville

0   25

appeared to be an entrenchment—but no sign of cannon or infantry in force. On the ground they found a slouch hat left by a rebel picket as he fled. Emboldened, Cross's men moved out, advancing into the village near the ford as the rebel horsemen kept their distance. Before long the Union cavalry, which had gathered on the far bank, splashed across the Rappahannock and galloped past the infantry, which re-formed and followed.

Infantrymen had always considered the cavalry as useless as a hand on a hog's back, but on this expedition the horsemen carried the burden. Eventually Cross's men heard firing, distant and sustained, and marched toward it. Emerging from woods near a railroad depot called Brandy Station, they found themselves sightseers at the biggest cavalry fight of the war. "We . . . saw in the plain to the left of us large bodies of our cavalry galloping, wheeling, and charging, and the horse artillery hotly engaged with the enemy," wrote Livermore. Doctor William Child was with the detachment, too. "The smoke of carbines suddenly shot out in elongated puffs," he wrote, "clouds of dust were thrown up by the moving troops, the sabres gleamed and flashed, and all the rush, fury and turmoil of battle were seen as if in a strange picture." The battle ended in a draw, a heartening outcome for Yankee horsemen long dominated by their opponents in arms. By nightfall the Union cavalry and the soldiers who watched them fight had recrossed the Rappahannock and camped. The day's events had relieved Livermore's worst fears for the mission, so on this night sleep came easily.

The next day Livermore's company was sent to support a cavalry detachment guarding Beverly Ford, in anticipation that the Rebels might stage their own raid across the Rappahannock. They did not, and Livermore's adventures were limited to toying with two Union horsemen who thought for a frightened, helpless moment that they had fallen into rebel hands. When Livermore's men rejoined the detachment, Cross invited the captain to dinner. "He informed me that 'the last pig of the Rappahannock' had 'just come in and surrendered himself,'" Livermore wrote, "and that he was being cooked, which was a good commentary on the condition of that region, which in March, '62, fertile and well stocked, was at this time almost bare of crops, houses and stock."

Hooker now knew for certain that Lee was on the move, although he could only guess at his destination. Cross's detachment watched in succeeding days as the Union Third Corps and then the First Corps marched past to shadow Lee's army. By June 14, the detachment was on the move too; on June 17 it was reunited with the rest of the Fifth, marching with the Second Corps. "The party of Col. Cross came in this P.M. and [he] assumes command of the brigade," Lieutenant Colonel Charles Hapgood wrote in his diary before adding another development of note: "Tooth out."

On June 20, the Fifth marched over the twice-contested battlefield of Bull Run. "It is a fearfull sight," Hapgood wrote. "The field is strewn with broken muskets, accouterments, shot, shell, canister & in many places the bones of men and horses." As on other battlefields, many corpses had been buried in graves so shallow that the earth mounded over them washed away. From almost every grave, Livermore said, "hands or feet projected, withered and brown, or the bones of them." More chilling still were the skulls that gazed at the marching men—comrades from the past, heralds of the future. Some in the Union column paused long enough to knock teeth from their grins.

The pursuit of Lee's army was physically and mentally wearing. The weather was hot, and the men marched many miles almost every day, uncertain where or when they might meet their formidable enemy. When the Fifth paused at Thoroughfare Gap, guarding against a possible rebel thrust through the mountains, Child was struck by the rocky terrain's resemblance to New Hampshire. But his distance from home and the anxieties of the campaign left him in a dark mood. Child worried in a letter to his wife Carrie about the prospects of resuming his medical practice in Bath after the war. He pressed her to refresh his image of their children, particularly little Bernard, now seven months old, whom he had never seen: "Tell me just how the baby looks. Is he growing? Will he be homely or good looking? Does he talk any yet?—I mean baby talk." Child said his health was good—none of the bowel troubles of the previous summer—but he could not shake a sense of foreboding: "We here are in the midst of dangers—may be killed or wounded any day, hence I cannot write a letter without a feeling of sadness coming over me. To know that those most dear to you and dependent on you may be left alone in the cold world will soften and make sad any man with a heart."

The Rebels, the marching, and the weather conspired to make June 25 a particularly trying day. At six in the morning, the men heard picket firing as rebel cavalry tested the Union position. By nine the regiment was on the move toward Gum Springs, twenty miles away. The Rebels followed closely enough to harass the Yankee column, and in midmorning a shell burst in another regiment killed one man and wounded eight. It was raining by the time the Fifth stopped for the night at half past eight. An Irish colonel serving as officer of the day assigned Captain Larkin command of the pickets. Later Larkin would entertain his comrades in the Fifth by mimicking the brogue in which his orders were delivered: "Now, captain, the enemy is close upon us and an attack by him is expected. Ye will put yer men at intervals of exactly four paces. Ye will pace the ground yerself and ye will keep a strict watch for the enemy." That night, however, there was nothing humorous in Larkin's lot. The rain fell in torrents, but the pickets were forbidden to keep a fire; they expected relief but received none. By morning, the sodden Larkin had fallen so ill that he had to be carried by ambulance. Three weeks would pass before he was well enough to rejoin the regiment.

June 25 proved eventful for Captain Livermore, too—surprisingly so. During a pause in the day's march he was approached by an old acquaintance from the First New Hampshire, Colonel R. N. Batchelder, now serving as quartermaster for the Second Corps. Batchelder asked Livermore if he would consider joining the Second Corps staff as chief of the ambulance corps. An offer of peace itself could not have been more startling. "The brigade or division staff was thought by company officers to be a fine one to serve in," Livermore wrote, "but the corps staff was something which not only was even more mysterious in its supposed advantages, but was thought (if thought was taken about it) to be about as hard to be appointed to as Congress or other high places of equal dignity." Staff duty, Batchelder explained, meant spacious quarters, horses at no expense, and substantial responsibilities. "This roseate prospect, opening up the romantic side of war . . . was at once contrasted with my present situation," Livermore wrote. "It was true I was captain of a good company in a good regiment, not disliked by my superiors, in good health, and up to that time contented. But that very day I had perspired in a hot and dusty march; that night I should lie on the ground with little if any shelter; my coffee would be drunk if at all from a tin cup; my meal would be rounded out with a slice of fat pork, salt beef, or fresh-killed meat boiled in an iron pot, and hardtack; if it rained while we were marching I should be soaked and my feet would be clogged with mud; and I had all the morning felt all the miseries of trudging slowly along with the enemy pelting our rear." Livermore knew that Colonel Cross hated to lose good officers to detached duty. But Cross now commanded the brigade, not the regiment, and the Fifth had more officers than its reduced numbers required, so Livermore approached Lieutenant Colonel Hapgood and requested permission to accept the offer. Hapgood did not hesitate. "Yes, captain, take it," he said. Livermore told Batchelder that he had his commander's permission, and watched with delight as his benefactor rode off to corps headquarters. Minutes later, however, Livermore noticed Hapgood approach Cross, and the two engaged in conversation. At its conclusion Hapgood sent for Livermore and told him he had changed his mind, saying he was new to command and needed Livermore's help. There was no telling if Cross had ordered Hapgood's reversal or simply advised it, but it was clear that the colonel—the mentor to whom Livermore had been unfailingly loyal—now stood between him and advancement. Embarrassed and disappointed, but ever dutiful, Livermore returned to his company "and in a few minutes trudged on at its head."

Politics was afoot at the army's highest levels, too. Hooker's performance at Chancellorsville left his command in jeopardy, and the general knew it. When the administration refused to reposition Union troops near Lee's path, as Hooker requested, he took it as an expression of no confidence and offered his resignation. On June 28, President Lincoln accepted the offer, replacing Hooker with Major General George Meade—the fourth army commander under whom the Fifth had served in twenty months in the field. Meade was a difficult, rumpled man with a record of success, but there was little time for him or those in the ranks to reflect on his prospects. The Fifth had walked from Virginia into Maryland as Union troops tracked Lee north; rebel troops were already on the loose in Pennsylvania, spreading alarm from the countryside to the capital, Harrisburg. When Doctor Child wrote home with news of Hooker's ouster, the Fifth was near the Antietam battlefield and a new fight seemed imminent. "I am discouraged," he told Carrie. "We do not yet find the man able to conduct the war successfully. I hope the North people are satisfied that southerners can fight—and wish all negroes in Africa."

As a critic of Hooker, Colonel Cross could not have been discouraged by his ouster, but there was complexity to the colonel's mood on the day Meade took command. Cross rode that day with Lieutenant Charles Hale, like Livermore a young officer and admirer whom the colonel had lifted from the ranks. Months before at Antietam, Hale had been a sergeant who thought Cross stood ten feet tall in battle. Now Cross had named Hale an aide on his brigade staff, an intimate association that Hale found thrilling. On the march they encountered an old comrade, Captain Frank Butler of the Fifth, now assigned to the Signal Corps. As the trio rode, Cross told Butler of the ceremonial sword, spurs, and watch the officers of the Fifth had purchased for him in response to Captain James Perry's dying wish for reconciliation at Fredericksburg. "As he spoke of the matter in a pleased animated way," Hale wrote, "I saw that the colonel had been touched and gratified." But as talk turned to the impending fight, Cross darkened. "It will be my last battle," the colonel said. He slipped into a distracted silence, then addressed Hale directly. "Mr. Hale, I wish you to attend to my books and papers, that private box of mine in the headquarters wagon," he said. "After the campaign is over, get it at once, dry the contents if damp, and turn it over to my brother Richard." It was not the first time Cross had had a presentiment of his death, but Hale, new to the colonel's inner circle, considered his fatalistic attitude shocking.

Livermore also found himself confounded by Cross that day. When Captain Welcome Crafts rejoined the Fifth after recovering from wounds suffered at Fredericksburg, Cross promptly recommended him for the Second Corps staff job that had been promised to Livermore. Crafts was a brave officer and a

Coos County man like Cross, but he had angered the colonel on the Peninsula by lending money to enlisted men at high interest and had fallen asleep and been captured the night before the battle of Malvern Hill. This left Livermore wondering if Cross wanted to be rid of Crafts or to reward him. In either case, Livermore decided the time had come to act on his own behalf—even if that meant defying Cross. The young captain found the baggage wagon, pulled out his dress uniform, and made his way to corps headquarters. "It was situated upon a beautiful lawn in front of a mansion of handsome proportions," he wrote. "Its wall tents, spacious and clean, were arrayed in lines of geometrical precision; a sentry paced to and fro in front of them; quietness reigned about the camp." Livermore presented himself to Batchelder, his benefactor; together they sought out the corps's medical director, who said a different officer had been named to the job. Batchelder pleaded his case, and when Livermore returned to the Fifth's camp, it was with the renewed expectation that the ambulance corps would soon be his to command.

By June 29 both Lee and Meade were concentrating their armies near Gettysburg, Pennsylvania, for different reasons and with no particular intention of fighting there. Lee's cavalry had ridden off on an extended jaunt, leaving him first blind and then surprised by word that Meade was close. Gathering his seventy thousand men near Gettysburg, a road hub, strengthened Lee's hand while maximizing his options for further movements. Meade's maneuvers were intended to block Lee's anticipated path to Baltimore or Harrisburg and, if possible, to force a battle with the Union army of ninety-three thousand on ground of Meade's choosing.

Doing that, of course, meant getting in position first. On the morning of the twenty-ninth, Meade ordered the Second Corps to march more than thirty miles to Frizzellburg, Maryland. The order was mishandled, which delayed the corps's start and led a frustrated General Hancock to drive his men all the harder. The column was forbidden even to pause on the banks of streams to remove footwear before crossing, a common indulgence for the men. "No one of us was permitted to stop long enough to remove our shoes or stockings," Livermore wrote, "and as we forded several early in the day and drenched our feet and their apparel, we became footsore very easily on the hard roads."

One regiment new to the army and Cross's command, the 148th Pennsylvania, displeased him by crossing a stream too slowly. The colonel drew his sword, leaned from his saddle, and struck a startled corporal on the back of his neck with the flat of his blade. It was not unprecedented behavior for Cross, and it could be said that he was only enforcing Hancock's sense of urgency. But the incident was enough to brand Cross a tyrant in the minds of the Pennsylvanians. "In five minutes every man in the regiment knew of the act," wrote Private Henry Meyer of the 148th. "I'll bet if Colonel Beaver were here he would not dare do that," another soldier grumbled. But Beaver was recovering from wounds suffered at Chancellorsville, the regiment's first battle, leaving his men feeling defenseless in the face of Cross's assault.

The long march carried the column through communities whose names seemed chosen to encourage those with sore feet or wounded spirits: Liberty, Mount Pleasant, and, finally, Uniontown. "Various rumors flew through the ranks," Livermore wrote. "We all knew that we were marching to battle. I never knew our regiment and indeed all the troops to have lighter hearts than on this day." As the hours wore on, however, even the lightest heart was encumbered by heavy legs. "Field after field and wood after wood were reached and passed," Livermore wrote, "and at last we realized the fact that it was not a good camping ground we were marching for, but a position." When Cross again spoke to his staff of his impending death, Lieutenant Hale was too tired to restrain himself. He told the colonel that he considered such talk foolishness. "It finally led to his having some sharp words with me," Hale wrote. The anger quickly faded but left distant formality in its place. Hapgood, at the head of the Fifth's column, at last made camp at eleven that night. It was two in the morning when Livermore arrived; only half his company had kept pace. Among those lost along the way was Private Hilas Davis, who dropped from the column just before Uniontown, chagrined by the failure of his well-tested lameness remedy: heavy doses of quinine and coffee as strong as he could make it. "I was pretty well used up," he wrote. Those who kept up covered thirty-two miles in a march that carried the Second Corps not to its goal, but near it. Fortunately the next day was one of leisure, marked by a welcome muster for pay and the gradual reappearance of stragglers, including Davis.

Colonel Cross decided that rest alone was not sufficient for the 148th Pennsylvania, which had provoked him on the march. He wanted the regiment under someone he could trust. To the great embarrassment of the 148th's officers, Cross placed the regiment under the command of Colonel Boyd McKeen of the Eight-first Pennsylvania, at whose side the Fifth had marched and fought for months. The change compounded the resentment among the men of the 148th. Having indicted them in the stream, Cross had convicted them in camp, and all before a shot was fired. Cross's judgment gave the Pennsylvanians someone to hate and something to prove.

Far removed from this turmoil, Livermore seized the opportunity to play a practical joke on Hale, who wore a simple infantryman's sword with a leather scabbard. Livermore's was an officer's sword with a steel scabbard, but the blade had broken about eighteen inches from the hilt. Without disclosing the weapon's unfortunate condition Livermore proposed an exchange, saying that Hale's lofty role on the brigade staff merited the better blade. Flattered, Hale accepted the offer. That evening Livermore—rearmed and refreshed by his mischief—drew picket duty and led his men into a field of ripe, belly-high wheat. The farmer was friendly despite the damage the pickets caused his crops, and he offered to let Livermore sleep in his house. Livermore chose the barn instead and settled for the night in hay heaped on the floor. A messenger woke him hours later: Livermore had been named chief of the Second Corps's ambulances and was to report for duty in the morning.

It was July 1, and battle was at hand, but Livermore's promotion was not the only piece of routine business carried out in the army that morning. At headquarters, Meade's staff processed a request from Hancock that Cross be named a brigadier general, the promotion for which the colonel had so bullishly campaigned. Support from Cross's military superiors had never been lacking, and now they expressed it again. "He has been distinguished during this war in many battles and has been recommended for promotion heretofore by his Brigade, Division, Corps and Army Commanders," Hancock wrote. Meade added a simple endorsement: "Recommended to favorable consideration."

The Fifth broke camp at half past six that morning and set off toward Taneytown, Maryland, just south of the Pennsylvania border. "Expect to meet the enemy very soon, perhaps today," Hapgood wrote in his diary. "May God in his mercy protect the Officers & Men of this command & cover our heads in the day of battle." But it was distance and not divinity that would shield the regiment on July 1; its camp was still thirty miles from Gettysburg. By midday, at Taneytown, word of a fight ahead reached the column, but the men could not hear the gunfire. It was an ambulance, accompanied by a single mounted officer, that provided confirmation of the clash. Inside was the body of Major General John Reynolds, commander of the First Corps and one of the army's finest leaders, shot by Rebels as he positioned his men shortly after the battle broke out.

Meade detached Hancock from the Second Corps and sent him ahead to assess the situation in Gettysburg. Hancock found that the day had begun with promise. A division of Union cavalry had slowed a column of rebel infantry approaching Gettysburg long enough for Reynolds to rush his First Corps to the scene. The Eleventh Corps had followed, as had rebel reinforcements, escalating the fight to a level neither Lee nor Meade had anticipated. After Reynolds's death, however, the Rebels had pressed their attack against the Eleventh Corps, the same troops who had run during Stonewall Jackson's surprise attack at Chancellorsville. They fought hard but failed to redeem their reputation, giving way and retreating through Gettysburg. Hancock arrived in time to help organize a new position on high ground behind the town. Despite the day's misfortune, Hancock considered the position a strong one, and he sent word to Meade urging that the army make a stand there.

The Fifth was three miles from Gettysburg when it halted at eight o'clock on the night of July 1. Hale noted with satisfaction that, with action imminent, Colonel Cross seemed to have regained his "usual lively spirits." But Hapgood and many in the ranks were done in, exhausted by the heat, the weeks of pursuit, and their second thirty-mile march in three days—a staggering effort in the best of circumstances. "Men were asleep as they marched, and here and there a fellow was falling down," Hapgood wrote. "My horse went to sleep, so that I dismounted and took the bridle over my arm. I was afraid to ride him."

For Livermore, the day brought an uneasy farewell to the Fifth and a hurried introduction to his new responsibilities. In the morning, having returned his pickets to camp, he received an acknowledgment from Cross of his reassignment. The colonel's tone was cool; there must be a mistake that would soon be corrected, Cross wrote, because he had recommended another officer for the position. Livermore snapped back. "I thought . . . his message was needlessly and purposely calculated to remind me of my supposed powerlessness to oppose his wishes," he wrote, "and for the first and last time I was perhaps disrespectful to him. I sent word to him, in answer to his suggestion that I doubtless would see the propriety of my being sent back on his recommendation, that I didn't see it." Livermore regretted his message as soon as he sent it, but there was little time to dwell on the exchange. He pulled on his dress coat, packed his valise, and hurried to Second Corps headquarters. There he found Batchelder, who lent him a horse and directed him toward the ambulance corps, already on the march. Livermore reached his command on the road to Taneytown, fell in alongside his second in command, a lieutenant from the Eighth Indiana, and began learning just what his assignment entailed. As a captain in the battle-worn Fifth, Livermore had commanded a company of thirty men. His new command comprised four hundred men, several hundred horses, and more than one hundred ambulances and wagons. The corps was divided into three trains, one attached to each division; its mission was to rush the wounded from the battle lines to the waiting surgeons. Livermore came to his new role with the disposition of an infantryman. He believed the ambulance corps was gun-shy, leaving wounded men bleeding on the battlefield for too long. "At the time I took command I had fully made up my mind to make the ambulance corps learn what fighting was from actual experience," he wrote. That experience, familiar and horrific, was about to engulf the Fifth once again.

Though the first day's fight had gone Lee's way, like so many before it, this much had to be said of the Army of the Potomac that evening: it was present in force on good ground, having lost all its innocence and most of its battles since the Fifth joined its ranks—but not its willingness to fight. Such resolve was evident in the Second Corps's orders, to move at earliest daylight toward a position in the Union line, and in the purposeful manner in which they were executed. Despite the exhausting march of the previous day, the men were roused at three in the morning. The Fifth ate breakfast, broke camp, and was on the Taneytown Road toward Gettysburg by half past four. The air was misty and already thick at six o'clock, when the column approached the Union position on the ominously named Cemetery Hill. The troops who had fought the day before were preparing for renewed battle. Cross rode out among them, questioned officers he found in the gray light, and returned in jangling excitement. "Gentlemen," he announced, eyes flashing, "it looks as though the whole of Lee's army is here in Pennsylvania. There will be a great battle fought today."

The corps was directed to fill a half-mile stretch of Cemetery Ridge, a long, low plateau running south of Cemetery Hill. From above, the federal line looked like a fishhook; Cemetery Ridge was its shaft. Brigadier General John Caldwell's First Division was assigned the left end of the Second Corps line, with Cross's brigade at the extreme left of the division. The men were not deployed in a line of battle, but instead remained grouped by brigade in a formation best suited to rapid movement. The arrangement sent a rumor rippling through the ranks: they were being held in reserve, and need not expect to fight that day. By eight the corps was settled in its position, with skirmishers deployed to the front. It was quiet. With no enemy in sight but his faith and his wife in mind, Lieutenant Colonel Hapgood returned to his diary. "Now lie near the front line," he wrote. "Very little firing just at present. God keep us and help Mary to be resigned to whatever may come [by] evening."

The men of the Fifth looked upon a pastoral setting. They were posted along the crest of Cemetery Ridge, whose openness promised security. The Rebels would have to come a long way over exposed ground to reach them. The ground fell away gently in their front toward a brook, called Plum Run. Beyond that was a road and then, a mile away, a wooded ridge parallel to their own. The fields before them were ripe in wheat and corn, with farmhouses, barns, and outbuildings scattered throughout their view. To the left of their position on the ridge were two hills, the Round Tops. The low-lying gap between the Second Corps and these hills, the end of the Union line, was soon filled by troops from the Third Corps under Major General Daniel Sickles, a former congressman who owed his position to political connections. Sickles, an impulsive man, was endowed with great confidence and limited judgment. This unfortunate brace of characteristics would soon shape the fate of thousands.

Meade's plan was to fight a defensive battle, inviting a rebel attack. Lee's record suggested he would take up the challenge; the question was where and when the rebel blow would fall. By midmorning the Rebels had sent skirmishers forward to feel the Union line. They emerged from the distant woods across the valley, advanced until drawing fire from their Yankee counterparts, then withdrew before trying their luck again farther down the line. By noon they had passed in front of the Second Corps and the Third Corps too, having determined the disposition of Union troops without revealing their own.

In general, matters other than the popping of skirmishers' muskets occupied the regiments along the line. Surgeons selected hospital sites and hunted for sources of fresh water. The provost guard delivered stragglers for duty. Officers inspected their men to see that each had his allotment of eighty cartridges. As the morning wore on, the men stacked arms, and some piled fence rails in a breastwork. A few, laden with strings of empty canteens, hurried forward to Plum Run and filled them. Others made campfires and boiled coffee in dippers, smoked, played cards, chatted, or curled on the ground to sleep. Captain Livermore, having positioned his ambulance crews close to the front, paused to check on his old comrades. He did not speak with Lieutenant Hale, who remained unaware that Livermore had traded him a broken sword. To Livermore's relief, however, Colonel Cross seemed to have put aside their sharp exchange over his promotion. "We shan't want any of your death carts here today!" Cross joked. By noon, Hale wrote, "the hot July day began to burn." Horses were unbridled and given oats in nosebags; the men also ate their midday meals. Reports reached the Second Corps staff of rebel troops moving on their left, beyond the looming Round Tops. "There was no noise, save occasionally slight picket firing," wrote Lieutenant Charles Fuller of the Sixty-first New York, "but it was not the silence of assured quiet." The Sixty-first, a tested outfit like the Fifth, was in Cross's brigade. "Boys, you know what's before you," Cross said as he paused by the Sixty-first's line. "Give 'em hell!" Fuller was among those who shot back with, "We will, colonel!"

The wait in the stillness of summer heat was hard even on veterans, so the best that could be said about what happened next was that it provided a welcome distraction. Sickles had been stewing over the Third Corps position for hours; his men held the lowest point of the Union line as well as its extreme left, and he felt vulnerable. Finally, at about two o'clock, based on a willful misreading of Meade's orders, Sickles ordered his corps forward toward higher ground based in a peach orchard. The advance was crisp and impressive, but Sickles was marching his men into an exposed position more than a half mile beyond the rest of the Union line. The advantage of higher ground was more than offset by the isolation and by Sickles's deployment, which stretched the Third Corps dangerously thin. Sickles had opened the Union left to an attack—one that was being readied precisely as his corps advanced. Hale, along with thousands of comrades along Cemetery Ridge, watched in fascination as blue aides galloped along the Third Corps line, guiding the men into position. "Our impatience was great and the strain intense," Hale wrote. Few knew that Sickles had advanced without orders; nevertheless, the judgment of senior officers on the ridge was quick in forming. "It is beautiful to look at," Hancock told his staff, "but gentlemen, they will not be there long."

The rebel attack would have landed whether Sickles had moved or not, but his advance gave events their shape. Rebel artillery soon found the Third Corps line and opened fire; Sickles's gunners answered. The Fifth was detached from Cross's brigade and ordered to the left down Taneytown Road, where it stood guard behind the Round Tops. The artillery exchange grew in fury, and at about half past four, the sustained rattle of musketry signaled that the day's fighting had begun in earnest at last. Smoke rose along the left side of Sickles's line, starting in the valley below the Round Tops and running like a fuse toward the peach orchard. Meade, who had gone forward to chastise his wayward subordinate, realized he had no choice now but to support him. The Second Corps was next in the line and, one way or another, soon figured to be engaged.

It was time for final checks—of gear, of emotions, of comrades. Sergeant William Welch seemed so ill that a friend, Corporal Frederick Barrett, suggested he stay behind, but Welch refused. Lieutenant Hale's spirits rose; the waiting was the worst, and it was nearly over. Cross, who had been pacing, hands behind his back, summoned the lieutenant to his side. He pulled a black silk handkerchief from his pocket, folded it on his knee and, having handed his hat to Hale, tied the bandanna on his head. "We had seen him do this on other fields with a red bandanna and it then amused me somewhat," Hale wrote. Given Cross's fatalism on the way to battle, however, Hale found the colonel's new choice of color appalling. Ever dramatic, Cross fussed with his headgear. "Please tie it tighter, Mr. Hale," he said. Hands trembling, Hale obliged. "Draw it tighter," the colonel insisted. Again Hale complied. The smoke was now thick and the noise tremendous along Sickles's line. Hancock approached for a look, his staff trailing. The general reined in his horse at Cross's side, ready with words of encouragement. "Colonel Cross," he said, "this day will bring you a star." Cross shook his head. "No, general," he said,

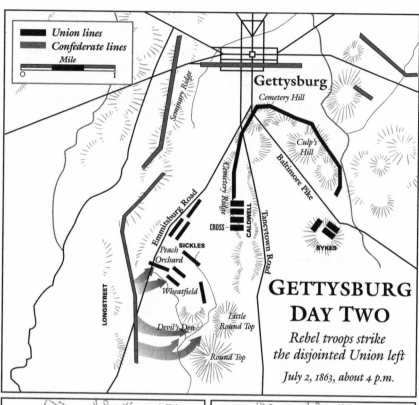

Union lines
Confederate lines
Mile
0   1

Gettysburg

Cemetery Hill

Culp's Hill

Seminary Ridge

Emmitsburg Road

Cemetery Ridge

Baltimore Pike

CROSS

CALDWELL

Taneytown Road

SYKES

SICKLES

Peach Orchard

Wheatfield

LONGSTREET

Devil's Den

Little Round Top

Round Top

GETTYSBURG DAY TWO

Rebel troops strike the disjointed Union left

July 2, 1863, about 4 p.m.

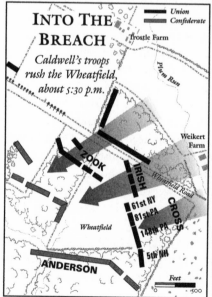

INTO THE BREACH

Caldwell's troops rush the Wheatfield, about 5:30 p.m.

Union
Confederate

Trostle Farm

Plum Run

Weikert Farm

ZOOK

IRISH

Wheatfield Road

61st NY

81st PA

CROSS

148th PA

5th NH

Wheatfield

ANDERSON

Feet
0   500

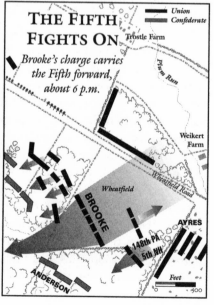

THE FIFTH FIGHTS ON

Brooke's charge carries the Fifth forward, about 6 p.m.

Union
Confederate

Trostle Farm

Plum Run

Weikert Farm

Wheatfield

Wheatfield Road

BROOKE

AYRES

148th PA

5th NH

ANDERSON

Feet
0   500

"this is my last battle." Hancock did not respond, but rode on, his eyes on the fight before him.

Sickles's men could not stop the attackers without help, creating a crisis into which other units were thrown without coordination. Meade dispatched the Fifth Corps from his reserve, and decided to commit a Second Corps division as well. Hancock's First Division, under Caldwell, was closest to the action and best positioned to move. Cross sent word to Lieutenant Colonel Hapgood and the Fifth to return from guard duty; the brigade was going in. Hapgood brought the regiment back on the run without waiting even for his pickets, leaving sixteen men to catch up later as best they could. Cross's brigade had the lead in Caldwell's advance but marched only a half mile before running into a Fifth Corps division also on its way forward. In the confusion someone ordered Caldwell to return to his original position; frustrated and bewildered, his men reversed their march. As the Fifth Corps division continued forward, a breathless general approached it with word that the Little Round Top, key to the Union line, was undefended. The first brigade in the division's line of march raced up the hill, taking position just in time to meet the onrushing Rebels. The struggle that followed would make heroes of Colonel Joshua Chamberlain and his Twentieth Maine Volunteers.

More help was needed almost immediately, because the Rebels were also pressing their attack in the bundle of boulders known as Devil's Den, the wheatfield to its right, and the peach orchard beyond that. At about five, Caldwell's division was ordered forward again. The need was so urgent that Caldwell simply faced his men to the left and marched toward the heaviest firing. "The column was soon swinging down through the fields, the ten hours of weary waiting now forgotten," Hale wrote. Still led by Cross's brigade, the division hurried past the neat white buildings of a farmer named George Weikert and through his woodlot. The men climbed over two stone walls and skirted a stream before entering a marshy pasture near the foot of Little Round Top. Only as they approached the battlefield did rebel cannonballs begin falling near, spraying dirt and grass in the air. Two aides rushed toward them with orders from the Fifth Corps commander, Major General George Sykes. One messenger struggled to control his horse, which plunged with the sound of every cannon. "The enemy is breaking in directly on your right!" he shouted. "Strike him quick!"

At Caldwell's order, Cross turned, spurred his horse and deployed his brigade along a dirt road that ran behind the wheatfield. There was no time for the maneuvers needed to arrange a typical battle line. The orders Cross barked—"By the right flank! March!" and then "Left face!"—left the formation inside out. The file closers were in the front, not the rear, and the front rank of riflemen was in the back. "Of course there was instant confusion," Hale wrote. The deployment alone might have defeated new troops, because formation was everything in an infantry line and this was nothing the men had ever practiced. But the veterans of Cross's brigade adapted; the file closers pushed through to the rear, and the line, its two ranks of riflemen still reversed, stood ready to advance. It had been only twenty minutes since they were ordered off Cemetery Ridge and into action. Caldwell had won his first battle of the day, delivering his division in time to make a difference.

The men of Cross's brigade scaled a fence and advanced toward the wheatfield, scene of the rebel threat. The Fifth held the extreme left of the line; the advance carried it into a stand of woods adjacent to the wheatfield. The men could hear heavy firing in the Devil's Den to their left and toward the peach orchard to their right. But the wheatfield was quiet, revealing only the scattered puffs of rebel skirmishers' fire as the brigade hurried forward. Convention called for Yankee skirmishers to lead the advance, but the rush left no time to deploy them. As a result, the battle line advanced so quickly that the rebel skirmishers were overwhelmed before they could withdraw. "Get a file of men for a guard and hold them, Mr. Hale," shouted Cross. "Look sharp, there's more in the edge of the woods by the wall; there's an officer, get his sword!" Before Hale could reach him, the Rebel laid his blade on the ground under his foot and snapped it in two, throwing the hilt into the dirt. Colonel McKeen sent three men to assist Hale, and together they herded twenty defiant captives toward the shelter of a sassafras thicket.

The rebel battle line was not in the wheatfield but controlled it from the shelter of a stone wall running along its edge. This position provided a distinct advantage over the advancing Yankees. As soon as the men in Cross's brigade appeared over a crest in the middle of the field, the Rebels opened up. The brigade stopped along the crest and returned fire. "The Rebs had their slight protection, but we were in the open, without a thing better than a wheat straw to catch a Minnie bullet that weighed an ounce," wrote Lieutenant Fuller of the Sixty-first New York. "Of course, our men began to tumble." Cross and his staff dismounted, so as to present a less conspicuous target. "Close it up! That's right!" Cross cried, tightening his formation as the blue soldiers fell. Bullets clipped the heads of wheat and flicked them in the air. Smoke settled over the field, and men lay down before firing so they could see. Their position was too exposed to be held for long, and Cross considered his options. Retreat was one. Attack was the other. "Boys!" he shouted to his staff. "Instruct the commanders to be ready to charge when the order is given! Wait here for the command, or, if you hear the bugles of the Fifth New Hampshire on the left, move forward on the run." Cross intended to initiate the attack himself, so he hurried down the line toward the left, where the Fifth was fighting in the woods. "Standing by my prisoners," wrote Hale, "I looked after him sort of regretfully as he vanished among the trees."

The Fifth was confronting soldiers from the First Texas and Fifteenth Georgia who had just fought their way through the Devil's Den. Beyond them was a brigade of Georgians commanded by General George T. Anderson. These were men who had already driven Union soldiers from the Third and Fifth Corps out of the wheatfield. At first the Fifth New Hampshire's advance into the woods had been unopposed. "Then the dropping shots began to come on us, and by looking down under the trees we could see the rebels lying on the ground," wrote Hapgood. The regiment and its foes were no more than a stone's throw apart as Cross approached Hapgood to begin the brigade's attack. The regiment was already taking casualties in the smoky, crackling woods. As always, the colors drew heavy fire and the color sergeant, Sampson Townsend, was shot in the right thigh. He passed the flag to Corporal Charles Reynolds and staggered to the rear. Sergeant George Gove was struck in the right shoulder and also made for the rear, his face white and his blue shirt dark with blood.

Hapgood noticed Cross hurrying his way, and so did a rebel marksman peering around a massive boulder only forty yards from the Fifth. The marksman had his eye out for officers. He had already sent a shot or two whizzing past Hapgood, who had sensed his presence among the many dangers in the woods. Hapgood was turning to meet Cross when the marksman fired again. The minié ball struck Cross in the belly button, ripped through his bowels, and emerged from his back near the spine. This punch in the stomach knocked Cross to the ground. The colonel had been wounded in every major engagement save Chancellorsville, and at Fair Oaks and Fredericksburg his injuries had been serious. He had always risen from these wounds, as if in defiance of death, but he and the comrades who knelt at his side could see that this injury was different. To be gut shot was to suffer a mortal wound, and a painful one. Hapgood detailed men to carry Cross to an ambulance at the edge of the wheatfield, and turned to Sergeant Charles Phelps with orders that were unusual in their particularity. He told Phelps to kill the marksman by the rock who had shot the colonel.

Phelps was something of a rock himself, a solid soldier whose qualities and experience typified the Fifth. Nineteen when the war broke out, he was among the sixteen Amherst boys celebrated in town for volunteering in the days just after Fort Sumter. His three-month enlistment having passed uneventfully, he signed on with Hapgood's company for service in the Fifth New Hampshire. In training camp Phelps's soldierly bearing had won Cross's approval, and he was named a fourth sergeant. Despite all the openings created by casualties since, however, Phelps had never advanced to an officer's rank. At Fredericksburg, he was shot just above the hip and hospitalized; he rejoined the regiment in March, four months later. Phelps was faithful to his family as well as his cause, writing every two weeks to his sister and sending his parents much of his pay by express. His letters revealed homesickness that time did not cure. Now the sergeant loaded a musket and positioned himself for a shot at the Rebel on the rock, no easy task in the threatening woods. When the man exposed himself to view, Phelps caught a glimpse and squeezed the trigger. He could not hear his own shot in the tumult of battle, but he felt the rifle push into his shoulder, and the familiar billow of white, foul-smelling smoke floated from the barrel. Phelps had found his mark. The rebel soldier fell.

Cross's wounding came at a critical moment. The attack he planned never materialized, leaving his brigade to bleed its strength slowly into the trampled wheat. By the time Colonel McKeen realized he was in command, the men (and their ammunition) were too spent to advance. Caldwell decided to relieve the brigade by committing his reserve under Colonel John Brooke. As the reinforcements swept into the wheatfield, McKeen's men fell back to safety. But Brooke's men marched only into the wheatfield, not the woods occupied by the Fifth and three companies of the 148th Pennsylvania. McKeen left these men where they were to protect Brooke's flank. When the fresh troops reached the wheatfield crest they paused to fire a volley; then Brooke ordered them forward, just as Cross had intended to. As the Union line surged, bayonets fixed, the Fifth and the 148th charged, too. This attack was well timed, because the Rebels had been weakened by their long engagement. Brooke's men cleared the wheatfield and raced into the woods beyond, continuing onto high, stony ground before halting in the face of a new rebel line. The Fifth and the 148th drove the larger rebel force in their front as well, advancing several hundred yards into the woods before stopping on a rise of their own, overlooking a stream called Rose Run. The charge was a triumph but an incomplete one, and thus contained the elements of its own undoing. The Fifth was vulnerable to attack by Rebels in Devil's Den, which was now not just on its left flank but also in its rear. Brooke's brigade was exposed to attack on its right. Caldwell, with no more troops of his own to send into action, scrambled to persuade other units to advance in support.

The Fifth's ranks, meanwhile, were badly depleted. Officers bent over stricken men, took their ammunition, and replenished the cartridge boxes of those who still stood and fired. When muskets grew foul with unburned powder, the soldiers discarded them for fresh weapons that had been carried by fallen comrades. Casualties mounted. Hilas Davis was shot with his right arm raised as he rammed a bullet home; the ball shattered his wrist and ripped the muscle from beneath his upper arm. Ned Stinson had been wounded at Fair Oaks and then shot in the chest at Antietam on the day he returned to duty. Now Stinson fell again, shot in the right leg. This time, he would not survive. John Butcher was struck in the chest, Reuben Gilpatrick in the shoulder. Frederick Barrett, who had tried to persuade his friend William Welch to report sick that day, watched in horror as Welch fell with a mortal wound. "We still kept up our fire," Hapgood said. "I do not know why, only because we were put in there for a purpose, and as long as the cartridges lasted, we were supposed to stay."

By the time Caldwell succeeded in bringing two Fifth Corps units into action in support of his men, it was too late. The reinforcements were just moving into position when the old Third Corps line anchored in the peach orchard finally gave way. That freed a fresh brigade of rebel troops to sweep down the wheatfield road, smashing Caldwell's exhausted soldiers in the right flank. The Union line collapsed and men raced for the rear, all semblance of order lost. The Fifth and the 148th held on tenaciously, helping to keep the path of retreat open. At last they were relieved by a division of regulars under Brigadier General Romeyn Ayres, but the weary volunteers and the fresh regulars both suffered from the heavy fire of the Rebels advancing on their flank. The Fifth's Sergeant Phelps, who had shot Cross's assailant, fell with a mortal wound in his back. A minié ball struck Private Samuel Crowther in the back as well, entering below his left shoulder blade and passing by his spine before emerging under his right arm. It was about half past seven, more than two hours after Cross's brigade had gone into action. The men of the Fifth had been among the first of Caldwell's troops on the field, and they were the last to leave.

The division's flight continued for nearly a mile. Unaware of its cause, Hancock fumed at what seemed a disgraceful performance by his old division. Captain Livermore, too, was shocked by the scene as he directed his ambulance crews forward. "I was grieved and surprised," he wrote, "to see coming across the Taneytown road hundreds and perhaps thousands of the 1st Division of our corps in hasty retreat and great disorder. There was no organization among them, and they bore the appearance of having been broken by the enemy." Finally, Colonel Brooke rallied the division behind its original line in a field along the Taneytown Road. The Fifth had broken apart in the chaos as it withdrew. Lieutenant Charles Liscomb had taken twenty-three men in Company A into action; in the first roll call afterward, only three answered.

Having at last driven Sickles's corps from the field, along with those who came to its assistance, the Rebels fell on the original Second Corps line on

Cemetery Ridge. The attackers were worn down, but the defenders had also been weakened by the loss of units already thrown into the evening's fight. Hancock filled one gap after throwing the First Minnesota forward against overwhelming odds to slow an attacking force. Meade himself led reinforcements into a second gap, where the Rebels briefly penetrated the Union line. At the other end of the line, on Culp's and Cemetery Hills, rebel troops pressed furious assaults into the darkness; there too, the Yankees held on. Finally the fighting came to an end, and the familiar but haunting cries of the wounded rose in the stillness. Twinkling ambulance lanterns were everywhere, like fireflies, as Livermore's men and other crews collected the injured. What had seemed a disastrous day for the Union army was, strategically speaking, a successful one: its line was intact. Someone remarked to Meade that the Rebels had nearly carried the day. "Yes, but it is all right now," he answered. "It is all right now." Later that night, Meade and his generals decided to hold their ground and fight again on July 3 if Lee remained willing.

Cross's brigade was ordered to re-form in its initial position on Cemetery Ridge, but it took hours for many men to find their units. A frustrated Lieutenant Hale had spent hours just looking for someone to take his prisoners off his hands. He missed the fight entirely and did not locate the brigade again until ten that night. "They were feeling very sore and dejected over the result of our fight," he wrote. "It certainly looked disheartening; we had held our own, but the loss had been frightful, and we had gained no ground." As Hale reported, Colonel McKeen took his hand and asked, "Lieutenant, where is the Fifth New Hampshire?" Hale could tell him nothing. Then, with "evident emotion," another officer delivered devastating news: "Colonel Cross was carried back from the line badly wounded within five minutes after he left us." Hale collapsed, "feeling that hope was dead."

It was midnight before Hapgood reported with the remnants of the Fifth. He had gone into action with 179 men; he emerged with about 100. What was worse, many of the wounded men remained where they had fallen, on ground now beyond Union control. The Rebels were certain to assist their own wounded first, so the prospects for the missing Yankees were grim. Confusion along the battle line diminished their chances even further. Livermore sent his ambulance crews as far forward into the wheatfield as he dared. He was unaware, however, that there had been fighting in the woods to the left, let alone that his own regiment had been engaged there, so he made no effort to recover the wounded from that portion of the battlefield. There was probably little he could have done in the darkness, but Livermore would later call this unwitting failure to assist his injured comrades "a source of regret to me."

An ambulance had carried Cross to a field hospital beyond the Taneytown

Road, located, fittingly enough, in a wheatfield. The wheat had been harvested and bound into sheaves, which remained on the field; several were gathered into a bed for the dying colonel. With nightfall campfires flickered throughout the field, casting the men around Cross in an otherworldly light. His brother Richard was at his side, as were two doctors, John Bucknam and William Child. Cross asked how his "brave boys" were doing; told the battle had gone well, he smiled. "Do you think I can live to get home?" he asked Bucknam, who had grown up with him in Lancaster. "I fear you will live only a few hours," the surgeon answered. "Oh, my mother!" Cross said. The colonel's wound was excruciating, and as he weakened he issued a stream of nonsensical commands. "I was kept awake by my own wound," wrote a New Yorker lying nearby, "and heard him in his delirium calling out to his comrades" from his pre-war days in Mexico. Around midnight, Cross's thoughts returned to the present. "I did hope I would live to see peace and our country restored," he said. And then: "I think the boys will miss me. Say goodbye to all." With that the colonel, a leader to the last, resumed his stream of disjointed commands.

Colonel Cross died at half past twelve. Bucknam folded the colonel's arms over his body, then closed his eyes. Livermore arrived soon after and was told that Cross had been asking for him; there was solace in that, but also a pang over his failure to get there sooner. Livermore pulled the blanket from the colonel's face and gazed at his features. "They were placid and exceedingly lifelike," he wrote, "and it was hard to persuade myself that the flush of life had gone from them. His lofty forehead was smooth, his long, silky beard lay upon his breast undisheveled, and he looked more as he would if he slept than seemed possible." Livermore sat beside his colonel's body. Nearby, mortally wounded in the peach orchard fighting, lay a lieutenant from the Second New Hampshire. Already a detail from the 148th Pennsylvania was preparing to drag the dead from this field of misery for burial. The third body these men picked up was Cross's. In writing about it years later, a member of the 148th's detail still referred to Cross as "the tyrant commander of our Brigade." To Livermore, however, the sense of loss seemed overwhelming. "If all the colonels in the army had been like him we should never have lost a battle," Livermore wrote later. "Other volunteer regiments, many of them, were composed of as good men as ours, but I do not think there were a half dozen in the army which were as good in every respect as ours, and we owed that to the colonel. In the first place, Colonel Cross taught us—by rough measures, to be sure, sometimes—that implicit obedience to orders was one of the cardinal virtues in a soldier. Then he imported several excellently drilled men into the regiment, who aided us exceedingly in acquiring a correct drill. He taught us to aim in battle, and above all things he ignored and made us ignore the idea of retreating. Besides this he clothed us and fed us well, taught us to build good quarters, and camped us on good ground, and in short did everything well to keep us healthy, well drilled, and always ready to meet the enemy."

As a fallen leader, Cross was not to be buried on the field. Before the night was out his body was sent to Baltimore in the care of Captain Crafts. By afternoon the captain had made his way to Fayette Street and a busy undertaker named J. H. Weaver, who embalmed Cross's body the next day along with the remains of a lieutenant colonel from Connecticut and a New Yorker whose jaw had been blown off by a shell burst. Prepared for their final journey, Cross's remains were shipped by train to Lancaster.

As Meade expected, General Lee was willing to continue the fight on July 3. Caldwell's shattered division was placed in reserve behind the Second Corps battle line. At daylight the fighting at the right end of the Union line resumed, having been suspended by darkness the night before. Five separate rebel attacks on Culp's Hill failed. Lee intended his main attack to fall on the Second Corps line, but it could not be organized until midday. It came, at last, in such form and with such fury that none who survived it would ever forget.

In the early afternoon, about 150 rebel cannon opened fire along Seminary Ridge, opposite the Second Corps. There had never been a cannonade like it in the war. Heavy smoke and considerable distance made accuracy difficult; soon many shots were arching over the battle line and into the rear. Doctor Child was laboring in a field hospital that seemed to have become a particular target. "The shell and solid shot fell all about us," he wrote, "but only two hit the house." Union artillery pieces returned fire, as much for morale's sake as anything; the infantrymen, like the men of the Fifth, hugged the ground and hoped for the best. Sergeant George Hersum was struck by a flying fragment the size of a nutmeg. Other fragments, he wrote his wife, "stove my haversach all to peaces. If they had all hit me fair, I guis I should [have] got a furlow home in a way I would not like." Somehow, Hapgood felt sufficiently secure amid the thudding concussions and whizzing shrapnel to open his diary. "A caisson blew up just besides us, 2 men were blown up," he noted. "We have thrown up a breast work and lay behind it—safe enough."

Finally, after two hours, the rebel cannon fell silent. As the smoke and dust cleared, the Yankees looking across the mile of undulating fields saw a daunting line of rebel infantry—nearly a mile from left to right—emerge from the woods along Seminary Ridge and begin to advance as if on drill. "They came up the slope like an avalanche," Hapgood said later, "and from where I stood, I thought the day was lost."

The advantage of numbers would be with the Rebels if they could reach the Union line to deliver their blow. The Yankee artillery along Cemetery Ridge opened fire on the attackers immediately. The rebel line began to shorten due to losses and the need to bear in on the focal point of its attack: a cluster of trees to the right of the Fifth. The Rebels paused to climb a fence along Emmitsburg Road, about four hundred yards in advance of the Union line. Rifle fire and canister shells began to rip the Rebels apart. Vermont troops directly in front of the Fifth advanced into the fields, pivoted, and delivered devastating fire into the flank of the attackers. Still the Rebels pressed on, reaching and then tangling with the Union line, but the long charge under fire had stripped them of order, energy, and numbers. Soon they fell back as yells of triumph erupted along the Yankee line. The Fifth moved forward to help the Vermonters round up prisoners. Half of the twelve thousand charging Rebels had been killed, wounded, or captured. Lee met the survivors with words of assurance not unlike Meade's the night before: "The fault is mine, but it will be right in the end." In truth he had suffered a disastrous defeat.

Unlike his old comrades in the Fifth, Livermore could find no room for rest or relief in the day's events. Because of the rebel cannonade, the Second Corps hospital was moved to the rear, and Livermore selected a new site near a hillside along Rock Creek. General Hancock was wounded during the rebel onslaught. Livermore escorted his ambulance to the hospital, pausing anxiously under fire while Hancock wrote a dispatch. A Second Corps brigadier complained that his wounded had been left on the field, and Livermore ventured beyond the skirmish line to investigate. Later in a cow shed, he found an artillerist lying face down, the flesh from his buttocks shot away. The man was strangely calm. "He said he hated to be shot in the rear, and seemed to care for that more than for being so grievously hurt," Livermore wrote. Livermore had had only a few hours of sleep since the battle began. "It was necessary for me to drink whiskey to keep myself up," he wrote, "and it was astonishing to see how much of it without water or sugar I drank without feeling it."

The next day was Independence Day, though the circumstances discouraged festivities. "You were right about my celebration of the 4th," Doctor Bucknam wrote his sister later. "It was at the amputation table." The Fifth was sent forward in light rain for picket duty along Emmitsburg Road. Hapgood and Child toured the battleground. "Dead men and horses, muskets, side arms, exploded caissons, dismounted cannon and thousands of those things that make the soldiers' equipment complete, covered the field," Child wrote. That night the rain grew heavy, as if trying to wash the awful mess away. Lee had expected a Union attack on the Fourth. During the night, grateful for the reprieve, he began to withdraw his army. The wagon train that carried the wounded was seventeen miles long. A picket from the Fifth, Lieutenant Liscomb, wondered why his rebel counterparts had grown so quiet. At three in the morning, "armed only with a stout stick," he crawled toward the rebel picket line. Finding it deserted, he hurried back to report the news. "Expect to move this morning," Hapgood wrote in his diary. "The enemy is in full retreat."

But Meade chose not to contest Lee's withdrawal on July 5, leaving his army to bury the dead and tend to its housekeeping in the downpour. Lieutenant Hale knew the time had come to comply with Cross's instructions regarding his possessions. He found the box containing the colonel's books and papers, checked its condition, and delivered the contents to Richard Cross. He asked—and received—permission to keep the colonel's copy of the Army regulations. On the inside cover Cross had recorded a favorite poetic passage. "'Tis sweet for our country to die," it began. Livermore sought out Hale to make amends for his sword prank, in which he had duped the lieutenant into trading for a broken blade. Had Hale had occasion to draw the new sword during the battle? he asked. Yes, Hale had. Livermore offered Hale's old sword back, thinking it was fortunate for them both that the lieutenant had not been engaged in hand-to-hand combat. Many soldiers made time to write home with news of the battle and assurances of their well-being. "I wish it might be that we could destroy the reb. army before they leave the Northern States," Child told his wife, Carrie. "I am well, only very tired. Our rations are rather short." Corporal Frederick Barrett gathered himself to deliver news no parent wanted to hear. "Mr. Welch," he began, "I take this opportunity of informing you of the death of your son William, which is a verry sad duty. He was shot on the Battle field July 2. I am verry sorry for you and his Mother, Sisters and Brothers. He was the best friend that I have, and now they have taken him. My Friends, you have one thing to Comfort you. He was a Soldier that has always done his duty. He died a Soldier's death. I have $20, a watch and some miniatures of his Sisters and Brothers. I can not write any more now. This is wrote in a hurrey."

The heavy rain itself became an enemy. The creek began to rise at the hospital site Livermore had selected. Some of the wounded men along its banks were too weak to move, and they drowned. That night Hapgood, Bucknam, and Child rolled up together to sleep in a single blanket. They were wet through, and Hapgood awoke the next morning feeling sick. At last the army set out after Lee, but Hapgood could neither march nor ride for long. He had to be carried by ambulance in pursuit of the enemy.

Lee's army reached the Potomac River on July 7 only to find that the rain had rendered it impassable. The Rebels turned and formed a defensive position, expecting an attack. But Meade's pursuit was both slow and roundabout, giving rise anew to criticism in Washington. Once again it seemed a damaged Confederate army might slip away before the Army of the Potomac delivered a crushing blow. Letters from the Fifth suggested that many in the ranks were looking back to their last fight and not forward to a new one. "Col Cross is gone and we feel very lonely," Lieutenant William Lyford wrote his mother from Frederick. By July 13, Meade's army was at last in position to strike Lee. "There seems to be no desire on either side to bring on the fight," Child observed. That night the Potomac had subsided enough for the rebel army to cross back into Virginia. Lee's second invasion of the North was over, having ended as the first did: in defeat.

Lee's escape prevented a decisive outcome to the campaign, but the Union victory at Gettysburg proved to be pivotal. In nearly two years of war to come, Lee was not able to take the offensive again. In time the rebel attack on the third day of the battle came to be called Pickett's Charge and remembered as the Confederacy's high-water mark. Yet without the action in the wheatfield, slowing the rebel attack on the second day, draining its strength, ultimately helping to preserve the Cemetery Ridge line, the third day's climactic charge might never have come. The Fifth's casualties at Gettysburg were a telling measure of the cost at which the day was won: twenty-seven killed, fifty-three wounded. Only one other regiment in Cross's brigade, much larger than the Fifth, suffered more heavily: the 148th Pennsylvania, whose character Cross had challenged.

On July 15, from a sickbed in Baltimore, Hapgood began a personal campaign to bring what remained of the Fifth home to recuperate. "The Reg't now numbers less than 100 fighting men," he wrote to the adjutant general in Concord, whose approval would be needed for the regiment to leave the field. "I deem it my duty to make an earnest request that it be permitted to return to New Hampshire for a short time at least. . . . Am I asking too much? Is it more than right that this [regiment] now reduced to less than a company is permitted a little respite?" Rest and recruits were clearly due, but for a time it appeared that the regiment would be assigned to guard a prison camp at Point Lookout, Maryland, while recovering. For the balance of the month the Fifth remained on the march with the army. On July 30, Hapgood was finally well enough to return to duty. "Assumed command of the Regt. this morning," he wrote in his diary. "Think we may go to N.H. yet." Though some in the regiment doubted it until the last, Hapgood was right.

On August 1, at four in the morning, the men of the Fifth boarded a train in Baltimore to begin their trip north. They would follow much the same route as they had on their way south in October of 1861. At that time the regiment had 1,012 men in its ranks. In the months since, 171 additional recruits had joined the regiment in the field, for a total enlistment of 1,183. Yet on that northbound train were only 165 men from the Fifth. Due to sickness or wounds, as many as 40 were not fit for duty.

Almost a month had passed since Colonel Cross's body was placed on a train for his trip north from Baltimore. The colonel had already been buried, as had Charles Phelps, the sergeant who avenged his shooting. One had defined the regiment while the other exemplified it. Both had endured long enough to participate in the Army of the Potomac's greatest victory, though neither had had the good fortune to survive it. In death each was celebrated as a hero in his hometown, with services that drew large crowds and evoked deep feelings. Henry Kent welcomed his closest friend home to Lancaster with an account of Cross's funeral in the *Coos Republican*. "Amid a throng of friends who had known him from boyhood," Kent wrote, "the brave soldier, the true friend, the impulsive and honorable man, was borne to his final resting place in the valley he loved so well, amid all his wanderings." At Phelps's funeral in Amherst a quartet sang "Bear Them Home Tenderly," and a simple line from the pastor's eulogy became his epitaph. It captured well the story of Cross and his regiment. "A young man," it said, "but an old soldier."

14 Before and After

"A man that lives through this war and
gets out all safe—there is not anything
that will kill him. He is bomb proof and
there is not any disease that can kill him.
He will live always or some time."
— Private Daniel George,
    July 4, 1864

NINE YEARS BEFORE A REBEL MARKSMAN MORTALLY wounded him at Gettysburg, Edward Cross wrote a story about an actual volunteer regiment recruited from New England to fight in the Mexican War. It was typical of Cross's early newspaper work: historical fiction in which outnumbered American soldiers won unlikely victories through strength of character and belief in cause. But from beginning to end, from its details to the motives of its characters, "The Young Volunteers" foretold Cross's experience leading the Fifth New Hampshire Volunteers in the Civil War. Though Cross fancied himself a mystic, he was no clairvoyant. This was a case of life imitating art, of a man given the chance to live events that he had previously imagined. By the age of twenty-two, when he wrote the story, Cross had already formed strong opinions, clear ideals, and deep prejudices; he was a character in search of a drama, and in the Civil War he found it. If the result was not quite as romantic as the young author had dreamed it, it was close enough—especially for a man who subscribed to the theory that "this world is a monstrous humbug."

"The Young Volunteers" chronicled the adventures of Tom and Harry, two New Hampshiremen who joined a New England infantry regiment bound for the Mexican War. Like Cross, Tom and Harry were printers—"adventurous beings" who enlisted in greater proportion "than any other class of our citizens." Nothing forced them to do so. "They had not been torn from

249

their homes to fight the battles of a king! No, they were simply answering their country's call—freely, joyfully, for her cause was their cause! They were volunteers!" As the regiment set sail for the war, the colors were unfurled and the band played "The Girl I Left Behind Me." "It was a noble, patriotic spectacle!—Fathers parting with their sons—brothers with brothers—with a feeling of patriotism and pride that swelled far over their sorrow." Yet Cross made it clear from the outset that Tom and Harry were destined to die soldiers' deaths in "the Bloody Ninth."

The leader of the regiment, Colonel Ransom, was a disciplinarian who drilled his men constantly to prepare them to fight. He also paid heed to their needs and to the privileges they earned through good work. Ransom "was proud of his regiment, proud of the intelligence, bravery, and good behavior of his men. And they, in turn, loved their Colonel, and respected him as a skillful, kind and gallant officer. Such was the mutual feeling of regard between officers and men that existed all through the volunteer portion of our army; and it was one great element of their efficiency. It is the right feeling, and renders an army almost invincible." Within a professional army, by contrast, such a bond was impossible. "The men looked upon their superiors as petty tyrants, whom they obeyed from compulsion, not from choice."

The Bloody Ninth of Cross's youthful story earned its nickname, but not all its triumphs were strictly military. The men were avid foragers in a hostile land; they overcame obstacles with ingenuity and determination. On one march to battle, the road led to a bridge that had been destroyed. The engineers said the regiment could not cross the river because the bridge could not be rebuilt. "All d——d nonsense," responded a captain in the Ninth. "Give me five hundred men and the tools, and I'll build a road there in one day." Like Cross's regiment at the Chickahominy River, the captain and his band had enough experience in "the lumber swamps" of New England to make good his boast.

The author of "The Young Volunteers" saw the Irish as an enemy within. Cross cast them as a rogue element in the army and even created a prototype—or stereotype—for Thomas Francis Meagher, the Irish general he reviled during the Civil War. The villains, a band of Irishmen commanded by "the infamous Riley," deserted and fought on the Mexican side as "Saint Patrick's Legion." Thirty of them were captured in battle, fighting against their countrymen. The Ninth had the pleasure of watching these thirty meet "a well merited fate"—a mass hanging. "As the colors which they had deserted were seen through the smoke to mount the fort, they were launched off the scaffold."

If there had been no Colonel Cross, no Antietam, Fredericksburg, or Gettysburg, the battle scenes in "The Young Volunteers" might seem far-fetched. As the Ninth marched toward the enemy on one field, grapeshot hit Tom's musket and sent him hurtling into a ravine. Harry's first impulse was to stop and check on his friend, but instead he obeyed the cry of "Forward!" Soon he heard Tom shouting in his ear, "All right!—tie this handkerchief round my head!" Cross took up this idea of a bandanna as a warrior's flourish in nearly every battle. In the story, Tom, Harry, and the Ninth were assigned to bury the dead after the battle. "Thousands of men had fallen, and the dead lay scattered singly or in great heaps over an extent of many acres," Cross wrote. "From the hundreds of wounded there arose a wail of agony fearful to hear. Villainous looking leperos, priests and prowling camp-followers wandered like ghouls over the field, plundering the dead and dying. The ground was strewed with mangled limbs, and all slippery with human gore." The dead "had come from their distant homes, strangers to each other, to fight the battles of their country, and together found a common grave in a hostile soil." The young author honored them with a poem that began "O, it is sweet to die for our country where ranks are contending"—a poem very similar to the one the Fifth New Hampshire's Lieutenant Charles Hale would one day find scrawled in his dead colonel's army regulations. In the story, Cross's heroes fought on, but during the decisive battle before the Mexican capital a shell burst killed Harry and mortally wounded Tom. Tom's death scene, like Cross's own, lasted for hours. He bore his pain bravely, and when General Pierce came to his bedside, Tom said, "General, when you get back to the old Granite State, tell my friends I died like a soldier." In his final delirium Tom spoke of mother and home and ended with a rallying cry: "Come on, boys. Harry, let's keep together. Our guns will open soon." Victory in hand, the regiment returned to New England eighteen months after its departure. "One day a lone vessel beat into the same harbor, came to her moorings at the pier, and from her deck one hundred and fifty men, ragged, sick, mutilated, marched silently forth, and entered the fort. They were the tattered remnants of the 'BLOODY NINTH!'"

The tattered remnants of the bloody Fifth reached the Concord railroad station at eight o'clock on the morning of August 3. Less than two years before, with the band playing "The Girl I Left Behind Me" and well-wishers lining the streets of the state capital, it had marched to the same station. That day, its colonel, a lanky erect man full of martial qualities that he had instilled in his volunteers, had ridden proudly down Main Street leading more than one thousand men—a regiment of citizen-soldiers heading south with a taste for glory but only a vague idea of the perils that lay ahead. Now Colonel Cross was dead, and the war had reduced the regiment that stepped off the train to roughly the number who returned in Cross's youthful story. There was no band to meet them, no crowd, no patriotic speech—nothing. No one knew the Fifth was coming home that day.

Colonel Charles Hapgood, whose promotion was dated the day after Cross's death, marched the regiment up Main Street to the State House yard. Asa McFarland, editor of the *Statesman*, recorded his surprise at seeing the regiment pass his office in the Phenix block. The Fifth's "thinned ranks and tattered flags" created "a spectacle of truly affecting character," he wrote, noting that "one of the officers, bereft of his right arm, carried his sword upon his left." This was John Crosby, who had returned to the Fifth with his lieutenant's commission after his elbow was shattered before Marye's Heights. McFarland wrote that the Fifth's "sad reduction brought home to all who saw it when marching through Main street more effective evidence of the desolating consequences of War than pen and ink descriptions are adequate to convey." In the State House yard, the men rested in the shade through the morning heat as state and city officials figured out what to do with them. By noon, a feast had been prepared at two hotels across Main Street—the Eagle, the political headquarters of the state, and the Phenix, where the late Major Edward Sturtevant had boarded before the war.

Hapgood, meanwhile, arranged for the men to go home the next day on a week's leave. For its returning contingent, Claremont prepared a reception at town hall and a banquet at the Tremont Hotel. Less than two years before, with townspeople gathered round to watch, eighty-one sons of Claremont had paraded on the green with Captain Charles Long's Company G. Now town hall filled to honor the returnees. Twenty-four men had been killed in action or died of disease, and wounds or illness had forced many more to leave the company. When townspeople applauded, the recipients of their tribute numbered twelve men.

In Concord, the failure to give the Fifth a rousing homecoming preyed on the consciences of the state's leaders, and they set out to rectify the oversight. Governor Joseph Gilmore had gone to the White Mountains with his family, knowing that the regiment was bound for Concord but believing that it could not possibly arrive before his scheduled return. "I desire to correct any wrong impression which may exist in the minds of the officers and soldiers of your command in regard to the want of some public demonstration of welcome on their return this morning," Gilmore wrote Hapgood. The governor had been "much surprised" upon reaching home to learn that the regiment had already arrived. "The first intimation which the citizens of Concord had of its coming was the sight of its tattered banners on Main St.," he wrote. Gilmore assured Hapgood that there was no regiment "of which the people of New Hampshire are more proud" and invited the Fifth to a dinner and public reception after the men had returned from leave.

On August 11, 1863, the capital made up for any slight the Fifth might have felt. In its edition reporting the event, the *Statesman* included an account from a Washington correspondent who had seen the regiment depart for home. "Rome, on her best days, would have marched out to meet such illustrious soldiers, strewed their way with palms, and built for them triumphal arches," he wrote. For the festival in Concord, flags flew everywhere along Main Street, and throngs from near and far stood along the way to hail the soldiers. Banners bedecked the State House, front and back. When the men of the Fifth marched into its yard, Governor Gilmore was there to greet them and to give the first of several patriotic speeches. It was left to editor McFarland to divine the melancholy truth beneath all the gaiety. "The occasion was one of mingled emotions," he wrote. "Joy and sorrow were twin sisters at the festal board. Speaking figuratively, the sparkling wine and the sugar-coated bridal cake were in close neighborhood with the bitter herbs and the baked meats of the house of mourning, and it was fit that it were so; for it is by such means, in the economy of Providence, that households, and communities, and States, are reminded, in this season of national disaster, that it is to be only through much tribulation [that] an afflicted people will, in God's own time, be conducted into the haven of rest."

McFarland's funereal tone suited the occasion more than he knew. Cross's regiment was no more. As much as the men respected the steady Hapgood, Cross had been the heart and soul of the Fifth. There would be no replacing him, and no replacing Edward Sturtevant or John Murray or James Perry or Charles Ballou or the hundreds of brave boys who had fallen in battle or died of infectious diseases. Captain Thomas Livermore, the Fifth's most eloquent chronicler, passed up the chance to return to Concord with its remnant, staying instead in the field as a member of the corps staff. "With Cross's death the glory of our regiment came to a halt," Livermore wrote. "The memory of its achievements were never effaced, and the veterans who fought under him never forgot their training, but the substitutes who came, the officers who commanded, and the fortunes of war which came afterwards, all served to make its history under him conspicuous in contrast for all that was soldierly and gallant." The key to Cross's success had been to instill in his regiment his own soldierly character and demeanor. "I believe that the regiment as little contemplated retreating as he himself did," Livermore wrote.

Cross's death in a crucial Union victory ensured his status as a hero in New Hampshire, but it did not foreclose debate about his character. Was he a tyrant? And why had such a successful regimental commander been denied promotion to brigadier general? The answers begin with Cross's temper. Even his admirers acknowledged that certain events seemed to "unbalance him with rage." He was ruthless in rooting out officers who resisted his ways, and at times his suspicious nature misled him. But the furies that some people never forgot or forgave—the whacks with the flat of the sword and the vicious upbraidings—detracted little from Cross's qualities as a commander. He led through intellect, experience, discipline, attention to detail, personal courage, and an earnest, expressive presence. He spelled out both his expectations and the consequences for not meeting them. He could be as tender as he was tough. Bluntness did not make Cross a tyrant, but it did make him enemies— including some who stood between him and his brigadier's star. His story "The Young Volunteers" provided another clue to why he was never promoted. The story made much of the voluntary aspect of its heroes' military service. Cross was not a West Pointer, and thus it took him time to earn the favorable attention of the professional soldiers who ruled the army. What's more, he had strong political views and was accustomed to expressing them; as a volunteer officer in a country founded on freedom of speech, he saw no reason to give up his. The professional generals carped and schemed, but at some level they exercised discretion—a point that escaped Colonel Cross. How Cross would have fared as a general is a matter of conjecture, but his success leading both a regiment and a brigade suggests that he would have excelled.

With Colonel Hapgood now in command, the Fifth New Hampshire stayed in Concord for two months to recuperate and recruit. In the last five months of 1863, nearly six hundred men joined its ranks. Many of these were bounty soldiers, and most proved unreliable. The law allowed draftees to pay other men to take their places. As Livermore explained it, the prices quickly rose, and "a class of 'substitute brokers' sprang up, who imported men from other states, chiefly from New York City, who enlisted for money." Because the brokers had no interest in the quality of the substitutes, "there came out to us crowds of disreputable rascals whose determination it was to desert at the earliest opportunity, as well as idiots and cripples whom these brokers foisted upon us by collusion with the medical and enlistment officers." The men built a fence around the camp in Concord to try to keep the recruits in. Hapgood recorded the first desertion in his diary on August 27, writing that the general was "mighty mad about it, and justly too"; desertions soon became so frequent that the colonel seldom saw fit to record them. During the siege of Petersburg a year later, so many deserted to the enemy that the Rebels put up a sign on their works reading "Headquarters, 5th New Hampshire Volunteers. RECRUITS WANTED."

This is not to suggest that the Fifth did not face danger or exhibit bravery after Gettysburg. The regiment spent nearly seven months guarding rebel prisoners at Point Lookout, Maryland, then joined Lieutenant General Ulysses Grant's campaign just days before Cold Harbor. There, on June 3, 1864, just a few miles from where Cross's regiment had first gone to battle at Fair Oaks, Hapgood sent the Fifth toward the rebel trenches. The men took the first line of defense, and Hapgood sent them forward again. This time they met heavy resistance and were cut off from the rest of the army. Overwhelmed, they broke for the rear. Forty-six members of the Fifth were killed that day, most of them recruits, and ten more died at Cold Harbor during the week that followed.

The Fifth's last battle, at Farmville, Virginia, on April 7, 1865, proved a tragic signature to the regiment's history. Captain John Ricker, who had distinguished himself under Cross, led six companies of the Fifth on a desperate charge against a large entrenched force. Ricker was shot in the shoulder and then the leg during an advance of nearly a quarter mile over rough ground. Unfortunately for him and his band, the other elements of Brigadier General Nelson Miles's division fell back. Despite his wounds Ricker led his men forward until a third bullet hit him in the groin and knocked him to the ground. The Rebels, who numbered at least in the hundreds, captured Ricker, the seventy men who remained in his command, and the flag of the Fifth New Hampshire Volunteers. Twenty-one members of the Fifth lost their lives that day. Livermore, now a staff officer, heard what had happened and hastened to Farmville to see after Ricker. "I could not bear to have the brave old fellow lie out on the field wounded, so I went out to find him," he wrote. "I walked as far as I dared to stand erect beyond our lines, and then crept until I could go no farther without venturing into the enemy's hands, but I could not find him, and came back with a very sad heart." Ricker crawled away from his captors in the night and Livermore found him the next morning in bed in a house, "full of courage." Although surgeons could not remove the bullet from Ricker's groin, he survived. The Fifth got its prisoners and its flag back just hours before General Robert E. Lee surrendered at Appomattox Courthouse on April 9.

For the members of Cross's regiment who lived to see war's end, service in the Fifth created a bond that lasted a lifetime. They met at reunions in their camp at The Weirs on Lake Winnipesaukee, they told white lies for each other in federal pension proceedings, and with misty eyes they remembered their fallen comrades as forever young. From the beginning, the story of the Fifth was not merely a war story but mainly a human story. Survivors of the Fifth, like those of many other regiments, sought to tell this story in an official history written a quarter of a century after the war by a member of the regiment.

The author was Surgeon William Child. His mission was to tell a noble tale—not a chronicle of what had happened but a reflection of how the men wanted to be remembered. Fortunately, Child and many others had already provided the grist for a real history in their letters home, in their diaries, and in their memoirs. A few of their personal stories, including Child's, are worth following beyond Cross's death at Gettysburg.

Child's most startling war experience came just after victory was won. He loved the theater, and his desire to celebrate the surrender of Lee's army led him to Ford's Theater in Washington on the same night as President Lincoln and the first lady. Immersed in the evening's comedy, Child was startled by a gunshot and the sight of a man leaping from the president's box to the stage, shouting to the stunned crowd, and making his escape. In the chaos that ensued, Child offered to assist the mortally wounded president but was rebuffed. He returned to his hotel and sat immediately to write his wife, Carrie. "Wild dreams and real facts are but brothers," he began. "This night I have seen the murder of the President of the United States." Child had opposed Lincoln's candidacy in 1860 because he thought it divisive; by 1864, he was a Lincoln man intent on seeing the war through. "We do not sufficiently realize the influence of our present acts on the future of our nation," he wrote Carrie just before the election. "Are we to be a great and powerful nation—or are we to be broken into weak and envious fragments? This is the great point to be considered."

Fortunately for Child and the weary nation, Lincoln's assassination did not re-ignite the war. But peace and the doctor's eventual discharge brought his personal conflicts to the surface. Child's insecure nature had caused him to doubt the prospects of reestablishing his practice in tiny Bath after the war. He was aware that some in town attributed his political transformation to his successful quest for promotion. And he resented the men who had stayed home, sent substitutes, or fled to Canada rather than enlist in the Union cause. "Bath needs to be taken by its corners and well shaken," he wrote in January of 1865. "I would tell every boy there to get up and go somewhere—anywhere."

Child entertained thoughts of moving his young family west but, apparently at Carrie's urging, soon put them aside as "foolish dreams" and returned home. It was a good decision. After the war, he was selected state representative from Bath twice and became a leader in veterans' affairs. He rose professionally as well, serving as president of the New Hampshire Medical Society, for which he prepared many articles. "These published papers show that he held advanced views on sanitary matters," a biographical sketch says, "had little faith in drugs, no faith in so-called disinfectants, claiming that to be 'clean' was the essence of modern sanitation and surgery." Child's practice was curtailed, however, by lingering wartime afflictions. Rheumatism sometimes made it hard for him to ride; he was prone to recurrent fevers and painful piles. There was pain in his personal life as well. Carrie, to whom he wrote longingly throughout the war, died in 1867. Child's second wife was Carrie's sister Luvia; in wartime letters he had called her Aunt Luv. His son Clinton, to whom he had written so tenderly from Antietam, died in 1880 at the age of twenty-one. Child lived until the age of eighty-four. He died in 1918 at the home of his daughter Kate, who cherished memories of the stories he told about his wartime days.

The man who provided the finest account of the Fifth New Hampshire under Colonel Cross was the precocious Thomas Livermore. He joined the regiment as a sergeant at seventeen years of age and left the army at war's end as a colonel. On March 31, 1867, Livermore set out to write a memoir of his war service. His habit was to reserve Sundays for leisure, and over the next eight years every word of his memoir—more than 150,000 words in all—was written on a Sunday. Livermore was a gifted man with a prodigious memory; it was he who, as a sergeant, had learned by heart the ninety-eight-man roll of his company so that he could call it in the dark. In writing his memoir, he made two concessions to his comrades in arms. In the style of a nineteenth-century novelist, he often blanked the names of those guilty of embarrassing behavior; in nearly every case, a knowledgeable reader using other sources can fill in the blanks. The other omissions are lost to history. Livermore wrote the memoir as "my talisman in years to come when I am at a loss to invoke the spirits of the past," but he knew it might one day become public. "Perchance when I am gone," he wrote, "this will come to the eyes of some who will not understand all there is to excuse some little wanderings from the path of morality on the part of the characters who will appear and of the one who writes, and it may be that over such events as these I shall pass in silence, saying, once for all, that soldiers who appreciated the fact that they wore their lives upon their sleeves generally were inclined to seize the pleasures of the world as old Time winged them on." This Victorian paean to privacy meant that Livermore left out any whoring the men might have done and the vulgarity of their language, but it seemed not to cover drinking, gambling, thieving, foolishness, or incompetence.

After the war, Livermore became the most successful veteran of the Fifth New Hampshire. Opportunity and responsibility sought him out, as they had during his military service. When he came home, his worldly possessions amounted to one thousand dollars, his faithful horse Charlie, his weapons, and his uniforms. He loved the outdoor life, and his pipe dream was to establish a business in Buenos Aires as an exporter of condensed beef. By happenstance and through a family connection, he fell into the study of law. "My old experience in the army had confirmed me in the habit of accommodating myself to the circumstances, and my long abstinence from the study of books had given me a zest for it which I never had before," he wrote. He was admitted to the bar in 1868 and practiced in Boston, but his real career was in business. He ran the Amoskeag Mills in Manchester, New Hampshire, for seven years and was vice president of a mining company for twenty-one.

Livermore was active in civic causes and scholarly avocations. He was chairman of the board of the Boston Park Commission and commander of the Military Order of the Loyal Legion for Massachusetts. He was also an amateur historian with a keen interest in shaping and preserving the meaning of the war. He wrote a statistical analysis of infantry regiments and the history of the Eighteenth New Hampshire Regiment, which he had commanded during 1865. In an article for the magazine *Granite Monthly* extolling the virtues of the volunteer army, he drew heavily on his own experience. An important advantage of the Union army, he wrote, was "that there was no class distinction between those who were officers and those who were in the ranks." This equality, and the regular promotion of line officers from the ranks, meant that "the men were very subordinate and amenable to discipline." In battle, "when exact and instant obedience to orders, even to death, was the price of victory, the soldier saw the benefit of discipline." Livermore summed up succinctly why the volunteer fought: "He did not fight for glory, and he did not love the trade of war, but his good name was his stake, and he had enlisted for the war to keep the Union whole." Many of these points reflected a moment that Livermore recounted early in his memoir. It was the day the governor presented the Fifth with its colors and Colonel Cross assured the men that many of them would die defending them. The colonel's speech stuck in Livermore's memory "because it proved so true, and was in the manly tone of a soldier who knew whereof he spoke." The regiment did not welcome the colonel's message, Livermore wrote, "because it predicted what finally came, death, hardship, and peril, but it was grand truth; and its sincerity was attested on every field by the wounds of the speaker, until at last he laid his lofty form down to die." After the war, one of Livermore's many outside endeavors was his long service as president of the Military Historical Society. In 1920, two years after his death at the age of seventy-three, his four children allowed the publication of his memoir under the society's seal. He had titled it *Days and Events*.

Another faithful storyteller of Cross's regiment was James Larkin, who wrote dozens of candid and poignant letters from the field to his wife, Jenny, and their children Bubby and Belle. Larkin was promoted to major after Gettysburg and to lieutenant colonel and command of the Fifth after a bullet in the arm sent Colonel Hapgood home in June of 1864. When the original regiment's three-year commitment ended four months later, Larkin finally went home to Concord and his beloved family. He was never wounded in battle, but the maladies of campaigning, including rheumatism so bad that Child often lent him his horse, caused Larkin pain for all the decades of his working life. He returned to painting Concord coaches at the Abbot and Downing factory but had to contort his body to do the job and suffered constantly. He gave up after two years. He won appointment through Republican patronage as Concord's postmaster and later as a federal revenue agent in Tennessee. "We made several raids into the mountains for the purpose of discovering illicit stills," recalled George Wilson, a colleague. "Always after these trips, Larkin was compelled to apply local treatments and remain in room or office for days." Finally, in 1884, Larkin sought and received a federal pension—twenty dollars a month. Thirteen years later, at the age of sixty-five, he had lost whatever money he had to bad investments and was desperate again. He appealed to J. G. Gallinger, a Concord physician who had once treated him and now, as a U.S. senator, served on the Committee of Pensions. "The fact is that I am more incapacitated from earning a living than with the loss of a leg or arm if I was otherwise well," Larkin wrote. Even with Gallinger's help, Larkin was past seventy before Congress approved a doubling of his pension. By then, doctors had reported that he used a cane and could hardly get around. "Hands show no use," one said. "He gets up and sits down with difficulty."

Through all his post-war tribulations, Larkin was a regular at reunions of the Fifth New Hampshire and basked in the honor due a survivor of such long, hard service. On the first Memorial Day in 1868, he led the solemn procession of the Edward E. Sturtevant chapter of the Grand Army of the Republic into the Eagle Hotel in Concord. On their left arms, the veterans wore black ribbons tied with bows of red, white, and blue. Each carried a wreath or bouquet. Businesses were closed for two hours that afternoon, and once Larkin and his comrades had listened to the benediction and a reading of the Gettysburg Address, they joined the schoolchildren of Concord in singing "America." The veterans led the march to the Old North and Blossom Hill Cemeteries to decorate twenty-five graves of men killed in the war, including seven nameless graves. Larkin took part in many more such observances before he died in Everett, Massachusetts, on August 7, 1911, fifty years after he joined the Fifth New Hampshire.

A chronicler of Cross's regiment who had even less luck than Larkin was

Miles Peabody, the corporal whose sickly father ran a hardscrabble mill on the North Branch of the Contoocook River. Peabody had been a faithful son, complaining bitterly about army life in his letters but dutifully sending home nearly all his pay. He wrote often that he would leave the army immediately if he could do so honorably, but in December of 1863, when the bounty rose to more than four hundred dollars, he reenlisted. On May 26, 1864, as the Fifth prepared to leave Point Lookout for Cold Harbor, he wrote home: "We are going to leave here today, and once more unite our future with the Army of the Potomac. I hope we shall be in season to go into Richmond with Grants victorious hosts." He added what seemed almost an afterthought: "My health is poor. My liver is out of order. If I am not better, I don't think I shall go far with the Regt."

Peabody soon found himself in a hospital in Alexandria, where he remained through the summer and into the fall, writing often to his father and also keeping a diary. His principal subject was the deterioration of his body. On July 10, he was suffering diarrhea for the fourth straight day. "The Liver Complaint, Intermitant fever, Diohrea, Bronchitis, Diohrea and now Diohrea again, and I don't know what will come next," he wrote home. Four days later, he wrote in his diary: "Pleasant but very hot, I went out on pass, visited the Cemetery and found a lot of Blackberrys, had all I could eat, my Diohrea very bad yet." It was his third visit to the soldiers' cemetery in three weeks. "You need not be alarmed about me for I am not dangerous yet," he informed his father, adding a note that indicated he was still keeping up with the war news: "Grant is a Gen of great resources, and as stuborn as a bulldog." As late as mid-September, Peabody sounded hopeful even while cataloging the chills and fevers that were ravaging him. By November 3, he lacked the strength even to write. To Harlan Thompson, a New York cavalry sergeant, Peabody dictated a letter saying he had received a furlough but could not take it on his own. He asked his father to come south to bring him home, "as I am entirely unable to make the journey without the assistance of some friend more devoted to my interest than even those who are willing to do what they conveniently can." Sergeant Thompson appended a note of his own. "I do not wish to unnecessarily excite your fears," he wrote, "but will join your Son in the request he makes, as I think he much needs your care, being a very sick man."

Five days later, Miles Peabody died. All his family could do was arrange to have his body sent home. The body arrived at the train station at Hillsboro with an $11.75 bill for transport. On the coffin was a message from "Drs. Brown and Alexander, embalmers, Washington, D.C.," to the undertaker in New Hampshire "or friends who open this coffin." The message read: "After removing or laying back the lid of the coffin, remove entirely the pads from the sides of the face, as they are intended merely to steady the head in travelling. If there be any discharge of liquid from the eyes, nose or mouth, which often occurs from the constant shaking of the cars, wipe it off gently with a piece of cotton cloth, slightly moistened with water. This body was received by us for embalmment in pretty good condition, the tissues being slightly discolored. The embalmment is consequently good. . . . The body will keep well for any length of time. After removing the coffin lid, leave it off for some time, and let the body have the air." Peabody was buried in a cemetery in Antrim under a small, government-issue stone. His father, who had long been ill, died less than a year later and was buried near him, leaving Mary Peabody, Miles's mother, with "no means of support except her labor and the charity of friends." In time, a claims agent helped her get a small pension to compensate for the loss of her son, who had been "a strong and healthy boy" when he enlisted in the summer of 1861.

Like Mary Peabody, many parents whose sons died in the Fifth turned to the government for assistance. Some found their claims subjected to rigorous review—including, remarkably enough, the parents of Colonel Cross. An investigator's report laid bare his father's financial failures and drinking habits while documenting the colonel's practice of quietly paying his mother's bills; in the end, her pension was granted. Other families were forced to submit as evidence precious letters in which their soldiers mentioned sending money home. Such was the case of Nancy Chase, a mother of eleven. Three of her sons served in the war, including Benjamin F. Chase of the Fifth, whom she called "our darling Bennie." In his letters home he had sought—and no doubt failed—to put her fears to rest. "Tell mother not to worry about me, not a mite," one letter said. "I stand one chance in 7 hundred thousand to not get killed, but perhaps I may get killed." The odds turned against Chase at Fredericksburg, where he died in the Fifth's futile charge—a blow from which his mother never recovered. "Before the war she was cheerful and singing about the house," her oldest daughter, Vittie, told pension authorities, "but afterward sad and dejected, and has never been heard to sing a word since the death of Benjamin F."

For every member of the Fifth who died in battle, more than two were wounded, and many of them found life was never the same after. Few suffered more grievously than Alonzo Allen, who was shot near the spine in the Fifth's first battle at Fair Oaks. The doctors decided not to remove the bullet for fear of causing paralysis, and he was left to languish in the wet grass outside a field hospital for several days with no food or water. A sympathetic doctor, Osmon Way, documented Allen's slow decline after the war. "He is still extremely nervous, excitable, timid and restless," Way wrote in 1875. "Sensation is abnormally acute over the whole surface of the body. He cannot handle his legs freely: they are woody. The brain is confused by a comparatively slight mental application. The tendency in this case is downward. . . . Just the nature of the injury the spine sustained I cannot tell, but the fellow is a poor sufferer." In 1877, Way reported that Allen was not sleeping more than three hours a night. "The back is painful constantly," the doctor wrote, "but the head seems most severely troubled." By 1883, Allen's walk had been reduced to a shuffle; by 1891, he had all but lost control of his bladder. He survived until June 13, 1900, just past the thirty-eighth anniversary of the battle in which he was dealt a crippling blow.

Rare was the Fifth survivor who was not diminished to some degree by illness and exposure in the field. Then, as now, it was hard for such veterans to prove their entitlement to a pension; as the years passed it grew harder, the question being whether their ailments were due to the ravages of war or old age. When Joseph Harris sought a pension increase for varicose veins in 1877, he submitted photographs of his badly disfigured right leg and an affidavit from his old lieutenant, Nathan Randlett, saying Harris had shown him a bulging vein while marching on the Peninsula. Hilas Davis's 1899 application for a pension increase due to rheumatism was met by a request for documentation, provoking this outburst in return: "I would respectfully suggest that the soldiers who got disabled and used up by exposure and the exhaustion of forced marches were not the ones who busied themselves in getting hospital records for such ailments as rheumatism. The only medical treatment we got in those days of desperate campaigning was a box of quinine stuffed in our pocket by an overworked surgeon with the injunction to 'cheer up,' 'make the best of it' and 'hold out anyway.' If we were forced to drop beside the road we got about as much 'treatment' (medical) as the abandoned war horses got. The troops passed on—an occasional call of 'Hello! See that poor devil.' . . . Possibly the ambulance picked him up but more likely it was either death or a weary drag till camp was reached." The pension office bureaucrats assessing these applications were in a difficult position. Certainly old soldiers were tempted to exaggerate or even lie to get something back from the government they had given so much. Rules were rules, and the taxpayers' interests were at stake, too. But public sentiment was behind the veterans, as evidenced by Congress's willingness to act on behalf of soldiers or their survivors when the pension office wouldn't. In 1900, the Fifth's George Hersum died of heart failure; his widow sought a pension, citing the malaria, chills, and diarrhea he endured in the service. The bureaucrats said no, but Congress said yes. "Upon the evidence as a whole the action of the Pension Bureau was technically correct," the committee report said. "It is highly probable, how-

ever, that the soldier's disease was largely contributed to by the disabilities in-
curred during his service. He has a good military record, and his widow is
now very poor and much in need of help."

An unfortunate few in the Fifth experienced more strife in civilian life than
they had in the midst of war. Barron Noyes was a sergeant who returned
home to Claremont after his discharge due to illness in 1862. By 1864, his wife,
Angelina, had requested a divorce and was taking nightly carriage rides with
her lawyer, a former Democratic congressman, newspaperman, and anti-war
extremist named Edmund Burke. One evening Noyes stepped out of the darkness to confront the couple. When Burke refused to stop his carriage, Noyes
raised a revolver and fired several shots in the air. Noyes was arrested, and
each man laid his side of the scandal before the public. Burke expressed himself through letters signed "Justice"; Noyes spoke for himself, but in terms
suggesting he had a clever lawyer's help. "I am a poor man," Noyes wrote in
the *National Eagle*. "I have a daughter seven years old, whom I desire to bring
up in the paths of rectitude and virtue; and it was to protect her name from
infamy and disgrace, and my own rights, that I interfered with Mr. Burke's
'pleasant' programme of evening rides with my wife." Buttressing Noyes's
defense was the fact that he had caused no injury. The same could hardly be
said of Thomas Wier, another veteran of the Fifth discharged for illness in 1862.
Upon enlisting Wier had awarded custody of his youngest daughters, Ellen,
eight, and Sarah, ten, to a Shaker religious community in Enfield. When he
returned he asked to have them back and was refused; his frequent requests
to see the girls were also denied. On July 16, 1863, Wier renewed his plea to
Caleb Dyer, a Shaker elder. Refused once again, Wier drew a revolver and
shot Dyer in the back. The Shaker died; Wier turned himself in. Wier was
convicted of first-degree murder and sentenced to be hanged. His cause was a
popular one, however, due to currents of sympathy for veterans and against
Shakers. Wier's friends argued that he had acted "in a fit of temporary insan-
ity" and petitioned successfully for a new sentence: thirty years in prison. In
1880, more petitions led to a pardon. Once freed, Wier sought a pension,
retroactive to his discharge. It was granted, and he used his $952 windfall to
buy a farm on Shaker Mountain.

Cross's best friend and correspondent, Henry Kent, was a success in post-
war life, but his military experience proved to be something of an embarrassment. In the fall of 1862, Kent was named colonel of the Seventeenth New
Hampshire. To his great frustration, the regiment never reached the field, its
ranks being stripped instead to bring the Fifteenth and Sixteenth regiments
up to strength before they left for war. No glory accrued to the stay-home
leader of a nonexistent regiment, and Kent knew this well. "Since the war—

save among its own members and the loyal *camaraderie* of veterans, the Regiment has not always been understood aright," Kent wrote in the Seventeenth's official history. "Indeed, it has been *mis*understood, and sometimes with a persistency and perversity not wholly agreeable." More agreeable, perhaps, was the respect accorded Colonel Cross's favorite horse, Jack, after the war. "He was a noble animal, undaunted by the roar of musketry or thunder of cannon," said an account in the *Coos Democrat* in 1889. Jack was wounded only once, the paper said, and not severely. After Cross died at Gettysburg, Jack was brought to Concord, where he was purchased by a Shaker from the Canterbury village. "He spent the remainder of his life in peace and quietness," the *Democrat* said, a warrior among pacifists.

The intemperate Richard Cross had risen in the Fifth due to his brother's influence; after the colonel's death he fell not just from grace but from the army. At Point Lookout in the spring of 1864 Colonel Hapgood and Major Larkin brought court-martial charges against Cross, then the Fifth's lieutenant colonel. It was the second time the Fifth's officers had turned on each other in such a way, and there was surely an element of revenge at work; before Fredericksburg, Richard Cross had played a part in the colonel's passing but sharp clash with Larkin. Now Hapgood and Larkin, among other officers, accused Richard Cross of wandering from camp at will, falling asleep drunk in a civilian's bed while wearing muddy boots, and demonstrating leniency toward a Southerner convicted of striking a black soldier. Their purpose may have been simply to force Cross from the regiment. If so it seemed to work; Cross used old regular army connections and received a new assignment. Unfortunately, in a demonstration of the bullishness that ran in the family, Cross tried to leave Point Lookout with the charges still pending. The base commander had him removed from a steamer; defiantly, Cross boarded another one. This led to more serious charges, to which Cross and Hapgood alike reacted with horror. Cross attempted to resign from the army; Hapgood, citing the regiment's reputation and the colonel's memory, asked that the resignation be accepted. It was too late. Cross was tried in June of 1864, convicted, and cashiered. In the years to come, he found civilian life a struggle. Cross lived briefly in New York, Canada, Lancaster, and Concord; he worked in the oil business, as a railroad contractor, and as a magnetic physician. When he sought a pension, citing minor wounds and illness, the bureaucrats were skeptical. Though some comrades had turned on Cross, others rallied behind him in this quest. Child was asked under oath why Cross left the army. "My impression is he resigned," the doctor answered carefully. Eventually Cross won a pension from the government—and more. At the time of his death in 1894, he was employed as a watchman at the Treasury Department in Washington.

For most survivors of the Fifth, of course, there was no need for reconciliation with their comrades or the government. The war long remained the central event in their lives. Service with the Fifth New Hampshire remained a source of lasting pride. And at the center of it all, even in distant memory, remained Colonel Cross. On July 2, 1886, a group of veterans from the Fifth gathered at Gettysburg to dedicate the official regimental monument there. It had been financed at their request by the state Legislature; when costs exceeded the budget, the men of the Fifth contributed the balance. Constructed of boulders from the field and an octagonal block of New Hampshire granite, the monument was erected on the spot where Cross fell. The day's main speaker was Elias Marston, who had served as regimental adjutant. He recounted the Fifth's role in the battle, Cross's death, and his qualities as a leader. The regiment Cross had fashioned, Marston said, died with him that day. "Like the granite boulder we consecrate today were those dead heroes of the Fifth New Hampshire," said Marston, "men of the Granite State, hard, enduring, patient, immovable—a living wall in defense of their native land." As for the survivors, Marston said, "For each of them it shall be the proudest boast, 'He was with Cross and the Fifth New Hampshire at Gettysburg.'" The monument was formally placed in the care of the Gettysburg Battlefield Memorial Association, and the ceremony concluded with the singing of "America."

The Fifth's survivors often assured themselves that the regiment's story would never be forgotten. In dedicating the Gettysburg monument, Marston said "the gratitude of a rescued nation" would cling to its stone as tenaciously as moss and lichen. He was wrong; nature is more persistent than memory. Now no retelling can fully recapture the experiences of the Fifth. For all its veterans said of their war, in letters, diaries, speeches, and books, many of their memories remained unspoken. These were lost forever when they died. What we have today are glimpses, as fleeting, flawed, and moving as an encounter between Charles Hale of the Fifth and General Winfield Scott Hancock at a parade in Philadelphia after the war. Hancock and his aides, who were to lead the march, waited for the opening gun in a crowd at the corner of Broad Street and Arch. Hale, who had ended the war as a captain, pushed his way through the throng to Hancock's side. The general extended his hand, saying, "I remember your face as one of my old division, but cannot recall your name." An aide at his side did. "It is one of the Fifth New Hampshire, General," the major said. "It is Captain Hale of the Fifth." Again Hancock offered his hand. "Captain," he said, "not long ago someone was telling me that at Gettysburg the color-bearer of the Fifth New Hampshire tied the staff of the colors to the stub of a sapling that had been shot away, and picked up a rifle and went to shooting." It was not true, but Hale chose a polite response. "I have never heard of that before, General," he said. "I was with Colonel Cross on the brigade staff at the time." "Ah, now I remember you perfectly," Hancock said. The general looked down from his horse; the colonel had been a favorite of his. "What a magnificent fighter Cross was," he said simply. At that the signal gun sounded, Hancock turned to his duties, and Hale fell back into the peacetime crowd.

Acknowledgments

When we began our research for this book in 1993, we had no idea how many people were out there waiting to help us along. We can't name them all, but we wish to acknowledge and thank as many of them as a short essay will allow.

We begin with three fellow travelers on the Fifth New Hampshire's trails.

The first is M. Faith Kent, granddaughter of Edward Cross's lifelong friend, Henry Kent. Faith gave our project both a head start and a finishing kick. She and the Lancaster Historical Society have preserved an extensive written record and many artifacts of Cross and his regiment, including Cross's wartime letters to Henry Kent. As we neared the end of our research and writing, Faith found a cache of fifty pre-war letters from Cross to her grandfather. One of the biggest of many thrills during our research was to unfold these letters for the first time in decades and read the unvarnished thoughts of an excited young man in a vast new country. We knew instantly the opportunity this presented us. Several accounts have been written of Cross's life over the years, and the same few dozen facts slosh around in nearly all of them. Faith Kent's careful preservation of Cross's letters to her grandfather enabled us to allow Cross himself to tell the story of his coming of age.

The most knowledgeable expert on Cross and the Fifth is Walter Holden. In his foreword to this book, Walter describes our first meeting from his perspective. When we walked up to his apartment that morning and saw the red trefoil—the Fifth's emblem—on his front door, we weren't quite sure what to expect. By the time we left, the still somewhat hazy idea that we might actually write a history of Cross and the Fifth had been transformed into something akin to marching orders. Walter shared with us the fruits of his long pursuit of the Fifth's story, including Cross's wartime journal. He became our colleague and friend during this project and carefully read and edited an early version of our manuscript.

The third Cross enthusiast we must thank is Bob Ross, who is working on a Cross biography. Initially we approached Bob warily, fearing that his project might interfere with ours. Soon we were trading information freely—an exchange that favored us greatly because we were ahead of Bob in our work and because he knew so much more about Cross than we did. Bob Ross is an amazing digger. In doggedness, pluck, and zeal, he is not unlike the man he is researching. His ever-expanding Cross archive and his knowledge of Cross's life have been of immense help to us.

Two other people provided significant caches of letters to us. One, Merrill "Tom" Sawyer, allowed us to copy and use more than one hundred wartime letters written by his ancestor, Dr. William Child. On a sunny morning after a rain in Bath, New Hampshire, Mr. Sawyer also took us to Child's grave and the house he had lived in. We thank him for his generosity. Many years ago, a descendant of Miles Peabody gave a friend thirty-five of Peabody's wartime letters. That friend, Mary Anne Zak, shared the letters with us, and Peabody became a major figure in our book. Although she had read the letters and developed a deep personal attachment to Peabody, in the end Mary Anne literally gave us the letters. In time we intend to donate them to the New Hampshire Historical Society. (We believe all such collections of letters—by far the best raw material for historians—belong in public archives. We found it distressing during our research that a burgeoning collectors' market, fanned by the reach of the Internet and its influence in driving up prices, means that many caches of Civil War letters are being dispersed across the country. It is sad to see such an important aspect of our national heritage thrown to the wind.)

On foot and by car, we followed the path of the Fifth from Concord to Gettysburg. On the battlefields, we had superb guidance from park rangers, volunteers, and historians. Especially helpful were Donald C. Pfanz on the Peninsula, Fredericksburg, and Chancellorsville; Paul Chiles, Ray Fournier, and Ted Alexander at Antietam; and Eric Campbell at Gettysburg. Stephen W. Sears, whom we consider the preeminent historian of the Army of the Potomac, answered several queries promptly and graciously. (More than once, he merely pointed us to the pertinent *Official Records*—the sort of veteran advice that reddens a rookie's face.)

Several people provided us invaluable assistance in the writing of history, in the writing of nonjournalistic prose, and in producing a clear manuscript. These included two poets, Donald Hall and Wesley McNair, columnist Ray Barham, and two colleagues at the *Concord Monitor*, Felice Belman and Ari Richter. Our history guru throughout the project has been a former colleague, Michael J. Birkner, who is chairman of the history department at Gettysburg College. Michael has advised us, cheered us on, cajoled us ("Get those endnotes right!"), and lent us lodging on many a night. With his colleague, Gabor Boritt, he has also allowed us entry into the world of American historians through official and social events at Gettysburg College.

The *Concord Monitor*'s newsroom artist, Charlotte Thibault, drew the maps and painted the image that appears on the cover. She also caught the Civil War bug from us. Our full confidence in her mapmaking ability freed us from the burden of describing the regiment's movements in detail. As anyone who has ever tried it can tell you, you can't write a map. We also benefited from the time and talent of another *Monitor* colleague, Melissa Monfet, who scanned and toned more than thirty historic photographs for use in this book.

When we first encountered the Fifth New Hampshire Volunteers re-enactment group, we thought, "Here's a group of men crazier than us!" Their devotion to accuracy in portraying Civil War soldiers is remarkable, as is their reverence for the Fifth's history. They helped us find a wealth of material about the regiment, but their unique contribution was in showing us how the men lived, what they wore, how they drilled, and how they formed for battle. During the summer of 1999, one of them, Greg Chase, allowed us to fire his musket so that we could accurately portray the experience in our book. We thank all these men, but especially Paul Levasseur, Bob Corrette, Randy Cook, Steve Allen, and John Hayward.

Probably a hundred other people have assisted us along the way—reference librarians, historical society clerks, archivists, researchers, town clerks, collectors. From Betsy Hamlin-Morin at the New Hampshire Historical Society to Michael Musick at the National Archives, from Rita D. Gross, Croydon's retired town clerk, to collectors Scott Hann and John Henry Kurtz, we are grateful to you all.

We must also acknowledge the aid and understanding of our families. Sven and Misha Pride and Ben Travis have walked battlefields with their fathers. Yuri Pride has likewise supported his father's ambitions for this project, while Leanna Travis has helped her father keep his perspective. Charlie and Robin Pride and Manapa and Mike Travis read early versions of the book and offered not only advice but also valuable encouragement. Monique Pride would make a fine editor were she not a dedicated teacher. She and Brenda Travis have indulged their husbands in a project that has consumed far more time and energy than any of them imagined it would.

Without the assistance of all these people and many others, this book would not have been possible. They share in whatever success we have had in telling our story, and they bear no blame for whatever errors of fact or judgment we have made. As nonprofessional historians, we have learned through this project a greater respect than ever for those who teach, research, and write history for a living. We therefore close by acknowledging the work of the many fine historians who helped us understand the big picture in which the Fifth New Hampshire played a small but—we think—significant role.

Notes

Our purpose in embarking on this project was to explore what struck us, a pair of New Hampshire journalists, as a compelling local story (albeit a dated one). Therefore the focus of the notes that follow, as of our research for *My Brave Boys*, is on the Fifth Regiment, New Hampshire Volunteers.

We were fortunate to be able to draw on standard secondary sources for our general understanding of the campaigns and battles in which the Fifth was engaged. We have chosen to acknowledge those works here and in our bibliography rather than citing them in the pages that follow. This has meant there are no citations for some paragraphs even when, for example, an exultant General McClellan is quoted after the discovery of Robert E. Lee's secret orders in September of 1862. Our intention is not to slight these secondary works but to focus our notes on the information we presume to be of greatest interest to readers and researchers: primary source material directly related to the Fifth's story.

Of these standard sources, none were of greater value than the works of Stephen W. Sears. His concise, readable, and balanced analyses are admirable in all respects.

Sears's *To the Gates of Richmond* and his biography of George B. McClellan shaped our view of the Peninsula campaign. For these battles, we also relied on Robert Underwood Johnson and Clarence Clough Buel's *Battles and Leaders of the Civil War*, the invaluable post-war collection of firsthand accounts that originally appeared in *Century Magazine*, and Frank Moore's *Rebellion Record*, a quirky but useful potpourri of articles, orders, and letters.

Our understanding of the Antietam campaign was shaped largely by Sears's *Landscape Turned Red*, supplemented by his discussion of Lee's lost order in *Controversies and Commanders*. Our view of the campaign was also influenced by the first full history written about it: *The Antietam and Fredericksburg* by General Francis W. Palfrey. We are indebted as well to a compilation of official reports, *The U.S. Army War College Guide to the Battle of Antietam*, edited by Jay Luvaas and Harold W. Nelson.

Our account of the battle of Fredericksburg was informed by Palfrey's book, *Battles and Leaders*, the *Rebellion Record*, and *The Fredericksburg Campaign*, one of a fine series of anthologies edited by Gary Gallagher, as well as William Marvel's biography of Ambrose Burnside.

Two recent books, Sears's *Chancellorsville* and Ernest B. Furgurson's *Chancellorsville, 1863*, gave us a firm grounding in Hooker's campaign. In Gallagher's *Chancellorsville: The Battle and Its Aftermath*, Carol Reardon's essay on General Winfield Scott Hancock's corps helped us focus on the role of Colonel Edward Cross and the Fifth New Hampshire during that battle.

Sears has not yet produced a history of Gettysburg, but his *Controversies and Commanders* does address Major General Daniel Sickles's decision to move off Cemetery Ridge, which so affected the fate of the Fifth. Harry W. Pfanz's *Gettysburg: The Second Day* was of weighty importance; useful too was his slim *Battle of Gettysburg* in the National Park Civil War Series. We drew as well on the *Guide to the Battle of Gettysburg*, another in the series edited by Luvaas and Nelson.

Finally, our understanding of the thoughts and experiences of Civil War soldiers was informed by a number of works, including two classics: *Hard Tack and Coffee* by John D. Billings and *The Life of Billy Yank* by Bell Irvin Wiley. We were also influenced by Reid Mitchell's *Civil War Soldiers* and *The Vacant Chair*; James M. McPherson's *For Cause and Comrades*; Gerald F. Linderman's *Embattled Courage*; and Earl J. Hess's *Union Soldier in Battle*.

To all these authors, and Sears in particular, we express our respect and gratitude. Any mistakes of fact or analysis in the application of their works in ours is, of course, our responsibility alone.

For brevity's sake, the following abbreviations have been employed in the notes.

DCL: Dartmouth College Library
HSP: Historical Society of Pennsylvania
LHS: Lancaster Historical Society
NA: National Archives
NHA: New Hampshire Division of Records Management and Archives
NHHS: New Hampshire Historical Society
OR: *War of the Rebellion: Official Records*
USAMHI: U.S. Army Military History Institute

I. THE FIGHTING FIFTH

P. 1, *Young Charles Wright*:   Charles A. Wright, "The Silent Neighbor," *New Hampshire Profiles*, May 1958, p. 30.

P. 1, *With that the veteran*:   Wright, "Silent Neighbor," p. 44. Leonard W. Howard, service record, NA. (The judgment that Howard embellished his tale is based in a comparison of the dramatic description of his chest wound in Wright's article with Howard's service record.) Fifth Regiment, New Hampshire Volunteers, regimental order book, May 22, 1863, NA.

P. 1, *As for the Fifth*:   Lt. Col. William F. Fox, *Regimental Losses in the American Civil War, 1861–65*, pp. 2, 139. *Farmer's Cabinet*, Aug. 6, 1863. Howard, pension file, NA.

P. 2, *Howard was luckier*:   William Child, *A History of the Fifth Regiment, New Hampshire Volunteers, in the American Civil War, 1861–1865*, part 2, p. 92. *National Eagle*,

Sept. 26, 1861. *Granite State Free Press*, Nov. 1, 1861. Thomas L. Livermore, *Days and Events, 1860–1866*, p. 189. Andy Sutherland, "A Survey of the Ages of the Original 5th NHV," *Charge Bayonets!* Apr. 1991, p. 5. Child, *History*, p. 21. *Farmer's Cabinet*, Nov. 26, 1863.

P. 3, *The regiment, a unit*:   Fox, *Losses*, p. 1.

P. 3, *Because they were composed*:   Maj. Gen. Winfield Scott Hancock to Sen. Daniel Clark, Dec. 19, 1862, courtesy of Walter Holden. Fox, *Losses*, p. 2. Bruce Catton, *Bruce Catton's Civil War*, pp. 123, 208.

2. CROSS

P. 5, *The Edward Ephraim*:   Edward E. Cross, "Private Journal of the Organization, March, and Services of the 5th New Hampshire Regiment," p. 2, courtesy of Walter Holden. Livermore, *Days*, pp. 25–26. Charles A. Hale, "With Colonel Cross in the Gettysburg Campaign," John Rutter Brooke Papers, HSP.

P. 5, *Cross had arrived*:   Cross, "Journal," p. 1. Edward Cross to Henry Kent correspondence, 1850–61. Edward Cross, writings in *Cincinnati Times, Cincinnati Dollar Times*, 1854–58. All Cross's letters to Kent cited in this chapter are used courtesy of M. Faith Kent.

P. 5, *The American*:   *Cincinnati Times, Cincinnati Dollar Times*, 1854–58. Natt Head, *Report of the Adjutant General, 1865*, vol. 1, pp. 799–802. Cross to Kent correspondence, 1850–61.

P. 6, *The young man*:   Cross to Kent correspondence, 1850–61.

P. 6, *Cross was born*:   Rev. A. N. Somers, *History of Lancaster*, pp. 114, 132, 135, 348–49. Cross to Kent, Jan. 15, 1853, Feb. 17, 1853, Mar. 1, 1857. U.S. Census tally sheet, Sept. 10, 1850, LHS.

P. 7, *At the age of*:   Somers, *History of Lancaster*, pp. 229, 232, 266, 454–58. Cross to Kent, Apr. 17, 1856.

P. 7, *Cross's brother Richard*:   Somers, *History of Lancaster*, 454–58. Artemus Ward, *Rocky Mountain News*, Sept. 10, 1859, reprinted from *Cleveland Plain Dealer*. Undated *Coos Republican* account in scrapbook of Edward R. Kent, LHS. Cross to Kent, Apr. 14, 1851.

P. 8, *In 1850, Cross*:   Cross to Kent, June 1, 1850, Apr. 14, 1851, May 15, 1852. Head, *Report, 1865*, p. 799.

P. 8, *The city offered*:   Cross to Kent, June 1, 1850, Dec. 9, 1852, Apr. 19, 1853.

P. 8, *Although Cross*:   Ibid., Dec. 9, 1852, Feb. 17, 1853, Mar. 15, 1853, Sept. 14, 1854.

P. 9, *Neither nightlife*:   Ibid, Jan. 15, Feb. 17, and Apr. 21, 1853.

P. 9, *Several of Cross's*:   *Cincinnati Dollar Times*, Nov. 10, 1854. Somers, *History of Lancaster*, p. 94.

P. 9, *"There is no class*:   *Cincinnati Dollar Times*, Nov. 10, 1854.

P. 10, *Beyond his writing*:   Our understanding of American Party politics is gleaned from writings by Cross and others in the *Cincinnati Times*; Michael F. Holt, *The*

Political Crisis of the 1850s, pp. 132–81, including the synthesis of William Gienapp's paper, "The Transformation of Cincinnati Politics"; Eric Foner, *Free Soil, Free Labor, Free Men*, pp. 223–41; and William B. Hesseltine and Rex G. Fisher, editors, "Trimmers, Trucklers and Temporizers," State Historical Society of Wisconsin.

P. 10, *Cross's loyalty*:   Cross to Kent, Mar. 16 and Apr. 19, 1853.

P. 10, *In his newspaper*:   *Cincinnati Dollar Times*, Nov. 10. 1854.

P. 11, *Beyond his political*:   Cross to Kent, Dec. 25, 1855, Mar. 28, 1857.

P. 11, *During the winters*:   *Cincinnati Dollar Times*, Feb. 22, Apr. 21, and May 1, 1856.

P. 12, *Although Cross*:   Cross to Kent, Apr. 3 and 7, 1855.

P. 12, *Cross left*:   *Cincinnati Dollar Times*, Feb. 29, 1856.

P. 12, *As the brotherhood*:   Cross to Kent, July 18, 1855, Mar. 24, 1856, Mar. 1 and 28, 1857.

P. 13, *Although Cross ran*:   Ibid., Aug. 26, 1856, Mar. 1, 1857.

P. 13, *Cross's new employer*:   Kenneth Hufford, "Journalism in Pre-Territorial Arizona," *The Smoke Signal*, pp. 80–81. Cross to Kent, July 28, 1857.

P. 13, *In a series*:   *Cincinnati Times*, Aug. 20–Dec. 21, 1858.

P. 14, *Cross's journey*:   Edward Cross, "A Journey to Arizona," *Cincinnati Times*, Letter No. I, Aug. 12, 1858. (The datelines used in these notes are Cross's; publication dates were slightly later.)

P. 14, *The departure*:   Ibid., Letters No. I, Aug. 12, 1858, and II, Aug. 18, 1858.

P. 14, *All across Texas*:   Ibid., Letters No. III, Aug. 26, 1858, and VI, Sept. 14, 1858.

P. 15, *In Texas's German*:   Ibid., Letters No. IV, Aug. 26, 1858 (Letters III and IV were dated the same day), and VII, Sept. 25, 1858.

P. 16, *On a less caustic*:   Ibid., Letters No. IV, V, Sept. 9, 1858, IX, Oct. 14, 1858, and X, Oct. 25, 1858.

P. 16, *The Rio Grande*:   Ibid., Letter No. XI, Nov. 1, 1858.

P. 16, *It was in El Paso*:   Ibid., Letter No. XII, Nov. 10, 1858.

P. 17, *As the party headed*:   Ibid., Letters No. VI and VII.

P. 17, *And yet in one*:   Ibid., *Cincinnati Dollar Times*, Letter No. XX, Feb. 3, 1859.

P. 18, *In early January*:   Hufford, "Journalism," pp. 78–79. Cross to Kent, Aug. 25, 1859. Edward Cross (writing as "Gila"), "The Humbug Exposed," quoted in various accounts from the *States*, Feb. 26, 1859.

P. 19, *While supplying*:   Hufford, "Journalism," pp. 81–82. *Weekly Arizonian*, Mar. 3 and July 7, 1859.

P. 19, *For an editor*:   *Weekly Arizonian*, Mar. 3, 1859. Cross, "Humbug Exposed." Sylvester Mowry to the *States*, Mar. 1, 1859.

P. 20, *Cross read into*:   Cross to the *States*, Apr. 24, 1859, published May 24, 1859.

P. 20, *By the time*:   Hufford, "Journalism," p. 85. Sylvester Mowry to the *States*, July 2, 1859, published July 24, 1859, quoted by David Dary, *Red Blood and Black Ink*, p. 112.

P. 20, *On the morning*:   "The Duel between Mowry and Cross—Exciting Scene," *Rocky Mountain News*, Sept. 10, 1859. *New Hampshire Patriot*, Aug. 25, 1859, reprinted from *Cincinnati Commercial*. Hufford, "Journalism," pp. 86–88. Dary, *Red Blood*, pp. 111–13. *Weekly Arizonian*, July 14, 1859. Cross to Kent, Aug. 25, 1859.

P. 21, *The combatants*:   *Weekly Arizonian*, July 14 and Aug. 4, 1859. Hufford, "Journalism," p. 88.

P. 21, *Cross offered*:   Cross to Kent, Aug. 25, 1859. *Weekly Arizonian*, July 21, 1859.

P. 21, *In the ensuing*:   Cross to Kent, Sept. 14, 1859. Artemus Ward, "The Fighting Editor," *Rocky Mountain News*, Sept. 10, 1859, reprinted from *Cleveland Plain Dealer*.

P. 22, *From the time*:   Cross to Kent, Sept. 14, Oct. 15, Dec. 14, and Dec. 30, 1859, Feb. 2, 1860. Edward Cross, pension file, NA. (An investigative report in this file details Edward Cross's father's financial and drinking problems and the extent to which the family relied on Edward Cross for financial assistance.) "Letter from Arizona," *San Francisco Daily Evening Bulletin*, July 1, 1860, published July 14, 1860. "Mexican Politics," *Weekly Arizonian*, Mar. 3, 1859. Head, *Report, 1865*, vol. 1, p. 802.

P. 22, *The wayward*:   Cross to Kent, July 10, 1858, Mar. 3 and Aug. 25, 1859.

P. 23, *Sooner than he expected*:   Ibid., July 3, 1861. Lieut. Charles N. Kent, *History of the Seventeenth Regiment, New Hampshire Volunteer Infantry*, p. 94.

P. 23, *By the time*:   Cross, "Journal," p. 1.

3. COMING TOGETHER

P. 24, *In September of 1861*:   *New Hampshire Patriot*, Sept. 25, 1861. Cross to Kent, Sept. 15, 1861, courtesy of M. Faith Kent.

P. 25, *Sturtevant was a natural*:   Henry McFarland, *Sixty Years in Concord and Elsewhere*, p. 70. Edward E. Sturtevant letters, 1844–60, collection of Mike Pride. *Statesman*, Dec. 20, 1862. James O. Lyford, editor, *History of Concord, New Hampshire*, pp. 481–82. The Rev. Stephen G. Abbott, *The First Regiment, New Hampshire Volunteers, in the Great Rebellion*, p. 102.

P. 26, *There were sixteen*:   Edward D. Boylston, *Amherst in the Great Civil Conflict of 1861–65*, pp. 5–9.

P. 26, *In Concord*:   Lyford, *History*, pp. 483–85. *New Hampshire Patriot*, Apr. 24, 1861.

P. 27, *In Claremont*:   *Northern Advocate*, Apr. 23, 1861. Otis F. R. Waite, *Claremont War History, April, 1861, to April, 1865*, pp. 16–23.

P. 27, *Lost in the frenzy*:   William Marvel, "Answering Lincoln's Call," *Historical New Hampshire*, fall/winter 1984, pp. 143, 145.

P. 27, *The combination of uncertain*:   First Regiment, New Hampshire Volunteers, records, NHA.

P. 28, *Despite the First's troublesome*:   Marvel, "Answering Lincoln's Call," pp. 144–46.

P. 28, *In the field*:   Capt. Charles Sawyer, June 13, 1861, First Regiment, records, NHA. Marvel, "Answering Lincoln's Call," pp. 146–47.

P. 28, *That was the end*:   Marvel, "Answering Lincoln's Call," pp. 149–50. *New Hampshire Patriot*, Aug. 7, 1861.

P. 29, *The question of how*: *National Eagle*, Oct. 17, 1861.

P. 29, *The war dominated*: *Journals of the Honorable Senate and House of Representatives*, June Session, 1861, Part 2, p. 208, Part 1, p. 114.

P. 29, *More critical still*: McFarland, *Sixty Years*, pp. 240–41. Livermore, *Days*, p. 22. *New Hampshire Patriot*, Aug. 28, Aug. 14, 1861. Lyford, *History*, pp. 1182–83.

P. 30, *For many in New Hampshire*: *National Eagle*, Aug. 8, 1861. *Northern Advocate*, Aug. 6, 1861. Waite, *Claremont War History*, pp. 59–61. *People's Journal*, Oct. 11, 1861.

P. 31, *Edward Sturtevant tapped*: *New Hampshire Patriot*, Sept. 25, 1861.

P. 31, *The Fifth was recruited*: Boylston, *Amherst*, p. 5. *Farmer's Cabinet*, Sept. 20, 1861.

P. 32, *Ira Barton was a captain*: Edward Wheeler, *The History of Newport, New Hampshire, from 1766 to 1878*, pp. 191, 196. (The judgment that Levi Barton used his connections to advance his son's career is ours, as is the assessment of his motives. Both are based on inferences in their correspondence.) T. W. Higginson to Ira Barton, Jan. 17, 1861, Barton papers, DCL. Abbott, *First Regiment*, p. 102. Levi Barton to Ira Barton, May 12, 1861, Barton papers, DCL. (The judgment as to the timing of Barton's marriage proposal is ours, based on the subsequent date of the marriage.)

P. 32, *State authorities named*: *National Eagle*, Aug. 29, Sept. 12 and 26, 1861.

P. 33, *As with April's volunteers*: *Granite State Free Press*, Nov. 1, Oct. 14, 1861. *Northern Advocate*, Oct. 1, 1861. *National Eagle*, Sept. 26, 1861.

P. 33, *Before meeting the enemy*: Child, *History*, pp. 6–7. Cross, "Journal," p. 2. General Order No. 1, Fifth Regiment, records, NHA.

P. 35, *The first company*: Child, *History*, pp. 6–7.

P. 35, *One of these men*: George A. Ramsdell, *The History of Milford*, p. 377. Livermore, *Days*, pp. vii, 4, 5, 10, 14, 24–25.

P. 37, *A private in Livermore's*: Child, *History*, Part 2, p. 142. Miles Peabody, pension file, NA. Miles Peabody, assorted letters, collection of Mike Pride. Miles Peabody to his parents, Sept. 29, 1861, USAMHI.

P. 37, *Peabody and his colleagues*: Fifth Regiment, records, daily calls, and General Order No. 1, NHA.

P. 38, *Colonel Cross knew*: Livermore, *Days*, p. 25. Cross, "Journal," p. 3.

P. 38, *Harshness was not*: Fifth Regiment, records, General Order No. 4, NHA.

P. 39, *The Fifth New Hampshire*: "P.S." to *National Eagle*, Oct. 3, Oct. 10, 1861. *Statesman*, as quoted in *People's Journal*, Nov. 8, 1861. Charles N. Kent, *History of the Seventeenth Regiment*, p. 71. Lyford, *History*, p. 1175.

P. 39, *The birth of the regiment's*: *People's Journal*, Dec. 6, 1861. Mary (Polly) Larkin to James Larkin, November 1861, James E. Larkin papers, NHHS. Livermore, *Days*, pp. 54, 154, 30. James R. Jackson, *History of Littleton New Hampshire*, vol. 3, p. 345. Hale to Crowley, May 5, 1897, *Report of the Ninth Annual Reunion of the 64th N.Y. Regimental Association*. Jackson, *History of Littleton*, vol. 1, p. 447. Thomas Wier, pension file, NA. Waite, *Claremont War History*, pp. 119–23. Benjamin Chase, pension file, NA. "X" to *Northern Advocate*, Oct. 1, 1861.

P. 40, *Some in the Fifth*: Waite, *Claremont War History*, pp. 106–7. Livermore, *Days*, p. 24.

P. 40, *Whether as individuals*: *Statesman*, Oct. 23, 1861. (The judgment that Cross was responsible for the rejection of the gray uniforms is our own, based on the implications of his journal and his personality.) Livermore, *Days*, p. 27. Child, *History*, p. 21. *Granite State Free Press*, Oct. 4, 1861. (Cross's chagrin is revealed in subsequent actions addressed in later chapters.) *Northern Advocate*, Oct. 15, 1861. *National Eagle*, Nov. 14, Oct. 10, 1861.

P. 41, *Between October 12*: Child, *History*, p. 9. Records of Harold E. Perkins, Newport (N.H.) genealogist. *National Eagle*, Oct. 3, Oct. 17, 1861. Waite, *History of Claremont*, p. 430.

P. 42, *The regiment's last days*: Child, *History*, p. 7. Fifth Regiment, records, General Order No. 5, NHA. *National Eagle*, Nov. 14, 1861.

P. 42, *Late that morning*: Livermore, *Days*, pp. 27–28.

P. 42, *The regiment was up*: Child, *History*, pp. 19–20. Cross, "Journal," p. 4.

P. 43, *Colonel Cross's spirits*: Cross, "Journal," pp. 3–4. *Northern Advocate*, Nov. 5, 1861. *National Eagle*, Oct. 29, 1861.

P. 43, *Overlooked in the excitement*: *Nashua Telegraph*, as printed in *Northern Advocate*, Nov. 5, 1861. Child, *History*, Part 2, p. 118.

P. 44, *The trip south*: Child, *History*, p. 20. Cross, "Journal," p. 4. "Volunteer" to *People's Journal*, Nov. 15, 1861. Livermore, *Days*, p. 29.

P. 44, *Before the capital*: Livermore, *Days*, p. 29. Child, *History*, p. 20.

P. 44, *It was October 31*: *National Eagle*, Nov. 7, 1861.

4. WINTER'S TRIALS

P. 46, *When Lieutenant James Larkin*: James Larkin to Jenny Larkin, Nov. 1, 1861, NHHS.

P. 47, *Larkin's first-day exuberance*: Child, *History*, p. 24. Cross, "Journal," p. 4. "Volunteer" to *People's Journal*, Nov. 15, 1861.

P. 47, *On the evening*: Cross, "Journal," p. 5. Fifth Regiment, regimental order book, Nov. 2, 1861, NA.

P. 47, *The coming Tuesday*: Child, *History*, pp. 24, 26. Cross, "Journal," pp. 5–7. Child, *History*, pp. 25–26.

P. 48, *Election day was*: Peabody to his parents, Nov. 10, 1861, USAMHI.

P. 48, *Despite the blisters*: Cross, "Journal," pp. 5, 8. Livermore, *Days*, p. 31.

P. 49, *Cross knew his men*: Fifth Regiment, regimental order book, Nov. 10, 1861, NA.

P. 49, *Drill was neither*: Ibid., Nov. 23, Nov. 16, 1861. (To add insult to injury, the record of Maley's court-martial misidentifies him as Patrick Malia.)

P. 49, *That intervention reflected*: Ibid., Nov. 19, 1861.

P. 50, *Soon it became clear*: Ibid., Nov. 11, 1861. Peabody to his parents, Jan. 20, 1862, courtesy of Mary Anne Zak. Livermore, *Days*, p. 30. Capt. Richard Welch and Lieut. J. B. David to Gov. Nathaniel Berry, Mar. 10, 1862, Fifth Regiment, records, NHA.

P. 50, *The Fifth had arrived*: *Farmer's Cabinet*, Nov. 28, 1861. Child, *History*, p. 27. James Larkin to Jenny Larkin, Nov. 27, 1861, NHHS. *Northern Advocate*, Nov. 30, 1861.

P. 51, *All these plans*: Livermore, *Days*, p. 31. Child, *History*, p. 28. "CHC" to *Farmer's Cabinet*, Dec. 12, 1861.

P. 51, *The Fifth put*: Child, *History*, p. 28. Cross, "Journal," p. 10.

P. 51, *The next morning*: Cross, "Journal," p. 9.

P. 52, *Camp California was located*: Mark M. Boatner III, *The Civil War Dictionary*, p. 818. (The judgment that the camp was named in Sumner's honor is our own.) Livermore, *Days*, pp. 31–32. Child, *History*, p. 35. "N." to *Farmer's Cabinet*, Dec. 12, 1861.

P. 52, *The regiment's routines*: Livermore, *Days*, pp. 35, 34, 39. Hale to Crowley, May 5, 1897, *Report of the Ninth Annual Reunion of the 64th N.Y. Regimental Association*. Child, *History*, p. 36.

P. 53, *Though just seventeen*: Livermore, *Days*, pp. 32–33, 36.

P. 53, *Although Sergeant Livermore*: Ibid., pp. 34–36.

P. 53, *A more pressing preoccupation*: George Worthington Adams, *Doctors in Blue*, pp. 222–23, 239. William Moore to Adams Moore, *People's Journal*, Jan. 3, 1862. Peabody to his parents, Nov. 11, 1861, USAMHI.

P. 54, *Cross's insistence*: Child, *History*, pp. 40–41. Fifth Regiment, daily reports, Company B, NA. William Moore to Elizabeth Moore, *People's Journal*, Dec. 11, 1861.

P. 54, *The men were exposed*: An unnamed officer to *Granite State Free Press*, as reprinted in *Statesman*, Jan. 18, 1862.

P. 54, *Often, there was little*: Ira Barton to Levi Barton, Jan. 15, 1862, DCL.

P. 55, *By the end of December*: Sgt. Maj. Daniel Cross to *Independent Democrat*, Jan. 6, 1862. Child, *History*, p. 36. Daniel Cross to *Independent Democrat*, Jan. 6, 1862. Cross, "Journal," p. 8. "P" to *Farmer's Cabinet*, Jan. 6, 1862. Ira Barton to "Mr. Waterman," *Granite State Free Press*, Feb. 7, 1862.

P. 55, *The threat of illness*: Unnamed soldier to *Farmer's Cabinet*, Dec. 5, 1861. "N" to *Farmer's Cabinet*, Dec. 19, 1861.

P. 56, *On December 6*: Child, *History*, p. 31. Livermore, *Days*, p. 41. William Moore to Elizabeth Moore, *People's Journal*, Dec. 11, 1861.

P. 56, *Most of the real action*: Livermore, *Days*, p. 43. Child, *History*, p. 31. Peabody to his parents, Dec. 14, 1861, courtesy of Mary Anne Zak. "P" to *Farmer's Cabinet*, Jan. 2, 1862. Cross to Kent, Dec. 17, 1862, courtesy of M. Faith Kent.

P. 57, *Cross was much less tolerant*: Cross to Kent, Dec. 17, 1862, courtesy of M. Faith Kent. Edward E. Cross to Nathaniel Berry, Nov. 11, Dec. 2, 1861, Fifth Regiment, records, NHA.

P. 57, *What outraged Cross*: Edward E. Cross to U.S. Rep. Thomas Edwards, *Farmer's Cabinet*, Feb. 6, 1862. *Keene Sentinel*, reprinted in *National Eagle*, Feb. 18, 1862. Fifth Regiment, regimental order book, Feb. 28, 1862, NA.

P. 58, *On the whole*: William Moore to Elizabeth Moore, *People's Journal*, Dec. 11, 1861. "N" to *Farmer's Cabinet*, Dec. 19, 1861. Charles Scott to "friend amie," Dec. 24, 1861, USAMHI.

P. 58, *The colonel had in mind*:   John Bucknam to Sally Bucknam, Dec. 25, 1861, LHS. John McCrillis's narrative, as printed in Child, *History*, pp. 41–42. William Moore to Adams Moore, *Farmer's Cabinet*, Jan. 3, 1862. James Larkin to Jenny Larkin, Dec. 25, 1861, NHHS. Camp Song No. 1, Dec. 25, 1861, courtesy of Paul Levasseur.

P. 59, *Beginning on the day after*:   Cross, "Journal," p. 13. Child, *History*, pp. 38–39. "Yaf Slohein & Co." to *Farmer's Cabinet*, Jan. 25, 1862.

P. 60, *Making life still more*:   Charles Long to *National Eagle*, Jan. 2, 1862. *People's Journal*, Jan. 3, 1862. James Larkin to Jenny Larkin, Jan. 15, Jan. 21, Jan. 24, 1862, NHHS.

P. 60, *One officer*:   Anna Bucknam to Deborah McIntire, Feb. 27, 1862, LHS.

P. 61, *All in all*:   *The People's Journal*, Jan. 3, 1862. Child, *History*, p. 41. Charles Long to *National Eagle*, Feb. 6, 1862.

P. 61, *Such was the intimacy*:   Levi Barton to Ira Barton, Feb. 16, 1862, DCL. An unnamed officer to *Granite State Free Press*, as reprinted in *Statesman*, Jan. 18, 1862. "Iago" to *Granite State Free Press*, Jan. 31, 1862.

P. 62, *On January 14*:   Child, *History*, p. 32. "Private" to *Farmer's Cabinet*, Jan. 30, 1862. Livermore, *Days*, p. 41.

P. 62, *The men left at half past*:   Child, *History*, p. 32. "Private" to *Farmer's Cabinet*, Jan. 30, 1862. Livermore, *Days*, p. 42. James Larkin to Jenny Larkin, Jan. 19, 1862, NHHS. Cross to Kent, Jan. 20, 1862, courtesy of M. Faith Kent.

P. 63, *In the meantime*:   Edward E. Sturtevant to Adj. Gen. Anthony Colby, Jan. 18, 1862, Fifth Regiment, records, NHA. James Larkin to Jenny Larkin, Jan. 24, 1862, NHHS. Livermore, *Days*, p. 45. Child, *History*, p. 32. "N" to *Farmer's Cabinet*, Feb. 27, 1862. James Larkin to Jenny Larkin, Feb. 9, 1862, NHHS. "N" to *Farmer's Cabinet*, Feb. 27, 1862. Peabody to parents, Feb. 19, 1862, courtesy of Mary Anne Zak. "WSD" to *Statesman*, Feb. 1, 1862. (The identification of WSD as Walter Drew is our own judgment, based on the context of the letter and an examination of the regimental roster.) "Sarepta" to *Farmer's Cabinet*, Mar. 6, 1862.

P. 65, *On February 23*:   Livermore, *Days*, pp. 37–39. Capt. Richard Welch and Lt. J. B. David to Gov. Nathaniel Berry, Mar. 10, 1862, Fifth Regiment, records, NHA.

P. 65, *Welch and David*:   Capt. Richard Welch and Lt. J. B. David to Gov. Nathaniel Berry, Mar. 10, 1862, Fifth Regiment, records, NHA. Edward E. Cross to Secretary of State Allen Tenney, Mar. 30, 1862, Fifth Regiment, records, NHA.

P. 66, *Although such friction*:   "Sarepta" to *Farmer's Cabinet*, Mar. 6, 1862. James Larkin to Jenny Larkin, Mar. 9, 1862, NHHS. Child, *History*, p. 34.

P. 66, *Anna Bucknam*:   Anna Bucknam to Deborah McIntire, Mar. 14, 1862, LHS.

5. ON TO RICHMOND

P. 68, *As these plans*:   Peabody to parents, Apr. 5, 1862, courtesy of Mary Anne Zak.

P. 68, *The first of April*:   Livermore, *Days*, p. 51. Cross, "Journal," p. 23.

P. 68, *By the time*:   Cross, "Journal," p. 23. Cross to Kent, Apr. 6, 1862, courtesy of M. Faith Kent. *Statesman*, Apr. 26, 1862 (quoting *New York Herald* account).

P. 69, *Fine spring weather*:   James Larkin to Jenny Larkin, Apr. 6, 1862, NHHS. Cross, "Journal," p. 23.

P. 69, *The Fifth's destination*:   Cross, "Journal," p. 23. Livermore, *Days*, 54. Peabody to parents, Mar. 9, 1862, courtesy of Mary Anne Zak.

P. 69, *Finally, on April 11*:   Livermore, *Days*, 54. Fifth Regiment, regimental order book, Apr. 13, 1862, NA. Henry Holt to his grandfather, Apr. 19, 1862, Stephen H. Holt, papers, DCL. James Larkin to Jenny Larkin, Apr. 10, 1862, NHHS.

P. 70, *As pleasant as*:   James Larkin to Jenny Larkin, Apr., 10, 1862. Peabody to parents, Apr. 18, 1862, USAMHI. Cross to Kent, May 3, 1862, courtesy of M. Faith Kent.

P. 71, *Sent to join*:   Cross, "Journal," p. 24. Livermore, *Days*, p. 58. James Larkin to Jenny Larkin, Apr. 30, 1862, NHHS.

P. 71, *Abruptly, on May 4*:   James Larkin to Jenny Larkin and children, May 2, 1862, to Jenny Larkin, May 4, 1862, NHHS. "Serepta" to *Farmer's Cabinet*, May 13, 1862, published May 22, 1862.

P. 72, *Not all*:   Benjamin Chase to Nancy Chase, May 4, 1862, Benjamin Chase, pension file, NA.

P. 72, *McClellan's triumph*:   Cross, "Journal," p. 26. Livermore, *Days*, p. 60. George Spalding to cousin Mary, May 18, 1862, *Charge Bayonets!* Jan. 1990. George Gove diary, in Child, *History*, p. 58. James Larkin to Jenny Larkin and children, May 9, 1862, NHHS.

P. 73, *The men had*:   "Serepta" to *Farmer's Cabinet*, May 13, 1862, published May 22, 1862. Thomas Law to sister Annie, May 18, 1862, Thomas Law, pension file, NA. George Spalding to cousin Mary, May 18, 1862, *Charge Bayonets!* Cross, "Journal," pp. 27–28.

P. 74, *Even as rumors*:   Livermore, *Days*, p. 63. Fifth Regiment, regimental order book, May 23 and 27, 1862, NA. *Northern Advocate*, May 13, 1862. James Larkin to Jenny Larkin and children, May 24, 1862, NHHS.

P. 74, *The colonel's attention*:   *Coos Democrat*, Nov. 20, 1889. Charles Hale to Rodney C. Crowley, May 5, 1897, printed in *Report of the Ninth Annual Reunion of the Regimental Association of the 64th N.Y. Regimental Association*.

P. 74, *Cross was at*:   Fifth Regiment, regimental order book, May 25, 1862, NA. Livermore, *Days*, p. 64.

P. 75, *At daybreak on May 28*:   Natt Head, *Report of the Adjutant-General, 1866*, vol. 2, p. 542. Edward Cross to father, May 26, 1862, courtesy of John Henry Kurtz. Child, *History*, pp. 63–64. Cross, "Journal," pp. 27–31.

P. 76, *Cross organized*:   Cross, "Journal," pp. 27–31. Livermore, *Days*, p. 63. Head, *Report, 1866*, vol. 2, 1866, p. 542. Child, *History*, pp. 65–72 (including first-person accounts by Charles Hapgood, William H. Weston, George Gove, and two anonymous soldiers).

P. 76, *Whether the bridge*:   Cross, "Journal," pp. 30–31.

P. 77, *On the other side*:   Adjutant Charles Dodd, quoted by Walter Holden, "The Blooding of the Best," pp. 26–27, *Military History Magazine*, January 1990. Cross, "Journal," p. 31.

P. 78, *Five minutes before* through *"If I fall*: James Larkin to Jenny Larkin and children, May 27, 1862 (postscript, May 31, 1862), NHHS.

P. 79, *For others*: Livermore, *Days*, p. 66. Weston account in Child, *History*, p. 66.

P. 79, *As had happened*: William Moore to Adams Moore, June 2, 1862, published in *People's Journal*, June 20, 1862. James Larkin to Jenny Larkin and children, June [2?], 1862, NHHS. Cross, "Journal," pp. 31–32. Livermore, *Days*, p. 65.

P. 79, *Preparing for*: William Moore to Adams Moore, June 2, 1862, *People's Journal*. James Perry to editor, *Granite State Free Press*, June 5, 1862, published June 20, 1862. Child, *History*, p. 79. Cross, "Journal," pp. 33–36.

P. 80, *But these were not*: Livermore, *Days*, p. 66. Cross, "Journal," pp. 36–38. William Moore to Adams Moore, June 2, 1862, *People's Journal*. James Larkin to Jenny Larkin and children, June [2?], 1862, NHHS.

P. 80, *With dawn approaching*: Cross, "Journal," pp. 38–40. Livermore, *Days*, pp. 66–67. *Farmer's Cabinet*, June 26, 1862.

P. 82, *As Cross waited*: Cross, "Journal," p. 40. Charles Phelps to sister Sophia, June 4, 1862, collection of Mike Pride. Child, *History*, p. 91. Ira McL. Barton to Levi Barton, June 6, 1862, published in *Northern Advocate*, June 17, 1862.

P. 82, *As the senior*: Cross, "Journal," pp. 41–42. *Statesman*, June 14, 1862 (reprint of *Boston Journal* account). Charles Phelps to sister Sophia, June 4, 1862, Pride collection. Ira McL. Barton to Levi Barton, June 6, 1862, *Northern Advocate*.

P. 83, *Cross, by contrast*: *Cincinnati Commercial* account, in Frank Moore, editor, *The Rebellion Record*, 1864, vol. 5, p. 92. *Statesman*, June 14, 1862. Cross, "Journal," p. 42. William Cook, pension file, Veterans Administration Regional Office, Manchester, N.H. James Larkin to Jenny Larkin, June [2?] and June 11, 1862, NHHS.

P. 83, *As the Fifth*: Cross, "Journal," p. 42. Livermore, *Days*, pp. 67–69. Charles A. Hale to Rodney R. Crowley, May 5, 1897, *Report of the Ninth Annual Reunion of the 64th N.Y. Regimental Association*. Charles Phelps to sister Sophia, June 4, 1862, Pride collection. George Spalding to cousin Mary, July 18, 1862, *Charge Bayonets!*

P. 84, *On the far left*: Ira McL. Barton to Levi Barton, June 6, 1862, *Northern Advocate*. Charles A. Hale to Rodney R. Crowley, Jan. 25, 1897, and Rodney R. Crowley to Charles A. Hale, Mar. 8, 1897, *Report of the Eighth Annual Reunion of the 64th N.Y. Regimental Ass'n*. (This 1897 exchange between Hale and Crowley might merely have been an irresolvable dispute between two old soldiers. Hale did not remember the incident. But Captain Barton's long letter to his father five days after the battle of Fair Oaks confirmed that his company had fired on friendly troops not once but twice that day. Although Colonel Cross wrote a scathing letter claiming that troops from the Irish Brigade had fired on his regiment at Fair Oaks, he made no mention of Barton's company's mistake in any of his reports or accounts of the battle.)

P. 84, *Once Barton's company*: Alonzo Allen to mother and sister, June 13, 1862, published in *National Eagle*, June 26, 1862.

P. 85, *Farther up*: James Perry to editor, *Granite State Free Press*, June 5, 1862, published June 20, 1862. (Statistics are from our analysis of the regimental roster and New Hampshire adjutant general's reports.)

P. 85, *The closeness*: Jacob W. Keller to friend Merrifield, June 1–2, 1862, published in *National Eagle*, June 19, 1862. James Larkin to Jenny Larkin and children, June [2?] and June 5, 1862, NHHS. Ira McL. Barton to Levi Barton, June 6, 1862, *Northern Advocate*. Alonzo Allen to mother and sister, June 13, 1862, *National Eagle*. Waite, *Claremont War History*, p. 114.

P. 85, *The soldiers learned*: Benjamin Chase to Nancy Chase, June 15, 1862, NA. George Spalding to cousin Mary, July, 18, 1862, *Charge Bayonets!*

P. 86, *The Confederate line*: *Statesman*, June 14, 1862 (*Boston Transcript* account). William Moore to Adams Moore, June 2, 1862, *People's Journal*. Cross, regimental report, Fair Oaks Station, June 2, 1862, LHS. Cross, "Journal," p. 43. *Cincinnati Commercial* account in *Rebellion Record*, vol. 5, p. 93.

P. 86, *By this time*: Alonzo Allen to mother and sister, June 13, 1862, *National Eagle*. Ira McL. Barton to Levi Barton, June 6, 1862, *Northern Advocate*. Cross, "Journal," p. 43. Waite, *Claremont War History*, pp. 110–11.

P. 87, *In the immediate*: George Spalding to cousin Mary, July 18, 1862, *Charge Bayonets!* George W. Smith letter, June 7, 1862, published in *People's Journal*, June 20, 1862. James Larkin to Jenny Larkin and children, June 5, 1862, NHHS.

P. 87, *The wounded Colonel*: Cross, "Journal," p. 45. Cross to Gov. Nathaniel Berry, *OR*, part 1—reports, vol. 2, serial no. 2, p. 142.

P. 88, *On June 2*: Ira McL. Barton to Levi Barton, June 6, 1862, *Northern Advocate*. Jacob W. Keller to friend Merrifield, June 1–2, 1862, *National Eagle*. George Spalding to cousin Mary, July, 18, 1862, *Charge Bayonets!* George W. Smith letter, June 7, 1862, *People's Journal*. Charles Phelps to sister Sophia, June 4, 1862, Pride collection. Waite, *Claremont War History*, pp. 114, 116. *National Eagle*, June 12, 1862.

P. 88, *The experience*: Alonzo Allen to mother and sister, June 13, 1862, *National Eagle*. George Gove diary, June 4, 1862, in Child, *History*, p. 87.

P. 89, *Wounded Rebels*: Livermore, *Days*, p. 71. Lloyd D. Forehand to mother, June 13, 1862, Nebraska State Historical Society.

P. 90, *Cross left the Peninsula*: J. Gregory Acken, editor, *Inside the Army of the Potomac*, p. 95.

P. 91, *The landing*: Ibid., pp. 95–98. William Cook, pension file, Veterans Administration Regional Office, Manchester, N.H.

P. 91, *Aboard the Spaulding*: Paul H. Hass, editor, "A Volunteer Nurse in the Civil War: The Letters of Harriet Douglass Whitten," *Wisconsin Magazine of History*, no. 48 (winter 1964–65), p. 143.

P. 91, *The good nature*: Cross to Kent, June 8, 1862, courtesy of M. Faith Kent. *Northern Advocate*, June 17, 1862.

P. 92, *No legislative proclamation*: *Dover Enquirer*, Oct. 16, 1862.

P. 92, *Shortly after*: Charles Phelps to sister Sophia, June 4, 1862, Pride collection.

P. 93, *The men of*: Ibid. George Spalding to cousin Mary, July, 18, 1862, *Charge Bayonets!*

6. RETREAT

P. 94, *As the men*:   Theron Farr to Philena Farr, June 9, 1862, typescript in Bath (N.H.) Public Library.

P. 95, *During this time*:   Ibid. Peabody to parents, June 14, 1862, courtesy of Mary Anne Zak.

P. 95, *The Fifth strengthened*:   Peabody to parents, June 14, 1862, courtesy of Mary Anne Zak. Livermore, *Days*, p. 75. William Moore to sister Bell, June 14, 1862, NHHS.

P. 95, *If minor accidents*:   Livermore, *Days*, p. 76. William Moore to sister Elizabeth, June 20, 1862, NHHS. James Larkin to Jenny Larkin, June 22, 1862, NHHS.

P. 96, *Letters home*:   Benjamin Chase to Madison Chase (father), June 24, 1862, and Benjamin Chase to Nancy Chase (mother), June 15, 1862, NA.

P. 96, *As Chase's description*:   Waite, *Claremont War History*, p. 145. James Larkin to Jenny Larkin, June 22, 1862, NHHS.

P. 97, *Private James Daniels*:   James Daniels diary, in Child, *History*, pp. 87–88.

P. 97, *On June 25*:   Head, *Report, 1866*, vol. 2, p. 544.

P. 98, *To the men of*:   Ibid. Charles Phelps to sister Sophia, June 27, 1862, Pride collection. Livermore, *Days*, p. 78–79. Child, *History*, p. 92.

P. 100, *The Fifth stopped*:   Charles Hale letter, *Granite State Free Press*, July 18, 1862. Livermore, *Days*, pp. 79–80.

P. 100, *McClellan had*:   William B. Franklin quotations from Robert Underwood Johnson and Clarence Clough Buel, editors, *Battles and Leaders of the Civil War*, vol. 2, pp. 369–75.

P. 100, *The Fifth took*:   Livermore, *Days*, pp. 82–83. Peabody to parents, July 13, 1862, courtesy of Mary Anne Zak.

P. 101, *Peabody also*:   Ibid. Peabody to parents, July 13, 1862, courtesy of Mary Anne Zak.

P. 101, *It was midnight*:   Head, *Report, 1866*, vol. 2, p. 544. Livermore, *Days*, p. 54.

P. 101, *The sleep*:   Charles Hale letter, *Granite State Free Press*, July 18, 1862. Livermore, *Days*, p. 87.

P. 102, *There was reason*:   Charles Hale letter, *Granite State Free Press*, July 18, 1862. Livermore, *Days*, p. 189.

P. 102, *The Confederate gunners*:   Livermore, *Days*, pp. 87–89. Charles Hale letter, *Granite State Free Press*, July 18, 1862. James Perry to *Granite State Free Press*, July 18, 1862. Rev. Charles A. Downs, *History of Lebanon, New Hampshire*, p. 340.

P. 102, *As Livermore*:   Livermore, *Days*, pp. 88–90.

P. 103, *For two other men*:   Ibid. Peabody to parents, July 13, 1862, courtesy of Mary Anne Zak.

P. 103, *After the Fifth*:   Charles Hale letter, *Granite State Free Press*, July 18, 1862.

P. 104, *Because they had*:   Ibid. Head, *Report, 1866*, vol. 2, p. 546. Livermore, *Days*, pp. 93–94. Welcome Crafts, pension file, NA.

P. 104, *In the night*:   Livermore, *Days*, p. 94.

P. 104, *In line of battle*:   Child, *History*, p. 96. Samuel Langley, pension file, NA. Livermore, *Days*, pp. 95–98.

P. 105, *McClellan's troops*:   OR, part 1—reports, vol. 2, serial no. 2, p. 142. Head, *Report, 1866*, vol. 2, p. 546.

P. 105, *This was a gloomy*:   Statistics come from an analysis of Fifth rosters in Child, *History*, and New Hampshire adjutant general Head's annual reports.

P. 105, *McClellan had glowing*:   George B. McClellan to Army of the Potomac, July 4, 1862, in Stephen W. Sears, editor, *The Civil War Papers of George B. McClellan*, p. 339. Henry M. Holden to Charles Holden, July 6, 1862, *Charge Bayonets!* Mar.–Apr. 1988, p. 5. Peabody to parents, July 6, 1862, courtesy of Mary Anne Zak. James Larkin to Jenny Larkin and children, July 5, 1862, NHHS.

P. 107, *Once this labor*:   Benjamin Chase to Madison Chase, July 28, 1862, NA. James Larkin to Jenny Larkin and children, July 13, 1862, NHHS.

P. 107, *In the relative*:   Livermore, *Days*, p. 104. Private Henry Holt to grandfather, July 13, 1862, DCL. William Moore to J. H. Kendrick, and Corporal T. H. Lane to Mary Kimball, both Aug. 6, 1862, *Granite State Free Press*, published Aug. 15, 1862. Benjamin Chase to Madison Chase, July 21 and July 28, 1862, NA.

P. 108, *As always*:   William Moore to Dr. Adams Moore, July 18, 1862, NHHS. Peabody to parents, July 13, 1862, courtesy of Mary Anne Zak. Benjamin Chase to Madison Chase, NA.

P. 108, *McClellan later*:   George B. McClellan to Abraham Lincoln, July 4, 1862, and to Mary Ellen McClellan, July 9, 1862, in Sears, editor, *Papers*, pp. 344–45, 348. Livermore, *Days*, p. 103.

P. 108, *Democratic editors*:   *New Hampshire Patriot*, July 9, 1862.

P. 109, *War news*:   Franklin McDuffee, *History of the Town of Rochester*, vol. 1, pp. 198–99.

P. 109, *Letters home*:   Peabody to father, July 13, 1862, courtesy of Mary Anne Zak. George Spalding to cousin Mary, July 18, 1862, *Charge Bayonets!*

P. 110, *The only*:   William Cook, pension file, Veterans Administration Regional Office, Manchester, N.H. Edward Sturtevant to New Hampshire Adjutant General Anthony Colby, July 14, 1862, NHA. James Larkin to Jenny Larkin, July 27, 1862, to Jenny Larkin and children, Aug. 1, 1862, NHHS.

P. 110, *As had happened*:   William Moore to Dr. Adams Moore, July 18, 1862, NHHS. Miles Peabody to parents, Aug. 15, 1862, *Charge Bayonets!*, Mar. 1992. Charles Phelps to sister Sophia, Aug. 10, 1862, Pride collection.

P. 111, *Back in New Hampshire*:   *Coos Republican*, July 8, 1862. Henry Kent account in *Coos Republican*, July 1862, LHS. Cross to Kent, Aug. 5, 1862, courtesy of M. Faith Kent. *New Hampshire Patriot*, Aug. 6, 1862.

P. 112, *By early August*:   Peabody to parents, Aug. 15, 1862, *Charge Bayonets!* Henry Holt to grandfather, Aug. 15, 1862, DCL. James Larkin to Jenny Larkin and children, undated, Aug. 1862, NHHS.

P. 112, *The hot and dusty*:   William Moore to Elizabeth Moore, Aug. 24, 1862, NHHS.

P. 113, *Other reminders*: Ibid. James Larkin to Jenny Larkin, Aug. 20, 1862, NHHS.

P. 113, *Then, at one*: William Moore to Elizabeth Moore, Aug. 24, 1862, NHHS.

P. 114, *Two days later*: Child, *History*, p. 97–98.

P. 114, *Upon his arrival*: Ibid., pp. 98–99. William Child to Carrie Child, Aug. 22, 1862, courtesy of Merrill Sawyer. Child, *History*, pp. 98–99.

P. 114, *The men welcomed*: Cross, "Journal," p. 46. Cross to Kent, Aug. 22, 1862, courtesy of M. Faith Kent.

P. 115, *Cross distributed*: Livermore, *Days*, p. 107. James Larkin to Jenny Larkin and children, Aug. 26, 1862, NHHS.

7. "RICHARDSON'S FOOT CAVALRY"

P. 116, *The men of the Fifth*: Janvrin Graves's narrative, in Child, *History*, p. 104.

P. 116, *Graves had neither*: Ibid.

P. 117, *On the night of August 27*: Livermore, *Days*, pp. 108–9. Child, *History*, p. 101.

P. 117, *The march carried the Fifth*: Edward O. Lord, editor, *History of the Ninth Regiment New Hampshire Volunteers*, pp. 34–35. Graves's narrative, in Child, *History*, p. 106.

P. 117, *The regiments did not*: Sgt. Lewis Fernald's narrative, in Child, *History*, p. 103. (The judgment that the order to march provoked renewed grumbling is our own, based on the Fifth's earlier interaction with the Ninth New Hampshire — Lord, editor, *Ninth Regiment*, p. 34.) Graves's narrative, in Child, *History*, p. 106.

P. 118, *The sad truth*: Livermore, *Days*, p. 109. Cross, "Journal," p. 46.

P. 118, *In the morning*: Livermore, *Days*, pp. 109–10. Report of Col. Edward E. Cross to Gov. Nathaniel Berry, Oct. 31, 1862, as printed in Child, *History*, p. 140. Cross, "Journal," p. 46.

P. 118, *The next day both discomfort*: Cross, "Journal," p. 47. Livermore, *Days*, p. 111.

P. 120, *The Fifth's march*: Cross, "Journal," pp. 48–49. Graves's narrative, in Child, *History*, p. 108.

P. 120, *In the case of the Fifth*: Graves's narrative, in Child, *History*, p. 108.

P. 120, *The exhausting march*: Ibid., p. 109. Livermore, *Days*, p. 112. James Larkin to Jenny Larkin, Sept. 4, 1862, NHHS.

P. 121, *Lee had again*: Cross, "Journal," p. 50.

P. 121, *For the Fifth*: Fernald's narrative, in Child, *History*, p. 103. Livermore, *Days*, pp. 113–15.

P. 122, *Refreshing as it may have been*: Fernald's narrative, in Child, *History*, p. 103. Ira Bronson's narrative, in Child, *History*, p. 132. Charles Bean to James Larkin, Sept. 15, 1862, NHHS.

P. 122, *On September 13*: Head, *Report, 1866*, vol. 2, p. 549. (The account of the Fifth's experiences in the report was written in large part by Livermore, and he is explicitly credited for recounting the Fifth's experiences in the Maryland campaign.) Graves's narrative, in Child, *History*, p. 109. Livermore, *Days*, p. 116.

P. 123, *The next morning*: Livermore, *Days*, p. 119. Graves's narrative, in Child, *History*, p. 110. Cross, "Journal," p. 51.

P. 123, *But as the regiment*: Livermore, *Days*, p. 120.

P. 124, *Major General Israel Richardson's*: Report of Col. Edward E. Cross, Sept. 18, 1862, *OR*, series 1, vol. 19, part 1, p. 287.

P. 124, *Though the men of the Fifth*: Cross, "Journal," pp. 51–52. Livermore, *Days*, p. 121. (The judgment of time required to reach the division's front is our own.)

P. 124, *It was a moment*: Cross's report, *OR*, series 1, vol. 19, part 1, p. 287. Cross, "Journal," p. 52. A. D. Richardson, *New York Tribune*, Sept. 19, 1862. Livermore, *Days*, p. 121.

P. 125, *The Fifth pushed beyond*: Richardson, *New York Tribune*, Sept. 19, 1862. Fernald's narrative, in Child, *History*, p. 104. Livermore, *Days*, p. 122.

P. 125, *Refreshed, the regiment*: Marvel, "Answering Lincoln's Call," p. 149. Graves's narrative, in Child, *History*, p. 110. Head, *Report, 1866*, vol. 2, p. 551.

P. 125, *On the ridge*: Richardson, *New York Tribune*, Sept. 19, 1862. Head, *Report, 1866*, vol. 2, p. 551. Livermore, *Days*, pp. 123–25.

P. 126, *Soon the rebel artillery*: Livermore, *Days*, p. 125. Graves's narrative, in Child, *History*, p. 111. Cross, "Journal," p. 54. Bronson's narrative, in Child, *History*, p. 132.

P. 126, *By three o'clock*: Graves's narrative, in Child, *History*, p. 111. Cross's report, *OR*, series 1, vol. 19, part 1, p. 287.

P. 126, *Despite the prospect*: *OR*, series 1, vol. 19, part 1, p. 287. Livermore, *Days*, p. 126.

8. ANTIETAM

P. 127, *On September 16*: Cross, "Journal," p. 53. Cross's report, Sept. 18, 1862, *OR*, series 1, vol. 19, part 1, p. 288. *Dover Enquirer*, Oct. 16, 1862. Livermore, *Days*, p. 126.

P. 127, *Doctor William Child*: William Child to Carrie Child, Sept. 16, 1862, courtesy of Merrill Sawyer. Child, *History*, p. 127.

P. 128, *With evening each man*: Cross, "Journal," pp. 54–55. Livermore, *Days*, pp. 129–30.

P. 129, *The battle began*: Livermore, *Days*, p. 131.

P. 130, *Cross was invited*: Cross, "Journal," p. 55. Livermore, *Days*, p. 131.

P. 130, *McClellan ordered the Second Corps*: Lee and Barbara Barron, *The History of Sharpsburg, Maryland*.

P. 131, *At 9:20 came the order*: Livermore, *Days*, p. 129. Child, *History*, p. 129.

P. 131, *Once off the high*: Child, *History*, p. 120. Report of Brig. Gen. Winfield S. Hancock, Sept. 29, 1862, *OR*, series 1, vol. 19, part 1, p. 277. Report of Brig. Gen. Thomas Francis Meagher, Sept. 30, 1862, *OR*, series 1, vol. 19, part 1, p. 293. Benjamin Chase to Nancy Chase, Sept. 28, 1862, NA.

P. 131, *When the lines were ready*: Meagher's report, *OR*, series 1, vol. 19, part 1, p. 294. Cross, "Journal," p. 56.

P. 131, *The order to follow*:   Cross, "Journal," p. 56. Livermore, *Days*, p. 133. Fifth Regiment, regimental order book, Apr. 21, 1863, NA. Benjamin Chase to Nancy Chase, Sept. 28, 1862, NA. Child, *History*, p. 121.

P. 133, *Richardson sent Caldwell's brigade*:   Report of Brig. Gen. John Caldwell, *OR*, series 1, vol. 19, part 1, p. 284. (This deployment is also depicted visually in the Antietam Battle Board's map 10.) Livermore, *Days*, p. 133. (On page 56 of his journal, the colonel recounts the same speech in grander terms: "Officers and soldiers, the enemy are in front and the Potomac River is in their rear. We must conquer this day or we are disgraced and ruined. I expect each one will do his duty like a soldier and a brave man. Let no man leave the ranks on any pretense. If I fall leave me until the battle is over. Stand firm and fire low. Shoulder arms. Forward march!" Cross's account is so clearly written with an eye toward posterity that we chose to accept Livermore's ungarnished version instead.)

P. 133, *At last Richardson*:   Report of Col. Francis Barlow, *OR*, series 1, vol. 19, part 1, p. 289. (Livermore, *Days*, p. 134, puts the wait at ten minutes.) Cross, "Journal," p. 57. Livermore, *Days*, pp. 137–38.

P. 133, *But the Irish Brigade*:   Barlow's report, *OR*, series 1, vol. 19, part 1, p. 289. (Caldwell's report makes no mention of Richardson's outburst and asserts that he repositioned the brigade on the general's order. In light of Cross, Livermore, and Barlow's accounts, however, the weight of evidence suggests Richardson directed the movement on his own.) Cross, "Journal," pp. 57–58. Chaplain Milo Ransom to *People's Journal*, Sept. 26, 1862. Livermore, *Days*, p. 141.

P. 134, *The Irish had suffered*:   Livermore, *Days*, pp. 146, 133–34. Charles A. Hale, "The Story of My Personal Experience at the Battle of Antietam," John Rutter Brooke Papers, miscellaneous papers, HSP, p. 1.

P. 134, *The Fifth's first challenge*:   Meagher's report, *OR*, series 1, vol. 19, part 1, p. 294. Head, *Report, 1866*, vol. 2, pp. 554–55. Livermore, *Days*, pp. 134–35.

P. 135, *In an instant*:   Livermore, *Days*, pp. 135–37.

P. 135, *The men of the Fifth*:   Hale, "Experience," p. 2. Livermore, *Days*, p. 146.

P. 136, *Hundreds of Rebels*:   Hale, "Experience," p. 2. Cross's report, *OR*, series 1, vol. 19, part 1, p. 288. (Cross places this devastating shell burst earlier in the battle, while Livermore, *Days*, p. 140, places it after the regiment swept over the Sunken Lane. Livermore's account seems more logical, given that the regiment did not come under heavy artillery fire until crossing the lane.)

P. 136, *As the men pushed*:   Livermore, *Days*, p. 138. Report of Maj. Gen. D. H. Hill, n.d., *OR*, series 1, vol. 19, part 1, p. 1024.

P. 136, *The Fifth had drawn apart*:   Head, *Report, 1866*, vol. 2, p. 555. Cross, "Journal," p. 58.

P. 136, *Cross ran to the left*:   Cross's report, *OR*, series 1, vol. 19, part 1, p. 288. Cross, "Journal," p. 59. Hill's report, *OR*, series 1, vol. 19, part 1, p. 1024. Edward E. Cross to the Rev. Elijah Wilkins, Nov. 10, 1862, as printed in Child, *History*, p. 217. Hale, "Experience," pp. 2, 5.

P. 137, *The rise between*:   Report of Maj. Gen. George B. McClellan, *OR*, series 1, vol. 19, part 1, p. 59. Hale, "Experience," p. 3.

P. 137, *The Fifth won the contest*:   Cross, "Journal," p. 59. Cross to Wilkins, Nov. 10, 1862, in Child, *History*, p. 219.

P. 137, *Cross moved the regiment*:   Head, *Report, 1866*, vol. 2, p. 555. Report of Maj. Harry Boyd McKeen, Sept. 20, 1862, *OR*, series 1, vol. 19, part 1, p. 292. Livermore, *Days*, p. 140. Hale, "Experience," p. 3.

P. 137, *The Fifth was ready*:   Graves's narrative, in Child, *History*, p. 112. Livermore, *Days*, pp. 146, 142. Charles Long, pension file, NA. "One of the Fifth Regiment" to *Farmer's Cabinet*, Oct. 16, 1862.

P. 138, *With the fight at its peak*:   Livermore, *Days*, p. 141. "One of the Fifth Regiment" to *Farmer's Cabinet*, Oct. 16, 1862.

P. 138, *Without orders but alert*:   McKeen's report, *OR*, series 1, vol. 19, part 1, p. 292. Livermore, *Days*, pp. 141–43. Cross, "Journal," pp. 59–60.

P. 138, *For ten minutes*:   Cross, "Journal," pp. 59–60. Hale, "Experience," p. 4.

P. 138, *For the second*:   Cross, "Journal," p. 60. Child, *History*, p. 129. Waite, *Claremont War History*, pp. 135–36. Livermore, *Days*, p. 134.

P. 139, *While his comrades rested*:   Hale, "Experience," pp. 4–5.

P. 139, *The rebel counterattack*:   Child, *History*, p. 127. Livermore, *Days*, pp. 144–45.

P. 139, *Hancock, who was to replace*:   Cross, "Journal," p. 61.

P. 140, *With dark*:   Ibid., pp. 60–61. Graves's narrative, in Child, *History*, p. 111.

P. 140, *Staggering as the numbers*:   Livermore, *Days*, p. 146. Cross, "Journal," p. 60.

P. 140, *With morning*:   Child, *History*, p. 335. Graves's narrative, in Child, *History*, p. 113.

P. 141, *For the surgeons*:   William Child to Carrie Child, Sept. 18, 1862, courtesy of Merrill Sawyer. Child, *History*, p. 129.

P. 141, *Cross also made the most*:   Pension file, Hilas Davis, NA. Cross's report to Berry, Child, *History*, p. 141. Livermore, *Days*, p. 147. Cross to Kent, Sept. 20, 1862, courtesy of M. Faith Kent. (Cross's claim to have rearmed the regiment with Springfields dropped on the battlefield is contradicted by official ordnance records and a reminiscence in the regimental history, which together suggest that the Fifth was armed with Enfields until November 1863. We are unable to resolve this contradiction beyond speculating that Cross's intentions may have been thwarted sometime after he wrote Kent.)

P. 142, *Some in the Fifth*:   Child, *History*, p. 125. Cross, "Journal," p. 62. Livermore, *Days*, p. 147. *The National Eagle*, Oct. 23, 1862.

P. 142, *As the hours passed*:   Livermore, *Days*, pp. 148, 142. Ransom to *People's Journal*, Sept. 26, 1862. *Manchester American*, as printed in *Nashua Gazette*, Oct. 28, 1862. *Northern Advocate*, Sept. 30, 1862.

P. 142, *Near day's end*:   Livermore, *Days*, pp. 148–49. Child, *History*, p. 126.

P. 143, *During the darkness*:   Cross to Kent, Sept. 20, 1862, courtesy of M. Faith Kent.

P. 143, *Cross harbored darker*:   Cross, "Journal," p. 63. Charges and Specifications against Col. Edward E. Cross, Larkin papers, NHHS. Caldwell's report, *OR*, series 1, vol. 19, part 1, p. 285.

P. 143, *On the morning*:   William Child to Carrie Child, Sept. 22, 1862, courtesy of Merrill Sawyer.

P. 144, *Eleven members*:   The casualty tally is our own, based on an analysis of the regimental roster. Thomas Law, Charles W. Bean, pension files, NA. Walter Holden, "The Granite Regiment," pp. 172–73. *Farmer's Cabinet*, Apr. 2, 1863. Benjamin Chase to Nancy Chase, Sept. 28, 1862, NA.

P. 144, *Child stayed*:   William Child to Carrie Child, Oct. 20, 1862, courtesy of Merrill Sawyer.

P. 145, *That night Child*:   William Child to William Clinton Child, Oct. 19, 1862, courtesy of Merrill Sawyer.

9. AUTUMN TEMPEST

P. 146, *On September 22*:   Cross, "Journal," p. 64. Fifth Regiment, regimental order book, Oct. 15, 1862, NA.

P. 147, *While awaiting*:   Livermore, *Days*, pp. 153–54.

P. 147, *The men had*:   Child, *History* (biographical), p. 321. William Moore to Elizabeth Moore, Oct. 20, 1862, NHHS.

P. 148, *Brigadier General*:   William Moore to Elizabeth Moore, Oct. 20, 1862, NHHS.

P. 148, *The Fifth*:   Ibid.

P. 149, *The next day*:   Livermore, *Days*, p. 153.

P. 149, *Despite this happy* through *However much Kent*:   Cross to Kent, Oct. 6, Oct. 14, and Oct. 24, 1862, courtesy of M. Faith Kent.

P. 150, *In late October*:   OR, part 1—Reports, vol. 2, serial no. 2, p. 142.

P. 151, *Two days after*:   Cross, "Journal," p. 65. Gove diary, in Child, *History*, p. 144. James Larkin to Jenny Larkin, Nov. 7, 1862, NHHS.

P. 151, *As abruptly*:   James Larkin to Jenny Larkin, Nov. 3, 1862, NHHS. Peabody to parents, Nov. 1, 1862, courtesy of Mary Anne Zak. Livermore, *Days*, p. 153. Frank Haskell, *Battle of Gettysburg*, pp. 60–61.

P. 153, *The trouble*:   Livermore, *Days*, pp. 153–57. William Moore to Adams Moore, Nov. 18, 1862, NHHS.

P. 153, *The Fifth soon*:   Livermore, *Days*, p. 159. William Moore to Adams Moore, Nov. 18, 1862, NHHS. Cross, "Journal," p. 66. Gove diary, in Child, *History*, p. 145.

P. 154, *For the Fifth*:   James Perry and James Larkin courts-martial, Dec. 5–6, 1862, NA.

P. 154, *To some of*:   Ibid.

P. 155, *The talk of*:   Ibid.

P. 155, *The Army of*:   James Larkin to Jenny Larkin, Nov. 10, 1862, NHHS. William Moore to Adams Moore, Nov. 18, 1862, NHHS.

P. 156, *The men resumed*:   Fifth Regiment, regimental order book, Nov. 11, 1862, NA. James Larkin to Jenny Larkin, Nov. 19, 1862, NHHS.

P. 156, *The disciplinarian*:   Fifth Regiment, regimental order book, Nov. 20 and 24, 1862, NA. James Larkin to Jenny Larkin and children, Nov. 23, 1862, NHHS.

P. 156, *By far the severest*:   James Perry and James Larkin courts-martial, Dec. 5–6, 1862, NA.

P. 157, *Neither company commander*:   Ibid. James Larkin to Jenny Larkin and children, Nov. 23 and Dec. 5, 1862, NHHS.

P. 157, *The two officers*:   James Larkin's charges vs. Edward Cross, Larkin papers, NHHS.

P. 158, *News of*:   Livermore, *Days*, p. 94. Ira McL. Barton to Edward Cross (and Cross's response), Feb. 20, 1862, Levi Barton to Ira McL. Barton, Oct. 15, 1862 (two letters), many letters on war claim business and petitions and letters of recommendation on Barton's behalf, Barton papers, DCL. Edward Sturtevant to Anthony Colby, July 14, 1862, NHA. Edward Cross to Colonel J. B. Fry, May 31, 1863, Barton papers, DCL. (Our views of Barton's behavior are a matter of judgment. References to his drinking, or his reputation for drinking, occur in three letters. The malingering reference we derive from correspondence about his efforts to leave the Fifth and from Captain Sturtevant's July 14, 1862, letter. While in command of the regiment at Harrison's Landing, Sturtevant wrote to the state's adjutant general that Barton was sick but added: "not very bad, and I think [confidentially] should be on duty." Cross's animosity toward Barton was clear in his letters blocking Barton's quest for a new commission after leaving the Fifth. On May 31, 1863, upon hearing that Barton was seeking to become a major or a colonel in the Invalid Corps, Cross wrote to Colonel Fry: "I beg leave to state that Capt. Barton has received no recommendation from me nor from the Brigadier under which he served, nor can he receive any." After Cross's death, with petitions of support from several officers of the Fifth and a surgeon's certificate asserting that he suffered from "Bilious Remittant Disease," Barton did receive a second chance, as an officer in the Second Company, New Hampshire Heavy Artillery.)

P. 158, *Barton had*:   Charles Hapgood to Ira McL. Barton, Dec. 3, 1862, Barton papers, DCL.

P. 158, *Cross's efforts*:   Ibid.

P. 159, *Back at Falmouth*:   Edward Sturtevant to John Wilson, quoted by Moses B. Goodwin in *Statesman*, Dec. 22, 1862.

P. 159, *This high opinion*:   James Perry and James Larkin courts-martial, Dec. 5–6, 1862, NA.

P. 159, *The courts-martial*:   Ibid.

P. 160, *Regardless*:   James Larkin to Jenny Larkin and children, Dec. 9, 1862, NHHS.

P. 161, *As caught up*:   Livermore, *Days*, 160–61. Cross, "Journal," p. 66. James Larkin to Jenny Larkin and children, Dec. 9, 1862, NHHS.

P. 162, *The next day*:   James Perry and James Larkin courts-martial, Dec. 5–6, 1862, NA.

10. FREDERICKSBURG

P. 163, *Fifteen months*: Peabody to parents, Dec. 1, 1862, USAMHI.

P. 164, *Private Peabody's view*: Livermore, *Days*, p. 166. William Moore to sister, Nov. 22, 1862, NHHS.

P. 164, *"Why don't* through *At this*: William Moore to sister, Nov. 22, 1862, NHHS.

P. 165, *General Lee, meanwhile*: Francis Winthrop Palfrey, *The Antietam and Fredericksburg*, pp. 161–62.

P. 165, *As the two*: Murat Halstead, *Cincinnati Commercial*, Dec, 17, 1862, in Moore, editor, *Rebellion Record*, vol. 6, pp. 94–96. Cross, "Journal," p. 68. (Although Halstead does not name Cross, it is clear he is visiting Cross. As Washington correspondents for their respective Cincinnati newspapers, the two covered the 1856 American Party council and many other events together. Cross mentioned in his journal the presence of a correspondent from Cincinnati, and the events Halstead described concur with the actions of the Fifth's officers and men during Dec. 10–12.)

P. 165, *No doubt*: Halstead, *Cincinnati Commercial*, in Moore, editor, *Rebellion Record*, vol. 6, p. 96. Livermore, *Days*, p. 166.

P. 167, *Halstead and*: Cross, "Journal," p. 69. Halstead, in Moore, editor, *Rebellion Record*, vol. 6, p. 96.

P. 167, *Before dawn*: Livermore, *Days*, p. 167. Edward Sturtevant to John Wilson, quoted in Moses B. Goodwin's account, *Statesman*, Dec. 22, 1862. Halstead, in Moore, editor, *Rebellion Record*, vol. 6, p. 97.

P. 167, *Then, just below*: Halstead, in Moore, editor, *Rebellion Record*, vol. 6, p. 97.

P. 168, *Just after*: Livermore, *Days*, 168–70. John W. Crosby, account from *Boston Transcript*, reprinted in *Charge Bayonets!* Jan.–Feb. 1987. Cross, "Journal," p. 71.

P. 169, *The men awoke*: Livermore, *Days*, pp. 166, 171–72. Child, *History*, p. 165. Cross, "Journal," pp. 71–72.

P. 169, *With the battle*: Sumner Hurd to Ira McG. Barton, Feb. 10, 1862, Barton papers, DCL. Waite, *Claremont War History*, pp. 121–22. Darius Couch account, Johnson and Buel, editors, *Battles and Leaders*, vol. 3, p. 110.

P. 169, *At 8:15*: Couch account, Johnson and Buel, editors, *Battles and Leaders*, vol. 3, pp. 105–20.

P. 170, *As the morning*: Col. Robert Nugent, "The Sixty-Ninth Regiment at Fredericksburg," 3rd annual report of the State Historian of the State of New York, Albany, 1890.

P. 170, *From Sophia Street*: William McCarter, *My Life in the Irish Brigade*, pp. 165, 226. Cross, "Journal," pp. 72–73.

P. 171, *At around*: Cross, "Journal," pp. 72–73. Livermore, *Days*, p. 172. Crosby account, *Charge Bayonets!*

P. 171, *In this ravine*: Cross, "Journal," pp. 72–73. Crosby account, *Charge Bayonets!*

P. 172, *By now the rebel*: Waite, *Claremont War History*, p. 101. *Northern Advocate*, Dec. 23, 1862. Cross, "Journal," p. 74. James Larkin to Jenny Larkin and children,

Dec. 16, 1862, NHHS. Cross, Fredericksburg account (widely published), *Granite State Free Press*, Aug. 15, 1863. Crosby account, *Charge Bayonets!* Edward Cross to W. H. Hackett Esq., Nov. 26, 1862, NHA. (Accounts of Sturtevant's death were conflicting and vague. New Hampshire newspapers reported the deaths of other officers but said only that Sturtevant was "missing and supposed dead." Livermore, who did not march to battle with the Fifth at Fredericksburg, wrote in 1866 that Sturtevant had been hit not far beyond the ravine "and died in a ditch." In *Days and Events*, his later memoir, he wrote that Sturtevant had died near the stone wall. According to his footnote in *Days and Events*, other officers in the regiment had "assured" him after the war that this was so and that his 1866 account was incorrect. But there is no evidence Sturtevant was with the regiment beyond the first artillery fire. James Larkin gave no specifics of Sturtevant's death in his letters to his wife. Although Janvrin Graves, George Gove, John McCrillis, and others wrote in detail of deaths beyond the Stratton house, none mentioned Sturtevant's. No contemporary account described any action by Sturtevant during the battle; in all other cases in which an officer of the Fifth was killed at Fredericksburg, there were such accounts. John W. Crosby's recollections of the battle, published in the 1880s but probably written earlier, seemed accurate in nearly all respects. Crosby wrote that Sturtevant was at the left of the regiment just as it cleared the ravine and was hit and killed at about the time Colonel Cross was wounded, possibly by a fragment of the same shell. This early demise is close to the careful Livermore's initial account and consistent with our reading of all the material we could find on the Fifth at Fredericksburg.)

P. 172, *Somehow the regiment*:   John McCrillis account, in Child, *History*, p. 156. John L. Smith, *History of the 118th Pennsylvania Volunteers*, p. 105.

P. 173, *Still more than*:   Crosby account, *Charge Bayonets!* Rodney Ramsey to father, Dec. 24, 1862, NHHS.

P. 173, *As the Fifth*:   Waite, *Claremont War History*, pp. 122, 127–28. Sumner Hurd to Ira McL. Barton, Feb. 10, 1863, Barton papers, DCL. Newspaper accounts in Moore file, NHHS. Edward Cross to Adams Moore, Dec. 18, 1862, NHHS.

P. 173, *Not every wound*:   Welcome Crafts and Charles Hale, pension files, NA. G. H. F. (George H. Farnum) to *Farmer's Cabinet*, Apr. 30, 1863.

P. 174, *The regiment angled*:   Crosby account, *Charge Bayonets!*

P. 174, *Lieutenant Janvrin Graves*:   Casualty figures are derived from our analysis of regimental roster in Child, *History*, and Head's reports (the New Hampshire adjutant general). Rodney Ramsey to father, Dec. 24, 1862, NHHS. Child, *History*, p. 165.

P. 175, *Like Graves and*:   Child, *History*, pp. 156–59.

P. 175, *Wherever they were*:   Waite, *Claremont War History*, p. 116. Cross, "Journal," pp. 75–76. Cross, Fredericksburg account (widely published), *Granite State Free Press*, Aug. 15, 1863. *Farmer's Cabinet*, Aug. 16, 1863. Crosby account, *Charge Bayonets!*

P. 176, *Under cover*:   Cross, regimental report, Dec. 15, 1862 (widely published), *Statesman*, Jan. 30, 1863. Ramsey to father, Dec. 24, 1863, NHHS. Child, *History*, p. 165.

P. 176, *General Burnside*:   Couch account, *Battles and Leaders*, vol. 3, pp. 117–18. Halstead, *Cincinnati Commercial*, in Moore, editor, *Rebellion Record*, vol. 6, p. 100.

P. 177, *The next day*:   Mark Nesbitt, *Through Blood and Fire*, pp. 41–42. Couch account, Johnson and Buel, editors, *Battles and Leaders*, vol. 3, p. 116.

P. 177, *Not until*:   McCrillis account, in Child, *History*, p. 165.

P. 177, *In at least*:   Maj. Charles P. Adams, First Minnesota Volunteers, to Dr. Adams Moore, Mar. 3, 1863, reprinted in *People's Journal*.

P. 177, *Dozens of soldiers*:   William Child to Carrie Child, Dec. 23, 1863, courtesy of Merrill Sawyer. Child, *History*, pp. 162–64.

P. 178, *Private Crosby*:   Crosby account, *Charge Bayonets!*

P. 179, *Back home in*:   Casualty figures from our analysis. William Child to Carrie Child, Dec. 18, 1862, courtesy of Merrill Sawyer. *Farmer's Cabinet*, Dec. 25, 1862. *Granite State Free Press*, June 13, 1863.

P. 180, *Until Fredericksburg*:   *Farmer's Cabinet*, Dec. 25, 1862, and Jan. 1, 1863.

P. 180, *Claremont, a much*:   *Northern Advocate*, Nov. 25, 1862. (Casualty figures are from our analysis of rosters and adjutant general Head's reports.) *Northern Advocate*, Dec. 30, 1862.

P. 180, *The Claremont casualties*:   *National Eagle*, Dec. 25, 1862. Waite, *Claremont War History*, pp. 119–23.

P. 181, *Twenty miles north*:   *Granite State Free Press*, Dec, 19, 1862. Chaplain Milo Ransom to Mrs. James Perry, *Granite State Free Press*, Dec. 26, 1862.

P. 181, *Not all bodies*:   Sumner Hurd to Ira McL. Barton, Jan. 11, 1863, and Elisha Towne to Barton, Feb. 14 and July 12, 1863, Barton papers, DCL.

P. 181, *Although the battle*:   Cross, Fredericksburg account (widely published), *Granite State Free Press*, Aug. 15, 1863. Cross, regimental report, Dec. 15, 1862 (widely published), *Statesman*, Jan. 30, 1863. James Larkin to Jenny Larkin and children, Dec. 16, 1862, NHHS. Edward Cross to Ephraim Cross, Dec. 21, 1862, courtesy of Walter Holden.

P. 182, *Over the years*:   Johnson and Buel, editors, *Battles and Leaders*, vol. 3, p. 118 (caption). McCarter, *My Life*, p. 225. (In accounts listing regiments whose men died nearest the stone wall, the Fifth New Hampshire is almost always named.)

P. 183, *The soldiers of*:   Augustus D. Sanborn to mother and brothers, June 10, 1863, courtesy of Terry Thomann. Charles Hapgood to Ira McL. Barton, Jan. 9, 1863, Barton papers, DCL. Winfield S. Hancock to New Hampshire's two U.S. senators, Dec. 29, 1862, courtesy of Walter Holden.

P. 183, *Although the regimental*:   Sumner Hurd to Ira McL. Barton, Jan. 5 and Feb. 10, 1863, Barton papers, DCL. Sumner Hurd, pension file, NA. Gove diary, in Child, *History*, p. 150. Sanborn to mother and brothers, Jan. 10, 1863, copy at LHS.

P. 184, *During the weeks*:   James Larkin to Jenny Larkin and children, Dec. 16 and Dec. 22, 1862, and to Jenny Larkin, Jan. 2, 1863, NHHS.

P. 185, *Not everyone*:   Anonymous and Luther M. Chase to *People's Journal*, Jan. 3, 1863. Luther M. Chase, pension file, NA.

11. "CAMP NEAR FALMOUTH"

P. 186, *The Emancipation*:   Lex Renda, *Running on the Record*, pp. 111–16. Peabody to parents, July 13, 1862, courtesy of Mary Anne Zak.

P. 187, *The men's closest*:   Livermore, *Days*, p. 178. Child, *History*, pp. 169–70.

P. 187, *Conditions in*:   Child, *History*, pp. 169–70.

P. 187, *Such encounters*:   William Child to Carrie Child, Oct. 22, 1863, courtesy of Merrill Sawyer.

P. 188, *Livermore, like Child*:   Livermore, *Days*, pp. 189, 214.

P. 188, *When words*:   Ibid., p. 104.

P. 189, *Practicality aside*:   Peabody to parents, Jan. 16 and Feb. 3, 1863, courtesy of Mary Anne Zak. Peabody to brother and sister, Feb. 14, 1863, USAMHI.

P. 190, *Colonel Cross's views*:   Edward Cross to Franklin Pierce, Apr. 14, 1863, NHHS.

P. 190, *In fact, defeats*:   *New Hampshire Patriot*, Jan. 7, 1863, and *Laconia Democrat*, Feb. 13, 1863, quoted in Renda, *Running on the Record*, pp. 112, 114.

P. 191, *New Hampshire Republicans*:   Renda, *Running on the Record*, p. 114. James O. Lyford, *Life of Edward H. Rollins*, pp. 147–54. William B. Hesseltine, *Lincoln and the War Governors*, p. 319.

P. 191, *In Virginia*:   Peabody to brother and sister, Feb. 14, 1862, and to parents, Mar. 3, 1862, USAMHI.

P. 192, *For two of*:   James Larkin to Jenny Larkin and children, Dec. 28, 1862, to Jenny Larkin, Jan. 2, 1863, NHHS. William Child to Carrie Child, Dec. 28 and 31, 1862, Jan. 7, 1863, courtesy of Merrill Sawyer.

P. 193, *The Fifth New Hampshire*:   James Daniels diary, in Child, *History*, p. 171. Peabody to parents, Jan. 16, courtesy of Mary Anne Zak, and Jan. 29, 1863, USAMHI. James Larkin to Jenny Larkin and children, Jan. 16, 1863, NHHS.

P. 193, *Fortunately for*:   William Child to Carrie Child, Jan. 30, 1863, courtesy of Merrill Sawyer. Peabody to parents, Jan. 26, 1863, courtesy of Mary Anne Zak. Livermore, *Days*, p. 179.

P. 194, *The debacle ended*:   William Child to Carrie Child, Jan. 26, 1863, courtesy of Merrill Sawyer.

P. 194, *Some of the sour*:   Chaplain Milo Ransom to *Statesman*, Feb. 13, 1863.

P. 195, *Captain Larkin's*:   James Larkin to Jenny Larkin and children, Jan. 13, 16, and 26, 1863, NHHS.

P. 196, *The changes*:   Frank Butler to Mr. and Mrs. John Fletcher, Jan. 1863, in Doris E. Hopkins, *Greenfield, New Hampshire*, p. 164. James Larkin to Jenny Larkin and children, Jan. 31, 1863, NHHS.

P. 197, *The men longed*:   Livermore, *Days*, p. 179. Head, *Report, 1866*, vol. 2, p. 561.

P. 197, *Before leaving*:   Kent, *History of the Seventeenth*, pp. 71–73. Cross to Kent, Oct. 24, 1862, courtesy of M. Faith Kent.

P. 197, *Cross left Concord*:   Cross to Pierce, Feb. 19, 1863, NHHS. Edward Rollins to Abraham Lincoln, undated, John Forney to Abraham Lincoln, Feb. 28, 1863,

Edward Cross to Edwin M. Stanton, Mar. 10, 1863, all in Edward Cross, adjutant general's file, NA.

P. 198, *Newly promoted*: Charles Hapgood to Nathaniel Berry, Feb. 10, 1863, NHA. Charles Hapgood, pension file, NA. Child, *History* (biographical), p. 318.

P. 198, *In his first*: Hapgood to Berry, Feb. 10, 1863, NHA. Charles Hapgood to Anthony Colby, Feb. 9, 1863, NHA. Fifth Regiment, regimental order book, Feb. 11, 1863, NA. Livermore, *Days*, pp. 179–80.

P. 199, *In early March*: Daniels diary, in Child, *History*, p. 172. Livermore, *Days*, pp. 184–85. Peabody to parents, Mar. 3, 1863, USAMHI.

P. 200, *Because it had*: Fifth Regiment, regimental order book, Mar. 16, 1863, NA.

P. 200, *Cross returned*: Ibid., Mar. 21, 1863. Daniels diary, in Child, *History*, pp. 172–75. James Larkin to Jenny Larkin and children, Mar. 22, 1863, to Jenny Larkin, Mar. 20, 1863, NHHS. Livermore, *Days*, p. 182.

P. 201, *Hooker's attention*: Fifth Regiment, regimental order book, Apr. 16, 12, and 19, 1863, NA.

P. 201, *As the Fifth*: Daniels diary, in Child, *History*, p. 173. Livermore, *Days*, pp. 179, 186. William Child to Carrie Child, Mar. 24, 1863, courtesy of Merrill Sawyer.

P. 202, *For Cross, Sumner's*: Cross to Pierce, Feb. 14, 1863, NHHS.

P. 202, *Meanwhile, all was not drill*: James Larkin to Jenny Larkin, Apr. 21, 1863, NHHS. Livermore, *Days*, 182–83.

P. 203, *Cross employed*: Fifth Regiment, regimental order book, undated circular ca. Apr. 21, 1863, NA.

P. 203, *While the Fifth*: James Larkin to Jenny Larkin, Mar. 30, 1863, NHHS. Charles Phelps to Sophia Phelps, Apr. 26, 1863, Charles Phelps, pension file, NA,

P. 203, *By mid-April*: Edward Cross, Chancellorsville account (addendum to journal), in Child, *History*, pp. 180–81. John Bucknam to Mary Bucknam, Mar. 23, 1863, typescript at LHS. James Larkin to Jenny Larkin, Apr. 13, 1863, to Jenny Larkin and children, Apr. 16, 1863, NHHS.

12. CHANCELLORSVILLE

P. 205, *For an aggressive*: Ramsdell, *History of Milford* (Livermore biography), pp. 442–44.

P. 206, *Brigadier's star*: Charles Hapgood to Captain George H. Caldwell, May 7, 1863, in Child, *History*, p. 179. Cross, Chancellorsville account, in Child, *History*, p. 181. Noel G. Harrison, *Gazetteer of Historical Sites Related to the Fredericksburg and Spotsylvania National Military Park*, Fredericksburg and Spotsylvania National Military Park, 1986, vol. 1, p. 220.

P. 207, *The job of*: Cross, Chancellorsville account, in Child, *History*, p. 181. Livermore, *Days*, p. 189. *Farmer's Cabinet*, Milford, May 21, 1863. Child, *History*, p. 189. Head, *Report, 1866*, vol. 2, p. 561.

P. 207, *Captain Livermore*: Livermore, *Days*, p. 189.

P. 207, *The easy duty*:   Charles Hapgood diary, Apr. 30, 1863, typescript courtesy of Robert Corrette. *Statesman*, May 7, 1863.

P. 208, *The Fifth marched*:   Hapgood diary, May 1, 1863. Livermore, *Days*, p. 190. John Bucknam letters, May 8, 1863, typescript at LHS.

P. 208, *Five miles*:   Livermore, *Days*, pp. 190–92.

P. 209, *Cross's brigade*:   Cross, Chancellorsville account, in Child, *History*, p. 182. Livermore, *Days*, p. 192. Hapgood diary, May 1, 1863.

P. 209, *The regiment*:   Carol Reardon, "The Valiant Rearguard: Hancock's Division at Chancellorsville," in Gary W. Gallagher, editor, *Chancellorsville: The Battle and Its Aftermath*, pp. 150–51. Cross, Chancellorsville account, in Child, *History*, p. 183. Gove diary, in Child, *History*, p. 176.

P. 210, *The next day*:   Reardon, "The Valiant Rearguard," p. 165. Hapgood diary, May 2, 1863. Livermore, *Days*, pp. 197–98.

P. 211, *The Fifth had*:   Livermore, *Days*, pp. 200–201.

P. 211, *For Bucknam*:   John Bucknam diary, May 2, 1863, typescript, LHS. (In a letter to his wife dated May 8, 1863, Bucknam copied several entries from his diary.)

P. 211, *Like Bucknam*:   Livermore, *Days*, p. 201.

P. 213, *Several of the*:   Cross, Chancellorsville account, in Child, *History*, pp. 184–85. Livermore, *Days*, p. 202. Bucknam diary, May 3, 1863.

P. 214, *The moonlight*:   Livermore, *Days*, pp. 202–3.

P. 214, *The shock*:   Hapgood diary, May 2, 1863.

P. 214, *After another night*:   Livermore, *Days*, p. 204. McCrillis, pension file, NA. Cross, Chancellorsville account, in Child, *History*, p. 186.

P. 215, *The vigorous*:   Cross, Chancellorsville account, in Child, *History*, p. 185. Livermore, *Days*, p. 205.

P. 215, *Before the Chancellorsville*:   Livermore, *Days*, p. 205.

P. 216, *The colonel*:   Livermore, *Days*, p. 206. Cross, Chancellorsville account, in Child, *History*, p. 185. William Child to Carrie Child, May 7, 1863, courtesy of Merrill Sawyer. Head, *Report, 1866*, vol. 2, p. 562.

P. 216, *In their haste*:   Bucknam diary, May 3, 1863.

P. 216, *The Fifth's retreat*:   Livermore, *Days*, pp. 206–7. Sumner Hurd to Ira McL. Barton, May 12, 1863, DCL.

P. 217, *When the Fifth*:   Hapgood diary, May 3, 1863. *Farmer's Cabinet*, May 14, 1863. Livermore, *Days*, pp. 208–9. Cross, Chancellorsville account, in Child, *History*, p. 187.

P. 217, *Although they*:   Child, *History*, p. 192. Livermore, *Days*, p. 207.

P. 217, *The captain's*:   Livermore, *Days*, pp. 207–8. Fifth Regiment, regimental order book, May 15, 1863, NA.

P. 218, *The men of*:   Hapgood diary, May 5, 1863. Livermore, *Days*, pp. 208–9.

P. 218, *It was 3:30*:   Cross, Chancellorsville account, in Child, *History*, p. 187. Gove diary, May 6, 1863, in Child, *History*, p. 177.

P. 219, *Several officers*:   Cross, Chancellorsville account, in Child, *History*, p. 187. Hapgood diary, May 6, 1863. William Child to Carrie Child, May 14, 1863, courtesy of Merrill Sawyer. James Larkin to Jenny Larkin and children, May 19, 1863, NHHS.

P. 219, *For the Fifth*: Fifth Regiment, records, May 10 and May 22, 1863, NA.

P. 220, *Life back in*: James Larkin to Jenny Larkin and children, May 19, 1863, NHHS. Livermore, *Days*, p. 213.

P. 220, *As the weeks*: Peabody to parents, June 6, 1863, courtesy of Mary Anne Zak. Hapgood diary, June 7, 1863.

13. GETTYSBURG

P. 222, *With his Chancellorsville*: John Bucknam to Sally Bucknam, June 16, 1863, LHS.

P. 222, *The concentration of rebel*: Child, *History*, pp. 198–99. Livermore, *Days*, p. 216. Boatner, *Dictionary*, p. 713. (The sense of Russell's toughness is drawn from Livermore, *Days*, p. 218. When one soldier's effort to keep his feet dry offended the general, he knocked him into the river.)

P. 223, *On the evening of June 8*: Child, *History*, p. 200. Livermore, *Days*, p. 217.

P. 223, *It was four*: Livermore, *Days*, pp. 218–19. Child, *History*, p. 201.

P. 225, *Infantrymen had always considered*: Livermore, *Days*, p. 219–21. Child, *History*, p. 202.

P. 225, *The next day Livermore's*: Livermore, *Days*, pp. 222–23.

P. 225, *Hooker now knew*: Child, *History*, p. 202. Hapgood diary, June 17, 1863.

P. 226, *On June 20*: Hapgood diary, June 20, 1863. Livermore, *Days*, p. 224. Charles A. Fuller, *Personal Recollections of the War of 1861*, p. 90.

P. 226, *The pursuit of Lee's army*: William Child to Carrie Child, June 17, 18, and 24, 1863, courtesy of Merrill Sawyer.

P. 226, *The Rebels, the marching*: Child, *History*, p. 203. Hapgood diary, June 25, 1863. Livermore, *Days*, p. 229. James Larkin, pension file, NA.

P. 227, *June 25 proved eventful*: Livermore, *Days*, pp. 227–29.

P. 228, *Politics was afoot*: William Child to Carrie Child, June 28, 1863, courtesy of Merrill Sawyer.

P. 228, *As a critic*: Hale, "Experience," p. 6. Charles A. Hale, "With Colonel Cross in the Gettysburg Campaign," John Rutter Brooke Papers, miscellaneous papers, HSP, pp. I–II.

P. 228, *Livermore also found himself*: Livermore, *Days*, pp. 232–33.

P. 229, *Doing that*: Report of Maj. Gen. Winfield Scott Hancock, n.d., *OR*, series 1, vol. 27, part 1, p. 367. Livermore, *Days*, p. 234.

P. 229, *One regiment*: J. W. Muffly, editor, *The Story of Our Regiment*, pp. 533, 716.

P. 230, *The long march*: Child, *History*, pp. 203–4. Livermore, *Days*, pp. 234–35. Hale, "Gettysburg," p. II. Hapgood diary, June 29, 1863. Hilas Davis, pension files, NA.

P. 230, *Colonel Cross decided*: Speech of Maj. R. H. Forster, Sept. 11, 1889, *Pennsylvania at Gettysburg*, vol. 2, pp. 712–21.

P. 230, *Far removed*: Livermore, *Days*, pp. 236–37.

P. 231, *It was July 1*: Edward E. Cross, adjutant general's file, NA.

P. 231, *The Fifth broke camp*:   Hapgood diary, July 1, 1863. Muffly, *Our Regiment*, p. 716.

P. 232, *The Fifth was three miles*:   Hapgood diary, July 1, 1863. Hale, "Gettysburg," p. II. "Fighting Fifth in Action," *Boston Herald*, Mar. 11, 1886. (This article is a detailed account of a speech about the Fifth's Gettysburg fight given by Charles Hapgood in Concord on Mar. 10, 1886.)

P. 232, *For Livermore*:   Livermore, *Days*, pp. 237–42.

P. 233, *Though the first day's*:   Statement of Lt. William P. Wilson, in David L. and Audrey J. Ladd, editors, *The Bachelder Papers*, vol. 1, p. 1193. Hapgood diary, July 2, 1863. Frank A. Haskell, *The Battle of Gettysburg*, p. 18. Hale, "Gettysburg," p. III.

P. 233, *The corps was directed*:   Report of Brig. Gen. John C. Caldwell, Sept. 5, 1863, *OR*, series 1, vol. 27, part 1, p. 379. Eric Campbell, "Caldwell Clears the Wheatfield," *Gettysburg*, July 1990, p. 29. Haskell, *Battle*, p. 23. Hapgood diary, July 2, 1863.

P. 233, *The men of the Fifth*:   Campbell, "Caldwell," p. 29. Haskell, *Battle*, p. 24.

P. 234, *Meade's plan*:   Haskell, *Battle*, p. 30.

P. 234, *In general, matters*:   Ibid., pp. 27–28. Livermore, *Days*, p. 247. Hale, "Gettysburg," p. V. Haskell, *Battle*, p. 31. Fuller, *Recollections*, p. 93.

P. 234, *The wait in the stillness*:   Hale, "Gettysburg," p. VI. Wilson, in Ladd and Ladd, editors, *Bachelder Papers*, vol. 1, p. 1194.

P. 235, *The rebel attack*:   Campbell, "Caldwell," p. 31. "Fighting Fifth," *Boston Herald*, Mar. 11, 1886. Hale, "Gettysburg," p. VI.

P. 235, *It was time*:   William Welch, pension file, NA. Hale, "Gettysburg," pp. VI–VII.

P. 237, *Sickles's men*:   Campbell, "Caldwell," p. 31. Child, *History*, p. 206. David L. and Audrey J. Ladd, editors, *John Bachelder's History of the Battle of Gettysburg*, p. 452.

P. 237, *More help was needed*:   Wilson, in Ladd and Ladd, editors, *Bachelder Papers*, vol. 1, p. 1195. Fuller, *Recollections*, p. 93. Hale, "Gettysburg," pp. VII–VIII. Campbell, "Caldwell," p. 33.

P. 237, *At Caldwell's order*:   Fuller, *Recollections*, p. 93. Hale, "Gettysburg," p. VIII. Campbell, "Caldwell," p. 35.

P. 238, *The men of Cross's brigade*:   Fuller, *Recollections*, p. 93. "Fighting Fifth," *Boston Herald*, Mar. 11, 1886. Wilson, in Ladd and Ladd, editors, *Bachelder Papers*, vol. 1, pp. 1195–96. Hale, "Gettysburg," p. IX.

P. 238, *The rebel battle line*:   Wilson, in Ladd and Ladd, editors, *Bachelder Papers*, pp. 1195–96. Report of Lt. Col. Amos Stroh, July 5, 1863, *OR*, series 1, vol. 27, part 1, p. 385. Fuller, *Recollections*, p. 94. Campbell, "Caldwell," pp. 35, 37. Muffly, *Our Regiment*, p. 536. Hale, "Gettysburg," p. X.

P. 239, *The Fifth was confronting*:   Campbell, "Caldwell," pp. 35, 33. "Fighting Fifth," *Boston Herald*, Mar. 11, 1886. Child, *History*, p. 204. Hale, "Gettysburg," p. X.

P. 239, *Hapgood noticed Cross*:   "Fighting Fifth," *Boston Herald*, Mar. 11, 1886. Child, *History*, p. 207. Hale, "Gettysburg," notes, p. III.

P. 239, *Phelps was something*:   Charles Phelps, pension file, NA. (The file details

Phelps's Fredericksburg wound and contains letters on which the inference about his sharing of pay and homesickness are based.) Hale, "Gettysburg," notes, p. III. "Fighting Fifth," *Boston Herald*, Mar. 11, 1886.

P. 240, *Cross's wounding*:   Caldwell's report, *OR*, series 1, vol. 27, part 1, p. 379. Report of Col. H. Boyd McKeen, Aug. 11, 1863, *OR*, series 1, vol. 27, part 1, pp. 381–82. Report of Col. John R. Brooke, Aug. 15, 1863, *OR*, series 1, vol. 27, part 1, p. 400. Statement of Lt. William P. Wilson, in Ladd and Ladd, editors, *Bachelder Papers*, vol. 1, p. 1032. Campbell, "Caldwell," p. 45.

P. 240, *The Fifth's ranks*:   "Fighting Fifth," *Boston Herald*, Mar. 11, 1886. Hilas Davis, Edward G. F. Stinson, John Butcher, Reuben Gilpatrick, and William Welch, pension files, NA. (The judgment as to the timing of these wounds is our own.) "Fighting Fifth," *Boston Herald*, Mar. 11, 1886.

P. 241, *By the time Caldwell*:   Campbell, "Caldwell," pp. 47–48. Wilson, in Ladd and Ladd, editors, *Bachelder Papers*, vol. 1, p. 1032. McKeen's report, *OR*, series 1, vol. 27, part 1, p. 382. *Farmer's Cabinet*, July 16, 1863. Samuel Crowther, pension file, NA. (The judgment as to the timing of Phelps's and Crowther's wounds is our own. Both having been shot in the back, they likely fell during the regiment's retreat.) Wilson, in Ladd and Ladd, editors, *Bachelder Papers*, vol. 1, pp. 1197–98.

P. 241, *The division's flight*:   Statement of Lt. Col. Charles H. Morgan, in Ladd and Ladd, editors, *Bachelder Papers*, vol. 1, pp. 1355–56. Livermore, *Days*, p. 252. Campbell, "Caldwell," p. 49. Downs, *Lebanon*, p. 342.

P. 242, *Cross's brigade was ordered*:   McKeen's report, *OR*, series 1, vol. 27, part 1, p. 382. Hale, "Gettysburg," p. XI.

P. 242, *It was midnight*:   Hale, "Gettysburg,, p. XI. Livermore, *Days*, pp. 253–54.

P. 242, *The ambulance*:   Child, *History*, pp. 211, 204, 208. Head, *Report, 1865*, pp. 806–7. Rodney R. Crowley to Charles A. Hale, Mar. 8, 1897, *Report of the Eighth Annual Reunion of the 64th N.Y. Regimental Ass'n*. (The accounts of Cross's final words in Child's *History* and Head's *Report* differ in detail. We have selected elements from both, discounting as unlikely, for example, this quote in the adjutant general's sketch: "Oh! welcome death!"

P. 243, *Colonel Cross died*:   Child, *History*, pp. 211, 325. Livermore, *Days*, pp. 254–56. Muffly, *Our Regiment*, p. 461.

P. 244, *As a fallen leader*:   Child, *History*, p. 211. *Baltimore Daily Gazette*, July 6, 1863.

P. 244, *As Meade expected*:   Child, *History*, p. 206, 208.

P. 244, *In the early afternoon*:   William Child to Carrie Child, July 5, 1863, courtesy of Merrill Sawyer. George Hersum to Ann Hersum, July 13, 1863, as quoted in *Charge Bayonets!* Sept./Oct. 1988. Hapgood diary, July 3, 1863.

P. 244, *Finally, after two hours*:   "Fighting Fifth," *Boston Herald*, Mar. 11, 1886.

P. 245, *The advantage of numbers*:   Child, *History*, p. 206.

P. 245, *Unlike his old comrades*:   Livermore, *Days*, pp. 258–59, 264–67.

P. 245, *The next day*:   John Bucknam to Deborah McIntire, July 17, 1863, LHS. Child, *History*, pp. 206, 204. Downs, *Lebanon*, p. 342. Hapgood diary, July 5, 1863.

P. 246, *But Meade chose*: Hale, "Gettysburg," p. XIII. Livermore, *Days*, p. 269. William Child to Carrie Child, July 5, 1863, courtesy of Merrill Sawyer. William Welch, pension file, NA.

P. 246, *The heavy rain*: Gerard A. Patterson, *Debris of Battle*, pp. 18–19. William Child and Charles Hapgood, pension files, NA.

P. 246, *Lee's army reached*: William O. Lyford, pension file, NA. William Child to Carrie Child, July 13, 1863, courtesy of Merrill Sawyer.

P. 247, *Lee's escape prevented*: "Return of casualties," n.d., *OR*, series 1, vol. 27, part 1, p. 175.

P. 247, *On July 15*: Lt. Col. Charles Hapgood to Adjutant General Anthony Colby, July 15, 1863, NHA. Child, *History*, p. 233. Hapgood diary, July 30, 1863.

P. 247, *On August 1*: Child, *History*, p. 234. (The tabulation of recruits is our own, based on the roster in Child's *History*.) *Farmer's Cabinet*, Aug. 6, 1863.

P. 248, *Almost a month*: *Coos Republican*, July 14, 1863. *Farmer's Cabinet*, July 30, 1863.

14. BEFORE AND AFTER

P. 249, *Nine years* through *If there had been*: "The Young Volunteers," *Cincinnati Dollar Times*, Nov. 11, 1854.

P. 251, *The tattered remnants*: *New Hampshire Patriot*, Aug. 5, 1863.

P. 252, *Colonel Charles*: "The week in Concord," *Statesman*, Aug. 7, 1863. Child, *History*, p. 234.

P. 252, *Hapgood, meanwhile*: Waite, *History of Claremont*, p. 260.

P. 252, *In Concord*: Joseph Gilmore to Charles Hapgood, Aug. 3, 1863, Fifth New Hampshire correspondence book, NA.

P. 253, *On August 11*: *Statesman*, Aug. 14, 1863. Child, *History*, p. 235. (Democratic Editor William Butterfield of the *New Hampshire Patriot* had a far different view of the celebration honoring the Fifth, but given the political lens through which he saw all events, his facts seemed questionable to us. The *Patriot* of Aug. 19, 1863, reported that a Republican state representative had said of Cross: "He was a damned Copperhead, and I'm glad he's dead." Butterfield also wrote that several Republican politicians used the occasion of the Fifth's welcome-home celebration for partisan harangues, including one in which Sen. John P. Hale urged the crowd to contribute not one cent to a proposed monument for Cross.)

P. 253, *McFarland's funereal*: Livermore, *Days*, p. 285, pp. 255–56.

P. 253, *Cross's death*: Child, *History*, p. 221. "The Young Volunteers," *Cincinnati Dollar Times*, Nov. 11, 1854.

P. 254, *With Colonel Hapgood*: Livermore, *Days*, pp. 399–400. Child, *History*, p. 235. Hapgood diary, Aug. 27, 1863.

P. 255, *This is not*: Child, *History*, pp. 253–54. Hapgood report, June 18, 1864, in Child, *History*, pp. 256–57. (The statistics come from our analysis of the regimental roster in Child, *History*, and Head's reports as New Hampshire adjutant general.)

P. 255, *The Fifth's last*:   Livermore, *Days*, pp. 454–56. Child, *History*, pp. 300–303.

P. 255, *For the members*:   Fifth Regiment, pension files, NA. Child, *History*.

P. 256, *Child's most startling*:   William Child to Carrie Child, Apr. 14, 1865, courtesy of Merrill Sawyer.

P. 256, *Fortunately for Child*:   Ibid., Oct. 29, 1864, Jan. 9, 1865, courtesy of Merrill Sawyer.

P. 256, *Child entertained thoughts*:   Ibid., Jan. 20, 1865, courtesy of Merrill Sawyer. Granville P. Conn, *N.H. Surgeons in the Rebellion*, pp. 66–69. William Child, pension file, NA. Mark Travis, "Wild Dreamer of Bath," *Dartmouth Medicine*, summer 1999, p. 39.

P. 257, *The man who*:   Livermore, *Days*, author's note, p. xi.

P. 257, *After the war*:   Ramsdell, *History of Milford*, pp. 442–44. Livermore, *Days*, pp. 483–84.

P. 258, *Livermore was*:   Ramsdell, *History of Milford*, pp. 442–44. Livermore, "The Northern Volunteers," *The Granite Monthly*, vol. 10, 1887, pp. 240–41, 244, 262. Livermore, *Days*, pp. 27–28, and foreword, p. v.

P. 258, *Another faithful*:   James Larkin, pension file, NA.

P. 259, *Through all his*:   Lyford, editor, *History*, vol. 1, pp. 532–33. James Larkin file, NHHS.

P. 259, *A chronicler*:   Miles Peabody letters, USAMHI, NA, and courtesy of Mary Anne Zak. Peabody to parents, May 26, 1864, courtesy of Mary Anne Zak.

P. 260, *Peabody soon*:   Miles Peabody, pension file, NA. Peabody diary, July 14, 1864, NA. Peabody to father (John Peabody), July 23, 1864, courtesy of Mary Anne Zak, Sept. 13, 1864, and Nov. 3, 1864, Peabody, pension file, NA.

P. 260, *Five days later*:   Embalmers' note and receipt, with Peabody letters, USAMHI.

P. 261, *Like Mary Peabody*:   Edward E. Cross, Benjamin F. Chase, pension files, NA.

P. 261, *For every member*:   Fox, *Losses*, p. 189. Alonzo Allen, pension file, NA.

P. 262, *Rare was the Fifth survivor*:   Joseph H. Harris, Hilas Davis, pension files, NA. U.S. Senate, 57th Congress, second session, report no. 2137 (George L. Hersum, pension file, NA).

P. 263, *An unfortunate few*:   Barron S. Noyes, pension file, NA. *National Eagle*, Aug. 13, 1864. Thomas Wier, pension file, NA. "Enfield Historical Society News," *Charge Bayonets!* June 1992, p. 6.

P. 263, *Cross's best friend*:   Kent, *History of the Seventeenth Regiment*, pp. 94–95, 121. *Coos Democrat*, Nov. 20, 1889.

P. 264, *The intemperate Richard Cross*:   "Charges and Specifications against Lt. Col. Richard E. Cross, Fifth Regiment New Hampshire Vols.," NHA. "Proceedings of General Court Martial Convened at Point Lookout, Md., Lieut. Col. Richard E. Cross, 5th N.H. Vols.," records of the Office of the Judge Advocate, Department of Virginia and North Carolina, NA. Richard E. Cross, pension file, NA.

P. 265, *For most survivors*:   Child, *History*, pp. 226–32.

P. 265, *The Fifth's survivors*:   Child, *History*, p. 231. Charles A. Hale, "General Hancock and the Fifth New Hampshire Volunteers," John Rutter Brooke Papers, miscellaneous papers, HSP, pp. 1–2.

Bibliography

BOOKS

Abbott, Rev. Stephen G. *The First Regiment, New Hampshire Volunteers, in the Great Rebellion*. Keene, N.H.: Sentinel Printing Co., 1890.

Acken, J. Gregory, editor. *Inside the Army of the Potomac: The Civil War Experience of Francis Adams Donaldson*. Mechanicsburg, Pa.: Stackpole Books, 1998.

Adams, George Worthington. *Doctors in Blue: The Medical History of the Union Army in the Civil War*. Baton Rouge and London: Louisiana State University Press, 1996.

Barron, Lee and Barbara. *The History of Sharpsburg, Maryland*. Privately printed, 1972.

Bilby, Joseph G., and O'Neill, Stephan D., editors. *"My Sons Were Faithful and They Fought": The Irish Brigade at Antietam*. Hightstown, N.J.: Longstreet House, 1997.

Billings, John D. *Hard Tack and Coffee*. Boston: George M. Smith & Co., 1887. Reprint, Time-Life Books, 1982.

Boatner, Mark M., III. *The Civil War Dictionary*. New York: David McKay Co., 1959.

Boylston, Edward D. *Amherst in the Great Civil Conflict of 1861–65*. Amherst, N.H.: E. D. Boylston, 1893.

Catton, Bruce. *The Army of the Potomac: Glory Road*. Garden City, N.Y.: Doubleday & Co., 1952.

———. *Bruce Catton's Civil War*. New York: Fairfax Press, 1984.

Child, William. *A History of the Fifth Regiment, New Hampshire Volunteers, in the American Civil War, 1861–1865*. Bristol, N.H.: R. W. Musgrove, 1893.

Cochrane, Rev. W. B. *History of the Town of Antrim, New Hampshire, from Its Earliest Settlement to June 27, 1877*. Manchester, N.H.: Mirror Stream Printing Press, 1880.

Conn, Granville P. *N.H. Surgeons in the Rebellion*. N.H. Association of Military Surgeons, 1906.

Dary, David. *Red Blood and Black Ink: Journalism in the Old West*. New York: Alfred A. Knopf, 1998.

Downs, Rev. Charles A. *History of Lebanon, N.H., 1761–1887*, Concord, N.H.: Rumford Printing Co., 1908.

Foner, Eric. *Free Soil, Free Labor, Free Men: The Ideology of the Republican Party before the Civil War*. New York and Oxford: Oxford University Press, 1970.

Fox, William F. *Regimental Losses in the American Civil War, 1861–1865*. Albany, N.Y.: Albany Publishing Company, 1889. Reprint, Morningside Bookshop, 1974.

Frassanito, William A. *Antietam: The Photographic Legacy of America's Bloodiest Day*. New York: Charles Scribner's Sons, 1978.

Fuller, Charles A. *Personal Recollections of the War of 1861*. Sherburne, N.Y.: News Job Printing House, 1906.

Furgurson, Ernest B. *Chancellorsville, 1863: The Souls of the Brave*. New York: Alfred A. Knopf, 1992.

Gallagher, Gary W., editor. *Antietam: Essays on the 1862 Maryland Campaign*. Kent, Ohio, and London: Kent State University Press, 1989.

———. *Chancellorsville: The Battle and Its Aftermath*. Chapel Hill and London: University of North Carolina Press, 1996.

———. *The Fredericksburg Campaign: Decision on the Rappahannock*. Chapel Hill and London: University of North Carolina Press, 1995.

———. *The Second Day at Gettysburg: Essays on Confederate and Union Leadership*. Kent, Ohio, and London: Kent State University Press, 1993.

Griffith, Paddy. *Battle in the Civil War*. Camberley, Surrey: Fieldbooks, 1986.

———. *Battle Tactics of the Civil War*. New Haven and London: Yale University Press, 1989.

Harrison, Noel G. *Fredericksburg Civil War Sites: December 1862–April 1865*. Vol. 2. Lynchburg, Va.: H. E. Howard, 1995.

Haskell, Frank A. *The Battle of Gettysburg*, edited by Bruce Catton. Boston: Houghton-Mifflin Co. Reprint, Cambridge, Mass., Riverdale Press, 1957, 1958.

Hayward, John. *A Gazetteer of New Hampshire*, Boston: John P. Jewett, 1849.

Head, Natt. *Report of the Adjutant General, Year Ending May 20, 1865*. Vols. 1 and 2. Concord, N.H.: Amos Hadley, state printer, 1865.

———. *Report of the Adjutant-General of New-Hampshire, Year Ending June 1, 1866*. Vols. 1 and 2. Concord, N.H.: George E. Jenks, state printer, 1866.

Hess, Earl J. *The Union Soldier in Battle: Enduring the Ordeal of Combat*. Lawrence, Kans.: University Press of Kansas, 1997.

Hesseltine, William B. *Lincoln and the War Governors*. New York: Alfred A. Knopf, 1955.

———, editor. *Three Against Lincoln: Murat Halstead Reports the Caucuses of 1860*. Baton Rouge: Louisiana State University Press, 1960.

——— and Fisher, Rex G., editors. *Trimmers, Trucklers and Temporizers: Notes of Murat Halstead from the Political Conventions of 1856*. Madison: The State Historical Society of Wisconsin, 1961.

Holt, Michael F. *The Political Crisis of the 1850s*. New York: John Wiley and Sons, 1978.

Hopkins, Doris E. *Greenfield, New Hampshire: The Story of a Town, 1791–1976*, Milford, N.H.: Greenfield Historical Society, Wallace Press, 1977.

Jackson, James R. *History of Littleton, New Hampshire, in Three Volumes*. Cambridge, Mass.: [Harvard] University Press, 1905.

Johnson, Allen, and Malone, Dumas. *Dictionary of American Biography: Authors Edition*. New York: Charles Scribner's Sons, 1937.

Johnson, Robert Underwood, and Buel, Clarence Clough, editors. The Century War Series." 1883–. Reprinted as *Battles and Leaders of the Civil War*, vols. 2 and 3, Castle, undated.

Journals of the Honorable Senate and House of Representatives. June session, 1861. Concord, N.H.: Henry McFarland, 1861.

Kent, Lieut. Charles N. *History of the Seventeenth Regiment, New Hampshire Volunteer Infantry, 1862–63.* Concord, N.H.: Rumford Press, 1898.

Ladd, David L. and Audrey J., editors. *The Bachelder Papers: Gettysburg in Their Own Words.* Vols. 1–3. Morningside, 1994.

———. *John Bachelder's History of the Battle of Gettysburg.* Morningside, 1997.

Linderman, Gerald F. *Embattled Courage: The Experience of Combat in the American Civil War.* New York: Free Press, 1987.

Livermore, Thomas L. *Days and Events, 1860–1866.* Boston and New York: Houghton Mifflin Co., 1920.

Lord, Edward O., editor. *History of the Ninth Regiment, New Hampshire Volunteers, in the War of the Rebellion.* Concord, N.H.: Republican Press Association, 1895.

Luvaas, Jay, and Nelson, Harold W., editors. *Guide to the Battle of Gettysburg.* Lawrence, Kans.: University Press of Kansas, 1994.

———. *The U.S. Army War College Guide to the Battle of Antietam: The Maryland Campaign of 1862.* Carlisle, Pa.: South Mountain Press, 1987.

———. *The U.S. Army War College Guide to the Battles of Chancellorsville and Fredericksburg.* Carlisle, Pa.: South Mountain Press Inc., 1988.

Lyford, James O. *Life of Edward H. Rollins.* Boston: Dana Estes and Co., 1906.

———, editor. *History of Concord, New Hampshire: From the Original Grant in Seventeen Hundred and Twenty-five to the Opening of the Twentieth Century.* Concord, N.H.: Rumford Press, 1903.

Marvel, William. *Burnside.* Chapel Hill and London: University of North Carolina Press, 1991.

McCarter, William. *My Life in the Irish Brigade,* edited by Kevin E. O'Brien. Campbell, Calif.: Savas Publishing Co., 1996.

McClintock, John N. *History of New Hampshire,* Boston: B. B. Russell, Cornhill, 1889.

McDuffee, Franklin. *History of the Town of Rochester, New Hampshire, from 1722 to 1890,* edited and revised by Sylvanus Hayward. Manchester, N.H.: John B. Clarke Co. (printer), 1892.

McFarland, Henry. *Sixty Years in Concord and Elsewhere.* Concord, N.H.: privately printed, Rumford Press, 1899.

McPherson, James M. *Battle Cry of Freedom: The Civil War Era.* New York and Oxford: Oxford University Press, 1988.

———. *For Cause and Comrades: Why Men Fought in the Civil War.* New York and Oxford: Oxford University Press, 1997.

Merrill, Irving R. *Concord City Directory, for 1860–61.* Concord, N.H.: Rufus Merrill & Son, publishers, McFarland & Jenks, printers, 1860.

Mitchell, Reid. *Civil War Soldiers: Their Expectations and Their Experiences.* New York: Viking, 1988.

———. *The Vacant Chair: The Northern Soldier Leaves Home.* New York and Oxford: Oxford University Press, 1993.

Moe, Richard. *The Last Full Measure: The Life and Death of the First Minnesota Volunteers.* New York: Henry Holt and Co., 1993.

Moore, Frank, editor. *The Rebellion Record*, New York: G. P. Putnam, 1863, 1864.

Muffly, J. W., editor. *The Story of Our Regiment: A History of the 148th Pennsylvania Vols.* Des Moines, Iowa: Kenyon Printing & Mfg. Co., 1904.

The National Cyclopedia of American Biography, edited by "distinguished biographers, selected from each state." New York: James T. White & Co., 1897.

Nesbitt, Mark. *Through Blood and Fire: Selected Civil War Papers of Major General Joshua Chamberlain.* Mechanicsville, Pa.: Stackpole Books, 1996.

Palfrey, Francis W. *The Antietam and Fredericksburg.* New York: Da Capo Press, 1996.

Patterson, Gerard A. *Debris of Battle: The Wounded of Gettysburg.* Mechanicsville, Pa.: Stackpole Books, 1997.

Pennsylvania at Gettysburg: Ceremonies at the Dedication of Monuments Erected by the Commonwealth of Pennsylvania to Mark the Positions of the Pennsylvania Commands Engaged in the Battle. Harrisburg, Pa.: E. K. Myers, state printer, 1893.

Pfanz, Harry W. *Gettysburg: The Second Day.* Chapel Hill and London: University of North Carolina Press, 1987.

Ramsdell, George A. *The History of Milford.* Concord, N.H.: published by the Town of Milford, printed by Rumford Press, 1901.

Renda, Lex. *Running on the Record: Civil War–Era Politics in New Hampshire.* Charlottesville and London: University Press of Virginia, 1997.

Robertson, James I., Jr. *Stonewall Jackson: The Man, the Soldier, the Legend.* New York: Macmillan Publishing USA, Simon and Schuster Macmillan, 1997.

Sears, Stephen W. *Chancellorsville*, Boston and New York: Houghton Mifflin Co., 1996.

———. *Controversies and Commanders: Dispatches from the Army of the Potomac.* Boston and New York: Houghton Mifflin Co., 1999.

———. *George B. McClellan: The Young Napoleon.* New York: Ticknor & Fields, 1988.

———. *Landscape Turned Red: The Battle of Antietam.* New Haven and New York: Ticknor & Fields, 1983.

———. *To the Gates of Richmond: The Peninsula Campaign.* New York: Ticknor & Fields, 1992.

———, editor. *The Civil War Papers of George B. McClellan.* New York: Ticknor & Fields, 1989.

Secomb, Daniel F. *History of the Town of Amherst.* Concord, N.H.: Evans, Sleeper & Woodbury, 1883.

Smith, John L. *History of the 118th Pennsylvania Volunteers.* Philadelphia: J. L. Smith, 1905.

Somers, Rev. A. N. *The History of Lancaster, New Hampshire.* Concord, N.H.: Rumford Press, 1899.

Swinton, William. *Campaigns of the Army of the Potomac.* 1866. Reprint, Secaucus, N.J.: Blue & Grey Press, 1988.

Thomas, Emory M. *Robert E. Lee: A Biography.* New York and London: W. W. Norton & Co., 1995.

Vinovskis, Maris A. *Toward a Social History of the American Civil War: Exploratory Essays.* Cambridge: Cambridge University Press, 1990.

Waite, Otis F. R. *Claremont War History; April, 1861, to April, 1865: With Sketches of New-Hampshire Regiments, and a Biographical Notice of Each Claremont Soldier, Etc.* Concord, N.H.: McFarland and Jenks, printers, 1868.

———. *History of the Town of Claremont.* Manchester, N.H.: published by authority of the town, John B. Clarke Co., 1895.

———. *New Hampshire in the Great Rebellion.* Claremont, N.H.: Tracy, Chase & Co., 1870.

War of the Rebellion: Official Records of the Union and Confederate Armies. Series 1. Washington, D.C.: Government Printing Office, 1887.

Wheeler, Edward. *The History of Newport, New Hampshire, from 1766 to 1878.* Concord, N.H.: Republican Press Association, 1879.

Wiley, Bell Irvin. *The Life of Billy Yank: The Common Soldier of the Union,* 1952. Reprint, Baton Rouge and London: Louisiana State University Press, 1978.

PAPERS, ARTICLES, AND MANUSCRIPTS

(The abbreviation "NA" in this section refers to the National Archives, Washington, D.C.)

Allen, Alonzo. Pension file and service record. NA.

Austin, Ruel G. Pension file. NA.

Barrett, Frederick. Letters. Pension file of William B. Welch, NA.

Barton, Ira McL. Letters and papers. Special Collections, Dartmouth College Library, Hanover, N.H.

———. Pension file. NA.

Bucknam, John. Letters. Lancaster Historical Society, Lancaster, N.H.

———. Pension file. NA.

Butcher, John. Pension file. NA.

Campbell, Eric. "Caldwell Clears the Wheatfield." *Gettysburg* magazine, July 1990.

Charge Bayonets! Newsletter of the Fifth New Hampshire Volunteers (re-enactors). Londonderry, N.H.

Chase, Benjamin F. Pension file. NA.

Chase, Luther M. Pension file. NA.

Child, William. Letters. In private hands.

———. Pension file. NA.

Chiles, Paul. "Artillery Hell! The Guns of Antietam." *Blue & Gray Magazine,* December 1998.

Cook, William W. Pension file. Veterans Administration Regional Office, Manchester, N.H.

Crafts, Welcome. Pension file. NA.

Cross, Edward E. Journal and letters. In private hands.

———. Pension file, adjutant general's file, and service record. NA.

Cross, Richard E. Pension file, service record, and court-martial transcript. NA.

Crowther, Samuel. Pension file. NA.

Davis, Hilas D. Pension file. NA.

Fifth Regiment, New Hampshire Volunteers. Regimental order book, letter book, daily reports, NA.

———. Regimental records. New Hampshire Division of Records Management and Archives, Concord, N.H.

First Regiment, New Hampshire Volunteers. Regimental records. New Hampshire Division of Records Management and Archives, Concord, N.H.

Forehand, Lloyd. Letter. Nebraska State Historical Society, Lincoln.

George, George Washington. Pension file. NA.

Gilpatrick, Reuben. Pension file. NA.

Gove, George S. Pension file. NA.

Hale, Charles A. "General Hancock and the Fifth New Hampshire Volunteers." John Rutter Brooke Papers, Historical Society of Pennsylvania, Philadelphia, Pa.

———. Pension file. NA.

———. "The Story of My Personal Experiences at the Battle of Antietam." John Rutter Brooke Papers, Historical Society of Pennsylvania, Philadelphia, Pa.

———. "With Colonel Cross in the Gettysburg Campaign." John Rutter Brooke Papers, Historical Society of Pennsylvania, Philadelphia, Pa.

Halstead, Murat. "Cincinnati Commercial Account" (of the Battle of Fredericksburg). In Frank Moore, editor, *The Rebellion Record, 1862*, New York: G. P. Putnam, 1863.

Hapgood, Charles. Pension file. NA.

Harris, Joseph H. Pension file. NA.

Hass, Paul H., editor. "A Volunteer Nurse in the Civil War: The Letters of Harriet Douglass Whitten." *Wisconsin Magazine of History*, no. 48 (winter 1964–65).

Hersum, George L. Pension file. NA.

Holden, Walter. "The Blooding of the Best." *Great Battles—Military History Magazine*, January 1991.

———. "Competely Outgeneralled." *Civil War Times Illustrated*, July/August 1995.

———. "The Granite Regiment." Unpublished manuscript.

Holt, Stephen H. Letters. Special Collections, Dartmouth College Library, Hanover, N.H.

Howard, Leonard W. Pension file. NA.

Hufford, Kenneth. "Journalism in Pre-Territorial Arizona." *The Smoke Signal, Journal of the Tucson Corral of the Westerners* (Tucson, Ariz.), no. 14, Fall 1966.

Hurd, Sumner. Pension file. NA.

Langley, Samuel. Pension file. NA.

Larkin, James E. Letters. New Hampshire Historical Society, Concord, N.H.

———. Pension file and court-martial records. NA.

Law, Thomas H. Pension file. NA.

Little, Samuel B. Pension file. NA.

Livermore, Col. Thomas L. "The Northern Volunteers." *The Granite Monthly* (Concord, N.H.), vol. 10, 1887.

Livermore, Thomas L. Service record. NA.

Long, Charles. Pension file. NA.

Lyford, William O. Pension file. NA.

Marvel, William. "Answering Lincoln's Call: The First New Hampshire Volunteers." *Historical New Hampshire* (Concord: New Hampshire Historical Society), fall/ winter 1984.

———. "The Battle of Fredericksburg." Civil War Series. Eastern National Park and Monument Association, 1993.

McCrillis, John. Pension file. NA.

Moore, William. Letters. New Hampshire Historical Society, Concord, N.H.

Murray, John. Pension file. NA.

Nettleton, George. Pension file. NA.

Noyes, Barron. Pension file. NA.

Nugent, Col. Robert. Article. "The Sixty-ninth Regiment at Fredericksburg." 3rd annual report of the State Historian of the State of New York, Albany, 1890.

Peabody, Miles. Letters. United States Army National Military History Institute, Carlisle Barracks, Pa., and in private hands.

———. Pension file and service record. NA.

Perry, James B. Pension file and court-martial record. NA.

Pfanz, Harry W. "The Battle of Gettysburg." Civil War Series. Eastern National Park and Monument Association, 1994.

Phelps, Charles. Letters. In private hands.

———. Pension file. NA.

Randlett, Nathan. Pension file. NA.

Report of the Eighth Annual Reunion of the 64th N.Y. Regimental Ass'n, Held at Franklinville, N.Y. August 19 and 20, 1896. Randolph, N.H.: Enterprise Press.

Report of the Ninth Annual Reunion of the 64th N.Y. Regimental Association Held at Buffalo, N.Y. August 24, 1897.

Richards, Donald H. "The Fifth New Hampshire Volunteers (Light Infantry)." *Historical New Hampshire.* Concord: New Hampshire Historical Society, winter 1973.

Scott, Charles. Letter. United States Army National Military History Institute, Carlisle Barracks, Pa.

Stinson, Edward G. F. Pension file. NA.

Sturtevant, Edward E. Letters. In private hands.

———. Pension file. NA.

Wright, Charles A. "The Silent Neighbor." *New Hampshire Profiles,* May 1958.

Welch, William B. Letters. Pension file. NA.

Wier, Thomas. Pension file. NA.

Youngholm, Janet R. "Edward E. Cross: A Biography of a Civil War Soldier." Senior thesis, Princeton University, 1976.

NEWSPAPERS

Cincinnati Commercial, Cincinnati, Ohio, 1862.
Cincinnati Dollar Times, Cincinnati, Ohio, 1853–58.
Cincinnati Times, Cincinnati, Ohio, 1853–59.
Coos Democrat, Lancaster, N.H., 1889.
Coos Republican, Lancaster, N.H., 1861–63.
Enquirer, Dover, N.H., 1862–63.
Farmer's Cabinet, Milford, N.H., 1861–63.
Granite State Free Press, Lebanon, N.H., 1861–63.
Independent Democrat, Concord, N.H., 1861–63.
Keene Sentinel, Keene, N.H., 1861–63.
Laconia Democrat, Laconia, N.H., 1862–63.
Nashua Telegraph, Nashua, N.H., 1861–63.
National Eagle, Claremont, N.H., 1861–63.
New Hampshire Patriot, Concord, N.H., 1861–63.
New York Tribune, New York, N.Y., 1862.
Northern Advocate, Claremont, N.H., 1861–63.
People's Journal, Littleton, N.H., 1861–63.
States, Washington, D.C., 1859.
Statesman, Concord, N.H., 1861–63.
Weekly Arizonian, Tubac, Ariz., 1859.

Index